The Russian Revolution:
When workers took power

Paul Vernadsky

The Russian Revolution:
When workers took power

Paul Vernadsky

Art selection and text: Hugh Daniels

ISBN: 978-1-909639-32-4

Published 2017 by Phoenix Press
20e Tower Workshops
Riley Road
London SE1 3DG

Printed by Imprint Digital, Exeter, EX5 5HY

This work is licensed under the Creative Commons Attribution 2.5 Generic License.
To view a copy of this licence, visit
http://creativecommons.org/licences/by/2.5
or send a letter to Creative Commons, 444 Castro Street, Suite 900, Mountain View, California, 94041, USA

"To face reality squarely; not to seek the line of least resistance; to call things by their right names; to speak the truth to the masses, no matter how bitter it may be; not to fear obstacles; to be true in little things as in big ones; to base one's programme on the logic of the class struggle; to be bold when the hour for action arrives — these are the rules of the Fourth International."

Leon Trotsky, *The Transitional Programme* (1938)

Contents

1. Introduction: great days **9**

2. The story of 1917 **19**

3. The party of victory **73**

4. Soviets, workers' democracy and workers' control **125**

5. Permanent revolution **143**

6. War and the myth of defeatism **177**

7. Consistent democracy and the national question **203**

8. Women's liberation and the Russian revolution **235**

9. The Communist International — school of strategy **267**

10. Stalin's counter-revolution **301**

11. Why is the Russian revolution relevant today? **339**

Recommended reading **353**

Index

Illustrations

Vladimir Tatlin, 'Monument to the Third International', 1919-20 **7**
Olga Rozanova, 'Suprematism', 1916 **17**
Lyubov Popova, 'Space-Force Construction', 1921 **71**
Lyubov Popova, 'Untitled Textile Design', 1924 **123**
Kazimir Malevich, 'Architecton Beta', c.1920 **141**
El Lissitzky, 'Beat the White Circle With the Red Wedge', 1919 **175**
Gustav Klutsis, Design for a Loud Speaker No.2, 1922 **201**
Alexandra Exter, 'Construction', 1922-3 **233**
Karl Ioganson, 'Cold Structure IX', 1921 **265**
Vera Mukhina, 'Worker and Kolkhoz Woman', 1937 **299**
Alexsandr Deineka, 'We Will See Who is Right', 1932 **237**
Aleksandr Rodchenko, 'Design for a Workers' Club', 1925 **351**

THE RUSSIAN REVOLUTION: WHEN WORKERS TOOK POWER

Vladimir Tatlin, 'Monument to the Third International', 1919-20

This was a model for an unrealised building, which was designed to stand at over 400m in height. If built it would have contained three enormous geometric structures, all of which would have constantly been in motion. At the bottom was a cube, to carry the legislature and rotate once per year. In the middle was a cylinder, to hold the executive and rotate once per month. At the top was a pyramid, to hold the media and rotate once per day.

1. Introduction: great days

The Russian revolution of 1917 was the greatest event in political history so far. It was the first occasion that working class people took political power and held it for a significant period. In 12 months that shook the world, Russia was transformed from an oppressive, war-mongering autocratic monarchy into a democratic workers' republic. The Russian revolution of 1917 is one of the inspirations for the Alliance for Workers' Liberty (AWL), which publishes this book. For anyone who wants to change the world today, understanding the lessons of the Russian revolution can help shape working class politics now and in the years ahead.

Why revolution?

Revolution is necessary because we live in a **capitalist world**, where the vast majority of humanity is exploited and oppressed to furnish the power and fortune of a tiny ruling class. Under capitalism, most people live and work as waged labourers, exploited by the central processes in production and bound by market imperatives in all aspects of their lives. Capitalism shackles us through its web of economic ties, the power of its states and the false ideas it foists on our thinking. Russian workers in 1917 came to understand these fetters and fought for their own liberation.

Karl Marx and Frederick Engels, the founders of working class socialism, explained that revolution is necessary "not only because the ruling class cannot be overthrown in any other way, but also because the class overthrowing it can only in a revolution succeed in ridding itself of all the muck of ages and become fitted to found society anew".[1] Revolution is so that there is free time and resources to fulfil ourselves. Revolution is a process of creative transformation to establish democratic self-rule in every facet of our lives, so that collective decisions to meet human needs can be made, to better the society we live in and the planet we live on.

Revolution in the modern world means **working-class people** making our own history. Through revolution, the great mass of working people come forward as active creators of a new social order. At such times working people perform things that seemed impossible before, transforming ourselves and society from bottom to top. In Russia in 1917, millions of people organised themselves through an unconstrained public life of conferences, committees, meetings and organisations. Everywhere people were talking, debating, assessing, so much so that "mitingovat" ("to meeting") became a new verb.

In 1917, the fight for socialism meant the struggle for "volia" — for **liberty**, for the space and light to emancipate themselves. Everywhere workers organised carnivals of liberty. They adorned themselves in the colour red to signify revolution: red armbands and ribbons, red banners and red symbols. They sang revolutionary songs such as the Marseillaise, recalling the French revolution more than a century before. Everywhere they critically questioned the existing order — social relations at work and at home, the terrible world war raging in Europe, the ownership of land and the oppression of minority peoples. And everywhere they made plans for a better present and an alternative future.

Vladimir Lenin, the central socialist leader in 1917, described revolutions as "festivals of the oppressed and the exploited". But the Russian Marxists did not play with revolution: they understood that revolutionary situations come about under definite conditions. Lenin argued that "it is only when the 'lower classes' do not want to live in the old way and the 'upper classes' cannot carry on in the old way that the revolution can triumph". It is essential first, that "a majority of the workers (or at least a majority of the class-conscious, thinking, and politically active workers) should fully realise that revolution is necessary, and that they should be prepared to die for it"; second, that "the ruling classes should be going through a governmental crisis", which draws masses of workers and the oppressed into political struggle, "weakens the government, and makes it possible for the revolutionaries to rapidly overthrow it".[2]

Why now?

The Russian revolution matters today for two central reasons. First, it demonstrates in real life that working class people can free ourselves from exploitation and oppression. 1917 shows that workers can become a revolutionary class with the capacity and motivation to halt the current order and create a new regime based on our own organs of **democratic self-liberation**. The Russian revolution shows that class matters: class relations that underpin every aspect of life but also working class agency in changing the world. The active role of the working class in shaping its own fate is the essence of revolutionary socialism. 1917 shows the heights workers can reach when we dare to fight.

The Russian revolution is important for active socialists now for another reason. Workers' Liberty fights for socialism in today's conditions. The assessments we make of the present moment, the strategies and tactics we advocate in current politics, and how we organise are distilled from the evolving Marxist method we espouse and the rich history of working class struggle we learn from. The central lesson of 1917, from our theory and our history, is that active socialists need to organise a party capable of leading workers' struggle for power. Leon Trotsky, another of the central leaders of the 1917 revolution, summed up the interconnection of class and party: "Without a guiding organisation, the energy of the masses would dissipate like steam not enclosed in a piston-box. But nevertheless what moves things is not the piston or the box, but the steam."[3]

Working class people need our **own independent party** to make history and to win. The Russian revolution is distinguished from other great working class revolts by the presence of a cadre of worker-activist-thinkers who carved out their goals and their methods within the working class movement before the conditions for revolution were present. These permanently active persuaders fought the class struggle on all three fronts: the economic, the political, and the ideological, so as to prepare the ground for working class self-liberation. They articulated the vision of an alternative future and they intervened in struggles to help workers gain the confidence and strength to take power into their own hands. This is a necessary condition for progress today.

Why this book?

There are many books on the Russian revolution. Trotsky wrote *The History of the Russian Revolution*, an outstanding account that remains essential reading. But the Russian revolution is also one of the most misunderstood and misrepresented events in human history. Many Western academic accounts portray 1917 as mainly a mutiny of peasant soldiers leading ultimately to a coup d'état, led by a small group of manipulative Marxist fanatics who trampled over democracy to establish a totalitarian state. Because Russia under Joseph Stalin from 1928 until the demise of the Soviet Union in 1991, really was a despotic and oppressive regime, the original revolution was dismissed as the beginning of this terror. Worse, the mirror image of 1917 became the foundation myth of the Stalinist state: the 1917 revolution was used both in Russia and across the world by "Communist" parties to glorify the terrible Stalinist regime that endured after workers' self-rule was extinguished in the 1920s.

These accounts treat the Russian workers as a lumpen mass, led by a monolithic Bolshevik party. Even sympathetic commentators —

including people who regard themselves as Trotskyists — have often uncritically reproduced this narrative. As one historian put it, "for too long Russian history has been written not only from the top down, but with the bottom left out completely".[4] Since the 1960s — and especially since the opening of archives in Russia from the 1990s, much more is now known about the Russian revolution.

This book aims to bring the original Marxist perspectives of the Russian revolution together with a wide range of scholarship. It draws on a series of recent studies published in the *Historical Materialism* book series, by authors such as Lars Lih, Paul Le Blanc, John Riddell, Richard Day and Daniel Gaido, Richard Mullin, Marcel van der Linden, John Marot and Tom Twiss. These studies combine pathbreaking interpretations with materials that overlap activist and academic questions. This book quotes directly from some of the key participants in the events, on various sides of the debates, from a range of translations in English, so readers can trace the discussions and make up their own minds. The book also draws on recent academic studies, such as the works of Barbara Evans Clements and Katy Turton on Bolshevik women in Russia, August Nimtz on Lenin's electoral strategy, Carter Elwood on Lenin, Inessa Armand and other Bolsheviks, Steve Smith and David Mandel on workplace politics, and Lars Fischer, Jack Jacobs and Enzo Traverso on anti-semitism. It incorporates the insights from heavyweight scholars such as Alexander Rabinowitch, Diane Koenker, William Rosenberg, Rex Wade, James White and Eduard Burdzhalov, who have added much to the history of the Russian revolution from below.

The book is organised into themes, intended to help those coming to the Russian revolution with little background knowledge, but also to offer more familiar readers serious and critical discussion. This chapter outlines the reasons to study the Russian revolution today, and the standpoint of working class socialism adopted to understand the events and their contemporary relevance. Chapter two is a broad narrative of the year 1917, concentrating on Petrograd without ignoring the wider Russian and international context. chapter Three explains how the Bolshevik party was built, through its fight on all three fronts of the class struggle — the ideological, the political and the economic. Chapter four examines the distinct forms of working class organisation that flourished in 1917 — particularly the soviets, factory committees and workers' control.

The next chapters take a wider vista, explaining the origin and development of Russian Marxists, debates that ultimately allowed the Bolsheviks to win the majority of workers to socialist politics in 1917.

INTRODUCTION: GREAT DAYS

Chapter five discusses the perspectives and strategies for taking power, especially Trotsky's powerful conception of permanent revolution. Chapter six examines the debates around war and imperialism, which were pivotal to orientating Russian Marxists in the tumultuous events before 1917. Chapter seven explains Lenin's consistently democratic approach to the national question and why it proved the most coherent method not only for tackling immediate national oppression in Russia but for wider questions in the rest of the world and for particular forms of oppression such as anti-semitism. Chapter eight discusses the Bolshevik attitude towards women's oppression and women's liberation, the distinctive forms of organisation and social programmes they adopted, and the contribution made by important thinkers such as Aleksandra Kollontai.

The final chapters reflects on some key questions that followed the Russian revolution. Chapter nine examines the contribution of the Communist International in developing Marxist parties, drawing on the experience of the Bolsheviks. Chapter ten grapples with what went wrong, particularly the rise of the Stalinist bureaucracy, which ultimately destroyed workers' rule a decade after 1917. A final chapter outlines the relevance of the Russia revolution for current Marxist debates, concluding that no contemporary activist, radical or socialist can afford to ignore the significance of the 1917 revolution. Recommended reading (and the footnotes) help anyone who wants to find or rediscover other vital texts in light of this interpretation.

Above all, this book is intended to educate the new generation of working class socialist activists, to provoke debate and help shape working class politics in the present. It puts forward what Lenin and Trotsky called the **"third camp"** independent working class socialist perspective on the Russian revolution. The Russian revolution marked a vital turning point in the development of our version of socialism. In 1917, the old property-owning classes, headed by the Kadet party, made up the first camp, while the Mensheviks and Socialist Revolutionaries in the Provisional Government made up the second camp. As Trotsky put it, "when, by the inner logic of the class struggle, our party, standing at the head of the proletariat, came to power, the third camp was brought to the test, the camp of the working class, which by its entire nature is alone capable of fulfilling the fundamental tasks of the revolution".[5]

This book presents a unique, critical, third camp Marxist assessment of the Russian revolution. It tries to explain some irreplaceable ideas developed a century ago — uneven and combined development, permanent revolution, democratic centralism, soviets (councils), workers' control, consistent democracy, socialist feminism, transitional demands, the united front and the workers' government. Such ideas can be adapted for our own times. Standing on the shoulders of these predecessors, this is the politics Workers' Liberty is developing for today's class struggle.

INTRODUCTION: GREAT DAYS

References

1. Karl Marx and Frederick Engels, *The German Ideology*, (MECW 5: 52-53).
2. Lenin, *Left-Wing Communism: an Infantile Disorder*, (LCW 31: 84).
3. Leon Trotsky, *The History of the Russian Revolution*, (1980: xix).
4. Ronald Suny, 'Revising the old story: the 1917 revolution in light of new sources', in Daniel Kaiser, *The Workers' Revolution in Russia, 1917: The View from Below*, (1987: 3).
5. Trotsky, [28 March 1918] 'Work, Discipline, Order', *Military Writings and Speeches of Leon Trotsky. Vol 1*, (1979: 28-30).

THE RUSSIAN REVOLUTION: WHEN WORKERS TOOK POWER

THE RUSSIAN REVOLUTION: WHEN WORKERS TOOK POWER

Olga Rozanova, 'Suprematism', 1916

2. The story of 1917

In October 1917 the Russian working class, led by the Russian Social Democratic Labour Party (RSDLP, Bolshevik party), took power through their mass, democratic soviets (councils).[1] The workers constituted their own state based on the collective and democratically-organised armed force of labour, allied with rank-and-file soldiers, mostly peasants in uniform.

The Bolshevik party established a workers' government that carried out exactly what the workers and peasants demanded: an end to the war, land to those who worked it, a shorter working day, and workers' control over production. They brought liberation to the oppressed, separating the church from the state, relaxing marriage and divorce laws, granting self-determination to nations previously imprisoned by the Russian empire.

They succeeded in shattering the old bourgeois state, most notably its army, gendarmerie and old state bureaucracy. They deconstructed capitalist relations of production and put in place an economic system where the imperative was social need, not private profit. The story of 12 months that shook the world, the first time that workers have taken power and held onto it for a period of years, deserves to be discussed and assimilated to every modern revolutionist's theoretical arsenal.

Russia in 1917
Few predicted at the start of 1917 that Russian workers would finish the year ruling their own state, and spark a worldwide surge for socialism. Yet Russia on the cusp of 1917 was a society rife with contradictions, a tinderbox ready to blow. In the words of a contemporary "everyone knew then that the country was living on a volcano".[2]

By 1917 the conditions for revolution were present. An incompetent government, a discredited monarch, divisions within the ruling elite, alienation of wide sections of society from the regime, deteriorating economic conditions, industrial strikes, extreme war-weariness, resentful armed forces, a revival of activity by revolutionary parties, widespread anxieties and a sense that something had to break soon.[3]

Russia was a backward country, but part of the capitalist world economy. There were an estimated 160 million people living within the Russian empire, 80% of them peasants. Around a fifth lived in urban spaces, with 30 cities reaching the threshold of 100,000 inhabitants. St Petersburg and Moscow both had around two million people, while Riga, Kiev and Odessa had half a million each.[4] Russians toiled under the yoke of the tsarist absolute monarchy, which forbade even the limited liberal freedoms found elsewhere in Europe and whose secret police (the Okhrana) and its Siberian prisons repressed those who raised their hands against the regime.

Russian economy and society were subject to the most extreme pressures from what Trotsky called the laws of uneven and combined development. Economically, politically and socially Russia consisted of "the most primitive beginnings and the latest European endings". In the three decades before the revolution, imperial Russia underwent an industrial revolution. Spurred by pressure from global capitalism and sponsored by the tsarist state, foreign and domestic capital jump-started a modern mode of production. At the centre of these contradictory processes were the workers, "thrown into the factory cauldron snatched directly from the plough".[5]

The working class consisted of about 3.5 million factory and mine workers (with 400,000 in St Petersburg and Moscow), together with construction workers, railway workers, dockers and various kinds of wage labourers. In all, there were about 18.5 million workers, or 10% of the population. It was a diverse working class, with more than 100 different ethnicities (including about 20 major nationalities) of widely differing size, culture, language, beliefs and economic development.

Working-class struggles erupted in these industrialised areas from the 1870s onwards. In June 1896 there was a mass strike movement in St Petersburg. Then, in 1905 workers rose in revolution as part of a wider social protest including liberal bourgeois forces criticising the tsar. Workers drove the movement, three million taking part in strikes and organising soviets — democratic workers' councils — based on workplaces in towns and cities, with directly elected, recallable representatives and loquacious assemblies. The uprising forced the autocracy to concede a toothless parliament (the Duma) and make some limited reforms. But it soon resorted to repression, beating down the peasants and workers, driving their organisations underground, without ever extinguishing the fire. In the first six months of 1914, some 1.3 million factory workers alone took strike action. Repressed and atomised by wartime conditions, they rose again with almost a million striking in 1916.[6]

Nationalist fever swept Russia on the outbreak of the First World War, throwing back the working class movement. The capital St Petersburg was renamed Petrograd to make it sound less "German", although anti-war socialists kept using the old name. The fighting took a terrible toll on the Russian population, after 15 million people were drafted into the army. By the end of 1916, Russia had lost about 5.7 million soldiers, 3.6 million of them dead or seriously wounded, with the rest prisoners of war. There was seething discontent at the front, with the death penalty used for deserters. In the rear, the Petrograd garrison had about 180,000 troops, with another 150,000 in the surrounding suburbs, and some two million in total.[7] Soldiers, conscripted peasants and workers in uniform, yearned for peace.

In the first two months of 1917, more than half a million workers took strike action, the lion's share of them in the capital. In spite of police raids, on 9 January 150,000 workers went on strike in the capital, led by metal-workers. On 14 February, the day the Duma opened, about 90,000 were on strike in Petrograd, and several plants stopped work in Moscow. Hundreds of university students, ignoring threats by the police, marched down the Nevsky Prospekt in the capital singing revolutionary songs. Bread rationing was introduced, sparking queues and the sacking of some bakeries. These were "the heat lightnings of the revolution, coming in a few days".[8] On 22 February, bosses locked out workers at the Putilov plant, throwing 30,000 onto the streets. The prologue to revolution was over.

Political forces

At the start of 1917 an autocracy ruled, although when the tsar took control of the army during the war, the government was left to tsarina Alexandra and her mystical adviser Grigori Rasputin. The largest forces in the Duma were the constitutional monarchist Octobrist party of Alexander Guchkov and Mikhail Rodzianko, the liberal bourgeois Constitutional Democrats (Kadets) led by Pavel Miliukov, and the bourgeois-liberal Progressist Party led by Ivan Efremov, Alexander Konovalov and Pavel Riabushinskii. During the war, even these forces of order become a focal point of opposition to the imperial regime.

The forces of the left were savagely repressed and existed legally only through a small number of representatives in the Duma and in some semi-legal trade unions. The largest left party was the Socialist Revolutionaries (SRs), a populist party with roots in the earlier Narodnik (people's) revolutionary movement, who considered themselves the union of the intelligentsia, the workers and the peasants. The Labour Group (Trudoviks), a peasant party, had 10 deputies in the Duma, including Aleksandr Kerensky. The other main forces were organised within the Russian Social Democratic Labour Party (RSDLP).

In the underground, SRs played a significant role in building trade unions, cooperatives, cultural-educational societies and other workers' organisations. The memoirist Nikolai Sukhanov, who shifted from the SRs to social democracy, estimated that the SRs had the allegiance of one-third of the working class before the First World War.[9]

The SRs were divided into factions and suffered splits, such as the SR-Maximalists. The right supported the tsar's government in the world war, while the left, led by Maria Spiridonova and Mark Natanson, opposed the conflict. Victor Chernov was the leading theorist of the party, but represented the party centre and was politically weak. The SR leaders were mostly in exile at the outbreak of revolution and much of its loose organisation was in disarray. Nevertheless, it represented a significant force in the Russian revolution.[10]

The RSDLP was formed in 1898 on the model of the German Social Democratic Party (SPD). Social democracy at that time meant a socialism strongly influenced by Marxist ideas. However, at the second congress in 1903, held in exile, the party split into two factions: the Bolsheviks (derived from the Russian for "majority") led by Lenin, and the Mensheviks ("minority"), headed by Iulii Martov. These factions reunited within the RSDLP in 1906-07, but diverged after the tsarist regime re-established itself, and they subsequently divided for good. Within the factions there were disputes about the character of the next revolution, about whether to "liquidate" the party into a broad labour congress, and over "otzovism" (recall-ism), withdrawing from work in the Duma and other legal organisations and concentrating exclusively on underground work (see chapter 3).[11]

These splits deepened from 1912 as working class militancy revived, and were further extended at the outbreak of war, despite attempts by conciliators to unify the factions. Some Menshevik liquidationists supported the war, whilst other Menshevik internationalists opposed it. Lenin favoured defeatism for Russia (in a reactionary imperialist war, revolutionaries should consider the defeat of their "own" government the lesser evil), while Trotsky took a more straightforward internationalist position, promoting slogans for peace. Within Russia the pro-war factions worked in the workers' group of the war industries committee, while Bolsheviks, the inter-district committee (*Mezhraionka*), and other social democrats managed to carry on the class struggle from their strongholds in the Vyborg district of Petrograd and the giant Putilov factory.[12]

There were also a small number of Russian anarchists, either in exile or active within the country. The anarchist-communists took their inspiration from Mikhail Bakunin and Peter Kropotkin, advocating a free federation of communes, while the anarcho-syndicalists looked to workplace organisation (and some individualist-anarchists rejected all forms of organisation). Anarchists took part with social democrats and SRs in fomenting strikes, distributing leaflets and agitating for the downfall of the regime.[13]

The February revolution

Thursday 23 February was international women's day in the Russian calendar (some 13 days behind the system used in the rest of Europe, where it was 8 March). Revolutionaries had planned demonstrations and strikes for this socialist festival, but the day was transformed by protests by working-class women, angry that after working for 12 hours they had to wait in food lines with no guarantee of getting any bread or provisions. Throngs of militant women workers marched on the large factories across Petrograd and brought out 90,000 workers to join the demonstrations on that day.

Factory activists organised strike committees and called for the continuation of strikes on Friday 24 February. Some 200,000 workers came out on strike in Petrograd, about half the industrial workforce. Besides calling for "Bread!", workers raised slogans such as "Down with autocracy!" and "Down with the war!" It was a popular revolt.

On Saturday 25 February, a general strike kicked off in Petrograd. The police shot at protesters, and revolutionists were arrested. The strikes spread wider, with a quarter of a million workers involved. Large numbers of students and middle-class elements swelled the demonstrations. Students from Petrograd university and the various technical institutes abandoned their studies for the streets. Women faced down soldiers with bayonets, urging them to join the protests. Clashes with the police escalated, and the demand went up to "Disarm the pharaohs!"[14]

On Sunday 26 February tsar Nicholas dissolved the state Duma and ordered soldiers to suppress the protests. But Cossack soldiers, long feared by the revolutionaries, winked to indicate their sympathy with the demonstrators — the forces of coercion were no longer willing to repress. Tens of thousands of workers were on the streets. Captain Lashkevich ordered the Petrograd-based Volynskii regiment to use sabres and whips to disperse the crowd and then, after the warning bugle, ordered soldiers to fire into the crowds. Chastened soldiers debated the killings in their barracks overnight and the following day they rebelled. They shot their commanding officer — the same Lashkevich who had ordered firing on the crowds the day before. On the same day in the Baltic fleet about 75 officers were killed, including

40 or more at fleet headquarters in Helsingfors (Helsinki) and 24 at Kronstadt.

On Monday 27 February the revolution reached its zenith. The temporary committee of the state Duma, headed by Rodzianko, was formed with a specific goal "to restore order". But the workers had not finished their work. Apparently at the suggestion of the Menshevik liquidator Fedor Cherevanin, prominent representatives of the trade union and co-operative movements, together with leftist Duma deputies, met to call for a soviet of workers' deputies to be formed. The Petrograd soviet was reconstituted that evening. The Duma committee and the Petrograd soviet met in opposite wings of the Tauride Palace, the meeting place of the state Duma, which became the physical focal point of the revolution.[15]

Tsarism had effectively been ousted (the tsar resigned on 2 March) and dual power (*dvoevlastie*) was being created, whereby a Provisional Government replaced the fallen autocracy but was "weak to the point of impotence". Effective power lay in the hands of the soviets. Petrograd bore the brunt of the fighting in the February revolution. The Petrograd city council estimated the numbers killed, wounded and injured at 1,315, of whom 53 were officers, 602 soldiers, 73 policemen and 587 citizens of both sexes.[16]

Who led the February revolution? The sympathetic American historian William Chamberlin described the collapse of the Romanov autocracy as "one of the most leaderless, spontaneous, anonymous revolutions of all times", while Stalin's *Short Course* claimed the credit entirely for the Bolsheviks.[17] Neither view stands up to scrutiny. Historian Michael Melancon provides copious evidence for socialist agency and leadership of the February revolution, but from a diverse and multifaceted range of organisations.

Despite constant repression, by autumn 1916 revolutionary leaders of various socialist groups had begun to coordinate their activities, because they considered the situation to be revolutionary. During February 1917 an all-socialist leadership group met regularly and continued to do so throughout the protests. Because of differences in outlook, "the left socialists also maintained a separate informational group and the socialist Duma faction performed the same role for the moderates". They encouraged demonstrations for bread, and attempted to transform these into revolutionary uprisings. All agreed on the overall immediate goal of overthrowing tsarism, although differences in goals and tactics remained.

As international women's day approached, the all-socialist group met but could not agree on slogans. The left socialists, especially the

SRs, Left Mensheviks, Mezhraionka, and Bolshevik groups, pushed for the demonstrations on 23 February, a socialist holiday. The right socialists, "still smarting at the defeat of their plans as regards the opening of the state Duma on 14 February, were hesitant". Socialists intervened on 23 February to prolong and deepen the protests. They "issued leaflets, led factory strikes and demonstrations in the streets, held meetings at all levels, including of the joint socialist groups, and agreed on slogans to be used each day". By 25 February, the right socialists joined the movement and began to urge the election of soviets.

On 27 February a group of right socialists, including the SR Kerensky and the Mensheviks Matvei Skobelev and Nikolai Chkheidze with others, formed the provisional executive committee of the soviet and issued calls for factories and soldiers to send elected deputies to the Tauride Palace. Meanwhile, left socialists issued leaflets urging the movement forward to full revolution and for workers and soldiers to send delegates to meet at the city's railway station, Finland station, out of the aegis of the Duma. But the rightists prevailed, and by evening the soviet executive committee was elected, replicating the composition of the joint socialist group and transforming itself into a proto-government.

Socialists had no specific plans in advance to launch revolutionary disturbances on 23 February and bring them to fruition on 27 February. What they did have, was "an orientation to promote strikes and demonstrations and, if they showed promise, to prolong them and push them toward revolution. Direct and organised socialist involvement and intervention occurred at every single stage".[18]

The Provisional Government

On 2 March the tsar abdicated, as did his nominated successor Grand Duke Mikhail a day later. The first Provisional Government was formed by the provisional committee of the Duma, with Prince Georgi Lvov as minister-president and a cabinet including Miliukov (Kadet) as minister of foreign affairs, Guchkov (Octobrist) as minister of war and Konovalov (Progressist) as minister of trade. It was supported by the Petrograd soviet leaders, and Kerensky was made minister of justice. On 3 March the Provisional Government announced the revolution to the world by radio, and installed itself in the Marinskii Palace.

During 1917 the term "Provisional Government" covers several successive governments, all of which were mired in governmental crisis. The Provisional Government was never a democratically-elected government, but made up of remnants of the old state machine who attempted to restore order. It took until September 1917 for the government to declare a republic and dissolve the old tsarist Duma. The government was "provisional" because it was meant to exist only to summon a Constituent Assembly. By the time elections had been organised, the Provisional Government had lurched from one disaster to the next and was overthrown by democratic soviets.

The forces unleashed by the revolution drove the Provisional Government to implement some reforms, which Lenin described as making Russia the "freest of all the belligerent countries in the world".[19] These included an amnesty for political prisoners, freedom of press and assembly, legal trade unions and strikes. As well as the call for a Constituent Assembly, it sanctioned elections for local self-government, the replacement of the police by local militias and civil rights for soldiers. On 12 March the Provisional Government abolished the death penalty. On 27 March it issued a declaration of war aims, repudiating the occupation of territories.

However, the Provisional Government was unable to meet the basic needs of the population. It continued with the war, could not revive the economy, did not tackle matters such as the oppression of national minorities, and most of all, it failed to enact the kind of land reform that would satisfy the peasantry.

The soviets

On 27 February Chkheidze was chosen as chair of the Petrograd soviet, a post he held until September. Two other Duma deputies, Skobelev and Kerensky, were elected as vice-chairs. The executive committee was composed mostly of anti-war socialist intellectuals, with formal party representatives from the Bolsheviks, the Bundists (secular Jewish socialists), the Mensheviks, the Trudoviks (right socialists), the Populist-Socialists, the Mezhraionka and the Latvian Social Democrats. The executive composition was diluted by nine representatives of the newly formed soldiers' section of the soviet.

The Petrograd soviet, as it was first constituted, was more like a mass meeting than a deliberative assembly. Chamberlin describes the sessions of the executive committee as "held under exhausting and chaotic circumstances. They began about one in the afternoon and lasted until late at night; and it was seldom that the questions on the order of the day were satisfactorily solved".[20] Sukhanov, who was a member of the executive throughout 1917, describes how during an early meeting two soldiers used their bayonets to tug down the portrait of the tsar that hung behind the chair's seat in the meeting room.

For many months an empty frame "continued to yawn in this revolutionary hall".[21]

The Petrograd soviet executive committee supported the Provisional Government from the outset. At the first sitting of the executive on 1 March the central question was merely the conditions for handing over of power. No voices were raised against the formation of a bourgeois government, despite the presence of 11 Bolsheviks, including their three leaders on the spot. In the soviet the following day, out of 400 deputies present, only 19 voted against the transfer of power to the bourgeoisie — although there were already 40 in the Bolshevik faction. As Trotsky argues in his *History of the Russian Revolution*, "the voting itself passed off in a purely formal parliamentary manner, without any clear counter-proposition from the Bolsheviks, without conflict, and without any agitation whatever in the Bolshevik press".

The executive committee of the soviet of workers' deputies created on 27 February had little in common with its name. The original soviet of 1905 arose out of a general strike. It directly represented the workers in struggle. The leaders of the strike became the deputies of the soviet. Its executive committee was elected by the soviet for the further prosecution of the struggle. It was this executive committee that discussed armed insurrection. By contrast, in February 1917 the revolution was victorious before the workers had created a soviet. The executive committee of 27 February was self-constituted, independently of the factories and regiments, after the victory of the revolution.[22]

The Petrograd soviet nevertheless began to assert itself. On Tuesday 28 February it published the first issue of *Izvestia* (*The News*). Political strikes and demonstrations spread to other cities. Socialists formed local soviets of workers' (and sometimes soldiers') deputies — but these bodies supported and usually participated in the work of public committees.[23] On Wednesday 1 March the Petrograd soviet issued Order No.1, drafted by Nikolai Sokolov, mandating the establishment of soldiers' committees in the armed forces. (Ironically Sokolov was later severely thrashed by the rebellious soldiers of a regiment on the front which he was endeavouring to recall to discipline.)[24] At its session of 6 March, the executive committee agreed a proposal by an old Menshevik, Mikhail Braunstein, to install its own commissars in all regiments and in all military institutions. These measures bonded the soldier and the soviet: the regiments sent their representatives to the soviet, the executive committee sent its commissars to the regiments and each regiment had an elective committee.[25]

Sukhanov reports that on 6 March, the executive committee proposed "the immediate liquidation of the strikes and the transition to the new pacific status", and "an enormous majority spoke up for a resumption of work". The executive resolution was passed in the soviet by 1,170 votes to 30. The drive came from the soldiers, who demanded "the curbing of the workers", and threatened to use force. Armed soldiers "begin visiting factories, carrying out inspections and using force". On 14 March the Petrograd soviet issued its "Appeal to the people of the world", declaring for "peace without annexations or indemnities".[26]

Towards the end of March the Petrograd soviet lurched further to the right. The Menshevik Irakli Tsereteli reached the capital from exile in Siberia on 20 March and constituted a "revolutionary defencist" majority in the soviet. He argued that the overthrow of the tsar meant that the character of the war had changed. Now "the revolution", including the soviet were threatened by imperial Germany. He concluded that the soviets, should support the war and cease domestic activities for peace. Tsereteli had staunchly opposed the war and taken part in the Zimmerwald international anti-war conference. However, by the end of March, he and his SR allies had carried this line at the executive committee and at the all-Russian conference of soviets, where there were about 400 provincial delegates, representing 82 cities and the executives of military units.[28]

Dual power

On 23 March, the "funeral of the victims of the revolution" took place in Petrograd. It was a one million-strong demonstration that the revolution had triumphed but was still ongoing. Chamberlin describes the outstanding features of the first period of the deepening of the revolution: "Loosening of discipline in the army, increasingly radical demands of the industrial workers, first for higher wages, then for control over production and distribution, arbitrary confiscations of houses in the towns and, to a greater degree, of land in the country districts, insistence in such non-Russian parts of the country as Finland and Ukraine on the grant of far-reaching autonomy."[29]

The critical tensions of the situation were captured by the idea of dual power. Trotsky defined this as "a distinct condition of social crisis, by no means peculiar to the Russian revolution of 1917, although there most clearly marked out... The two-power régime arises only out of irreconcilable class conflicts — is possible, therefore, only in a revolutionary epoch, and constitutes one of its fundamental elements". The question of power stood thus: "Either the bourgeoisie will actually dominate the old state apparatus, altering it a little for its purposes, in which case the soviets will come to nothing; or the soviets will form the foundation of a new state, liquidating not only the old governmental apparatus but also the dominion of those classes which it served."[29]

Lenin rearms the Bolshevik party

The Bolshevik party was slow to assess the new context and was internally divided in its strategy and tactics immediately after the February revolution. Of course, Bolshevik militants had played their part in the February strikes and demonstrations, but probably no more than other socialist organisations. However, they were recognised as a significant minority party in the soviets and began to operate openly in the new political conditions. They established a headquarters in the mansion belonging to the famous ballet dancer Mathilda Kshesinskaia. On 5 March the Bolsheviks in Petrograd published the first issue of *Pravda* (*Truth*), as a central organ of the party. Similarly, the Petrograd party agreed to revive the Bolshevik women's paper *Rabotnitsa* (*Woman Worker*) as part of a drive to organise working class women. On 31 March the Bolshevik military organisation was founded. It organised "Club Pravda", a non-party soldiers' club, opened in the basement of the Kshesinskaia mansion, and published a special newspaper, *Soldatskaia Pravda*.[30]

On 3 April Lenin arrived in Petrograd from exile, speaking to both Bolsheviks and Mensheviks at the soviet conference. The next day he presented the party with a short written exposition of his views, *The Tasks of the Proletariat in the Present Revolution*, later known as the *April Theses*. Trotsky summarised Lenin's argument in his *History*:

> The republic which has issued from the February revolution is not our republic, and the war which it is now waging is not our war. The task of the Bolsheviks is to overthrow the imperialist government. But this government rests upon the support of the Social Revolutionaries and Mensheviks, who in turn are supported by the trustfulness of the masses of the people. We are in the minority. In these circumstances there can be no talk of violence from our side. We must teach the masses not to trust the compromisers and defencists. "We must patiently explain". The success of this policy, dictated by the whole existing situation, is assured, and it will bring us to the dictatorship of the proletariat, and so beyond the boundaries of the bourgeois régime. We will break absolutely with capital, publish its secret treaties, and summon the workers of the whole world to cast loose from the bourgeoisie and put an end to the war. We

are beginning the international revolution. Only its success will confirm our success, and guarantee a transition to the socialist régime.[31]

Lenin fought at every level of the party to rearm its political perspectives. This would be achieved at the party conference, which met in Petrograd on 24-29 April (see Chapter five for further discussion).

The Provisional Government in crisis

The first Provisional Government came to an end quickly. On 18 April foreign minister Miliukov sent a note to the Allied governments promising to continue the war until victory on the old terms. On 20 and 21 April thousands of armed soldiers, bearing slogans such as "Down with Miliukov" and "Down with annexationist policies", demonstrated outside the government's headquarters in the Marinskii Palace.[32]

As Sukhanov observes, the April days "marked a boundary and a turning point: they infinitely deepened the crack in the soviet; having broken the petty-bourgeois away from the proletarian groups, they — on the other hand — almost closed the gap between the petty and the big bourgeoisie". The all-Russian conference of Mensheviks, which opened in Petersburg on 9 May, approved their members' entry into the coalition and promised the new cabinet "complete confidence and support". The presidium of the Petrograd soviet was "concentrated into a continuously operative, quasi-official though still backstage institution, that had been given the name of the 'star chamber'. It consisted not only of the members of the presidium but also of a kind of camarilla, loyal intimates of Chkheidze and Tsereteli".[33]

On 1 May the Petrograd soviet voted for a coalition government, after two days earlier rejecting coalition with the bourgeoisie. On 5 May just such a government was announced. Five additional socialists, including Tsereteli, Skobelev and Chernov, joined Kerensky in the government. Ten non-socialists, including four Kadets, completed the government. A wealthy young Ukrainian sugar manufacturer, Mikhail Tereshchenko, replaced Miliukov as minister for foreign affairs.[34]

The workers organise

The working class was the chief motive force of the February revolution. Despite the efforts of the Provisional Government and its friends in the soviets, workers deepened the militancy of their representative bodies. They were strengthened by the return of more revolutionary leaders from exile. For example, Trotsky was freed from a British prison camp in Canada, and returned to Russia on 4 May.

One innovation was the Red Guards, involving both men and women. During March, *Pravda* articles by Vladimir Bonch-Bruevich and Vladimir Nevskii called for a permanent, autonomous, revolutionary, class-orientated armed force, harking back to the experience of 1905. The article by Bonch-Bruevich, on 18 March, contained the first printed use of the term Red Guard in 1917. On 29 April the Bolshevik-led industrial district Vyborg soviet approved regulations for a district-wide workers' guard organisation. In May a meeting in the Peterhof district formed a district Red Guard and similar initiatives were taken elsewhere. A conference of the Petrograd people's militia was held on 27 May and a council of the Petrograd people's militia established on 3 June.[35]

On 30 May a conference of the factory committees of the capital and its suburbs opened in the White Hall of the Tauride Palace. The conference grew from the bottom up: it was planned in the factories without the participation either of the official organs of labour or of the soviet institutions. It was initiated and organised by the Bolshevik party, which made a direct appeal to the workers. According to Sukhanov, the conference really represented "workers from the bench". For two days this workers' parliament debated the economic crisis and social ruin throughout the country. The Bolsheviks developed their slogan of "workers' control". When the vote was taken, 335 of the 421 workers voted for the Bolsheviks. The conference of the factory committees resolved to "organise in Petersburg an all-city centre of the representatives of all factory committees and trade unions".[36]

During May and June more and more factories went over to the Bolsheviks, passing similar resolutions on workers' control and sending Bolsheviks as their representatives in the soviet. A significant though little noted date in the history of the revolution is 13 June, when the workers' section of the Petrograd soviet passed, by 173 votes to 144, a resolution with the Bolshevik formula that power should be in the hands of the soviets.[37] Only weak, mostly illegal trade unions had existed before the revolution. After February they developed somewhat slower than the factory committees, but more than 2,000 were created in the course of the year.[38]

On 3 June, the first all-Russian congress of workers' and soldiers' soviets began a three-week-long session. It elected a central executive committee, which was dominated by Mensheviks and SRs. Of the 777 delegates definitely committed to a party, 105 were Bolsheviks.

Sukhanov recalled that the Menshevik internationalists didn't even number 35; all the rest were supporters of Tsereteli and Tereshchenko. Also represented were the United Internationalists, "which [Iuri] Steklov was trying to turn into a party and which the Interdistrictites led by Lunacharskii and Trotsky had joined. But this fraction didn't have more than from 35 to 40 people either".[39] A lively clash took place after Tsereteli claimed there was no party that would say "Give us the power". Lenin leapt to his feet to argue that "the Bolshevik party is ready at any moment to assume full power... They say we cannot get on without the financial support of England and France. But this 'supports' us just as a noose supports the man who is being hanged".[40]

The June demonstration

The Provisional Government went through further crises in June. They faced a serious challenge to their authority from militant workers and soldiers, who were taking matters into their own hands with some audacious expressions of direct action.

On 5 June, a group of anarchists seized a printing press, prompting the legal authorities to act. On 7 June the minister of justice gave notice to evict the anarchist-communists from their headquarters in the Durnovo villa. The anarchists refused to comply and appealed to the Vyborg factory workers and soldiers to support them. The next day thousands of workers went on strike: 28 factories came out. Representatives of 150 factories and military units attended an anarchist meeting on 12 June. Stalin, in a *Pravda* article (14 June), condemned the activities of the anarchist-communists as "ruinous to the workers' revolution". He argued that "we must suppress all anarchist demonstrations in order to prepare that much more vigorously for the 18 June demonstration".[41]

The Bolshevik military organisation took the initiative for a demonstration on 10 June, as an expression of mass opposition to the Provisional Government's preparations for an early military offensive. The party took steps to organise the demonstration and won the support of the Mezhraionka. Stalin wrote a leaflet and Bolshevik agitators toured workplaces. However, the day before it was due to take place, the all-Russian congress of soviets opposed the demonstration and the Bolsheviks reluctantly cancelled it. Some rank-and-file Bolsheviks tore up their party membership cards in disgust.

On 12 June, during the same session at which the Bolsheviks were censured for their part in the abortive 10 June demonstration, the congress of soviets voted to stage its own march on Sunday 18 June. The

Bolsheviks recycled their literature from the aborted demonstration and mobilised their forces. The huge demonstration, more than 400,000 strong, marched under the slogans, "All power to the soviets!", "Down with the 10 capitalist ministers!" and "Peace for the hovels, war for the palaces!"

Historian Alexander Rabinowitch states that it was "turned into a clear indication of the attractiveness of the Bolshevik programme and the effectiveness of Bolshevik techniques".[42]

The anarchists intervened in the demonstration. They decided to lead a crowd of 1,500-2,000 armed men to the Crosses [Kresty], the Vyborg prison in which the Bolshevik military organisation leader Flavian Khaustov was held, securing his release at gunpoint. The following day, the Provisional Government sent troops to the Durnovo villa, arresting all 60 of the workers, soldiers and sailors present and taking them to prison.[43]

Meanwhile, the all-Russian conference of Bolshevik military organisations opened on 16 June and closed on 23 June. Some 107 delegates, mostly rank and file soldiers and representing 26,000 party members from 43 front and 17 rear units, deliberated just as the government launched its ill-fated military offensive. Lenin spoke at the conference on 20 June, warning the Bolshevik militants to avoid provocations. He argued that the Bolsheviks were "an insignificant minority" and therefore it was naïve to think they could immediately take power and hold it at that moment.[44] This was wise counsel but it went unheeded. Militants pressed on, precipitating the July days and giving the Provisional Government the opportunity to stabilise itself.

The July Days

The "July Days" — a half-cocked uprising — was a pivotal moment in the history of the Russian revolution. For the Provisional Government it was the chance to repress the Bolshevik party, with the intention of destroying it as a force.

On 2 July the Kadets resigned from the government over the question of Ukrainian autonomy and general unhappiness with the administration. Over the next two days, hundreds of thousands of workers and soldiers demanded that the Petrograd soviet take governmental power. Then on 7 July Prince Lvov resigned as minister-president when the government, now overwhelmingly socialist, adopted a programme statement promising more sweeping social and economic reforms than he felt was within the rights of the Provisional Government to do.[45]

The July uprising was initiated in the First Machine Gun Regiment, which feared the Provisional Government was preparing to send them to join the disastrous military offensive at a newly launched front in the war. They argued that because of the large quantity of machine guns at their disposal, the regiment could easily overthrow the Provisional Government by itself. On 2 July the Bolshevik military organisation appealed to the party central committee for directives and was instructed not to participate and to take all possible steps to prevent an uprising. The following day the committee voted again against participating in a demonstration, with Trotsky and the Mezhraionka supporting this position.[46] On 3 July, in Anchor Square, Kronstadt's revolutionary forum, two prominent anarchists addressed a crowd of workers, sailors and soldiers who had gathered there in anticipation of radical action against the government. Efim Yarchuk and Iosif Bleikhman exhorted the First Machine Gun Regiment to overthrow the bungling Provisional Government.[47]

On the evening of 3 July, soldiers from the First Machine Gun Regiment began demonstrating in Petrograd. They were joined by other soldiers from Petrograd's garrison, by workers from the striking Putilov works, and, the next morning, by 20,000 sailors from the Kronstadt naval base. The demonstrators numbered probably 60-70,000. Opposing them, the force defending the Tauride Palace was negligible. The soldiers shouted the Bolshevik slogan "All power to the soviets". They were well armed and ignored the Bolsheviks' appeal to call off their action. The Bolshevik central committee reversed its position opposing street demonstrations in the early morning hours of 4 July, with the Petersburg committee and the all-Russian bureau of the military organisation already involved in the protests. Contemporaries estimated the number of demonstrators on 4 July were as high as half a million, while some 400 were killed or wounded over the two days.[48]

One celebrated incident summed up the mood of the July actions. Demonstrators arrived at the Tauride Palace and began to agitate about Anatoli Zhelezniakov, a truculent anarchist and Kronstadt sailor, who had been arrested at the Durnovo villa. Unable to find the justice minister Pavel Pereverzev, they instead collared the SR minister of agriculture, Victor Chernov. In the course of the altercation, a fist-shaking protester exclaimed: "Take power, you son-of-a-bitch, when it's given to you!"[49] Chernov was then "arrested" by the sailors with a view to taking him away.

Trotsky, accompanied by the Kronstadt sailors' leader Fedor Raskolnikov, reached the car in which Chernov was being held.

Raskolnikov describes what happened next:

> *It is difficult to say how long the turbulent excitement of the masses would have gone on... comrade Trotsky then jumped on the bonnet of the car and with a wave of his arm signalled to the crowd to be quiet.*
>
> *In the twinkling of an eye everything became silent and a deathly hush reigned. In a loud, distinct, metallic voice, rapping out every word and carefully articulating every syllable, comrade Trotsky made a short speech... 'I am sure that not one of you is in favour of this arrest... Whoever is for violence, let him raise his hand'. Comrade Trotsky stopped speaking and cast his eye over the whole crowd, as though throwing down a challenge to his opponents...*
>
> *'Citizen Chernov, you are free', said comrade Trotsky, turning round towards the minister of agriculture with a motion of his hand inviting him to get out of the car. Chernov was half-dead. I helped him get out of the car: with a sluggish, exhausted look and unsteady, irresolute gait he walked up the steps and disappeared into the entrance-hall of the palace.*[50]

There were echoes of the July days in a handful of other places across Russia — in Ivanovo-Voznesensk (the "Russian Manchester"), Nizhni Novgorod, Kiev, Astrakhan and other towns. Only in Ivanovo-Voznesensk, an overwhelmingly working class textile town with a long record of revolutionary activity, was there a conscious assumption of authority by the local soviet.[51] The isolation of the movement in Petrograd afforded the Provisional Government the prospect of rolling back the whole movement, and it took to its task with alacrity.

The Minister of Justice Pereverzev circulated claims that the Bolsheviks had deliberately provoked the July uprising on instructions from the German general staff, while the ex-Bolshevik Grigori Alexinskii accused Lenin of being in the pay of the enemy. The accusation that the Germans had facilitated Lenin's return in order to weaken the war effort was amplified. That some Mensheviks and SRs were present on the same train bringing Lenin back to Russia, and that others, such as Martov and Pavel Axelrod, followed via the same route after Lenin, counted for nothing. The government's offensive against the Bolsheviks was launched at dawn on 5 July, when a detachment of soldiers arrived at *Pravda's* publishing plant, only a little too late to catch Lenin. However, approximately 200 individuals were arrested and indicted by the Provisional Government for complicity in the July uprising, including most members of the Bolshevik military organisation.[52]

On Thursday 6 July, leading SRs led a scratch detachment to the Kshesinskaia mansion and the Peter-Paul fortress. They were about to lay siege and ready to open fire when it turned out that the Bolsheviks had already abandoned the house. At the Peter-Paul fortress, the Kronstadters had left, and the fortress was "taken" without a shot. The Durnovo villa was taken in the same fashion during the afternoon. The anarchists had left. A few weapons and a great deal of literature were found there.[53]

Yet the impact of the reaction should not be underestimated. Official Stalinist histories suggest that the July attacks — the combination of repression and slander — barely left a trace. But Bolshevik leaders such as Lenin and Grigori Zinoviev were forced into hiding, while others such as Trotsky and Lev Kamenev were arrested. Varvara Iakovleva wrote that "all the reports from the localities described with one voice not only a sharp decline in the mood of the masses, but even a definite hostility to our party". In some cases, Bolshevik speakers were beaten up. She recalled that "the membership fell off rapidly, and several organisations, especially in the southern provinces, even ceased to exist entirely".[54]

On 7 July a second Provisional Government, a so-called socialist "government of salvation of the revolution" was formed with Kerensky as minister-president. Sukhanov writes that this coalition "didn't last long — a fortnight in all". The entire period "was spent in an uninterrupted, frenzied, self-forgetting hunt by Kerensky and Tsereteli for new bourgeois ministers".[55]

On 12 July the government authorised the closure of newspapers advocating disobedience of military orders, and provided for administrative arrest of "persons whose activity constitutes a particular threat to the defence and internal security of the state". On the same day the government restored the death penalty in the army. Kerensky ordered a special military expedition to the Volga river city of Tsaritsyn to suppress the Bolshevik-led radical soviet there and the exceptionally mutinous local army garrison. The military cadets even executed a raid on the government Mensheviks themselves, whose party was headed by the minister of the interior.[56]

Kerensky managed to form a new, third coalition government on 23 July, which included both Kadets and Chernov. Trotsky commented in his *History* that "in the first coalition, formed on 6 May, the socialists had been in the minority, but they were in fact masters of the situation". However, in the ministry that met on 24 July, "the socialists were in a majority, but they were mere shadows of the liberals". For good reason, Trotsky defined Kerensky as "the mathematical centre of Russian Bonapartism" — meaning an authoritarian leader seeking to balance between conflicting forces.[57]

The counter-revolution

Russian capitalists took the opportunity presented by the July days to press forward with their own counter-revolution. Although they were hopelessly weak and divided under the tsar, they were united in their exploitation of the working class. Foreign investment in Petrograd and southern Russia, mainly in heavy industries, coal mining and the extraction of oil, tied these sections of capital to international finance and made them heavily dependent on the autocracy for government contracts. However, in Moscow and elsewhere, capital in industries such as textiles was a product of native, Russian accumulation, and some were more liberal in their politics.[58]

In Petrograd the leading bourgeois organisations were the Society for the Economic Rehabilitation of Russia and the Republican Centre. Both had ties to the armed forces. In Moscow the all-Russian union of trade and industry functioned in close cooperation with the Kadets. The Russian landowning class was also represented through its chief organisation, the Landowners' Union. The Kadets pushed for a government with "unlimited power", and even "dictatorship" was not baulked at. On 15 July Kerensky met with leading Kadets and industrialists. The coordination of all the various groups took place chiefly at the Moscow conference and at separate meetings shortly before, such as the "conference of public men" on 8 August.[59]

The Moscow state conference took place on 12-13 August. Kerensky called the gathering in an effort to strengthen his government and the state, but instead it displayed deep divisions. The bourgeoisie were corralling their forces, but the workers emphatically demonstrated a continued willingness to fight. The conference opened in a mostly shut-down city when the Bolshevik Moscow regional bureau took the lead in organising a wildcat protest strike for the opening day. The strike was subsequently endorsed by trade union leaders, by the Bolshevik Moscow committee, representatives of Moscow district soviets and district Bolshevik committees. By a vote of 312 to 284, however, a joint meeting of the Moscow workers' and soldiers' soviets opposed such action.[60] Osip Piatnitskii, a member of the Bolsheviks Moscow committee, subsequently wrote: "The strike came off magnificently. There were no lights, no tramcars, the factories and shops were closed and the railroad yards and stations, even the waiters in the restaurants had gone on strike." Miliukov added "the delegates coming to the conference could not ride on the tramways, nor lunch in the restaurants".⁶¹

Behind these conflicts was the social polarisation of Russian society, still at war, racked with economic crisis and lacking in political legitimacy. It was symbolised by Kerensky's decision on 18 July to move the Provisional Government and his own residence to the tsar's Winter Palace, while the Tauride Palace could be refurbished. In a concomitant move on 4 August, the Petersburg soviet and central executive committee moved to the Smolny Institute, previously a school for daughters of the nobility.⁶²

But Kerensky was unable to resolve even the basic problems of democracy. The demand for a Constituent Assembly had hung over the Provisional Government since its inception. On 22 July Kerensky announced that the elections would be held on 30 September and the convocation of the assembly on 12 December. However, on 22 August, citing problems with compiling the electoral lists, Kerensky ordered the postponement of the elections until 25 November, with the assembly scheduled to open on 12 December. The absence of legitimacy dogged Kerensky's administration, fuelling the suspicion of his own Bonapartist intentions while providing ample ammunition for the Bolsheviks to promote a more thoroughgoing democracy based on the soviets.

Kornilov or Lenin?

In his retrospective history of the Russian revolution, the Kadet Miliukov subtitled his second volume: Kornilov or Lenin? The insight accurately reflected the realities of power in August 1917. Who was the Kornilov of Miliukov's title?

General Lavi Kornilov was not a newcomer to the events of 1917. When the tsar abdicated in March, Kornilov was commanding the 48th artillery division in Galicia. One of Rodzianko's last acts was to appoint Kornilov commander of the Petrograd garrison. When demonstrations took place in the capital on 20-21 April in connection with the Miliukov note to the Allies, Kornilov ordered troops under his command to open fire on the demonstrators. When the order was not carried out because the Petrograd soviet had not given its consent Kornilov resigned his post in disgust.⁶³

On 18 July Kerensky appointed Kornilov to the post of commander-in-chief, also appointing the SR Boris Savinkov as assistant minister of war. After Kerensky's offensive against the Bolsheviks, there was a resurgence of the right — groups of army officers, industrialists, conservative politicians and others wanted to reverse the "rot". They sought out a strong man to take control and rescue Russia. The idea of a military dictator to accomplish these goals gained ground. The conservative press began to build Kornilov as a national hero and saviour of the country. At his arrival in Moscow for the state conference in August, Fedor Rodichev, a prominent Kadet, declared "Save Russia, and a grateful people will revere you".[64]

Kornilov wanted a strong government, purged of socialists, and either led or dominated by himself. He wanted to dispense with democracy in the army and to reorganise and strengthen Russia's war offensive. On 11 August, Kornilov argued that it was "high time to hang the German agents and spies headed by Lenin", and to "disperse the soviet of workers and soldiers in such a way that it would not reassemble anywhere". He toyed with idea of outright military seizure of power, while looking to act on behalf of the existing government against a Bolshevik provocation.[65]

On 27 August false rumours circulated of a Bolshevik uprising to coincide with the upcoming six-month anniversary of the February revolution. Kerensky sought Kornilov's support to enforce martial law in Petrograd, only to backtrack and announce Kornilov's removal as commander-in-chief. Kornilov then issued a statement denouncing Kerensky, the soviet and the Bolsheviks and ordered General Krymov, with the so-called "savage division", made up of mainly Muslim fighters from the Caucasus, to take Petrograd.[66]

Kornilov's rebellion posed an existential threat to the revolution and required a reaction commensurate with the danger of the situation. The right-Menshevik Simon Weinstein proposed that the executive committee of the soviets create an extraordinary military defence organ, the "committee for struggle against the counterrevolution", which began to function on the afternoon of 28 August. It was composed of three representatives from the SRs, the Mensheviks and the Bolsheviks. It set in motion masses of armed workers and soldiers as the only organised force that could repulse the reactionaries.[67]

The role played by the Bolsheviks was crucial at this juncture, as even their opponents testified. Sukhanov argues that the Bolsheviks were "the only organisation that was large, welded together by elementary discipline, and united with the democratic rank-and-file of the capital". Without them the committee was "impotent", and "it could only have passed the time with makeshift proclamations and flabby speeches by orators who had long since lost all authority". The Bolsheviks sent their representatives into the committee for struggle, although they were a minority there. They voted against a resolution to give Kerensky a free hand, but declared that if the government were really going to fight against the counter-revolution, they were ready to co-ordinate their entire activity with the Provisional Government, and conclude a military alliance with it. The Bolsheviks showed "extraordinary tact and political wisdom, to say nothing of devotion to the revolution".[68]

A Bolshevik central committee cable of 29 August stated: "In the interests of repulsing the counterrevolution, we are working in collaboration with the soviet on a technical and informational basis, while fully retaining our independent political position." As Lenin put it: "We shall fight, we are fighting against Kornilov… but we do not support Kerensky."[69] Some 240 revolutionary committees sprang up between 27 and 30 August in various parts of Russia, often on the initiative of local soviets. Within hours, alarm whistles were sounded in factories throughout Petrograd. Acting on their own, without instructions from higher authorities, workers reinforced security around plant buildings and began to form fighting detachments. During the Kornilov days, many of the newly recruited Red Guards received military training from the Bolshevik military organisation.[70]

Rabinowitch describes how swift action by rail and telegraph workers prevented reactionary leaders in the capital from establishing communications with advancing counterrevolutionary forces. The "savage division" were encircled by local workers and peasants, who berated them for betraying the revolution. The troops had not been told the real reason for their movement northward. Most had little sympathy for Kornilov and no desire to oppose the Provisional Government and the soviet. On 30 August the troops hoisted a red flag inscribed "Land and Freedom" over the headquarters. Rail workers held back rolling stock, wrecked bridges and track, and effectively blocked communications between Krymov's forces.[71]

By 31 August Kornilov's revolt had collapsed. He was placed under house arrest, although guarded by his own loyal bodyguards. Sukhanov described the extraordinary spectacle of representatives of the "savage division" addressing the Petrograd soviet to condemn Kornilov and explain their own role:

> The "bureau" was packed tight with Caucasian greatcoats, fur caps, felt cloaks, galoons, daggers, glossy black moustaches, astounded prawn-like eyes, and the smell of horses. This was the elite, the cream, headed by "native" officers, in all perhaps 500 men. The crowd kept the deepest silence while the delegates of the individual units, with their caps in their hands, made broken speeches in the names of those who had sent them.

On the whole they all said one and the same thing. In naively grandiloquent language they extolled the revolution and talked about their devotion to it to the tomb, to the last drop of their blood. Not one man in their units, not one of their people had gone or would go against the revolution and the revolutionary government. A misunderstanding had taken place, dissipated by the simple establishment of the truth. The "savages" were the bearers of solemn vows.[72]

Historian Rex Wade argues that the radical left gained new popularity from the Kornilov affair and this was "quickly translated into an elected majority for a Bolshevik-led radical left coalition in the Petrograd soviet and in many other city soviets and army committees". That in turn set the stage for the October revolution. The Bolsheviks "became the political alternative for the disappointed and disenchanted, for those looking for new leadership". But their appeal was not merely negative. They also drew support for the policies they advocated.[73]

The Bolshevik resurgence

The Bolshevik resurgence made visible by the response to Kornilov's rebellion had begun a month earlier. On 26 July to 3 August, 150 delegates met for the sixth congress of the RSDLP, under illegal conditions, and saw the fusion of the Bolsheviks with the Mezhraionka. The party's chief organiser Iakov Sverdlov reported that the party had grown from 80,000 members in 78 local organisations in April to 200,000 members in 162 local organisations. The congress discarded the slogan "all power to the soviets" in favour of a policy of "dictatorship of the proletariat and the poorest peasantry".[74]

The measure of the Bolshevik resurgence was registered across the labour movement and in bourgeois elections. At the end of July the Moscow conference of factory and shop committees adopted a Bolshevik resolution. A Moscow delegate, Podbelskii, reported to a party conference: "Six district soviets out of ten are in our hands… Under the present organised slanderous attacks only the worker mass which firmly supports Bolshevism is saving us". At the beginning of August, in elections at the Moscow factories, Bolsheviks were elected in place of Mensheviks and SRs.[75] On 7 August the second Petrograd conference of factory committees opened in Smolny and again the leadership was completely in the hands of Bolsheviks.[76]

Trotsky reported on a regional conference of trade unions in the Urals in the middle of August, uniting 150,000 workers, and where Bolshevik resolutions were carried. On 20 August at a conference of the factory and shop committees in Kiev, a Bolshevik-backed resolution was carried by a majority of 161 votes against 35, with 13 abstaining. At the democratic elections for the city Duma of Ivanovo-Voznesensk, which coincided exactly with the Kornilov revolt, the Bolsheviks won 58 seats out of 102, the Socialist Revolutionaries 24, the Mensheviks 4. In Kronstadt a Bolshevik, Lazar Bregman, was elected president of the soviet.[77]

On 31 August a Bolshevik-sponsored resolution passed in the Petrograd soviet for the first time. A heated debate through the night on the merits of creating an exclusively socialist government ended at about 5am on 1 September, when the delegates rejected the SRs' resolution and adopted Kamenev's statement. The vote was 279 deputies in favour, 115 opposed, with 51 abstentions. Rabinowitch argues that the number of deputies present and voting on this occasion constituted a relatively small fraction of the Petrograd soviet's total membership. This was "at least partly because many military representatives were still on duty with their regiments, defending the capital against Kornilov". However, "many rank and file left Mensheviks and SRs with no organisational loyalty to the Bolsheviks sided with the Bolsheviks on this issue". Nonetheless "the vote of the Petrograd soviet on 31 August reflected a gradual, although by no means negligible, leftward shift in the deputies' orientation".

The old soviet SR-Menshevik pro-war politicians put their leadership to a vote of confidence on 9 September and lost. They had not reckoned with the changes in workplaces or within the Petrograd garrison, where control of many regimental committees passed into the hands of the Bolsheviks. The moderate socialists who comprised the old presidium walked out in a huff, and on 25 September the leadership of the Petrograd soviet was completely reorganised. Making up the new presidium were two SRs, one Menshevik, and four Bolsheviks (Trotsky, Kamenev, Alexei Rykov and G F Fedorov); Trotsky replaced Chkheidze as chair.[78]

Sukhanov described the new relation of forces in the Petrograd soviet. In his first speech as chair Trotsky said that actually he had not taken Chkheidze's place, but, on the contrary, Chkheidze had been occupying his place: Trotsky had last chaired the Petersburg soviet during the 1905 revolution. For the workers, the Bolsheviks "had become their own people, because they were always there, taking the lead in details as well as in the most important affairs of the factory or barracks". They had become "the sole hope". On the new executive committee of 44 members, two-thirds were Bolsheviks. The Mensheviks numbered five in all, while the Menshevik-Internationalists did not get a single seat. However, at its first session the Bolshevik-led executive co-opted the latter group with a consulting voice, including Sokolov, Martov, Sukhanov himself and others.[79]

Soviet power had spread rapidly. In Trotsky's words, the soviet system "had been raised up over a human ocean which was billowing powerfully and driving its waves leftward". At the end of August, the secretariat of the executive committee counted as many as 600 soviets.[80] As early as 1 September the Bolshevik newspaper *Rabochii* announced that 126 soviets had requested the soviet central executive committee to take over power. On 5 September a Bolshevik resolution carried in the Moscow soviet, and two weeks later it elected a new executive committee with a Bolshevik majority and Viktor Nogin as chair. On 5 September a congress of soviets in Krasnoyarsk in Siberia revealed a Bolshevik majority. The following day a message from Ekaterinburg, the main city of the Urals and an important mining and industrial region, announced that power had passed into the hands of the soviets. On 10 September a regional congress of soviets in Finland adopted Bolshevik resolutions by big majorities.[81]

The mass support enjoyed by the Bolsheviks was also evident in the elections to city and district government councils during 1917, where the Bolsheviks received a third of the votes for the Petrograd city council on 20 August, despite the absence of top party leaders. This was second only to the SRs, who got 37%. In Moscow, Bolsheviks gained an absolute majority (51%) in voting for city district councils on 24 September, a dramatic rise from June when they had obtained only 12% of the vote for the city council. The SRs won 58% in June but only 14% in September. Polarisation was also evident: for example, the Kadets increased their vote in Moscow (though not in Petrograd).[82]

The September crisis

Although September opened with the defeat of Kornilov, there was no respite for Kerensky. On 1 September the Provisional Government ministers turned the running of the government over to a council of five, which was immediately dubbed "the directory" (alluding to the five-member executive set up during the French revolution). But the government no longer had an operable peace policy and had failed to meet the aspirations of the peoples of Russia. A sense of general crisis pervaded life, a feeling that things could not go on as they were. On 14-22 September Kerensky attempted to shore up his increasingly Bonapartist rule by holding a "'democratic conference", which elected a "council of the republic", or pre-parliament. A fourth Provisional Government was formed on 25 September. It was headed by Kerensky and included Kadets, Mensheviks, SRs and other moderate socialists and liberals.[83]

With growing Bolshevik support and the crisis of the Provisional Government, Lenin — who was still in hiding — decided in September that the time was right to agitate for an insurrection. On 15 September, the top Bolshevik leadership received two letters, 'The Bolsheviks must assume power' and 'Marxism and insurrection', in which Lenin summoned the party to make preparations for an immediate armed uprising. The central committee felt the letters so incendiary that they considered destroying them, although one copy was preserved. On 22 September, Lenin wrote 'Heroes of Fraud and the Mistakes of the Bolsheviks', in which he argued that the Bolsheviks should have walked out of the democratic state conference in protest. The following day, in 'From a publicist's diary: the mistakes of our party', he commented: "Trotsky was for the boycott [of the pre-parliament]. Bravo, Comrade Trotsky!" A steady stream of communications from hiding came to a head on 29 September, when Lenin tendered his resignation from the central committee in order to campaign among the rank and file of the party and at the party congress on the matter of insurrection. In 'The crisis has matured' he wrote, "for it is my profound conviction that if we 'wait' for the congress of soviets and let the present moment pass, we shall ruin the revolution".[84]

The conditions for insurrection

The most significant essential element of the situation by September 1917 was the revolt of labour. Workers already had "the mood of bitterness" generated by memories of class oppression. There were queues and shortages, all the elements of irritation that came with the collapse of national economic life. After July employers' attitudes had hardened. This was summed up in the speech given by the industrialist Riabushinskii. Addressing a congress of business people in Moscow on 16 August, he warned of "the bony hand of hunger", which "would grasp by the throat the members of the different committees and soviets" and bring them to their senses. The phrase obtained wide circulation and served to spur on the workers' revolt.

The conditions for an insurrection were also evident in the ongoing mutiny of the Russian army. While the fighting continued at the front, as historian Christopher Read put it, "the plight of troops went from the unbearable to the unimaginable".[85] Chamberlin argues that between spring and autumn this army, the largest ever put into the field by any country, was transformed into "an enormous, exhausted, badly clothed, badly fed, embittered mob of people, united by thirst for peace and general disillusionment". The mutiny of the Russian armed forces was protracted and varied. Sometimes it assumed relatively mild forms: "refusal to obey orders or to go into the trenches, desertion". Sometimes it found expression in the lynching and beating of officers and commissars.

The outstanding feature of the post-revolutionary Russian army was its far-flung network of committees. Although few had a Bolshevik majority (most who professed any political allegiance were SRs), the Bolsheviks were able to influence it through their military organisation, clubs and newspapers such as *Okopnaya Pravda* (*Trench Truth*). The troops understood that the fault for continuing the war lay with the Provisional Government, which by refusing to give up the utopian formula "war to the victorious end" assured themselves revolution to the bitter end. A congress of the Baltic fleet wrote to the premier: "To you, betrayer of the revolution, Bonaparte Kerensky, we send our curses".[86]

The third great element of the social revolutionary movement were the seizures of landed estates by the peasantry. These events took place across Russia, had much in common, and proceeded with a similar rhythm after they began at the end of March. A striking feature was the speed with which the peasants created new forms of organisation, particularly the local *volost* or township committees. A congress of peasant deputies met in Petrograd from 17 May to 10 June. Of the 1,115 delegates, 537 were SRs, while there were only 14 Bolshevik delegates. On every question except land the executive committee elected by the congress of peasant soviets was rather moderate. It "severely condemned the Bolshevik demonstration in the July Days, adopted a definitely defencist attitude in regard to the war, supported the idea of a coalition government to the end and was violently hostile to the Bolshevik overturn in November". But in the autumn a distinct change came over the peasant movement: it became at once less organised and more violent. The single month of October witnessed 42% of all cases of sacking and destruction of country homes reported for the whole eight months after the overthrow of the tsar.[87]

Sukhanov describes the peasant upsurge:

> "Disorders" were taking on absolutely unendurable, really menacing proportions in Russia. Anarchy was really getting under way. The city

and the countryside were both in revolt. The first was demanding bread, the second land. The new coalition was met with hunger riots and savage pogroms throughout Russia. I happen to have in front of me reports of such riots in Zhitomir, Kharkov, Tambov, Orel, Odessa, etc., etc. Troops were sent everywhere, Cossacks whenever possible. There were repressions, shootings, martial law. But nothing helped. Petersburg was quiet; it simply hungered and waited.

But the peasants, finally losing patience, began settling the agrarian question at first hand by their own methods. It was impossible not to give them land: it was impossible to torture them any longer by uncertainty. It was impossible to make speeches to them about the "regulation of rural relations without the destruction of the existing forms of land-holding".

But this was the essence of the coalition. And the peasants began acting on their own. Estates were divided up and tilled, herds were slaughtered and driven off, country-houses were destroyed and set on fire, arms were seized, stores were plundered and destroyed, trees and orchards were chopped down, there was murder and violence. These were no longer "excesses", as they had been in May and June. It was a mass phenomenon of tidal waves heaving and billowing throughout the country.[88]

On 6 September the Bolshevik military organisation issued detailed instructions for organising and training "workers' *druzhiny*" (voluntary guards or militia) in its newspaper. After the Bolsheviks won the leadership of the Petrograd soviet in late September they created a department for the workers' guard, chaired by Konstantin Iurenev. On the eve of the October revolution they worked out an elaborate city-wide structure for this Red Guard, headed by a general staff. The Red Guards — some 200,000 by October — were active together with soldiers in guarding factories and policing the streets. Red Guards were therefore vital for winning soviet power.[89]

Workers undertook militant forms of direct action. Among the major strikes were that of the Moscow leather workers, which began at the end of August and was not fully settled at the time of the October revolution, and that of the textile workers of the Ivanovo-Voznesensk and Kineshma, which was also in progress at the time of the insurrection.[90] Workers' control took on more expansive forms as employees sought to shut down production. The factory committees took on a wide range of functions, including guarding factory property, overseeing hiring and firing, labour discipline, and organising food supplies. By October, two-thirds of enterprises with 200 or more workers had such committees. Similarly, the soviets were the principal organs of political expression for the workers and soldiers. By October there were 1,429 soviets, of which 455 were soviets of peasants' deputies.[91]

The October government crisis

The government crisis deepened as October began, while the labour movement coalesced around the need for soviet power. On 6 October the government announced plans to send around half of the Petrograd garrison to defend the approaches to the city from opposing armies. Bread had been rationed since spring, but in mid-October incoming bread supplies fell dramatically below daily demands. By mid-October Petrograd had only three or four days of food reserves and little prospect of improvement. Long queues snaked out from food shops. The spectre of starvation was real for the city's workers.

But Russia's labour movement was in no mood to acquiesce. In Baku, a six day general strike against 610 firms in September-October radicalised workers. Successive workers' organisations became thoroughly Bolshevik. The issue before the workers by mid-October was not whether to have a socialist government, but when and how. The call for soviet power meant a government that would use state power in the workers' interests. Workers' support for a socialist government — soviet power — and Lenin's insistence on an armed seizure of power by the Bolsheviks were not the same thing, but they would converge in response to Kerensky's actions in late October.[92]

The pompously entitled "provisional council of the Russian republic", better known as the pre-parliament, opened on 7 October in the luxurious surroundings of the Marinskii Palace. The "democratic" majority consisted of 308 people, of whom 66 were Bolsheviks, about 60 official Mensheviks and 120 SRs, about 20 of whom were Left SRs. Then there were some co-operators, who included extreme right Mensheviks and SRs, about 30 Menshevik-Internationalists and 75 Cadets. Sukhanov reflected that this pre-parliament was "officially powerless, a concoction unworthy of the revolution and pathetic as an institution". Trotsky convinced the Bolshevik faction that the boats should be conclusively and publicly burnt and won a majority of two or three votes for the Bolsheviks to leave the pre-parliament immediately. When the chair called the pre-parliament meeting to order, Trotsky read out the party's declaration, and the Bolsheviks walked out.[93]

The Bolshevik debate on soviet power

From 27 September onwards the main Bolshevik newspaper carried across the front page the headline: "Prepare for the congress of soviets on 20 October!" Unlike earlier in the year, there was now widespread support for an all-socialist government taking power through the soviets. In Kazan on the Volga river, soldiers of the garrison had voted almost unanimously for a soviet regime. In Baku, the large oil centre of the Caucasus, a meeting of the soviet and of labour and army organisations voted, 238 to 55, for non-confidence in the Provisional Government and for the transfer of power to the soviets. In Nikolaev, a town in South Ukraine, the Bolsheviks obtained 13 seats out of 15 in the re-elected soviet executive committee.[94]

On 10 October the Bolshevik central committee met and for the first time since July, Lenin was able to leave hiding and attend. The meeting took place in the apartment of Galina Flakserman, a Bolshevik activist since 1905, a member of staff at *Izvestia* in 1917 and an aide to the central committee secretariat. Flakserman was also married to Sukhanov, who recounted the special steps taken to have him spend the night away from home so the Bolsheviks could deliberate without interruption. The resolution to make armed insurrection the order of the day was carried by ten votes to two, with Zinoviev and Kamenev opposed. This represented a shift in policy towards Lenin's view that any delay in insurrection would mean a disastrous acceleration of military and economic collapse and that the working-class would lose any chance to seize power. However, the resolution did not commit the party to a seizure of power before the congress of soviets or at any other specific time.[95]

Trotsky recalled in his short book *On Lenin* (1924) that there were three groups formed in the central committee: the opponents of the seizure of power by the party; Lenin, who demanded the immediate organisation of the rising, independent of the soviets; and the last group who considered it necessary to bind the rising closely with the second congress of soviets and in consequence wished to postpone it until the latter took place. Although no date appeared in the resolution, Trotsky revealed in 1924 that the committee decided that the rising should take place not later than 15 October, at least before the soviet congress, which was still expected to convene on 20 October. (Stalin disputed the claim about 15 October because it implied the Bolsheviks had let their own resolution slip.)[96]

Lenin thought that the congress of soviets of the northern region (CSNR) meeting on 11-13 October could be used to launch the armed insurrection against the Provisional Government. According to Vladimir Antonov-Ovseenko, the idea was that the proposed congress would "throw around revolutionary Petrograd an iron ring, which would defend the centre of the revolution, the capital, if the need arose". The first session of the CSNR opened in the Smolny Institute in the afternoon on 11 October. It brought together representatives of 23 soviets, including Petrograd, Moscow, Kronstadt, Revel, Helsingfors, the northern, Western and South-Western fronts and the Baltic Fleet.

Trotsky's speech was the highlight of the congress. He began by referring to the recent elections in which the Bolsheviks had gained majorities in the soviets. He attributed this to public disillusionment with previous soviet positions, such as support for the continuation of the war. Trotsky argued that the Petrograd soviet was now in conflict with the Provisional Government over the question of withdrawing some of the garrison from Petrograd, which he argued would leave the revolutionary capital undefended. He contrasted the actions of the Provisional Government, who were ready to abandon Petrograd to the Germans, with those of the Baltic sailors, who had resisted a German attack.

Historian James White argues that the logic of the proceedings at the congress was that "some new body would be created, attached to the Petrograd soviet, which would exercise control over the military authorities in the capital, just as similar organisations monitored the military authorities in towns in the Baltic area". Until 9 October the organisers of the CSNR had intended to propose the establishment of a body of this kind. On that day, however, the Mensheviks on the executive committee of the Petrograd soviet had suggested setting up of a "committee of revolutionary defence", which would concern itself with the question of the defence of Petrograd. This body became the military revolutionary committee (MRC). White points out that the CSNR voted to set up a northern executive committee, many of whom became members of the Petrograd MRC. These included the Bolsheviks Antonov-Ovseenko, Raskolnikov, Pavel Dybenko, Nikolai Krylenko and others.

The CSNR's decision was significant as part of a coherent sequence of events running from September 1917 right to the October revolution. It was a major landmark in a process that brought the Bolsheviks to power through the soviets. This in fact was *Trotsky's* strategy (as opposed to Lenin's more direct approach). It was also the approach that ensured the success of the revolution with minimal bloodshed over the following weeks.[97]

Preparation to seize power continued, with the Kiev, southwest regional soviet congress at Minsk and Ural regional soviet congress declaring for soviet power. When the Bolshevik central committee meeting reconvened on 16 October Lenin delivered a strong defence of the committee's decision to organise an immediate insurrection. He was opposed again by Zinoviev, who insisted that "there are fundamental doubts about whether the success of an uprising is assured", and by Kamenev, who declared that the experience of trying to organise an uprising confirmed that the conditions for one did not exist. Nineteen participants in the meeting supported Lenin's resolution, with two opposed and four abstentions. So preparations continued at pace.[98]

Wade argues that two decisions by their opponents played into the Bolsheviks' hands. First, on 18 October the moderate socialist leaders decided to postpone the opening of the congress of soviets from the 20 to the 25 October. This in fact helped because the Bolsheviks were not ready to seize power before 20 October. Second, Kerensky made a fateful decision to strike at the left again; this was implemented on 24 October and allowed the Bolsheviks to present the insurrection in explicitly defensive terms. Without those events the October revolution as we know it could not have occurred.[99]

The military revolutionary committee

The military revolutionary committee (MRC) was conceived on 9 October, arising from the soviet power, contrary to Stalinist histories, which imply it was the result of the 10 October Bolshevik central committee's decision to prepare for an uprising. Western historians have tended to view the MRC as merely a Bolshevik front organisation. This assessment is also inaccurate. The MRC held its first meeting on 20 October and its headquarters was in the offices of the Petrograd council of trade unions (the parallel committee in Moscow had its base in the Moscow union of metal workers' building). Of its 66 original members, 48 were Bolsheviks, 14 Left SRs and four anarchists. Its principal figures were Trotsky, Mikhail Lashevich, the leaders of the Bolshevik military organisation (Nevskii, Iurenev, Nikolai Podvoiskii, Konstantin Mekhonoshin) and the Left SR Pavel Lazimir.[100]

Sukhanov provides a vivid picture of the constant round of meetings Trotsky and other MRC leaders engaged in to convince key sections of the working class and the army in Petrograd to support soviet power against the reactionaries and the Provisional Government. Trotsky, "tearing himself away from work on the revolutionary staff, personally rushed from the Obukhovsky plant to the Trubochny, from the Putilov to the Baltic works, from the riding-school to the barracks; he seemed to be speaking at all points simultaneously".

On 21 October the Petersburg garrison acknowledged the soviet as the sole power and the MRC as the immediate organ of authority.

This was reinforced the following day when, in the name of the soviet, the MRC messaged: "No orders to the garrison, not signed by the military revolutionary committee, are valid... Vigilance, firmness, and unwavering discipline is the duty of every soldier of the garrison. The revolution is in danger!" On the same day Trotsky spoke at the People's House. He formulated a brief resolution, "we will defend the worker-peasant cause to the last drop of our blood", and asked for a vote. The crowd of thousands raised their hands, the "burning eyes of men, women, youths, soldiers, peasants, and typically lower middle-class faces". They vowed to defend the revolution — and countless other meetings throughout the city made similar pledges.[101]

On 23 October the MRC turned its attention to winning the Peter and Paul fortress. Trotsky described his activity in a little book, *History of the Russian Revolution to Brest-Litovsk*, published just three months after the events:

> *In the courtyard a meeting was being held. The speakers of the right wing were most cautious and evasive, carefully avoiding any question about Kerensky, whose name, even in soldiers' circles, always gave rise to cries of protest and indignation. They, however, listened to us and adhered to us. At four o'clock the cyclists held a battalion meeting in a neighbouring place, in the Modern Circus. Amongst the speakers was the quartermaster-general Paradeloff. He, too, spoke very, very cautiously. Far gone were the days when the official and semi-official orators never spoke of the workers' party otherwise than as a band of traitors and hirelings of the German Kaiser. The assistant-chief of the staff came up to me and said: "Let us, for goodness' sake, come to some understanding." But it was now too late. Against only thirty votes, the battalion declared itself, after a debate, in favour of the assumption of authority by the soviets.*[102]

The MRC's activities were prescient because the Provisional Government was preparing to move against the soviets and their leaders. On 17 October the minister of the interior, Nikolai Kishkin, reported that the government had sufficient reliable forces to put down disturbances once they broke out, but lacked the forces necessary to start an action against the left. However during the night of 23-24 October, the government decided to act. Kerensky proposed arresting the MRC. The government instead agreed to initiate legal proceedings against some MRC members and Bolsheviks, including Trotsky, and to close two Bolshevik newspapers, *Rabochii put'* and *Soldat*. As Wade puts it, "Kerensky unexpectedly handed Lenin his seizure of power before the congress of soviets".[103]

The seizure of power

In the early hours of 24 October the soviet seizure of power began. This was not a response to the government's ill-conceived decision to launch punitive action against the Bolsheviks. The blueprint had already been drawn up by the MRC; insurrectionary forces were to seize the Marinskii Palace and disperse the pre-parliament. Then the Winter Palace was to be surrounded, ministers arrested and the Provisional Government overthrown. Red Guards and pro-soviet soldiers were mobilised to control the bridges over the river and key buildings such as railway stations were occupied. Trotsky's plan focused on defensive measures designed to guarantee that the congress of soviets opened as scheduled on the following day.

Around midnight the insurrection shifted from defensive to offensive action. This was connected to two events: (1) a growing realisation that the government was much weaker than had previously been thought and that the city was coming under the physical control of soldiers and Red Guards rallying to the defence of the soviet, and (2) the arrival of Lenin at soviet headquarters. Lenin's arrival dramatically changed the situation. The Bolshevik soviet leaders shifted from a defensive posture about 2am on the morning of 25 October.[104]

In response, the government managed to assemble only a small force of military cadets, officers, Cossacks, and a detachment of the women's battalions to protect the Winter Palace and key buildings. Kerensky's exit was pathetic. On the morning of 25 October he paced the rooms of the Winter Palace in an overcoat, issuing ministers with instructions. He wanted to leave the city to meet the troops coming from the front for the defence of the Provisional Government. One of his adjutants requisitioned a car belonging to the American embassy. Kerensky "made off in this car, which carried the American flag and aided by this disguise, slipped through the numerous Bolshevik patrols which were already active in the city".[105]

On the afternoon of 25 October the Winter Palace was besieged. However, the socialist journalist John Reed and three other Americans bluffed their way in and wandered around the palace talking to various people, before walking back out past Red Guards and soldiers. The battleship Aurora, then anchored in the Neva river, responded by firing a blank round from its bow gun. Most of the shells fired exploded spectacularly but harmlessly, but one shattered a cornice on the palace and another smashed a third-floor corner window, exploding just above the room in which the government was meeting. Finally, during the late evening, the insurgents filtered into the palace in small numbers, rather than actually "storming" it (as depicted in subsequent fictional romanticised paintings and films). The losses in the taking of the Winter Palace were negligible: five sailors and one soldier killed and a number slightly wounded among the assailants.[106]

The second congress of soviets

While the Provisional Government was under siege the second congress of soviets began to assemble. In his recollections of Lenin published in 1924, Trotsky wrote: "The first session of the second congress of soviets was sitting in Smolny. Lenin did not appear here. He remained in one of the rooms of Smolny in which… there was for some reason no furniture, or almost none. Later somebody spread blankets on the floor and put two cushions on them, Vladimir Ilych and I took a rest there lying side-by-side."[107]

According to a preliminary report to the credentials committee, 300 of the 670 delegates were Bolsheviks, 193 were SRs (of whom more than half were Left SRs), 68 were Mensheviks and 14 were Menshevik-Internationalists. More than 500 came to Petrograd committed in principle to supporting the transfer of "all power to the soviets". The wait for the Winter Palace to be taken meant the opening of the congress was delayed. The congress endorsed Martov's motion, calling for the creation of a democratic coalition government by negotiation. However, a succession of speakers, representatives of the formerly dominant moderate socialist bloc, rose up to denounce the Bolsheviks. These speakers declared their intention to immediately walk out of the congress as a means of opposing the Bolshevik action.[108]

Sukhanov reported on the debate among the Menshevik-Internationalists on whether to walk out. His own view was that boycott was a mistake. First "no one contested the legality of the congress. Second, it represented the most authentic worker-peasant democracy". He added that the congress still retained some of those who participated in the first congress in June, including some Kadets. Sukhanov believed that a Bolshevik regime would be ephemeral and the Mensheviks should propose a "united democratic front". But this "could be achieved only in the arena of soviet struggle".

The [Menshevik] fraction divided and by 14 votes to 12 Martov's motion to leave the congress was carried. Martov denounced the overthrow of the Provisional Government as a "coup d'état" and his fraction walked out. Trotsky famously replied with venom:

> *A rising of the masses of the people... needs no justification. What has happened is an insurrection, and not a conspiracy. We hardened the revolutionary energy of the Petersburg workers and soldiers. We openly forged the will of the masses for an insurrection, and not a conspiracy. The masses of the people followed our banner and our insurrection was victorious. And now we are told: renounce your victory, make concessions, compromise. With whom? I ask: with whom ought we to compromise? With those wretched groups who have left us or who are making this proposal? But after all we've had a full view of them. No one in Russia is with them any longer. A compromise is supposed to be made, as between two equal sides, by the millions of workers and peasants represented in this congress, whom they are ready, not for the first time or the last, to barter away as the bourgeoisie sees fit. No, here no compromise is possible. To those who have left and to those who tell us to do this we must say: you are miserable bankrupts, your role is played out; go where you ought to be: into the dustbin of history!*[109]

Trotsky stated in his *History* that the minutes of the congress were not preserved. The stenographers abandoned Smolny along with the Mensheviks and SRs, and the secretarial notes "were lost without a trace in the abyss of events". There remain "only the hasty and tendentious newspaper reports, written to the tune of the artillery or the grinding of teeth in the political struggle". Lenin's speeches have suffered especially. The initial statement which John Reed puts in the mouth of Lenin, "We shall now proceed to construct the socialist order", does not appear in any of the newspaper accounts, but it was in Trotsky's view "wholly in the spirit of the orator". Reed "could not have made it up".[110]

By pulling out of the congress, the moderate socialists paved the way for a government which had never been publicly broached before — an exclusively Bolshevik regime. A new soviet central executive committee was elected, with the Bolsheviks initially taking 62 seats, the Left SRs 29 and 10 were divided among the Menshevik-Internationalists and other left groups. The soviet cabinet was dubbed the "council of people's commissars" (Sovnarkom) by Trotsky and began to outline a programme of government.

First acts of workers' self-rule

The new workers' government was extremely productive in the first two months of its existence. It issued no fewer than 116 different decrees by the turn of the year. On the first day after the seizure of power decrees on land and peace were passed and the death penalty abolished. On 27 October a temporary decree establishing press control was passed and two days later the new government decreed an eight-hour work day. On 2 November it issued the "declaration of the rights of the peoples of Russia", for the right of self-determination for Russia's various nationalities. A decree on 10 November abolished the many social, legal and civil distinctions, ranks and titles that were part of old Russia, while church schools were transferred to the people's commissariat of education by decree on 11 November. Full separation of church and state followed in January. The decree on workers' control was passed on 14 November. On 22 November the old judicial system was abolished and replaced by new "people's courts". On 16 December a decree abolished all ranks and titles in the army and provided for the election of commanders. The marriage decree on 18 December introduced civil marriages and non-religious weddings, and made it easier to get divorced.[111]

The old regime did not go quietly and some sections took up arms to fight the new workers' government. The Petrograd city council formed a "committee for salvation of the fatherland and revolution". On the morning of 29 October Petrograd awoke to sporadic bursts of rifle fire and the fighting was considerably bloodier than on the day of the revolution. About 200 were killed and wounded on both sides in the storming of the Vladimir junker school (a military academy), which put up especially stubborn resistance. Some of the junkers were thrown from the roofs and killed by enraged red forces, although Antonov-Ovseenko kept his word to ensure the safety of the junkers who had arrested him in the telephone station when they were obliged to surrender.[112]

Meanwhile Kerensky managed to obtain the support of a small Cossack force under General Pyotr Krasnov's command and persuade them to march on Petrograd. Ironically, these were units of the same cavalry corps that Kornilov had relied on against Kerensky in August. The key battle between Krasnov's thousand-strong Cossack force and the revolutionary forces army ten times larger, made up of workers' detachments, soldiers of the Petrograd garrison, and Baltic sailors, took place on 30 October on the Polkovo Heights, 12 miles from Petrograd. The leader of the Baltic sailors, Pavel Dybenko, offered the demoralised Cossacks a deal: swap Kerensky for safe passage to their homes in the south. Learning of this, Kerensky fled once more, disguised in a sailor's uniform wearing driving goggles. He was utterly discredited.

Other opposition came from within the labour movement. On 29

October Vikzhel, the all-Russian executive committee of the union of railway workers, issued an ultimatum, calling for negotiations between the Bolsheviks and the parties that had voluntarily withdrawn from the soviet. The Bolsheviks for their part felt that they needed to accept the proposal and entered into talks. However, the Mensheviks and SRs took a hard position, demanding repudiation of the seizure of power on 25 October and insisting that the new all-socialist government formed must not include Lenin or Trotsky.

In Moscow the Bolsheviks were less prepared for a revolutionary seizure of power. They had a majority in the workers' soviet, but not the separate soldiers' soviet, and so support from the garrison was uncertain. However the Moscow workers' soviet voted to support the Petrograd MRC's seizure of power and to create its own version. The fighting in Moscow was bitter, symbolised by the shooting of several dozen pro-soviet fighters after they surrendered in the Kremlin on 28 October. Red Guards fought with tenacity. The total number of deaths in Moscow was never established, but probably ran to several hundred dead and others wounded. By 2 November, when victory was assured in Moscow, the Bolsheviks had gained tentative control over a belt of territory across north-central European Russia.[113]

The spread of workers' power was highly uneven. In some places the soviets assumed power relatively simply, while in others there was a serious fight. Moscow was the sole place in central and northern Russia where the Bolshevik seizure of power encountered serious, sustained and bloody resistance. In factory towns such as Ivanovo-Voznesensk and Vladimir, taking power was bloodless and straightforward. In Kazan and Saratov there were short fights with the junkers and adherents of the Provisional Government, which ended in victories of the local Bolsheviks. In provincial centres such as Penza and Simbirsk, a Bolshevik-led administration was only established in December. The Ural and Siberian towns accepted the soviet regime in the main without serious opposition, although remote Blagoveschensk was an exception. In Tashkent, the main city of Russian central Asia, the first Siberian regiment and armed workers from the local railroad workshops overcame the resistance of the junkers and Cossacks to set up a soviet government.[114]

The soviet government consolidates

On 9 December the Left SRs finally joined the council of people's commissars, establishing a coalition government with the Bolsheviks that lasted until April 1918. The Bolsheviks and the Left SRs held an "extraordinary congress" on 13 November, where they agreed to create a restructured and much enlarged all-Russia central executive committee of workers', soldiers' and peasants' soviets. This new expanded CEC included 108 representatives from the old executive elected in October at the congress of soviets of workers', soldiers' and peasants' deputies (101 original and seven co-opted members), and an equal 108 from the left-dominated congress of peasants' deputies, 100 from army and navy units and 50 from the trade unions.

The new government was established in the aftermath of the Constituent Assembly elections, which began on 12 November, lasting a fortnight. After the seizure of power in October some Bolsheviks including Lenin wanted to cancel the Constituent Assembly elections, but other leaders disagreed and the elections were allowed to proceed. The elections probably bought valuable time for the new Bolshevik regime. Overall the Bolsheviks obtained only about a quarter of the total votes, although they received the majority of workers' votes and 42% of the soldiers' votes. For the assembly itself, the breakdown by membership shows that, of about 700 or so members, the SRs had 370-380 (including about 81 Ukrainian SRs), the Left SR party 39-40, the Bolsheviks 168-175, the Kadets and the Mensheviks each about 17, nationality candidates about 77-86, with the rest scattered among other parties.

There were many problems with the elections. The lists of candidates had been drawn up months before and did not reflect the split in the SRs and the breakaway of the Left SRs. The elections had been delayed by the Provisional Government and finally took place only after the soviet seizure of power. Lenin argued in *Pravda* on 13 December that a republic of soviets were a "higher form of democracy" compared with a bourgeois parliament. Both the Bolsheviks and the Left SRs began to talk of dispersing the assembly.

The Constituent Assembly finally opened on the afternoon of 5 January 1918 in the Tauride Palace. Victor Chernov, leader of the SRs and former minister in the Provisional Government, was elected president, standing against Maria Spiridonova of the Left SRs. The assembly refused to support the programme of the new soviet government. Raskolnikov read a statement and the Bolsheviks and Left SRs walked out in protest. Around 4am the commander of the guard at the palace, the anarchist Zhelezniakov (previously prominent in the Durnovo villa and July days), approached Chernov and asked that the deputies disperse, "since the guard is tired". The delegates duly vacated the building. When they returned the next day they found it locked and the assembly was dissolved by the soviet government. Then the third congress of soviets was called, which ratified the dissolution and ended the Constituent Assembly.[115]

Conclusion

The Russian revolution remains the high point of working class history. In October 1917, the Russian working class, led by the Bolshevik party, made a revolution, took power, smashed the old state and proceeded to build a new state based on workers' democracy. This socialist political and social revolution not only showed that working class power was possible, but unleashed an enormous democratic festival of the oppressed — poor peasants, minority nationalities and women.

The precious months of 1917 still have much to teach the current generation of activists. The debates about power and resistance, strategy and tactics, about the ebb and flow of struggle, all resonate beyond the immediate context. To examine 1917 in Russia is to glimpse the immense potential of working class revolution. To understand why it was possible for the Russian workers to win remains a vital part of learning the lessons of the past, so as to change the world in the present.

References

1. Russia used the Julian or old style calendar until 24 January 1918, when this system was replaced by the Gregorian or new style calendar used elsewhere in Europe. Dates in this book are old style before 24 January 1918 and new style after that. To convert old style dates to new style dates, add 13 days.
2. Alexander Rabinowitch, [1968] *Prelude to Revolution*, (1991: 24).
3. Rex Wade, *The Russian Revolution, 1917*, (2005: 28).
4. James Bater, 'St. Petersburg and Moscow on the eve of revolution'. In Daniel Kaiser, *The Workers' Revolution in Russia 1917*, (1987: 21-25).
5. Leon Trotsky, [1931] *The History of the Russian Revolution, Vol.1*, (1980: 468-469).
6. Wade, (2005: 90; 146-7; 25).
7. Allan Wildman, *The End of the Russian Imperial Army*, (1980: 95).
8. Trotsky, *HRR Vol.1*, (1980: 43-44).
9. Michael Melancon, '"Stormy Petrels": The Socialist Revolutionaries in Russia's Labour Organisations 1905-1914', *The Carl Beck Papers in Russian and East European Studies*, (1988: 38-41).
10. Sarah Badcock, 'Support for the Socialist Revolutionary Party during 1917'. Doctoral thesis, Durham University, (2000: 34-35).
11. Brian Pearce, 'Building the Bolshevik Party: Some Organisational Aspects', *Labour Review*, (February 1960).
12. Tsuyoshi Hasegawa, *The February Revolution: Petrograd 1917*, (1981: 118-133).
13. Paul Avrich, *The Anarchists in the Russian Revolution* (1973).
14. Eduard Burdzhalov, *Russia's Second Revolution: The February 1917 Uprising in Petrograd*, (1987: 105, 113, 122-26).
15. Wade, (2005: 29-44).
16. William Chamberlin, [1935] *The Russian Revolution, Volume I: 1917-1918*, (1987: 85, 100).
17. Chamberlin, (1987: 73); *Stalin, History of the CPSU(B) (Short Course)*, (1939: 177, 180).
18. Michael Melancon, 'Rethinking the February Revolution, Anonymous Spontaneity or Socialist Agency?' *Carl Beck Papers in Russian and East European Studies*, (2000: 33-35).
19. Lenin, [4 April 1917] 'The Tasks of the Proletariat in the Present Revolution', (*LCW* 24: 22).
20. Chamberlin, (1987: 109-110).
21. Nikolai Sukhanov, [1918-21] *The Russian Revolution 1917*, (1984: 74; 80-82).
22. Trotsky, *HRR Vol.1*, (1980: 216, 285).
23. Wade, (2005: 50).
24. Chamberlin, (1987: 86, 144).
25. Trotsky, *HRR Vol.1*, (1980: 281).
26. Sukhanov, (1984: 195, 232-33).
27. Sukhanov, (1984: 242, 255).
28. Chamberlin, (1987: 142).
29. Trotsky, *HRR Vol.1*, (1980: 206, 214).
30. Rabinowitch, (1991: 51-52).
31. Trotsky, *HRR Vol.1*, (1980: 295, 300).
32. Rabinowitch, (1991: 43).
33. Sukhanov, (1984: 321, 349-50, 359).
34. Wade, (2005: 86).
35. Rex Wade, 'The Red Guards: Spontaneity and the October Revolution'. In Edith Rogovin Frankel et al, *Revolution in Russia: Reassessments of 1917*, (1992: 57-60).
36. Sukhanov, (1984: 373).
37. Chamberlin, (1987: 155).
38. Wade, (2005: 94).
39. Sukhanov, (1984: 378-79).
40. Chamberlin, (1987: 159-60).

41. Rabinowitch, (1991: 65, 100-01).
42. Rabinowitch, (1991: 54, 71, 76, 79, 97, 105).
43. Rabinowitch, (1991: 107-08).
44. Rabinowitch, (1991: 111-12, 121-22).
45. Rex Wade, *The Russian Revolution, 1917*, (2005: 196).
46. Alexander Rabinowitch, [1968] *Prelude to Revolution*, (1991: 135, 137, 157).
47. Paul Avrich, *The Anarchists in the Russian Revolution*, (1973: 133-134).
48. Rabinowitch, (1991: 164-65, 172, 178, 200).
49. Paul Miliukov, [1921] *The Russian Revolution, Vol.1*, (1978: 202).
50. Fedor Raskolnikov, [1925] *Kronstadt and Petrograd in 1917*, (1982: 167).
51. William Chamberlin, [1935] *The Russian Revolution, Volume I: 1917-1918*, (1987: 178).
52. Rabinowitch, (1991: 191, 207, 221).
53. Nikolai Sukhanov, [1918-21] The Russian Revolution 1917, (1984: 469).
54. Trotsky, [1933] *The History of the Russian Revolution, Vol.2*, (1980: 250-51, 256).
55. Sukhanov, (1984: 485, 488).
56. Wade, (2005: 198-199); Sukhanov, (1984: 487).
57. Trotsky, *HRR Vol.2*, (1980: 126-7, 154).
58. James White, 'Moscow, Petersburg and the Russian Industrialists', *Soviet Studies*, 24, 3, (1973: 414-15).
59. James White, 'The Kornilov Affair. A Study in Counter-Revolution', *Soviet Studies*, 20, 2, (1968: 196-97, 187-89).
60. Alexander Rabinowitch, [1976] *Bolsheviks Come to Power: The Revolution of 1917 in Petrograd*, (2004: 111).
61. Trotsky, *HRR Vol.2*, (1980: 149).
62. Sukhanov, (1984: 498, 23 N.1).
63. White, (1968: 193).
64. Wade, (2005: 197-8, 201-202).
65. Rabinowitch, (2004: 109).
66. Wade, (2005: 205-206).
67. Rabinowitch, (2004: 132).
68. Sukhanov, (1984: 505-06).
69. Lenin, [30 August 1917] 'To the Central Committee of the RSDLP', (*LCW 25*: 290).
70. Rabinowitch, (2004: 138, 142).
71. Rabinowitch, (2004: 145, 148-149).
72. Sukhanov, (1984: 519).
73. Wade, (2005: 208).
74. Chamberlin, (1987: 186).
75. Trotsky, *HRR Vol.2*, (1980: 266).
76. Sukhanov, (1984: 492).
77. Trotsky, *HRR Vol.2*, (1980: 276).
78. Rabinowitch, (2004: 162, 175).
79. Sukhanov, (1984: 528-531).
80. Trotsky, *HRR Vol.2*, (1980: 296).
81. Chamberlin, (1987: 278-79).
82. Wade, (2005: 214-15). The August and September elections saw a dramatic falling off of voting.
83. Wade, (2005: 216-218).
84. Rabinowitch, (2004: 178, 191-194).
85. Christopher Read, *From Tsar to Soviets*, (1996: 138).
86. Chamberlin, (1987: 223-24, 228-29, 235-36, 240).
87. Chamberlin, (1987: 242-251).
88. Sukhanov, (1984: 533).
89. Wade, (1992: 62-67).
90. Chamberlin, (1987: 265-68).
91. Steve Smith, *The Russian Revolution: A Very Short Introduction*, (2002 p.16-17).

92. Wade, (2005: 218-222).
93. Sukhanov, (1984: 535-540).
94. Wade, (2005: 226); Chamberlin (1987: 301).
95. Rabinowitch, (2004: 202, 206).
96. Trotsky, [1924] *On Lenin*, (1971: 86-87); Trotsky, [1933] *The History of the Russian Revolution, Vol.3*, (1980: 155-56).
97. James White, 'Lenin, Trotskii and the Arts of Insurrection', *The Slavonic and East European Review*, 77, 1, (1999: 120, 126-127, 130-01, 135, 139).
98. Rabinowitch, (2004: 220-222).
99. Wade, (2005: 230).
100. Rabinowitch, (2004: 233, 239); Chamberlin, (1987: 274, 300); Sukhanov, (1984: 560-562).
101. Sukhanov, (1984: 578, 583-85, 591-92).
102. Trotsky, *History of the Russian Revolution to Brest-Litovsk*, (1918: 81-82).
103. Wade, (2005: 233-34).
104. Wade, (2005: 235-38).
105. Chamberlin, (1987: 314).
106. Wade, (2005: 240-41); Rabinowitch, (2004: 289); Chamberlin, (1987: 319).
107. Trotsky, *On Lenin*, (1971: 91); Trotsky, *HRR Vol.3*, (1980: 306).
108. Rabinowitch, (2004: 291-93).
109. Sukhanov, (1984: 631-32, 645, 639-40).
110. Trotsky, *HRR Vol.3*, (1980: 323-24).
111. Wade, (2005: 270). The Bolsheviks also passed important laws on ecology. The decree on land, issued two days after taking power, declared all forests, waters and subsoil minerals to be the property of the state and arrogated these resources to the state's exclusive use. The law "On Forests" (14 May 1918) created the Central Administration of Forests of the Republic to manage planned reforestation, erosion control, protection of water basins and "the preservation of monuments of nature". On 4 May 1920 the inaugural national *zapovednik* was created, the first protected territory anywhere created by a government exclusively in the interests of the scientific study of nature. Lenin signed a new law, 'On the Protection of Monuments of Nature, Gardens, and Parks' on 16 September 1921. By 1929 there were 61 *zapovedniki* covering four million hectares. These achievements were smashed by Stalin's "revolution from above". See Douglas Weiner, *Models of Nature: Ecology, Conservation and Cultural Revolution in Soviet Russia*, (1988: 29, 61).
112. Chamberlin, (1987: 328-29).
113. Wade, (2005: 248-249, 253-54, 256).
114. Chamberlin, (1987: 341).
115. Wade, (2005: 280, 282-85).

Twelve months that shook the world[1]

Date	Government	Labour movement
9 January 1917		On the anniversary of Bloody Sunday (1905), 186,000 workers across Russia, including 40% of the industrial workers of Petrograd, took strike action.
14 February		Another strike brought out about 84,000 workers and closed more than 50 factories.
23 February		International Women's Day demonstrations and strikes.
24 February		200,000 workers on strike in Petrograd.
25 February		General strike in Petrograd. Shootings and arrests of revolutionists.
26 February	Tsar Nicholas dissolves the Duma (parliament) and order soldiers to suppress the protests.	Tens of thousands of workers in the streets.
27 February	Mutiny of the Guard regiments. Provisional Committee of the Duma announced.	The Petrograd Soviet of Workers' deputies formed.
28 February		First issue of *Izvestia* — "The News of the Soviet."
1 March		Petrograd Soviet Order No. 1 is issued to the soldiers. Soldiers' section of the Petrograd Soviet formed. First session of the Moscow soviet.
2 March	The tsar abdicates. Provisional Government is formed by the Provisional Committee of the Duma, with the support of the Soviet and with Kerensky as Minister of Justice.	Political strikes and demonstrations spread to other cities. More soviets formed.

1. The Russian calendar in 1917 was 13 days behind the calendar used in most of Europe.

Date	Government	Labour movement
3 March	The Grand Duke Mikhail abdicates. The Provisional Government announces the revolution to the world by radio.	
5 March		The first issue of *Pravda*, central organ of the Bolshevik Party.
12 March	Provisional Government abolishes death penalty.	
14 March		Petrograd Soviet "Appeal to the People of the World" declares for "peace without annexations or indemnities".
22 March		Tsereteli and "revolutionary defencists" win majority in the Petrograd Soviet.
23 March		Funeral of the Victims of the Revolution becomes one million-strong demonstration.
27 March	Under pressure from the Petrograd Soviet, the Provisional Government issues a declaration of war aims, repudiating occupation of territories.	
29 March		All-Russian conference of the Soviets.
April		Beginning of peasant land seizures.
3 April		Lenin, Zinoviev and other Bolsheviks arrive from Switzerland.
4 April		Lenin's April Theses outline his policy of proletarian revolution.
18 April	"April Days" crisis: Foreign Minister Miliukov sends a note to the Allies promising war to victory on the old terms.	Demonstrations in Moscow and Petrograd to coincide with international workers' day also oppose war.

Date	Government	Labour movement
20 April		Armed demonstrations of protest against the Miliukov note.
24 April		Beginning of an All-Russian conference of the Bolshevik Party.
1 May		The Petrograd Soviet votes for a coalition government.
4 May		Trotsky arrives from America. Joins Mezhrayontzi, while working with Bolsheviks. All-Russian Congress of Peasants' Deputies opens in Petrograd.
5 May	Coalition government is organised, with Kerensky as Minister of War, and members of the Petrograd Soviet.	
30 May		First conference of factory and shop committees opens in Petrograd.
2 June	Kadet ministers resign from the Provisional Government, formally over a disputed agreement to grant autonomy to Ukraine.	
3 June		First All-Russian Congress of Workers' and Soldiers' Soviets opens for three weeks. Elects a Central Executive Committee dominated by Mensheviks and SRs.
8 June		8 factories shut in protest and government attempts to evict the Petrograd Federation of Anarchist-Communists from the Durnovo villa.
10 June	Ukrainian Central Rada issues First Universal Order.	Planned Bolshevik demonstration in Petrograd banned by the Soviet.

THE RUSSIAN REVOLUTION: WHEN WORKERS TOOK POWER

Date	Government	Labour movement
18 June	Russian military offensive begins.	A half-million strong Petrograd Soviet demonstration called by the Mensheviks and SRs is dominated by Bolshevik slogans: "Down with the Ten Capitalist Ministers" and "All Power to the Soviets".
1 July	Provisional Government delegation and Central Rada reach agreement on limited self-government for Ukraine.	
2 July	Kadet ministers resign over Ukraine issue — new government crisis begins.	
3-5 July		"July Days" — mass, armed demonstrations in Petrograd calling for "All Power to the Soviets". Differences between local and leading Bolsheviks; party takes responsibility for retreat.
5 July	Military offensive collapses. Second Universal of Ukrainian Rada. Finnish parliament votes to assume governing authority in Finland.	
7 July	Prince Lvov resigns. Socialist "Government of Salvation of the Revolution" formed with Kerensky as minister-president.	
12 July	Kerensky launches an offensive against Bolsheviks, with arrests, meetings and newspapers closed and restoration of the death penalty in the army.	
16 July	General Kornilov appointed commander-in-chief of the army.	
18 July	Members of the Duma gather at the Tauride Palace to discuss how to "save" Russia.	Petrograd Soviet moves to Smolny Institute.

Date	Government	Labour movement
20 July	Provisional Government extends the right to vote to women.	
24 July	New coalition government with Kadets.	
26 July		Sixth Congress of the Bolshevik Party; fusion with Mezhrayontzi; new Central Committee elected.
7-12 August		Second Conference of Factory Committees of Petrograd.
12 August	State Conference begins in Moscow, aimed at restoring order.	Moscow strike to coincide with opening of the State Conference.
20 August		Elections held for a new Petrograd City Duma; Bolsheviks make gains.
21 August	German offensive drives Russian army from Riga.	
27 August	Kerensky tries to remove Kornilov; Kornilov marches on Petrograd.	Soviet Committee for Struggle against Counter-revolution formed.
28-30 August		Kornilov coup collapses as workers sabotage his advance and troops desert.
31 August		Petrograd Soviet passes a Bolshevik resolution calling for an all-socialist government excluding the bourgeois parties.
1 September	Government "directory" of five ministers headed by Kerensky established.	
5 September		Bolshevik resolution carries Moscow Soviet.

Date	Government	Labour movement
9 September		Petrograd Soviet confirms Bolshevik resolution. Old leadership resigns.
14-22 September	Last coalition government formed, Kerensky president.	
25 September		Petrograd Soviet elects Trotsky chair with a Bolshevik majority leadership.
7 October	Council of the Republic, or preparliament opens.	Bolsheviks walk out of the preparliament.
9 October		Petrograd Soviet forms the Committee for Revolutionary Defence, which becomes the Military Revolutionary Committee.
10 October		Fourth Conference of Factory Committees of Petrograd. Bolshevik Central Committee adopts Lenin's resolution on armed insurrection.
13 October		Petrograd Soldiers' Soviet votes to transfer military authority to the Military Revolutionary Committee. Northern Regional Soviet Congress endorses coming All-Russian Congress and declares for Soviet power.
15 October		Kiev Soviet backs Soviet power.
16 October		Southwest Regional Soviet Congress at Minsk declares for Soviet power. Bolshevik Central Committee reaffirms Lenin's resolution on the insurrection against the opposition of Zinoviev and Kamenev.
17 October		Zinoviev and Kamenev attack insurrectionary policy in the public press. All-Russian Central Executive Committee postpones All-Russian Soviet Congress from 20 to 25 October. First All-Russian Conference of Factory Committees opens.

THE RUSSIAN REVOLUTION: WHEN WORKERS TOOK POWER

Date	Government	Labour movement
19 October		Ural Regional Soviet Congress declares for Soviet power.
20 October		Military Revolutionary Committee begins active preparations for the insurrection.
22 October		"Day of the Soviet" with rallies for soviet power.
23 October		Peter and Paul Fortress comes over to Soviets.
24 October	Provisional Government issues orders against Military Revolutionary Committee and to suppress Bolshevik press.	
25 October	Kerensky flees.	Insurrection begins at 2am. Second All-Russian Congress of the Soviets opens at 11am.
26 October	Provisional Government ministers arrested.	Winter Palace falls and Provisional Government arrested at 2am. New government of the Council of People's Commissars (Sovnarkom) set up. Decrees on land and peace, death penalty abolished.
27 October	Kerensky and General Krasnov attack but are defeated by Soviet forces.	Decree establishing press control.
29 October		Union of Railroad Employees (Vizkhel) appeals for a broad socialist government and forces negotiations.
31 October		Three days of fighting in Moscow end with Bolshevik victory.
2 November		Bolsheviks reject Vizkhel demands. "Declaration of the Rights of the Peoples of Russia" promises national self-determination.

THE RUSSIAN REVOLUTION: WHEN WORKERS TOOK POWER

Date	Government	Labour movement
7 November	Third Universal proclaims Rada the government of Ukraine.	
10 November		Abolition of civic ranks and titles.
12 November	Constituent Assembly elections begin.	
19 November		Formal armistice talks begin.
20 November		Bolsheviks take over army general staff headquarters.
24 November	Kerensky flees.	Existing law courts replaced.
28 November		Arrest of Kadet leaders ordered.
2 December		Formal armistice agreed with Germany and Austria-Hungary.
7 December		Cheka formed.
12 December		Left SRs join the government.
16 December		Decrees on marriage, divorce and civil registration. Decrees abolish all ranks and titles in the army.
Mid-December		Spread of soviet power in the south and at the front.
1 January 1918		Attempt to assassinate Lenin.
4 January		Soviet government officially accepts Finnish independence.
5 January	Constituent Assembly opens.	
6 January	Constituent Assembly disbanded.	

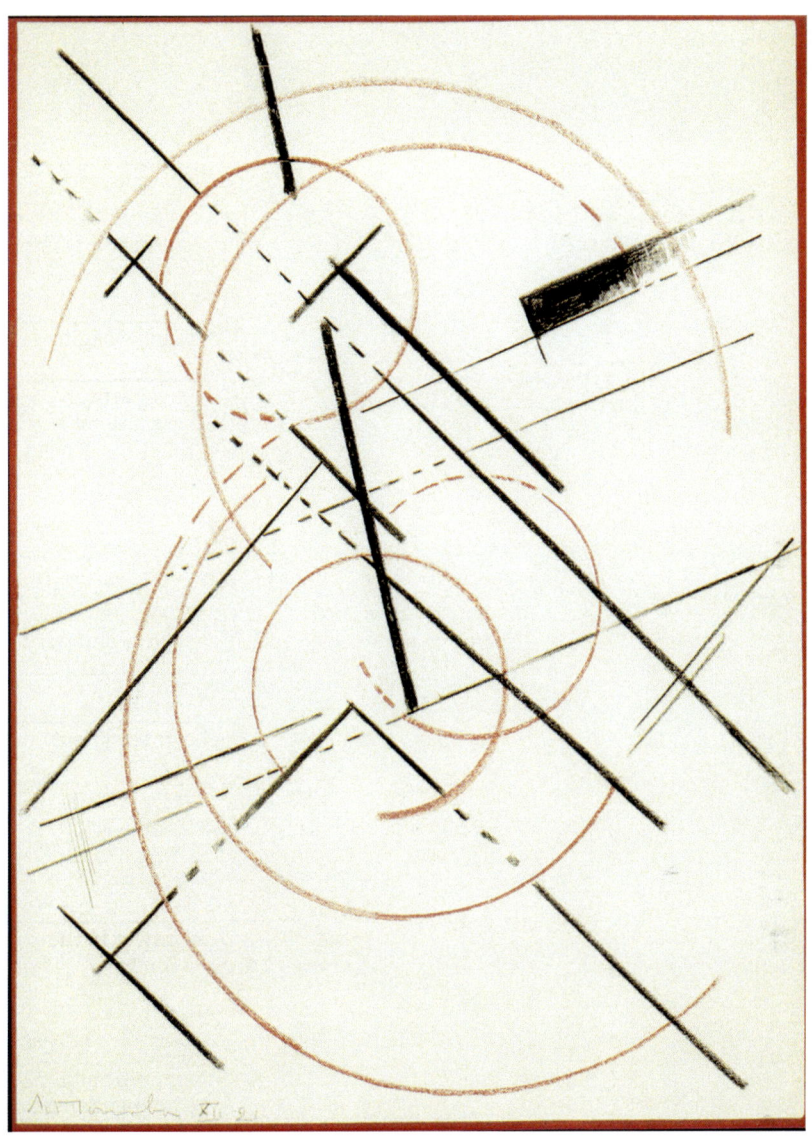

Lyubov Popova, 'Space-Force Construction', 1921

3. The party of victory

The Russian Social Democratic Labour Party (RSDLP), headed by the Bolsheviks, led the workers to power in 1917. The party was the product of decades of educating and organising, carried out under conditions of illegality inside Russia and in exile across Europe. Its formation is an heroic story of ideological battles for clarity, splits and fusions, of factional debate coupled with intervention in the class struggle. The lessons from how this party was built are the greatest legacy of the Russian revolution to future generations. Trotsky summed up well the irreplaceable role of the party:

> *But the events have proved that without a party capable of directing the proletarian revolution, the revolution itself is rendered impossible. The proletariat cannot seize power by a spontaneous uprising… there is nothing else that can serve the proletariat as a substitute for its own party… Without a party, apart from a party, over the head of a party, or with a substitute for a party, the proletarian revolution cannot conquer. That is the principal lesson of the past decade.*[1]

Yet the real history of the party is almost entirely buried under the weight of its opponents, right down to the present day. The dominant picture of what the party represented is derived from Stalin's book, the *Short Course* (1938). The RSDLP is reduced to the Bolshevik faction, the Bolsheviks portrayed as a fully formed party from 1903, monolithic and totalitarian. Stalin's version of party "history" was used to shore up the legitimacy of his own terrible rule. Later, Cold War academics took the same picture and inverted it, so as to condemn the party for its lack of democracy, its fanatical members and the evil outcome of its rule. Even more sympathetic accounts — such as by the British SWP's founder Tony Cliff — took much from the Stalinist version, helping to cut off the Trotskyist movement from the real history of Marxist party building in Russia. Revisionist historians have done much to restore the central role of workers' action to the history of the revolution, but often by erasing the role of the party in shaping the class struggle.

But the RSDLP was the product of decades-long organising. This history of the party's ideological battles, its strategy and tactics up to 1917 and how it became a mass party, is highly relevant to today's conditions, where there are thousands of aspiring revolutionaries but no authoritative Marxist centre anywhere across the globe.

How the RSDLP was built

The RSDLP was inspired most visibly by the German Social Democratic Party (SPD). In Russia its origins can be traced to a small group of exiles who came out of the utopian socialist Narodnik movement. That movement has also been described as populist revolutionaries. The RSDLP's organisational history can be summarised tersely from its publications and gatherings, by the splits and fusions that melded the party into a force capable of leading a workers' revolution.

On 12 September 1883, the Emancipation of Labour Group (*Gruppa Osvobozhdenie Truda*, GOT) was launched in Switzerland by a handful of former members of *Chernyi Peredel*, a split from the Russian populists that had fought the tsarist autocracy for almost two decades. The founders were Georgi Plekhanov, Pavel Axelrod, Vera Zasulich, Leo Deutsch and Mikhail Ignatov. From the beginning, the GOT sought to establish circles of sympathisers inside Russia, but these ambitions were thwarted. In 1884 Deutsch was arrested in Germany and dispatched to Russia, where he was sentenced to hard labour for previous involvement in terrorist activity. The group lost virtually all organisational contact with Russia for almost six years.[2]

Despite these problems, the GOT did not waste their time in exile. Plekhanov wrote *Socialism and the Political Struggle* (1883) and *Our Differences* (1884), devastating critiques of the populist movement that mapped an alternative socialist path. The GOT elaborated draft programmes to clarify their revolutionary goals. The group aimed to spread socialist ideas in Russia and organise a Russian socialist workers' party. They produced a newspaper, *Sotsial-Demokrat*, in Geneva and founded the Library of Contemporary Socialism.

Inside Russia, despite the repression, socialists continued to meet, educate themselves and intervene in the class struggle. In 1883 Dimitar Blagoev, a Bulgarian studying at Petersburg University, formed the Party of Russian Social Democrats. The group produced its own draft programme and statutes. It established direct contact with the GOT, with Plekhanov and Axelrod contributing articles to the two issues of its paper, *Rabochii* (*The Worker*), published in 1885-86. Around 30 students from the university, the Technological Institute and the Medical Academy organised circles dedicated to political education among the local working class, until the police broke it up.

In 1889 Mikhail Brusnev organised a social democratic society circle at the Petersburg Technological Institute. Brusnev was an ardent admirer of the German SPD, defining the objective of the group as "developing future Russian Bebels". In 1891 Brusnev's circle organised a May Day celebration involving around 100 workers and students in the woods outside Petersburg. Women weavers such as Vera Karelina and Anna Boldyreva received assistance from the Brusnev organisation in 1890-91. Brusnev also helped establish circles in Moscow until imprisoned in 1892. In 1893 Vladimir Ulianov (later known as Lenin) joined a Marxist circle of Technological Institute students.[3]

Social democratic circles were not confined to the capital. In Vilna (now Vilnius), Jewish workers formed a revolutionary circle in 1885. It supported the struggle of women hosiery workers, including collecting strike fund money from synagogues. In Kiev, Abramovich Sokolov organised 30 workers and founded a clandestine library, although it was destroyed by arrests in 1889.[4] In 1892, Olga Varentsova established the first women workers' study circles, meeting in her flat in Ivanovo-Voznesensk. In 1895 this circle was incorporated into the local branch of the Union of Struggle, which the police crushed the following year. In 1893 the Social Democracy of the Kingdom of Poland (SDKP, later SDKPiL), was formed in the Russian-ruled part of Poland.[5]

Social democratic circles became more influential during the mid-1890s. The Petersburg Union of Struggle for the Emancipation of the Working Class was formed in 1894. It combined around 20 propaganda circles, which taught workers Marxist theory, and how to intervene in strikes using leaflets. In 1894, the GOT created a wider organisation of exiles, the Union of Russian Social Democrats Abroad. It began to publish a paper, *Rabotnik* (*The Worker*) and *Listok Rabotnik* (*The Worker Supplement*), with six issues published between 1896 and 1899. The Petersburg Union of Struggle founded an underground newspaper inside Russia, *Rabochee Delo* (*Workers' Cause*), but the main people involved (including Lenin, Nadia Krupskaia, Iulii Martov and Aleksandr Potresov) were arrested in December 1895. With the arrest of the Petersburg group, economists gained the ascendency in Petersburg social democracy, publishing *Rabochaia Mysl*.

In May 1897, 30 social democrats united as the Kiev Union of Struggle and contacted other Russian cities with the aim of re-establishing a nationwide organisation. They published the underground newspaper, *Rabochaia Gazeta* (*Workers' Paper*). In August 1897, Jewish workers in Warsaw issued the newspaper *Arbeter Shtime* (*Labour Voice*). In autumn 1897 a Jewish social-democratic party, the General Jewish Labour Union of Poland and Russia (the Bund), was founded.[6]

The fight for the RSDLP

The Russian Social-Democratic Labour Party (RSDLP) was founded on 1 March 1898 in Minsk. Boris Eidelman and Natan Vigdorchik from the Kiev group convened the gathering. The congress took place over three days, where nine delegates approved a centralised party structure and central committee. The party newspaper *Rabochaia Gazeta* would be edited by Petr Struve. They recognised the Union of Russian Social Democrats Abroad as the sole foreign organisation. Plekhanov was unanimously acclaimed the chief ideologist. The Bund was granted autonomy within the party in all matters pertaining to Jewish workers. Almost immediately after the first congress, hundreds of social-democrats were arrested, including seven of the nine delegates. Only two out of three members of the central committee, Stepan Radchenko and Arkadi Kremer, remained free and managed to publish the party manifesto written by Struve.[7]

In October 1898, the first congress of the Union of Social Democrats Abroad took place and an opposition of younger members, who were publishing *Rabochee Delo* paper, defeated the GOT. Plekhanov responded with his 'Vademecum' for the Editorial Board of *Rabochee Delo* (February 1900), a devastating critique of revisionism and economism. In April supporters of *Rabochee Delo* attempted but failed to organise a party congress. Plekhanov, Axelrod and Lenin began publishing *Iskra* (*The Spark*) newspaper in December 1900. It aimed to be an all-Russian political newspaper that would build a clear and unified party. The GOT walked out of the second congress of the Union of Social Democrats Abroad to form its own organisation, "The Social Democrat". In June 1901, Russian social democrats met in Geneva to reunify the exile organisation. In October 1901, at another reunification meeting held in Zurich, the League of Revolutionary Social Democrats Abroad was established.

During 1902, preparations began in earnest to organise a party congress, the highest decision-making body in the party. Plekhanov and Lenin drafted the proposed programme. In January 1902, a conference of *Iskra* supporters held in Samara founded the Russian *Iskra* organisation. Lenin's pamphlet *What is to be Done?* (March 1902) was published in Germany as a summary of *Iskra's* party-building project. Also in March, the Belostok conference began preparation for the congress, but most participants were arrested. In November 1902, the Pskov conference established the organising committee for the second party congress. Approximately 3,500 people had participated in social-democratic organisations in all the years prior to the second congress.[8]

THE PARTY OF VICTORY

The second congress of the RSDLP took place between 17 July and 10 August 1903. The first week was held in Brussels, but after it drew police attention, a new venue was found in London. Some 43 delegates from 26 organisations were present, as well as 14 others who had speaking rights. *Iskra* supporters held the majority of mandates, although they did not remain united. Among the leading contributors were Lenin, Plekhanov, Martov, Trotsky, Deutsch, Axelrod and Zasulich. Other notable attendees were the Economists Vladimir Akimov and Aleksandr Martynov, the Bundists Kremer, Mark Liber and Vladimir Medem, Iakov Hanecki, Dimitri Ulianov (Lenin's brother), Petr Krasikov, Krupskaia, Nikolai Bauman, Potresov, Ekaterina Alexandrova and Konstantin Takhtarev. Eight of those present were women.

The first sessions were dominated by debates between *Iskra* supporters and their opponents, principally the Bund and the economists over the party programme. However, *Iskra* delegates disagreed about paragraph one of the statutes defining membership. Martov's formula read "all who recognise the programme and offer it assistance under the supervision of a party organisation are considered party members", while Lenin's was "all who recognise the programme and personally participate in one of the party's organisations". Lenin's formulation was rejected by 28 votes to 23, with Martov's adopted by 28 to 22, with one abstention.[9]

On 5 August, Liber announced that the Bund delegation was leaving the congress and the Bund would withdraw from the RSDLP. Both Akimov and Martynov also departed. Then the *Iskra* split widened over the issue of membership of the editorial board of the party paper (known as the central organ) and the composition of the central committee. The central committee in the constitution was not the supreme body between conferences (that was the party council). Rather it was a practical body charged with distributing literature, organising local committees and literature distribution. Lenin's supporters wanted continuity between the Russian *Iskra* organisation and the new central committee. Martov insisted on the reappointment of the "old" editorial of six people (himself, Plekhanov, Lenin, Axelrod, Zasulich and Potresov), while Lenin wanted the election of the first three alone. Lenin won the votes for the composition of the central organ and the central committee, but Martov refused to serve as an editor. This was the origin of the split into "Bolsheviks" (majority-ites), who won the vote on the leading bodies, and the "Mensheviks" (minority-ites), who lost those votes.[10]

In September 1903, the minority founded the Menshevik faction.

In October they convened the second congress of the League of Russian Revolutionary Social-Democracy Abroad, seeking to circumvent the decisions of the second RSDLP congress. In October-November 1903, Plekhanov defected to the Mensheviks, who had been boycotting *Iskra* since the congress. Lenin resigned from the editorial board. Plekhanov published *Iskra* on his own for one issue and then with an editorial board including the three former members, now Mensheviks, who had been voted off at the congress. In December 1904, after a year of organisational wrangling, the Bolshevik faction announced the formation of an organising committee and the convening of the third congress of the RSDLP. The Bolshevik faction also began publishing their paper *Vpered (Forward)*.

Historian David Lane estimates that almost 1,100 had joined the RSDLP before the 1905 revolution. In Petersburg, at the third RSDLP congress (April 1905), Bolshevik circles reported more than 700 members, while the Mensheviks claimed 1,200 members in the capital.[11] However, RSDLP militants led strikes and demonstrations, trade unions and ultimately soviets (see chapter 5). In April 1905, both factions organised their own separate congresses. The Bolshevik-led third RSDLP congress was held in London, 12-27 April 1905, while the Mensheviks held their own gathering in Geneva. A united Bolshevik-Menshevik gathering, called the "first conference of the RSDLP", was held in Tammerfors (now Tampere, Finland) on 12-17 December 1905 and attended by delegates from 26 social democratic organisations. It approved Lenin's call for an active boycott of the tsar's Duma. On 11 February 1906, 65 delegates met for the Petersburg RSDLP city conference, the majority voting for an active boycott of the Duma.

The fourth RSDLP congress (involving both factions) took place in Stockholm (10-25 April 1906). The congress was attended by 112 delegates representing 57 local party organisations and 22 additional consultative delegates. The congress adopted Menshevik resolutions on the majority of issues, including participating in the Duma elections and forming a social-democratic parliamentary fraction. It also approved Lenin's 1903 definition of party membership. The congress elected a central committee of three Bolsheviks and seven Mensheviks, with a Menshevik editorial board. RSDLP membership consisted of 13,000 Bolsheviks and 18,000 Mensheviks. In addition, social democratic parties from Latvia (14,000), Poland and Lithuania (26,000) and the Bund (33,000) joined the party. By October 1906 the party as a whole had around 150,000 members.[12]

Throughout 1906, RSDLP gatherings took place across Russia,

with discussions centring on the attitude to the state Duma. In June the Social-Democratic Party of Poland and Lithuania held a congress in Zakopane. The Petersburg RSDLP conference was held in Terijoki (Finland, now Zelenogorsk in Russia) on 11-12 June. The Moscow RSDLP regional conference took place the same month. In July, RSDLP meetings were held in Kuokkala (Finland) and Kostroma. In August, a party meeting in Terijoki voted against the Menshevik slogan of a "labour congress" and proposed convening the fifth RSDLP congress.

The second RSDLP conference was held in Tammerfors on 3-7 November 1906. It was attended by 32 delegates — 11 Mensheviks, seven Bundists, six Bolsheviks, five Polish and Lithuanian social democrats and three Latvian social-democrats. The conference adopted the Menshevik resolution on "Tactics of the RSDLP in the Election Campaign", which allowed for blocs with the Kadets. Later the same month the RSDLP military organisations held their first conference.

The beginning of 1907 was again dominated by debates around the Duma. The Petersburg RSDLP city and gubernia conference met on 6 January 1907, attended by 70 delegates (39 Bolsheviks and 31 Mensheviks). The Mensheviks walked out after the majority decided to oppose agreements with Kadets in elections to the second Duma. Another Petersburg RSDLP conference was held in Terijoki on 25 March, attended by 133 delegates (92 Bolsheviks and 41 Mensheviks).

The fifth RSDLP congress was held in London (30 April-19 May 1907). Some 336 delegates attended: 105 Bolsheviks, 97 Mensheviks, 57 Bundists, 44 Polish social-democrats, 29 Latvian social-democrats and four "non-factional". The Bolsheviks, supported by the Polish and Latvian delegates, had a majority at the congress.

The third RSDLP conference was held in Kotka (Finland) on 21-23 July 1907, and followed a crackdown on political opposition by the Tsar's interior minister Pyotr Stolypin inside Russia. Twenty-six delegates attended, nine Bolsheviks, five Mensheviks, five Polish social-democrats, five Bundists and two Latvian social-democrats. The conference supported Lenin's resolution in favour of participation in elections to the third Duma (and therefore opposing any boycott). The fourth RSDLP conference was held in Helsingfors (Helsinki) on 5-12 November 1907, shortly after the elections to the third Duma. Some 27 delegates attended: 10 Bolsheviks, four Mensheviks, five Polish social-democrats, five Bundists and three Latvian social-democrats. It also favoured Bolshevik resolutions.

Lenin described 1908 as "a year of disintegration, a year of ideological and political disunity, a year of party driftage". The RSDLP was wracked with crises, as the reactionary autocracy stabilised itself. There were debates with "liquidators", who sought to abandon the RSDLP's illegal work and take refuge in legal organisations, softening the party's politics. At the other pole, supporters of Aleksandr Bogdanov within the Bolshevik faction wanted to abandon legal work and boycott the Duma, recalling the social democrats elected in spite of tsarist restrictions. In between and within factions were conciliators, who believed that the RSDLP should unite all the factions. The fifth RSDLP conference held in Paris on 21-27 December 1908 involved 16 voting delegates: five Bolsheviks, three Mensheviks, five Polish social-democrats and three Bundists. Lenin gave the main report at the conference and his motion condemning liquidationism and recallism was carried.[13]

In early 1909 the disagreement on tactics towards the Duma within the Bolshevik faction came to a head. The Bolsheviks held a conference of the extended editorial board of their paper *Proletarii* in Paris (8-17 June 1909), attended by nine delegates. Lenin's supporters opposed Bogdanov's *otzovist* (recallist) stance towards the social-democratic Duma faction. The conference also debated philosophical differences and Bogdanov's plans to organise a party school on the island of Capri in Italy. Alexi Rykov, Mikhail Tomskii and others took a conciliatory position. However, Bogdanov refused to accept the Bolsheviks' decisions and was excluded from the faction (though not from the RSDLP).[14]

By 1910, with the malaise in the RSDLP continuing, its forces had seriously depleted. It had perhaps 10,000 members, but Trotsky estimated that Lenin had regular contact with only 30-40 reliable organisers.[15] Committees inside Russia had been broken by the police, its central organ (*Sotsial-demokrat*) appeared irregularly, and the central committee had met only twice since the fifth party congress. On the initiative of Trotsky, the RSDLP central committee plenum was organised on 2-23 January 1910 in Paris. In the interests of party unity, the plenum ordered that the Bolshevik "centre" and *Proletari* dissolve, on condition that the Mensheviks' *Golos Sotsial-demokrata* also close down. The factions were to cooperate in the revival of the central organ and other joint party work. Representatives of the Bund, Polish, Lithuanian and Latvian social democrats held the deciding votes. However, the plenum opposed both liquidationism and otzovism (recallism), and agreed to a party conference.[16]

Lenin regarded the plenum as an exercise in "idiotic conciliationism", enforcing the "utmost concessions" on organisational issues. However, he managed to reverse the setbacks, in part due to the errors and miscalculations of his rivals. In February 1910 Martov and Dan, the Menshevik faction representatives on the new editorial board of *Sotsial-demokrat*, protested at Lenin's editorial (called 'Towards Unity') and withdrew from further activities on the central organ. This left the party's most prestigious paper in Lenin's hands and he used it to get Plekhanov (an opponent of liquidationism) to contribute. Trotsky failed to take the practical steps necessary to bring about a party conference. Meanwhile Lenin used the central organ to promote his own efforts to call the conference.

Lenin organised a meeting of RSDLP central committee members living abroad in Paris from 28 May to 4 June 1911. The meeting opened with only eight of the 45 central committee members present. Liber (the Bund) and Boris Gorev (Mensheviks) walked out, while M V Ozolin (Latvian social democrats) remained but abstained on most issues. This meant that the decisions were made by the remaining five members: Lenin, Zinoviev, Rykov, Leo Jogiches and Felix Dzerzhinskii (the Polish representatives). The gathering established a foreign organising commission and a technical commission to organise the party conference. However, Lenin feared these bodies would organise an all-inclusive conference, including both liquidators and otzovists. Lenin, Krupskaya and Inessa Armand organised a Bolshevik school in Longjumeau near Paris during summer 1911. Lenin sent three of the Longjumeau students — Evgenii Shvarts, Boris Breslav and Sergo Ordzhonikidze — to Russia with instructions to establish the Russian organising commission. After multiple arrests, this commission was finally convened in Tiflis, on 3 October, in Elena Stasova's apartment.[17] On 14-17 December 1911, a Bolshevik faction meeting took place in Paris in preparation for the forthcoming party conference.

On 5-17 January 1912, the sixth RSDLP conference convened at the Workers' House of the Czech social democrats in Prague. Of the 18 participants at the conference, 14 claimed to represent 10 local organisations inside Russia, while another 10 organisations either had elected representatives who were arrested or had expressed solidarity with the meeting. However, Trotsky (who was not present) claimed only one of the 14 delegates had been legitimately elected by a recognised party organisation. The delegates consisted of 12 Bolsheviks — two of whom, Roman Malinovskii (Moscow) and A S Romanov (Tula), were police agents — as well as two "pro-party" Mensheviks (supporters of Plekhanov), V Zevin (Ekaterinoslav, now Dnipropetrovsk in Ukraine) and D M Shvartsman (Kiev). The four non-voting representatives were Lenin, Kamenev, Nikolai Semashko and Osip Piatnitskii.

The conference condemned liquidationism, formally resolving that "the group around *Nasha zaria* and *Delo zhizni* has once and for all placed itself outside the party". A new central committee of seven members was elected (Lenin, Zinoviev, Ordzhonikidze, Spandarian, Fillip Goloshchekin, Malinovskii and Shvartsman), with five candidate members (Shaumian, Stasova, Bubnov, Ivan Smirnov and Mikhail Kalinin) who would join the committee if any member were arrested. Although Mensheviks and otzovists repudiated the conference, it was clear that Lenin had stolen a march on his rivals in re-establishing the RSDLP under Bolshevik leadership. This became clear in April, when the RSDLP was able to bring out a legal daily paper *Pravda*.[18]

Although Trotsky managed to organise a conference in August 1912 in Vienna, including the editors of *Golos Sotsial-demokrata* and Bogdanov's group, they were unable to constitute an alternative centre to the Bolshevik-led RSDLP. The RSDLP central committee under Lenin's leadership convened in Krakow (26 December 1912-1 January 1913). The gathering included three of the six Bolshevik Duma deputies, Aleksei Badaev, David Petrovskii and Nikolai Shagov. The central committee held a further conference from 23 September to 1 October 1913, in the village of Poronin (near Krakow). The conference discussed the intervention of the Duma deputies and their separation from the Mensheviks, as well as the national question and the burgeoning strike movement.

The RSDLP's history might have been very different had the Second International got its way in 1914. The international bureau invited Russian social democratic groups to attend the Brussels 'unity' conference on 16 July 1914. Emile Vandervelde chaired the meeting, flanked by Karl Kautsky, Edward Anseele (Belgium), Antonin Nemec (Czechoslovakia) and Ilya Rubanovich (SRs). Some 22 delegates representing 11 different Russian organisations attended, including Armand, Mikhail Vladimirskii and Dimitri Popov for the Bolshevik faction. Lenin refused to attend. Armand delivered the Bolshevik report and was opposed by Plekhanov, Trotsky, Axelrod and Martov. Kautsky drafted a unity motion, which included the call for a party congress to resolve the differences. The Bolshevik delegation abstained, which upset both Lenin and the bureau.[19]

The First World War, the cancellation of the Second International's Vienna conference, and its collapse into social-chauvinism cut across these developments. The RSDLP factions led by Lenin (Bolsheviks), Martov (Mensheviks), and Trotsky (advocates of across-the-board unity) all opposed the war. But Plekhanov (anti-liquidationist Mensheviks and Potresov (liquidators) backed the Russian government. The Bolshevik faction organised conferences in Berne in February 1915, with debates between the Baugy group of exiles in Switzerland (including Nikolai Bukharin and Iuri Piatakov), Lenin and the Russian-based organisations over the precise stance in opposition to the war (see chapter 6). In February-June 1916, Lenin debated the Bolshevik lefts who used their analysis of imperialism to oppose democratic demands such as national self-determination.[20]

War hit the RSDLP hard. The Bolsheviks had almost 6,000 members in Petrograd immediately before the war, but repression left them with about one hundred by December 1914. Membership climbed to 1,200 by the end of 1915, 2,000 in autumn 1916 and 3,000 in early 1917. By then, the Bolshevik organisation throughout Russia had about 24,000 members, over 60% of whom were workers.[21]

RSDLP militants played a crucial role in the overthrow of the tsar, even while the bulk of their leaders were in prison or exile. The Bolsheviks grew to 80,000 members in April, 240,000 in July and 350,000 in October 1917. The seventh RSDLP conference in 24-29 April adopted Lenin's theses, rejecting unification with the Mensheviks but proposing unity with the Inter-district committee (Mezhraionka). The sixth RSDLP congress on 26 July-3 August 1917 brought Bolsheviks, Mezhraionka and some Mensheviks around Iuri Larin together, electing a new central committee. In October 1917 the RSDLP resolved to lead the working class to power.[22]

The German social democratic model

The German SPD was, from the inception, the RSDLP's mighty example of how an independent mass working class party led by Marxists could be built. The SPD was founded at the Eisenach congress in 1869, uniting a group around August Bebel and Wilhelm Liebknecht with some dissident supporters of Ferdinand Lassalle. This party and the remaining Lassallean organisation united at Gotha in 1875, claiming 25,000 members. After twelve years of illegality, the SPD emerged in 1890 with 290,000 members. It would reach half a million in 1907 and over a million by 1914. The SPD was instrumental in establishing the Second International in 1889. For Russian Marxists, the SPD provided ideological guidance, material support as well as an unrivalled example of how to build a party.

Despite his political mistakes, Lassalle made a significant contribution to the pre-history of the SPD. He took critical realism from Marx and Engels, summed up by his aphorism: "All great political action consists in the stating of that which is, and begins with, such a statement. All political pettifogging consists in concealing and cloaking that which is." Lassalle's 'Open Letter' (March 1863) argued that "the working class must constitute itself an independent political party". Workers should "peacefully but untiringly demanding continual agitation for the introduction of the universal and direct suffrage". He urged socialists to "raise this cry in every workshop, in every village, in every hut... by debate and discussion, daily, and without cession". The workers' party should have its own finances, spread the word through pamphlets and paid agents. He insisted "let your voice continually be heard; in season and out of season; perpetual, never tiring; in place and out of place, a continual presence, compelling people to listen".[23]

What was the secret of the SPD's success? Engels identified the advantage the SPD had as early as 1874. This was their theoretical seriousness, namely their work on the ideological front of the class struggle. For Engels, in fact, there were three fronts of the class struggle and the German party's fusion of these fronts made it the model for socialists to follow. Engels wrote:

> It must be said to the credit of the German workers that they have utilised the advantages of their situation with rare understanding. For the first time in the history of the labour movement the struggle is being so conducted that its three sides, the theoretical, the political and the practical economical (opposition to the capitalists), form one harmonious and well-planned entity. In this concentric attack lies the strength and invincibility of the German movement...[24]

Kautsky's commentary on the SPD's 1891 Erfurt programme concluded with a section 'Social democracy as the merger of the worker movement and socialism'. He argued that "in order for the socialist and the worker movements to become reconciled and to become fused into a single movement, socialism had to break out of the utopian way of thinking". The task of social democracy was "to make the class struggle of the proletariat aware of its aim and capable of choosing the best means to attain this aim".[25]

Marxists, argued Kautsky, recognised that scientific socialist ideas had developed separately from the working-class movement. The role of Marxists was the "fusion" or "combination" of these socialist ideas with organic working class struggles.[26] In 1901 Kautsky explained further with his critical remarks on the new draft programme of the Austrian social-democratic party:

> But socialism and the class struggle arise side by side and not one out of the other; each arises under different conditions. Modern socialist consciousness can arise only on the basis of profound scientific knowledge. Indeed, modern economic science is as much a condition for socialist production as, say, modern technology, and the proletariat can create neither the one nor the other, no matter how much it may desire to do so; both arise out of the modern social process. The vehicle of science is not the proletariat, but the bourgeois intelligentsia: it was in the minds of individual members of this stratum that modern socialism originated, and it was they who communicated it to the more intellectually developed proletarians who, in their turn, introduce it into the proletarian class struggle where conditions allow that to be done. Thus, socialist consciousness is something introduced into the proletarian class struggle from without [von Aussen Hineingetragenes] and not something that arose within it spontaneously [urwüchsig].[27]

The SPD elaborated party programmes in 1869, 1875 and then 1891. It published its own central newspaper, with titles such as *Volksstaat (People's State)*, *Sozialdemokrat* and *Vorwärts (Forwards)*, as well as local (and factional) newspapers. It published large quantities of socialist books and a theoretical journal, *Die Neue Zeit (The New Times)*.

A defining characteristic of the SPD press was its openness, with party members encouraged to air their diverse views. Wilhelm Liebknecht insisted on free expression for all party members. In 1885, he told the staff of *Der Sozialdemokrat:* "As comrades you have the same right as every other comrade to judge, to condemn, and to attack, but as editors of the party organ you do not have the right to take sides within the party." *Vorwärts* hailed the invigorating effect of the debate, adding that socialists were "too good democrats" to tolerate the "intellectual autocracy" implicit in a central organ that dictated orthodoxy in all contested issues. "The central sheet belongs to the entire party", Liebknecht pointed out in 1896, "and if various currents prevail in the party... I do not consider myself entitled to damn or excommunicate deviating opinions from my editorial desk".[28]

The most famous and inspiring activity of the outlawed socialists during the heroic period 1878-90 was the distribution system set up to smuggle the *Sozialdemokrat* into Germany from Switzerland. Supervised by the "red postmaster", Julius Motteler, this system used trusted persons (*Vertrauenspersonen*) to smuggle copies into the country by various means. In 1895, Motteler wrote a guide for Italian socialists on how to smuggle literature. The papers created the scaffolding for local organisation, education and the dissemination of the message to party members and new supporters.

Decision-making in the SPD was highly democratic. The sovereign annual congress made the party's major political decisions, with controls over the executive committee alongside strong local organisations. The party press "debated problems at great length, and opened its pages to the representatives of all divergent opinions", at least until 1911. But for most of the period before the war "almost any view could get a public airing. At the party congresses there were no attempts to restrict the expression of opinions other than those dictated by time". The SPD congress jealously guarded its rights and privileges: "there was no guillotine and the chairman's [sic] rules of order were lax. Above all the opposition had many opportunities of putting its views to meetings in various localities all over the country". Local party secretaries were "more concerned with having interesting and provocative speakers in order to provide a worthwhile evening for their members than with any attempt to impose a party line". Up to 1900, the party only expelled seven people for violations of the rules.[29]

A member was someone who "actively supports the party", advocates the party programme and pays monthly dues. Early on Bebel argued passionately for regularly monthly dues to finance party activities, but the dues were waived for subscribers to the party's official organ. Local branches were not bound by the statutes to support the national apparatus financially, nor did the party leadership have statutory control over the local press, the selection of electoral candidates or any other aspect of local party activities.[30] Such extreme decentralisation was not a model for a serious party to follow.

The party was also instrumental in utilising all possibilities on the "cultural front" of the class struggle. The party sponsored extensive social, cultural and educational endeavours. It ran insurance programmes, burial societies and travel clubs. It sponsored facilities in which itinerant workers could find shelter and support. There were "socialist taverns and cafes, socialist theatres, socialist athletic clubs, and in some heavily industrialised areas, even entirely socialist neighbourhoods". There were walking and hiking clubs. By 1912 "there were at least a dozen national federations and one super organisation of sports clubs (gymnasts, cyclists, athletes and swimmers), the latter called the central commission for workers' sports and physical fitness".[31]

The young Lenin was suitably enamoured by the SPD model when he visited Germany in 1895. In exile he wrote 'The Tasks of the

Russian Social Democrats' (1897) advocating the German SPD party model and calling for the unification of Russian circles into a single social democratic party. At the height of the 1905 revolution he argued that the German social-democratic movement ranked "first in respect of organisation, integrality and coherence, and the extent and rich content of its Marxist literature". Responding to Russian critics in 1905, he argued "when and where did I ever claim to have created any sort of special trend in international social-democracy not identical with the trend of Bebel and Kautsky? When and where have there been brought to light differences between me, on the one hand, and Bebel and Kautsky, on the other". The Prague RSDLP conference in January 1912 sent greetings to the SPD, heralding its recent electoral successes.[32] At least until the outbreak of the First World War, the SPD remained the model to aspire to.

The Emancipation of Labour group

The Emancipation of Labour Group (GOT) emerged from populism and did not simply repudiate Russia's previous revolutionary traditions. Thus Plekhanov took from Nikolai Chernyshevskii the aphorism: "there is no abstract truth, truth is always concrete". This commitment to base politics on reality was also one of the many fusions Plekhanov made in adapting SPD wisdom to Russian conditions.[33]

The GOT's central political mission was to form a workers' party. In *Our Differences* (1884) Plekhanov, systematically rejected the dominant peasant-oriented politics of Russia's socialist intellectuals, stating that "the earliest possible formation of a workers' party [is] the only means of solving all the economic and political contradictions of present-day Russia. On that road success and victory lie ahead; all other roads can lead only to defeat and impotence". He bluntly told socialist intellectuals to place their hopes first and foremost in the working class. Revolutionaries should "exert all their energy so that in the very opening period of the constitutional life of Russia our working class will be able to come forward as a separate party with a definite social and political programme". The detailed elaboration of that programme must "be left to the workers themselves", but "the intelligentsia must elucidate for them its principal points". This could be done "only by intensive work among at least the most advanced sections of the working class, by oral and printed propaganda and the organisation of workers' socialist study groups".[34]

Plekhanov asserted that "without revolutionary theory there is no revolutionary movement in the true sense of the word".[35] The GOT elaborated draft programmes in 1884 and in 1887 to clarify the goals workers should take up. The aim was "the transfer to collective ownership by the working people of all means and products of production and the organisation of all the functions of social and economic life in accordance with the requirements of society". In Russia, workers suffered the "double yoke" of capitalism and tsarist "police-despotic state". The overthrow of absolutism was the first political task and "obligatory" for the embryo of the future Russian workers' party.[36]

The GOT pioneered the immensely fertile idea of the hegemony of workers leading other exploited classes towards revolution against the tsar. Plekhanov made this fundamental point at the founding of the Second International: "the revolutionary movement in Russia will triumph only as a working-class movement or else it will never triumph". Axelrod was similarly unequivocal, arguing that "if there is no possibility of assigning to the Russian proletariat an independent, pre-eminent role in the struggle against police tsarism, autocracy and arbitrariness, then Russian social democracy has no historical right to exist".[37] This conception informed Lenin's conception of a revolutionary democratic alliance of the working class and the peasantry and Trotsky's strategy of permanent revolution (see chapter 5).

The central task was to create what Plekhanov and Axelrod called "worker intellectuals". This would prevent the workers' movement from "following in the tail of the so-called intelligentsia circles", (what they called 'tailism'). Marxist literature should "clarify in people's minds the aims and means that will most surely lead to their well-being". The task of the 'Workers' Library' was "principally to explain to the worker intelligentsia its tasks and the conditions through which they can best be accomplished". Axelrod wrote *The Workers' Movement and Social Democracy* (1885) designed to serve as a handbook for the "workers' intelligentsia".[38]

Plekhanov explained the differences between propaganda and agitation. The propagandist "conveys many ideas to a single person or to a few people, whereas the agitator conveys only one or a few ideas, but s/he conveys them to a whole mass of people, sometimes to almost the entire population of a particular locality". Propaganda involves training revolutionaries, "leaders in theory". But to become leaders in reality, "they must know how to become agitators". The task of the agitator "involves putting into circulation in each particular case the maximum possible number of revolutionary ideas in a form accessible to the mass".[39]

Plekhanov also introduced an evocative metaphor from Aleksandr Herzen for strategy and tactics. Strategy was the "algebra of the revolution", in contrast to the tactical "arithmetic" of revolution. Binding together the struggle for political freedom (i.e. overthrowing tsarism) and preparing the working class for future socialist revolution, meant following "the splendid example of the German communists" (Marx and Engels). Plekhanov paraphrased the *Communist Manifesto*, which he said advised communists to fight "with the bourgeoisie whenever it acts in a revolutionary way, against the absolute monarchy", and yet "never cease, for a single instant, to instil into the working class the dearest possible recognition of the hostile antagonism between bourgeoisie and proletariat". Acting thus, the communists wanted "the bourgeois revolution in Germany" to "be but the prelude to an immediately following proletarian revolution".[40] In short the GOT furnished Russian Marxism with its mental furniture, clarifying the road ahead and inspiring revolutionaries inside Russia to develop independent working-class politics.

The ideological front

The ideological front of the class struggle would be central to the RSDLP's existence. The primacy of ideas in the party's political life is evident from the sheer quantity of their literature. Newspapers, pamphlets, journals and books were staple, integral tools arming the working class to fight for socialism. Ideological clarity required unceasing arguments over political ideas. Littered throughout Lenin's collected works are references to stating what is and telling the truth. He argued that "it is unworthy of a socialist to conceal or blur the truth concerning a serious political matter. We must call a spade a spade. We must expose all subterfuges and pretences, so that the mass of the workers may clearly understand what is going on". Bluntly, as the Germans put it: *"aussprechen was ist"*.[41]

An outstanding example of Lenin's approach is an early essay, 'What the "Friends of the People" Are and How They Fight the Social-Democrats' (1894) in which he argues that the hallmark of social-democratic views were "the conformity of theory with reality and the history of the given, i.e., the Russian, social and economic relations". He brilliantly summarised what Marxists bring to the organised labour movement:

> "There can be no dogmatism where the supreme and sole criterion of a doctrine is its conformity to the actual process of social and economic development; there can be no sectarianism when the task is that of pro-

moting the organisation of the proletariat, and when, therefore, the role of the 'intelligentsia' is to make special leaders from among the intelligentsia unnecessary".

In other words, Marxists, however "intellectual" they may be, always take their cue from, and are in tune with the conditions, needs and interests of the working-class: a central role of Marxist intellectuals is to make other Marxist intellectuals in the working-class movement. Lenin also supported the strategic perspective of working class hegemony.[42]

Early debates: revisionists, legal Marxists and economists
The Marxist perspective of independent working-class politics had to be fought for in the context of an almighty ideological struggle within the international working-class movement at the end of the nineteenth century. The debate took an acute form among Russia Marxists, making it difficult to untangle. Historian Richard Mullin's has recently provided vital documentary material in English for the first time, which helps unpack the issues.

From 1896, SPD leader Eduard Bernstein began publishing a series of articles challenging various aspects of Marxist doctrine. He rejected the perspective of socialist revolution, advocating instead the democratisation of capitalism and the struggle for piecemeal reforms. As Bernstein expressed it: "the ultimate aim of socialism is nothing, but the movement is everything". Plekhanov unleashed a barrage of criticism, warning that "Bernstein will bury social democracy or social democracy will bury Bernstein". The SPD's Stuttgart (1898) and Hanover (1899) congresses overwhelmingly opposed Bernstein's views. However Bernstein pressed on, expanding his views in the book, *The Preconditions of Socialism* (1899), including dismissing the Marxist phrase for working-class political rule, the "dictatorship of the proletariat". (Plekhanov would include the term in his draft programme for the RSDLP and it would pass at the second congress).[43]

Russian social democrats had home-grown revisionists to tackle. Ekaterina Kuskova's infamous *Credo* (1899) baldly stated that fundamental law of the working-class movement was "the line of least resistance". In Russia, "the line of least resistance will never tend towards political activity". She described the Russian working-class movement as "still in the amoeba state and has not yet acquired any form". Kuskova wrote that "discussion of an independent workers' political party is in essence nothing more than the consequence of transferring foreign tasks and foreign outcomes onto our soil". Instead Russian radicals should assist "the economic struggle of the proletariat and participation in liberal-oppositional activity". Kuskova concluded that "to speak now, to propagandise the overthrow of the autocracy among workers – and this means out-and-out revolution – means exposing them to the greatest historical danger". She portrayed revolution in Russia "as a sea of blood that will submerge the movement for a long time":

> *The abstract preaching of socialism and solidarity can be of little help here. There is no doubt that the hearts of the Russian masses are closed to the "overthrow" and "socialism"... At present, socialism is good for the evocation of a prayerful and blissful state in the masses by means of reflections on this future, but it is not good for active, conscious and determined struggle.*[44]

Zemah Koppelson confessed admiration for Sergei Prokopovich, who did not "leave a stone unturned in his criticism of the established programmes of European social-democratic literature" and "completely agrees with the view of Bernstein". The ambition of many social democrats "to seize political power in the immediate future… [was] a utopia". Therefore, "to speak now about 'the death agony of capitalism', as many now habitually put it, is at best merely funny". For Prokopovich, "talking to the working masses in Russia about the abolition of capitalism, about socialism and, finally, about the abolition of the autocracy, is in general absurd and it amounts to an unproductive waste of energy". Rather than a workers' party, he advocated "the formation of a united opposition party of all the revolutionary forces in Russia". Prokopovich proposed the "slow, gradual but uninterrupted development within these peaceful organisations — mutual aid, entertainment, consumer and educational societies", as the best way to "make so many reliable soldiers for the proletarian army".[45]

Lenin plunged into these debates while in exile. On receiving a copy of Kuskova's *Credo*, he organised a vigorous letter of protest signed by other imprisoned social democrats. If the Russian workers followed "the line of least resistance" and confined themselves to the economic struggle, this was "tantamount to the political suicide of Russian social-democracy" and would "greatly retard and debase the Russian working-class movement and the Russian revolutionary movement". Politically, the "line of least resistance" would mean determining tactics entirely by opportunistic circumstances, rather than by evaluating the situation in light of principles and programme.[46] In

February 1900 Plekhanov published his *Vademecum*, a collection of unpublished correspondence by Kuskova, Prokopovich and Koppelson and his own commentary. Plekhanov's verdict was searing but accurate. They had repudiated the foundational belief of Russian Marxism, he said — that the working class as the only force capable of bringing down tsarism. They were "narrow-minded pedants and political castrates". Plekhanov echoed Lenin — their programme was "equivalent to the political suicide of Russian social democracy".[47] So it proved: Kuskova and Prokopovich soon became liberals.

Another current inside Russia were the "legal Marxists". Petr Struve published an academic defence of Marxist economics, *Critical Notes on the Economic Development of Russia* (1894), which the censor allowed on the grounds that it criticised populism and did not draw explicitly revolutionary conclusions from the argument that Russia had already become capitalist. Struve represented Russian social democrats at the 1896 congress of the Second International alongside Plekhanov. In the late 1890s he edited the legally-permitted journals, *Novoe Slovo* and *Nachalo*. He drafted the *Manifesto of the RSDLP* (1898) requested at the first party congress, although he did not attend the meeting. As late as the spring of 1900, Struve and his co-thinker, Mikhail Tugan-Baranovskii, discussed co-operation on a social-democratic newspaper. However, Struve was arrested in March 1901 having attended a student demonstration in Petersburg, and nothing came of this project. Struve and his supporters became increasingly keen on revising Marxist ideas and moved rapidly to the right, embracing the Kadets during 1905.[48]

Economism became a catch all term for opponents of the GOT. Economists did not reject politics in general, although some did repudiate independent working-class politics. Economist views were articulated in *Rabochaia Mysl* (*Workers' Thought*), *Rabochee Delo* and by the Bund. They emphasised the struggle for immediate economic improvements at the level of individual enterprises, whilst ignoring or evading the task of preparing workers for a revolutionary uprising.[49] Konstantin Takhtarev's article 'Our Reality' in *Rabochaia Mysl* supplement (September 1899) summed up its economist approach. He ridiculed those who made overthrowing the autocracy the immediate task of the Russian workers' movement. Instead he advocated work in trade unions and consumer associations, dismissing the fight for socialism as a matter for great-great grandchildren.[50]

Lenin's response was a full-blown defence of the SPD and the GOT's methods of applying it in Russian conditions. He used Kautsky's formula, in which social-democracy represented "the merger of socialism and the working-class movement" and argued that it was necessary "to concentrate all forces on establishing a regularly appearing and regularly delivered organ [newspaper]". Without a revolutionary newspaper, "no broad organisation of the entire working-class movement is possible". The paper was the pivot for basic activities: study, propagandise, organise — "studieren, propagandieren, organisieren".[51]

The German party during the period of its prescription (1878-90) had ensured "the regular transport across the frontiers of a weekly illegal newspaper and to deliver it to the houses of all subscribers, so that even the ministers could not refrain from admiring the social-democratic post ('the red mail)". Lenin urged comrades to ensure the party newspaper appear 10-12 times a year and was "regularly delivered in all the main centres of the movement to all groups of workers that can be reached by socialism".[52]

Similarly, Lenin implored Russian Marxists to adopt the example of the German SPD's programme. He wrote: "We are not in the least afraid to say that we want to imitate the Erfurt programme: there is nothing bad in imitating what is good, and precisely today, when we so often hear opportunist and equivocal criticism of that programme, we consider it our duty to speak openly in its favour". Imitating" must under no circumstances be simply copying". Russian Marxists "must not, under any circumstances, lead to our forgetting the specific features of Russia which must find full expression in the specific features of our programme".[53]

He criticised *Rabochaia Mysl* for failing to understand the relationship between social-democracy and the labour movement. He argued that at first "socialism and the working-class movement existed separately in all the European countries". The separation of the working-class movement and socialism gave rise to weakness and underdevelopment in both. For this reason "we see in all European countries a constantly growing urge to fuse socialism with the working-class movement in a single social-democratic movement". When this fusion takes place "the class struggle of the workers becomes the conscious struggle of the proletariat to emancipate itself from exploitation by the propertied classes, it is evolved into a higher form of the socialist workers' movement — the independent working-class social-democratic party". By directing socialism towards the merger with the working-class movement, Marx and Engels did their greatest service: "they created a revolutionary theory that explained the necessity for this fusion and gave socialists the task of organising the class struggle of the proletariat".

Similarly, in Russia, "socialism has been in existence for a long time, for many decades, standing aside from the struggle of the workers against the capitalists, aside from the workers' strikes, etc. On the one hand, the socialists did not understand Marx's theory, they thought it inapplicable to Russia; on the other, the Russian working-class movement remained in a purely embryonic form". The foundation of Russian social-democracy by the Emancipation of Labour Group and the establishment of the RSDLP "marked the biggest step forward towards this fusion". The principal task for all Russian socialists and all class-conscious Russian workers was "to strengthen this fusion, consolidate and organise the social-democratic labour party". Those who did not recognise this fusion or who tried to draw an artificial demarcation between the working-class movement and social-democracy "renders no service but does harm to workers' socialism and the working-class movement in Russia".[54]

Another economist publication proved a bigger threat than the *Credo* and *Rabochaia Mysl*. *Rabochee Delo* was founded out of the ideological and organisational conflict within the Union of Russian Social Democrats Abroad. The new board was made up of Boris Krichevskii, Vladimir Ivanshin and Pavel Teplov. Ivanshin was involved with *Rabochaia Mysl*. Another key figure was Vladimir Akimov. Some 12 issues of *Rabochee Delo* (and eight of its supplement, *Listok Rabochego Dela*) appeared between April 1899 and February 1902. The 'Programme of Rabochee Delo' contained almost no analysis of capitalism or socialism. It was "tactically committed to a 'gradualist' approach, arguing that workers could not acquire sophisticated political ideas prior to lengthy experience of state brutality acquired in the course of campaigns for economic improvements".

In *Rabochee Delo* No.5 (September-December 1899), the editorial board announced its intention of publishing a collection of articles from the German SPD's revisionist controversy. In *Rabochee Delo* No.7, Krichevskii returned to the theme of political consciousness and the way it was acquired by workers as a result of direct participation in strike struggles over "economic" issues, such as the length of the working day, fines for inaccurate work, wages and holidays. He argued that, because these activities were illegal, workers would face with police and judicial persecution and gradually understand that the entire state apparatus served the interests of the factory owners.

The newspaper *Iskra* (*The Spark*) was conceived in the context of the stalled progress of the RSDLP and the ongoing faction fight within the Union Abroad. In August 1900 Lenin and Plekhanov agreed to produce *Iskra*, an "unofficial central party newspaper" for the RSDLP, along with a theoretical journal, *Zaria* (*Dawn*). The ideological approach was plain from the 'Declaration of the Editorial Board of *Iskra*' (September 1900), which announced that "before we can unite, and in order that we may unite, we must first of all draw firm and definite lines of demarcation". To obtain clarity, "open polemics, conducted in full view of all Russian social-democrats and class-conscious workers are necessary and desirable in order to clarify the depth of existing differences".[55]

But the economists continued to attack. In *Rabochee Delo* No.10 (October 1901), Krichevskii justified sharp tactical "turns" detached from "principles", which he viewed primarily as statements about the "final goal" of socialism. Krichevskii attacked the idea of a general revolutionary strategy, arguing they were too inflexible to connect with working-class consciousness. In the same issue of the paper, an article by Martynov criticised the notion that a political newspaper produced by émigrés could serve as an organisational centre for the unification of the RSDLP.[56]

This was the context in which Lenin wrote *What is to be Done?* (1902). The famous pamphlet represents another stout, explicit defence of the German model and the GOT's application to Russian conditions. In the first chapter Lenin refers to Plekhanov's dictum that without revolutionary theory there is no revolutionary movement, reproducing Engels' appreciation of the primacy of ideological struggle in shaping the three fronts of the class struggle.[57] It is the decisive conclusion that unites the successes of both the SPD and RSDLP. Lenin would echo Kautsky's conception of the origins and limits of class consciousness — and hence the active role of Marxists in developing it. He wrote:

> *We have said that there could not have been social-democratic consciousness among the workers. It would have to be brought to them from without. The history of all countries shows that the working class, exclusively by its own effort, is able to develop only trade union consciousness, i.e., the conviction that it is necessary to combine in unions, fight the employers, and strive to compel the government to pass necessary labour legislation, etc. The theory of socialism, however, grew out of the philosophic, historical, and economic theories elaborated by educated representatives of the propertied classes, by intellectuals. By their social status the founders of modern scientific socialism, Marx and Engels, themselves belonged to the bourgeois intelligentsia.*[58]

Far from scandalous as many subsequent decriers of Lenin have argued, these passages were an honest, realistic approach to the shape and limits of working-class consciousness. Lenin never repudiated these conceptions, contrary to an interpretation by historian Marcel Liebman, picked up by the British SWP's Tony Cliff. They suggested that Lenin was so inebriated by the spontaneous movement in 1905 that decided workers would always and at all times hold social-democratic consciousness instinctively.[59] That's a fable. Of course Lenin was hugely enthusiastic about the possibilities opened up by the 1905 revolution. But he recognised that the "instinctive" socialist consciousness of workers was the result of years of active socialist propaganda rather than just generated spontaneously by class conflict. Experience at the time and afterwards confirm rather than obliterate the view of class consciousness Lenin inherited from the international Marxist movement and expressed in *What Is to be Done?*

Lenin was a keen student of the GOT's literature and references to these conceptions occur throughout his works, including propaganda and agitation, strategy and tactics.[60] Lenin also assimilated the idea of the political lever of the Marxist vanguard organisation, able to move far larger class forces. In *What is to be Done?* (1902), Lenin utilised the Archimedean metaphor, exclaiming: "give us an organisation of revolutionaries — and we will overturn Russia". A decade later, when mocked by the Mensheviks for only having two or three hundred underground members, he retorted that "a decision drawn up by half a dozen members of the executive commission of the Petersburg committee — a leaflet printed and circulated by 'two or three hundred' — two hundred and fifty thousand people rise as one in Petersburg". From such small beginnings, "the two million inhabitants of Petersburg see and hear these appeals for revolution which go to the hearts of all toiling and oppressed sections of the people".[61]

But Russian conditions were different to German conditions. Russian revolutionaries were subject to the oppressive pressure of the tsarist state and therefore had to master the art of *konspiritsiia*. Historian, Lars Lih translates this as "the fine art of not getting arrested". Social-democratic *konspiritsiia* set out to achieve political freedom, which would make conspiracies unnecessary. Such *konspiritsiia* created the publications and the organisational space for politics even under police-state conditions. To attempt underground work with *kustarnichestvo* (amateur) methods was the attitude of charlatan, not a professional revolutionary.[62]

Lenin also described *Iskra*'s methods in 'A Letter to a Comrade on Organisational Tasks' (September 1902), including plans to reorganise the local RSDLP organisation in Petersburg, having won control over it. According to Zinoviev, the *Iskra* apparatus contained between 100 and 150 members. Mullin concludes that "if *Iskra* was evidently capable of a hard inter-factional fight within the framework of a common party, there is no evidence that it sought to split this party with the aim of securing control over one part of it, as is sometimes alleged".[63] On the contrary, the ideological fight waged by *Iskra* laid the theoretical basis for the second RSDLP congress and efforts to transform the party into a genuine force inside Russia.

Debates with the Mensheviks

The Menshevik faction emerged out of divisions at the 1903 RSDLP congress in which the *Iskra* group split and a number of its leaders linked up with former economists such as Martynov. Mullin argues that in the immediate post-congress period, Martov's initial refusal to serve on the editorial board elected by the congress "matured into a broad ranging boycott of the leading party institutions — a refusal to co-operate with them or obey their instructions — and the creation of a 'Menshevik' factional apparatus to agitate for a similar boycott on the part of the local committees". They carried out what became known as "the general strike of the generals". Martov's faction succeeded in calling a second congress of the League Abroad in October 1903. At this meeting Plekhanov broke with Lenin when faced with the predictably charged atmosphere of the meeting, announcing his willingness to co-opt Martov and reinstate the three previous editors.[64]

After more than six months of Menshevik shenanigans and his own efforts to bring about party unity, Lenin published his book, *One Step Forward, Two Steps Back* (May 1904) about the second congress and its aftermath. Whereas the Menshevik accounts are politically vague and rhetorically venomous, Lenin's account is forensic, factual and concrete. He concluded that the disagreements that divided the two wings for the most part concerned, "not questions of programme or tactics, but only organisational questions". The organisational principle he upheld was not ultra-centralism, but that everyone should go by the decisions of the congress, convened with such pains, rather than self-appointed stars calling the shots.[65] However he did not believe the differences were sufficient for two separate parties. In October 1905 he wrote to Plekhanov: "We are in agreement with you on approximately nine-tenths of the questions of theory and tactics, and to quarrel over one-tenth is not worthwhile".[66]

Indeed the ideological differences were not vast before the 1905 revolution. As discussed in chapter 5, it was strategic differences between Bolshevik and Mensheviks over the role of the bourgeoisie in the bourgeois revolution that ultimately separated the two factions. This emerged theoretically and practically during 1905, particularly regarding how social-democrats should relate to the bourgeois Kadet party in the context of the tsar's limited parliamentary body, the state Duma.

Were differences over the definition of RSDLP membership crucial? Clearly not on the basis of subsequent history. In fact, Lenin won the membership debate. The Mensheviks' all-Russian conference on 20 November 1905 passed a resolution defining a member according to Lenin's logic, as someone who was a member of a party organisation. At the united fourth RSDLP congress on 25 April 1906, the Mensheviks had a majority and one of its supporters moved the organisational report. A new set of rules containing Lenin's definition was passed unanimously and without dispute. Both sections of the party wanted a more-or-less "tight" definition of membership. Nor did Lenin's definition have the dire practical consequences predicted by its opponents. RSDLP membership was not restricted to committee members or professional revolutionaries alone.[67]

What about the much-vaunted fear of Lenin's organisational methods, as summed up by the formula "democratic centralism"? The term "democratic centralism" was first put forward and adopted at the *Menshevik* all-Russian conference on 20 November 1905. The Menshevik resolution 'On the Organisation of the Party' stated, "The RSDLP must be organised according to the principle of democratic centralism". They probably acquired the expression from the SPD. At the Bolshevik conference of 12-17 December 1905, the resolution 'On Party Organisation' recognised "as indisputable the principle of democratic centralism". At the fourth RSDLP congress on 25 April 1906, the unified party resolved that "all party organisations are built on the principles of democratic centralism".[68]

Lenin explained what "democratic centralism" meant in practice. He advised that "the duty of every social-democrat is to strive to ensure that the ideological struggle within the party on questions of theory and tactics is conducted as openly, widely and freely as possible, but that on no account does it disturb or hamper the unity of revolutionary action of the social-democratic proletariat". Democratic centralism did not restrict revolutionary socialists from organising around or publicising their ideas, even if they were in a small minority.[69] Lenin argued that "there can be no mass party, no party of a class, without full clarity of essential shadings, without an open struggle between various tendencies, without informing the masses as to which leaders and which organisations of the party are pursuing this or that line".[70] Hence the importance of open factions within parties:

In our party Bolshevism is represented by the Bolshevik faction. But a faction is not a party. A party can contain a whole gamut of opinions and shades of opinion, the extremes of which may be sharply contradictory. In the German party, side by side with the pronouncedly revolutionary wing of Kautsky, we see the ultra-revisionist wing of Bernstein. That is not the case within a faction. A faction in a party is a group of like-minded persons formed for the purpose primarily of influencing the party in a definite direction, for the purpose of securing acceptance for their principles in the party in the purest possible form. For this, real unanimity of opinion is necessary. The different standards we set for party unity and factional unity must be grasped by everyone who wants to know how the question of the internal discord in the Bolshevik faction really stands. The conference did not declare a split in the faction.[71]

Lenin held to this view up to and including his time in power. In 1921, he argued that "it is, of course, quite permissible (especially before a congress) for various groups to form blocs (and also to go vote chasing)" and that "ideological struggle within the party does not mean mutual ostracism but mutual influence".[72] From Lenin's account in *One Step Forward* it is clear that the falling out was over the Lenin's refusal to accept the reversal of a decision of the conference to restore the old *Iskra* editorial board of six. Lenin thought this showed a lack of respect for party decision-making, and consequently seriousness toward building the party. So much for the anti-democratic Lenin!

Liquidators, recallists and conciliators
During the period of reaction after the 1905 revolution until the 1912 strike wave, Lenin waged many ideological battles, organising factions where necessary to convince the majority of party activists who were often disoriented under the pressure of tsarist reaction and a submerged class struggle. The first battle Lenin fought was against the majority of his supporters, who continued to argue for a boycott of the tsarist Duma, long after the tide of revolution had ebbed. An ultra-left grouping associated with Aleksandr Bogdanov, Gregori Alexinskii and Anatoli Lunacharskii also developed a wider fetish for purely underground work and cultivated heterodox views on philosophy and culture.[73]

Lenin accepted that there were legitimate differences of opinion over the Duma. However he believed the issue had been settled by the experience of the second Duma and the reaction imposed by Stolypin. By then, the RSDLP had voted for a parliamentary fraction and had helped elect its own. This convinced Lenin that the boycott tactic was no longer viable, as it had been when revolution and the soviets were immediate alternatives. He spent two years, publishing articles and pamphlets, seeking to persuade errant Bolsheviks to accept the need for parliamentary work. But Bogdanov and his supporters were not convinced. They proposed *otzovism* — the demand to recall the Duma deputies — and wanted to issue an ultimatum. This was rejected at the RSDLP conference in December 1908.

In January 1909 Lenin launched a "relentless ideological war" against the *otzovists*. He argued that "*otzovism* is not Bolshevism, but the worst political travesty of Bolshevism".[74] In June 1909, Lenin organised a meeting of the extended editorial board of *Proletarii*, the Bolsheviks' factional paper. The conference reiterated opposition to *otzovism*. Rather than accept the majority decision, Bogdanov refused to submit. The conference therefore passed a resolution "disclaiming all responsibility for the political actions [of Bogdanov]". This effectively expelled Bogdanov from the Bolshevik faction — though not from the RSDLP.[75] Bogdanov's faction did not cease. They organised schools at Capri (1909) and Bologna (1910), published their views and attended party conferences. By then, the value of the RSDLP's parliamentary work was unassailable. But the ideological fight against *otzovism* had been necessary to ensure RSDLP deputies could carry out their role.

Lenin and other RSDLP factions had to simultaneously fight liquidationism. These were mostly Mensheviks around Potresov, Larin, Levitsky and others, who reacted to the defeats suffered after the 1905 revolution by retreating politically and organisationally. Liquidationism was defined by the fifth RSDLP conference in December 1908 as "an attempt on the part of a group of party intellectuals to liquidate the existing organisation of the RSDLP and to replace it at all costs, even at the price of downright renunciation of the programme, tactics, and traditions of the party, by a loose association functioning legally".[76]

In the following four years liquidationism worsened. Liquidationism "consists ideologically in negation of the revolutionary class struggle of the socialist proletariat in general, and denial of the hegemony of the proletariat in our bourgeois-democratic revolution in particular". Organisationally, liquidationism meant "denying the necessity for an illegal social-democratic party" and renouncing the RSDLP. It mean "fighting the party in the columns of the legal press, in legal workers' organisations, in the trade unions and co-operative societies, at congresses attended by working-class delegates". Finally, the liquidators actively refused to implement the decisions of the 1907 RSDLP congress and its subsequent conferences. Instead they "sabotaged the work of the Russian central committee".[77]

Lenin argued that the liquidators' behaviour was far worse than the opportunism elsewhere in European social-democracy — worse than even Bernstein. Other Russian social-democrats agreed. In 1909, Mensheviks around Plekhanov joined the struggle against liquidationism. Plekhanov wrote in his paper *Dnevnik Sotsial-Demokrata*, (August 1909) that Potresov already "spoke like a convinced liquidator" in the autumn of 1907. Plekhanov resigned from the editorial work with other Mensheviks over these differences, concluding that "Potresov is no comrade of mine... he and I do not go the same way".[78]

By the RSDLP plenary meeting in January 1910, the liquidator publications, *Nasha Zarya* and *Dyelo Zhizni* were "belittling... the importance of the illegal party", declaring that the party was "extinct" and "already liquidated". They said reviving the illegal party was "a reactionary utopia" and regarded the nuclei of party structures as "dead". Ultimately, Lenin concluded that the liquidators "serve as conductors for bourgeois influence among the proletariat". Kamenev authored an important pamphlet in the summer of 1911 entitled *The Two Parties* (1911), which argued that the liquidators were "endeavouring to 'substitute' for the RSDLP an 'amorphous' legally existing federation".[79]

Finally, after four years of ideological combat, the sixth RSDLP conference in Prague declared that "by its conduct the *Nasha Zarya* and *Dyelo Zhizni* group has definitely placed itself outside the party". The conference called on all party members, "irrespective of tendencies and shades of opinion, to combat liquidationism, explain its great harmfulness to the cause of the emancipation of the working class, and bend all their efforts to revive and strengthen the illegal RSDLP".[80] This dealt a mortal blow against the liquidationists and helped diminish their influence just as the class struggle on the economic and political fronts was about to revive.

The contrasting fortunes of the Bolshevik-led RSDLP and the liquidators was evident six months after the Prague conference. Lenin's supporters managed to publish one hundred newspapers during that period, compared to the liquidators' 21 publications. Over the same period Lenin's supporters received over 500 contributions from workers' collections, compared with only 15 for the liquidators.[81] The

RSDLP had sunk roots within the Russian working class, while the liquidators remained isolated.

Lenin also did ideological battle with the conciliators during this period. These were RSDLP members who favoured unity of most (if not all) factions within the sheath of the party. Lenin defined conciliationism as "the totality of moods, strivings and views... during the period of the counter-revolution of 1908-11". He argued that "Trotsky expressed conciliationism more consistently than anyone else", seeking unity through "agreements concluded between all the 'intellectual' factions". Conciliators included Mensheviks, Bolsheviks and non-factionalists. Bolshevik militants such as Alexi Rykov, Victor Nogin and Stalin all pushed for unity within the party. There was a strong conciliationist tendency among the Polish social-democrats around Leo Jogiches. [82]

According to recent research by historian Alice Pate, there was a significant trend towards conciliationism within Russia itself, partly because of the arduous conditions. Pate argues that "party activists and workers inside Russia rejected party factionalism and infighting. They collaborated in trade union activities, strikes and worker associations voting for 'Marxist' slates". In elections to insurance institutions "the labour movement reaffirmed the desire for unity". Activists from both party factions "utilised the slogan, but defined it differently". Leninists "called for unity of all anti-liquidationist elements in hopes of claiming centre stage as the true social democrats". Trade unionists "still retained the hope that party workers in legal and illegal arenas could work together".[83]

The desire for reconciliation between Bolshevik and Menshevik factions within the RSDLP did not disappear with the onset of war, despite differences of tactics and strategy. The war brought further ideological battles, including on how best to frame socialist opposition (see chapter 6). And the ideological struggle around conciliationism extended into 1917, starting with the joint conference held by the two main factions at the time of Lenin's return in April. Conciliationism was only settled once the Mezhraionka joined the Bolsheviks and the Menshevik factions all opposed the October revolution.

The role of the revolutionary newspaper
Lenin was convinced that the central newspaper was the answer to the ideological and practical fragmentation of the RSDLP. A workers' newspaper should contain "everything pertaining to the theory of socialism, science, politics, questions of party organisation, etc.", and not leave that "to a periodical for the intelligentsia". It should go be-

yond matters that immediately and directly concern the spontaneous working-class movement". Questions of high theory should be combined with concrete matters, or as he put it: "the light of theory must be cast upon every separate fact". In 'Where to Begin?' (May 1901) he explained that the role of a newspaper, included "the dissemination of ideas, to political education, and to the enlistment of political allies". However it was not limited to those tasks. A newspaper was "not only a collective propagandist and a collective agitator, it is also a collective organiser". Lenin compared the paper to scaffolding round a building under construction, which "marks the contours of the structure and facilitates communication between the builders, enabling them to distribute the work and to view the common results achieved by their organised labour". He would repeat the same idea in his pamphlet *What is to be Done?*[84]

Just before the war, Lenin reflected on the range of newspapers he had been had been involved with. In 1895, a paper produced abroad, *Rabotnik* and in Petersburg *Rabochee Delo*. Famously, he was an editor of *Iskra* (and the journal *Zaria*) between 1900 and 1903. After the split, the Bolshevik faction published *Vperyod* and *Proletarii* (Geneva, 1905), *Novaia Zhizn* (Petersburg, 1905), *Volna, Ekho*, (Petersburg, 1906), *Proletarii* in Finland (1906-07), Geneva (1908) and Paris (1909), *Sotsial-Demokrat* in Paris (1909-12)... the newspapers *Zvezda* (1910-12), *Pravda* (1912- Petersburg), and the periodicals *Mysl* (1910 Moscow) and *Prosveshcheniye* (1911-13 Petersburg).[85] He might have added *Rabochaia Gazeta* (Paris) and *Nash Put* (Moscow) around that time. More publications were produced during the war. If nothing else, the Bolsheviks fought the ideological front of the class struggle with newspapers in hand.

While the Bolsheviks insisted on publishing socialist papers, they often combined legal and illegal forms, often producing factional organs alongside papers involving broader forces. A good example is the legal daily newspaper launched at the sixth RSDLP conference. Lenin arranged with social-democratic Duma deputies, who had parliamentary immunity, to serve as publishers. Originally Lenin intended that *Zvezda*, a collaboration between the Bolsheviks and Plekhanov's Mensheviks, would become the legal daily. However *Zvezda* ceased publication in April, at the same time as Petersburg social-democrats began publishing *Pravda* as a legal daily paper.

Historian Carter Elwood burst a number of myths around *Pravda*. The paper did not begin life as a Bolshevik factional organ and probably started with a significant donation from a wealthy social-democrat, Viktor Tikhomirnov. Although initially successful, circulation fell from 60,000 in the spring to 20,000 in the summer of 1912. Stalin's opening article was significantly conciliationist and the paper did not print 47 of Lenin's articles in its first two years. In July 1912 Lenin complained:

> A socialist paper must carry on polemics: our times are times of desperate confusion, and we can't do without polemics... You can't hide differences from the workers (as Pravda is doing): it's harmful, fatal, ridiculous... Pravda will perish if it is only a 'popular', 'positive' organ, that is certain... It would certainly be victorious if it were not afraid of polemics, talked straight... became lively through argument... A paper must be a step ahead of everyone.[86]

Lenin persevered with *Pravda* because it outflanked the Menshevik and liquidator competitors in terms of circulation and workers' donations. He insisted Sverdlov replace Stalin as editor, only for both to be arrested. The new editor Miron Chernomazov and new publisher Vasily Shurkanov turned out to be police agents. Nevertheless under Kamenev's editorship, *Pravda* revived, reaching a circulation of 130,000 on its second anniversary and creating a significant layer of worker-intellectuals.[87] After two years' work, the majority of the social democratic workers in Russia now apparently identified themselves with *Pravda*. Lenin's opponents (and even the police) recognised the gains of Bolshevism had made on the cusp of war.

The political front

Building a revolutionary socialist party is a political act, but such a party cannot be built by proclamation, it may have to be built by carving out political space in the most difficult or unlikely terrains. This was just how it was for the RSDLP. Lenin told delegates at the second Comintern congress in 1920 that the RSDLP had "participated in the most counterrevolutionary parliaments, and experience has shown that this participation was not only useful but indispensable to the party of the revolutionary proletariat", both for the overthrow of the tsar and the October 1917 socialist revolution.[88] Two recent books by historian August Nimtz exhaustively explain Lenin's strategy of "revolutionary parliamentarism" and its relevance for activists today.[89] Lenin's electoral strategy was a vital component of the party's fight on the political front of the class struggle.

Marxists analyse parliaments from the class perspective. In capitalist societies, all state bodies, including parliaments, are part of the apparatus of power that dominates the working class and cements its exploitation. Bourgeois parliaments cannot introduce socialism — workers have to create their own, more democratic institutions to overthrow the old state and establish their own forms of self-rule before socialist measures can be implemented. At the same time, political freedom represents the best environment for organising a working class movement. It provides space — the "light and air" — for workers' to combine collectively. Therefore Marxists support maximum democracy under capitalism and fight for reforms to loosen the shackles on the working class.

Marx and Engels bequeathed these attitudes after decades of experience with parliaments in the nineteenth century. They lambasted as "parliamentary cretinism" the attitudes which came to see bourgeois legislatures as the hub of all politics, and warned against careerists who became deputies for personal advancement. Lenin was also acutely aware of the limits of bourgeois parliaments. He argued that economic distinctions were "aggravated and intensified under the freedom of 'democratic' capitalism". Parliamentarism "lays bare the innate character even of the most democratic bourgeois republics as organs of class oppression". Parliaments helped "to enlighten and to organise immeasurably wider masses of the population than those which previously took an active part in political events".[90] He told Bolshevik opponents of work in the Duma that "the specific task of the party becomes to master the parliamentary weapon of struggle", not because parliamentary struggle is higher than any other forms of struggle, "but because it is lower than mass strikes and uprisings".[91]

Why stand in elections?
From the beginning, Lenin believed that Russian communists "should more than any others call themselves social-democrats, and in their activities should never forget the enormous importance of democracy".[92] He agreed with Marx and Engels that socialists should stand in elections, into order "count their forces" and "lay before the public their revolutionary attitude and party standpoint". Elections under universal suffrage provided a "thermometer" to register the "boiling point" among the workers.[93] Lenin argued that class-conscious workers would have "no illusions" about the significance of democracy. Democracy could not "eliminate the class struggle and the omnipotence of money". But democracy was important because "it makes the class struggle broad, open and conscious".[94] He explained why revolutionary socialists take part in bourgeois elections:

> *Firstly, to rally and politically enlighten the mass of the workers during the elections, when party struggles and the entire political life will be stimulated and when the masses will learn politics in one way or other; and, secondly, to get our worker deputies into the Duma. Even in the most reactionary Duma, in a purely landlord one, worker deputies have done, and can do, a great deal for the working-class cause, provided they are true worker democrats, provided they are connected with the masses and the masses learn to direct them and check on their activity.*[95]

Finally, another advantage of parliamentary work was to develop "good 'leaders', reliable, tested and authoritative". The difficulties of Russian conditions could be overcome by "testing the 'leaders', among other ways, in parliaments".[96] Lenin was clear that the ultimate aim of socialism should guide electoral work. He argued that "the main tasks of the party in elections and of social-democratic deputies in the Duma was "socialist, class propaganda and the organisation of the working class".[97] The raw results of RSDLP parliamentary activity in the Dumas is summarised in the table:

Duma	Date	RSDLP deputies	
First	14 April 1906 — 8 July 1906	18/478	All Mensheviks (Bolshevik boycott)
Second	20 February 1907 — 3 June 1907	65/518	18 Bolsheviks, 36 Mensheviks
Third	7 November 1907 — 9 June 1912	18/442	
Fourth	15 November 1912 — 6 October 1917	13/442	6 Bolsheviks, 7 Mensheviks

Although for Lenin and others the general rule was that socialists should participate in bourgeois elections, there were exceptions. After the bloody Sunday demonstrations in 1905, the tsarist minister Bulygin came forward with proposals for an advisory Duma. Elections would be indirect and voters based on a very limited suffrage. Deputies were to be elected from electoral colleges (known as "curiae") of various categories of the population: landowners (including the clergy), urban property owners, peasants on communal land and city residents. High property qualifications excluded Russia's working class.[98]

While the Mensheviks favoured participation even under such restrictions, the Bolsheviks were adamantly opposed. Lenin accused the Mensheviks of "playing at parliamentarism when no parliament whatever exists", joking that "we have no parliament as yet, but we have parliamentary cretinism galore".[99] He urged Bolsheviks to "fight in a revolutionary way for a parliament, but not in a parliamentary way for a revolution".[100] At the end of 1905, in the context of the creation of workers' soviets and the uprising in Moscow, the Bolshevik cadres understandably voted for an active boycott of any Duma. They carried this position into the first Duma elections in early 1906.

Despite the restrictions and the Bolshevik boycott, 18 social-democrats were elected as deputies in the first Duma elections. The three-month first Duma was sufficient to convince Lenin to change his line. In the first issue of *Proletarii*, his article 'The Boycott' (August 1906) began: "the left-wing social-democrats must reconsider the question of boycotting the state Duma".[101] Lenin published a twenty-page pamphlet, 'The Social-Democrats and Electoral Agreements' (November 1906) explaining his views on electoral work, justifying the previous boycott but calling for participation in light of the ebb of the revolution. The central theme detailed his opposition to electoral "blocs" or agreements with bourgeois parties such as the Kadets. In another pamphlet, 'Against Boycott' (26 June 1907) Lenin argued that the boycott was "not a line of tactics, but a special means of struggle suitable under special conditions".[102]

The debate reached a turning point in the second Duma, when Stolypin demanded the arrest of virtually the entire social democrat fraction on the ground of their military and expropriation activity. After the Duma refused to comply with the trumped up charges, Stolypin announced the dissolution of the second Duma, with new elections for a third Duma by November. As Nimtz argues, "the absence of any kind of real protest against Stolypin's 'coup d'état' of 3 June signalled the end of the revolution of 1905. The all-important energy 'outside' the walls of Tauride Palace had dissipated". Many of the fraction members, including Irakli Tsereteli and Grigori Alexinskii, were arrested, brought to trial six months later and sentenced to hard labour or exile.[103]

The third RSDLP conference (July 1907) held a debate about the third Duma. The Mensheviks favoured participation, while most Bolsheviks favoured boycott. The Menshevik resolution was defeated by the Bolshevik majority at the congress, but then Lenin crossed over to vote with the Mensheviks to defeat Bogdanov's boycott resolution. Finally Lenin's proposal that the party should take part in the Duma was passed with Menshevik support.[104]

How to campaign in elections

Lenin was effectively the party's electoral and parliamentary director during this period. He claimed that from the beginning of the social-democratic group in the third Duma, "the Bolshevik faction, through its representatives authorised by the central committee of the party, has all the time assisted, aided, advised, and supervised the work of the social-democrats in the Duma". He added that the paper's editorial board played the same role, underlining his involvement.[105]

Lenin supervised parliamentary activity, particularly around the fourth Duma, from beginning to end. In October 1911 he urged the party to launch its election campaign a year ahead of the vote. Lenin observed that "a platform is something that has existed long before the elections; it is not something specially devised 'for the elections,' but an inevitable result of the whole work of the party, of the way the work is organised, and of its whole trend in the given historical period". He learned from Engels that "very often it may be useful, and sometimes even essential, to give the election platform of social-democracy a finishing touch by adding a brief general slogan, a watchword for the elections, stating the most cardinal issues of current political practice". This would provide "a most convenient and most immediate pretext, as well as subject matter, for comprehensive socialist propaganda". The watchwords he advocated for the 1912 elections in Russia were: a republic, confiscation of all landed estates, and the eight-hour day. In short, "the substance and mainspring of the social-democratic election platform can be expressed in three words: for the revolution!"[106]

The election was an opportunity to campaign and renew the party. In the summer of 1912, Lenin and Krupskaia moved to Krakow to be closer to the work. They sent Inessa Armand and Safarov to re-establish the Petersburg branch of the party, get the *Pravda* editors on board and begin preparations for the workers' curiae elections. Armand, working undercover, scored a success with workers at the Putilov plant. After hearing her report on the Prague conference, they decided to support the Bolshevik line and take part in the elections. She arranged a meeting to select a slate of six Bolshevik candidates. Although she and others were arrested, the intervention helped

Badaev win the Petersburg seat for the RSDLP (and the Bolshevik faction).[107]

Lenin also had very clear conceptions of how to approach electoral agreements with other parties. In the workers' curia, he argued that "the social-democratic party must come out absolutely independently and refrain from entering into agreements with any other party".[108] He rejected the lesser evil logic of supporting other parties in order to keep out the Black Hundreds in Petersburg. He accepted that in other curia, it was acceptable for the party to support democratic peasant candidates from the Trudovik party, but he opposed support for Kadets. He argued that "the tactics of the democrats should be to unite first with the liberals to defeat the Rights, and then with the Rights to defeat the liberals, so that neither are able to secure the election of their candidates".[109]

How should deputies work?

Initially, Lenin faced the practical difficulty of managing the Duma fraction's work when most deputies had been elected without support or help from the exiles. In the case of the first Duma, he recognised the distance between those elected and the party. The 15 deputies who constituted the 'Workers' Group' were "not nominated by workers' organisations. The party did not authorise them to represent its interests in the Duma. Not a single local organisation of the RSDLP adopted a resolution... to nominate its members for the State Duma". The worker deputies got into the Duma "through non-party channels" with nearly all "by direct or indirect, tacit or avowed, agreements with the Kadets". However he welcomed the declaration of Mikhailichenko, the leader of the group, who proclaimed himself a social-democrat, dissociated the group from the Kadets and sought to become a genuine social-democratic group.[110]

Lenin was particularly concerned with how the RSDLP parliamentary fraction conducted itself when the Duma opened. At the beginning of the second Duma, he praised Tsereteli, the Menshevik faction leader from Georgia, along with Bolshevik faction leader Alexinskii, for roundly denouncing Stolypin. However at the outset of the third Duma, Lenin was critical of the social-democratic deputies for supporting the Kadets over the gerrymandered franchise.[111] He argued that social-democratic deputies should use their platform to act as tribunes for the working class, agitating on the key issues of the day, using their legal position to help publish newspapers and express their solidarity with strikes.[112] Finally, the parliamentary fraction was tasked with opposing imperialist war, which it duly carried out in July 1914.

In light of these problems, Lenin was convinced the party needed to hold deputies to account. He was mindful of the history of western European socialist parties and the instances of "abnormal relations between the parliamentary groups and the party". Social-democratic parliamentarism in Russia would be different. He argued that "every social-democratic deputy" must "really feel that he has the party behind him", that "the party is deeply concerned over his mistakes and tries to straighten out his path". The solution was for every party worker to take part in the general Duma work of the party, "learning from the practical Marxist criticism of its steps, feeling it his duty to assist it, and striving to gear the special work of the group to the whole propaganda and agitation activity of the party".[113] At the fourth RSDLP congress (1906), the Bolsheviks tried to amend the Menshevik resolution to ensure deputies actually represented the working class, particularly given the restrictions in Russia on workers' public political activity. Lenin advocated "triple control" over members of parliament:

> *First, the general control that the party exercises over all its members; secondly, the special control of the local organisations who nominate the parliamentary candidates in their own name; and thirdly, the special control of the central committee, which, standing above local influences and local conditions, must see to it that only such parliamentary candidates are nominated as satisfy general party and general political requirements.*[114]

Although the Bolsheviks were unsuccessful on this occasion, they returned to the matter two years later. Lenin argued that to ensure the Duma fraction was "a really party organisation" required a real party, with "a strong illegal organisation of the party centres, systematic illegal publications and — most important of all — local and particularly factory party groups, led by advanced members from among the workers themselves, living in direct contact with the masses".[115]

Of course the RSDLP parliamentary fraction suffered setbacks, including the loss of Bolshevik leader Roman Malinovskii in May 1914 (later revealed as a police spy). It would split formally in 1913 over the papers deputies backed and finally (after the joint declaration against the outbreak of war), when the Menshevik deputies backtracked. Nevertheless the fraction was pivotal to the revival of the RSDLP after the period of reaction, including for the publication of

Pravda and the support for the strike wave. The RSDLP's parliamentary work made real gains on the political front of the class struggle.[116] And the party would again use bourgeois elections in 1917 as a barometer to measure its support.

The third camp
How did Lenin sum up independent working class political representation during the elections of 1912? The RSDLP was faced with an array of hostile forces in the Duma. First, the Octobrist party were advocates of constitutional monarchy. Second, the Kadet party, apparently liberal and subject to police harassment, but actually pro-monarchist and bourgeois. There were also the Trudovik party, representing peasant interests and ostensibly a democratic force. Furthest to the left were of course the social-democrats, but how would they relate to the other forces? Throughout the election campaign, hostility towards the Octobrists was taken for granted. Lenin continuously sought to distinguish the liberals from the democratic forces — or what he dubbed the "third camp". He wrote:

> *Marxists long ago defined their fundamental attitude to the elections. The right-wing parties — from Purishkevich to Guchkov — the liberal-monarchist bourgeoisie (Kadets and Progressists) and the democrats (worker democrats and bourgeois democrats, i.e. Trudoviks) are the three principal camps contesting the elections. The distinction between these camps is a basic one, for they represent different classes and have entirely different programmes and tactics.*[117]

Summing up after the vote, Lenin argued that there had been "three camps in the elections to the fourth Duma and three camps in the country". The third camp was "the democrats... led by the working class".[118] This was a crisp formulation for independent working class politics, standing apart from both ruling conservative and bourgeois-liberal forces, with workers at the head of their own forces, rallying other exploited and oppressed behind them in a democratic alliance. The phrase would be used by Lenin again and picked up by others such as Trotsky in different contexts. It was a durable expression for working-class politics.

The economic front
The Bolsheviks are often accused of underestimating the spontaneous protests of workers, downgrading the role of trade unionism and largely ignoring the economic exploitation of workers. This is a myth

invented by their opponents within the contemporary Russian labour movement, spread by cold war historians and echoed by anarcho-syndicalists.

The myth usually begins with two "scandalous" passages from Lenin's *What is to be Done?* (1902). Explaining the common ideas inherited from the international socialist movement, he remarked that "social-democratic consciousness could only have been brought to the workers from without". He added, "the history of all countries shows that the working class exclusively by its own effort is able to develop only trade-union consciousness". Further on Lenin argued that "the task of social democracy is to combat spontaneity, to divert the working class movement from this spontaneous, trade-unionist striving to come under the wing of the bourgeoisie, and to bring it under the wing of revolutionary social democracy".[119]

Lenin's views are perfectly explicable and suggest no downgrading of the economic front of the class struggle. Lenin's early political activity was characterised by the close attention to workers' economic struggles, to the particular conditions found in the factories and by practical support to the strike movement in the mid-1890s, in the form of newspapers and leaflets. Far from not paying attention to the conditions of the working-class, Lenin was a strong advocate of the elemental, unstoppable natural force of class struggles implied by the Russia term, *stikhiinyi*, translated as spontaneous.

However compressed in these passages from *What is to Be Done* are a number of different issues that can only be understood in context. First, Lenin is reiterating the basic Marxist proposition that in bourgeois society, the ruling ideas of the epoch are those of the ruling class. This was Marx and Engels' insight, found in the *German Ideology* and the *Communist Manifesto*, which forms a key part of their understanding of capitalism. The role of bourgeois ideas in dominating working-class consciousness is a key explanation for why workers do not simply draw socialist conclusions from the experiences of their exploitation. It is also crucial to explaining why even organised working-class movements, such as the trade unions, do not automatically become socialist and often end up with bureaucratic leaders tied to bourgeois politics.

In the circumstances of fin-de-siècle labour movements, this was evident from the "pure-and-simple" trade unionism of the US trade union leader Samuel Gompers, or the trade unionism-only attitudes "nur-Gewerkschaftlerei" found in Germany.[120] It was these limitations Lenin sought to combat. In Russian conditions, Lenin was fighting those who wanted to confine socialist activity to local workers' support work and those who assumed that economic battles were sufficient to develop socialist consciousness. Instead, Lenin wanted to assert that without the active intervention of socialists, the spontaneous militancy of the workers would be diverted into bourgeois politics, to demoralisation and ultimately defeat.

The activity of the RSDLP intimately connected with workers in their workplaces. This is evident from the role RSDLP militants played in leading strikes and building other forms of working class organisations such as soviets and factory councils. For example the strike in Ivanovo-Voznesensk that created the first soviet of workers' deputies (April-May 1905) was led by Bolsheviks, whose members made up a third of its leading committee.[121] Lenin wrote *Strike Statistics in Russia* (1910), a brilliant analysis of the mass strike movement during the 1905-07 revolutionary period.[122]

The importance of the economic front of the class struggle for the RSDLP was illustrated by the strike wave of 1912-14. On 4 April 1912 striking miners in the Lena goldfields in Siberia were mowed down by soldiers. Some 230 died and 540 were wounded.[123] The massacre sparked an explosion among Russian workers that would once more rock the tsarist monarchy and ultimately prepare the ground for the 1917 revolution. Two and half million workers participated in more than thirty political strikes from April 1912 to the end of 1916, while another 1.8 million workers engaged in economic strikes. The epicentre of this movement was Petersburg, where 23 large strikes involving 50,000 workers or more occurred for various political causes. The Bolsheviks provided a significant catalytic role to this strike movement.[124]

Lenin's response to these developments was unrefracted enthusiasm. He lauded the strikes and sought to develop them. He welcomed the strikes that greeted the opening of the fourth Duma in November 1912. Lenin recognised that the "massive offensive against the capitalists and the tsarist monarchy" was a turning point, signalling the end of the reaction since 1907. He undertook a careful statistical analysis of the 1912 strikes, estimating that while "the number of political strikers reached one million", in a number of cases workers "put forward economic and political demands simultaneously [and] the period of economic strikes was succeeded by a period of political strikes and vice versa".[125] Lenin's attitude contrasted with caution of the Mensheviks, who warned about the "dangerous frittering away of forces", "nothing is to be gained by outbreaks" and howling against "playing at strikes". He celebrated the mass, elemental force of workers' action:

> *That means is revolutionary strikes, stubborn strikes shifting from place to place, from one part of the country to another, recurrent strikes, strikes which rouse the backward to a new life of struggle for economic improvements, strikes which brand and lash every salient act of violence or tyranny, every crime of tsarism, strike-demonstrations which unfurl the red banner in the streets of the capital cities and bring revolutionary speeches and revolutionary slogans to the crowd, to the mass of the people. Such strikes cannot be called forth artificially, but neither can they be stopped once they have begun to involve hundreds and hundreds of thousands.*[126]

The dialectic of economic and political struggle was captured by the opposition to further armaments spending in 1914. Social-democratic deputies in the Duma were denied the right to protest at this expenditure, so they promptly obstructed the debate on the government's budget. They were then suspended by the Duma president, which provoked strikes and demonstrations by tens of thousands of workers in Petersburg and Moscow as well to protest the suspensions.[127] This fed action already planned for May Day a few days later, sparking the largest protests since 1905-07.

Trade unionism revived after 1912, mostly adopting industrial over sectional forms. By 1914 there were 30 legal trade unions in Petersburg, with a membership of over 29,000, including unions of metalworkers, printers, bakery, confectionary and textile workers. During 1912-14, Bolshevik militants increasingly won majorities on union executive bodies — epitomised by the Petersburg metalworkers. Even where they didn't win a majority, such as among the printers, Bolsheviks still made up significant minorities on the leadership bodies.[128] These developments, temporarily thrown backwards at the beginning of the First World War, would be reasserted during 1917.

Conclusion

Without the RSDLP, the Russian revolution in October 1917 would never have occurred. The party led by the Bolshevik faction and by Lenin in particular adopted sharp, principled and yet flexible political ideas. This party took the best of European social democracy and applied it to Russian conditions. The course of the RSDLP's adaptation was not linear — the RSDLP had to adapt and change under the many different conditions of Russian society and politics. That 40-year adaptation was not a simple facsimile of the SPD, not least because the model itself underwent degeneration. The SPD by 1914 was not the party that had emerged from illegality in 1890 — or even the party it was in 1905. By the outbreak of war it was heavily bureaucratised, increasingly reticent in politics, its left-wing marginalised, the leadership cautious in industrial relations and fearful of the state it had once appeared to threaten. While it retained merits, Lenin recognised it showed signs of disease.[129]

Socialist historian Paul Le Blanc sums up the status of the RSDLP prior to the 1917 revolution. The Prague conference "did not declare the existence of a new Bolshevik party. It declared the reorganisation and renewal of the RSDLP". Lenin supporters "were propagating the party principle as it had always been understood in the Second International". Their goal was "an organisation conforming to the idealised notion of the German social democratic party". Yet what emerged in 1912 was nonetheless "a Bolshevik party, with a Bolshevik leadership, following a Bolshevik line".[130]

The RSDLP was not the "party of a new type", as the Stalinists and their cold war imitators would have it. The party fought the class struggle on all three fronts: the economic, political and ideological. It published open, critical publications that debated matters in public. It ran an efficient party regime commensurate with conditions of illegality in Russia, but still went to extraordinary lengths to democratically decide the central questions of the day. It was a party of factions and free-flowing discussion, coupled with serious intervention into every sphere of Russian life. It was a combat party, but simultaneously a party of ideas. Members were "professional revolutionaries" in the elaborate ways they sought to elude the tsarist police. The revolutionaries maintained their essential principles, but adapted their methods to the circumstances. The party contested elections, used every available platform, supported and led strikes, built broad workers' organisations and allied with other oppressed and exploited forces. Lenin summed up the approach:

> *We must train people who will devote the whole of their lives, not only their spare evenings, to the revolution; we must build up an organisation large enough to permit the introduction of a strict division of labour in the various forms of our work. Finally, with regard to questions of tactics, we shall confine ourselves to the following: social-democracy does not tie its hands, it does not restrict its activities to someone preconceived plan or method of political struggle; it recognises all methods of struggle, provided they correspond to the forces at the disposal of the party and facilitate the achievement of the best results possible under the given conditions. If we have a strongly organised party, a single strike may turn into a political demonstration, into a political victory over the govern-*

ment. If we have a strongly organised party, a revolt in a single locality may grow into a victorious revolution. We must bear in mind that the struggles with the government for partial demands and the gain of certain concessions are merely light skirmishes with the enemy, encounters between outposts, whereas the decisive battle is still to come.[131]

The RSDLP led by the Bolsheviks has been demonised for generations. Millions have been miseducated by academics, Stalinists, anarchists and even those purporting to be "Leninists". But the party will not lie down. The historical truth about this party endures because the Russian revolutionaries who composed it dared to fight, to take power — dared to win. This party is the most valuable legacy of the 1917 revolution. No socialist activist today can afford to ignore it.

References

1. Trotsky, [1924] 'The Lessons of October'. In *Challenge of the Left Opposition*, (1975: 201, 252).
2. Samuel Baron, *Plekhanov: The Father of Russian Marxism*, (1963: 130, 122-127); Franco Venturi, *Roots of Revolution*, (1960: 581).
3. Neil Harding, *Marxism in Russia*, (1983: 379-81, N.42, 48, 49, 67).
4. Vladimir Akimov [1905] 'A Short History of the Social Democratic Movement in Russia'. In Jonathan Frankel, *Vladimir Akimov on the Dilemmas of Russian Marxism 1895–1903*, (1969: 205, 216, 221, 285, 292).
5. Jane McDermid, 'The Evolution of Soviet Attitudes towards Women and the Family', University of Glasgow PhD thesis, (1988: 160-68, 281-82); Anna Hillyar, 'Revolutionary Women in Russia, 1870-1917: a prosopographical study', University of Southampton PhD thesis, (1999: 65).
6. Frankel, (1969: 22, 24); Barbara Norton, 'Eshche raz ekonomizm: E D Kuskova, S N Prokopovich, and the Challenge to Russian Social Democracy', *The Russian Review*, 45, 2, (1986: 187-88).
7. Vadim Medish, 'The First Party Congress and Its Place in History', *The Russian Review*, 22, 2, (1963: 172-78).
8. Lars Lih, *Lenin Rediscovered — "What Is to Be Done?" in Context*, (2008: 443).
9. Richard Mullin, *The Russian Social-Democratic Labour Party, 1899-1904*, (2016: 36-44); Brian Pearce, *1903 — Second Congress of the Russian Social-democratic Labour Party*, (1978).
10. Mullin, (2016: 341, 357); Pearce, (1978: 399-402).
11. David Lane, *The Roots of Russian Communism*, (1968: 12-14, 72-74).
12. Lenin, [10 November 1906] 'On Convening an Extraordinary Party Congress', (*LCW* 11: 264-65).
13. Lenin, [28 January 1909] 'On the Road', (*LCW* 15: 345).
14. Lenin, [8-17 June 1909] 'Report on the Conference of the Extended Editorial Board of Proletary', (*LCW* 15: 431-432).
15. Paul Le Blanc, [1993] *Lenin and the Revolutionary Party*, (2015: 155); Leon Trotsky, [1939] 'Against the Stream', Sean Matgamna, *The Two Trotskyisms Confront Stalinism*, (2015: 132).
16. Ralph Carter Elwood, (2011) *The Non-Geometric Lenin*, (2011: 17-19).
17. Elwood, (2011: 19-25).
18. Elwood, (2011: 29-33).
19. Elwood, (2011: 73-85).
20. Olga Gankin and Hal Fisher, *The Bolsheviks and the World War*, (1940).
21. Le Blanc, (2015: 208).
22. Le Blanc, (2015: 228).
23. Ferdinand Lassalle, [17 November 1862] 'What now'? *Speeches of Ferdinand Lassalle: Voices of Revolt*, Vol.3, (1927: 46); Lassalle [1 March 1863] 'Open Letter to the National Labour Association of Germany'. In Frank Macklenburg and Manfred Stassen, *German Essays on Socialism in the Nineteenth Century*, (1990: 79, 101-102).
24. Engels, [1874] 'Addendum to The Peasant War in Germany', (*MECW* 23: 630-31).
25. Kautsky, [1892] *Das Erfurter Programm*. In Lih, (2008: 85, 88-89).
26. Lih, (2008: 120, 142-44).
27. Kautsky, Karl [1901] 'Die Revision des Programms der Sozialdemokratie in Österreich', in Lenin, [March 1902] *What is to be Done?* (*LCW* 5: 383-84).
28. Raymond Dominick, *Wilhelm Liebknecht and the Founding of the German Social Democratic Party*, (1977: 290-92).
29. Peter Nettl, 'The German Social Democratic Party 1890-1914 as a Political Model', *Past and Present*, 30, (1965: 72-73).
30. Gary Steenson, *Not one man! Not one penny! German Social Democracy, 1863-1914*, (1981: 27-28; 84). See also Vernon Lidtke, *The Outlawed Party: Social Democracy in Germany, 1878-1890*, (1966).

31. Vernon Lidtke, *The Alternative Culture: the Socialist Labor Movement in Imperial Germany* (1985).
32. Lenin, [September 1905] 'The Jena Congress of the German Social-Democratic Workers' Party', (*LCW* 9: 290); Lenin, [June-July 1905] *Two Tactics of Social-Democracy in the Democratic Revolution,* (*LCW* 9: 65-66); Lenin, [5-17 January 1912] 'Resolutions of the Sixth (Prague) All-Russia Conference of the RSDLP', (*LCW* 17: 486}.
33. Georgi Plekhanov, [22 July 1884] *Our Differences,* (*SPW* 1: 135); Plekhanov, [January 1895] *The Development of the Monist View of History,* (*SPW* 1: 703).
34. Plekhanov, *Our Differences,* (*SPW* 1: 391); 'Socialism and the Political Struggle', (*SPW* 1: 117-118).
35. Plekhanov, [1883] 'Socialism and the Political Struggle', (*SPW* 1: 102).
36. Plekhanov, [1884] 'Programme of Social-Democratic Emancipation of Labour Group', (*SPW* 1: 400); Plekhanov, [1885] 'Second Draft Programme of the Russian Social-Democrats', (*SPW* 1: 408).
37. Plekhanov, [July 1889] 'Speech at the International Workers' Socialist Congress in Paris', (*SPW* 1: 454); Pavel Axelrod, (December 1897) 'On the Question of the Present Tasks and Tactics of the Russian Social Democrats (Draft Programme)', in Harding, (1983: 237).
38. Plekhanov and Axelrod (1884) 'From the Publishers of the 'Workers' Library'', in Harding, (1983: 68, 71, 380, N.52); Abraham Ascher, *Pavel Axelrod and the Development of Menshevism,* (1973: 95).
39. Plekhanov, [1891] 'The Tasks of the Social Democrats in the Struggle against the Famine in Russia'. In Harding (1983: 104-105).
40. Plekhanov, 'Socialism and the Political Struggle', (*SPW* 1: 78-79, 119).
41. Lenin, [13-14 January 1907] 'The Social-Democrats and the Duma Elections', (*LCW* 11: 444-45); Lenin, [27 February 1907] 'The Imminent Dissolution of the Duma and Questions of Tactics', (*LCW* 12: 187).
42. Lenin, [13-14 January 1907] 'The Social-Democrats and the Duma Elections', (*LCW* 11: 444-45); Lenin, [27 February 1907] 'The Imminent Dissolution of the Duma and Questions of Tactics', (*LCW* 12: 187).
43. Henry Tudor and J. Tudor, Marxism and Social Democracy: The Revisionist Debate 1896-1898, (1988); Eduard Bernstein, [1899], *The Preconditions of Socialism* (1993: 145); Plekhanov, [October 1898] 'What Should We Thank Him For?' (*SPW* 2: 351).
44. Plekhanov, [February 1900] *Vademecum*. In Mullin, (2016: 88-89, 116-19).
45. Plekhanov, *Vademecum*. Mullin, (2016: 133-37).
46. Lenin, [September 1899] 'A Protest by Russian Social-Democrats', (*LCW* 4: 172, 178).
47. Plekhanov, *Vademecum*. Mullin, (2016: 107, 123).
48. Mullin, (2016: 166); Lenin, [1898] *Once More on the Theory of Realisation*, (*LCW* 4: 13-93).
49. Mullin, (2016: 28).
50. Lih, (2008: 243-45); Konstantin Takhtarev [September 1899] 'Our Reality'. In Harding, (1983: 242-50).
51. Lih, (2008: 143-52); Lenin, [1899] 'Our Immediate Task', (*LCW* 4: 217-20).
52. Lenin, [1899] 'An Urgent Question', (*LCW* 4: 224).
53. Lenin, [1899] 'A Draft of Our Party Programme', (*LCW* 4: 235).
54. Lenin, [1899] 'A Retrograde Trend in Russian Social-Democracy', *LCW* 4: 257-59).
55. Lenin, [September 1900] 'Declaration of the Editorial Board of *Iskra*', (*LCW* 4: 354-55).
56. Mullin, (2016: 224-28, 258-59).
57. Lenin, [March 1902] *What is to be Done?* (*LCW* 5: 369-370).
58. Lenin, [March 1902] *What is to be Done?* (*LCW* 5: 375).
59. Lars Lih, 'Lenin Disputed', *Historical Materialism*, 18, (2010: 147); Marcel Liebman, [1973] *Leninism under Lenin*, (1975: 45-49); Tony Cliff, *Lenin: Building the Party*, (1975: 173-75).
60. Lenin, [March 1902] *What is to be Done?* (*LCW* 5: 409-10).
61. Lenin, [March 1902] *What is to be Done?* (*LCW* 5: 467); Lenin, [15 June 1913] 'May Day Action by the Revolutionary Proletariat', (*LCW* 19: 224-25).
62. Lih, *Lenin Rediscovered*, (2008: 447-449).
63. Lenin, [September 1902] 'A Letter to a Comrade on Organisational Tasks', (*LCW* 6: 229-

50); Grigorii Zinoviev, History of the Bolshevik Party, (1973: 75).
64. Mullin, (2016: 50-51).
65. Lenin, [May 1904] *One Step Forward, Two Steps Back*, (*LCW* 7: 205-06).
66. Lenin, [October 1905] 'Letter to Plekhanov', (*LCW* 34: 364).
67. Carter Elwood, Resolutions and decisions of the Communist Party of the Soviet Union, 1898-1917, (1974: 82-83, 93-94); Lih, (2008: 518-519).
68. Elwood, (1974: 83, 87, 94).
69. Lenin, [25-26 April 1906] 'An Appeal to the Party by Delegates to the Unity Congress Who Belonged to the Former "Bolshevik" Group', (*LCW* 10: 310-11).
70. Lenin, [5 November 1907] 'But Who are the Judges?' (*LCW* 13: 159).
71. Lenin, [8-17 June 1909] 'Report on the Conference of the Extended Editorial Board of Proletary', (*LCW* 15: 430) translation tweaked.
72. Lenin, [19 January 1921] 'The Party Crisis', (*LCW* 32: 52); Lenin, [25 January 1921] 'Once Again on the Trade Unions', (*LCW* 32: 106).
73. Le Blanc, 'The Birth of the Bolshevik party in 1912', *Links: International Journal of Socialist Renewal*, (17 April 2012).
74. Lenin, [28 January 1909] 'On the Article "Questions of the Day"', (*LCW* 15: 357
75. Lenin, [8-17 June 1909] 'Report on the Conference of the Extended Editorial Board of Proletary', (*LCW* 15: 431-32).
76. Lenin, [5-17 January 1912] 'Resolutions of the Sixth (Prague) All-Russia Conference of the RSDLP', (*LCW* 17: 480).
77. Lenin, [11 July 1909] 'The Liquidation of Liquidationism', (*LCW* 15: 454); Lenin, [December 1910] 'Letter to the Russian Collegium of the Central Committee of the RSDLP', (*LCW* 17: 17).
78. Lenin, [21-27 December 1908] 'Statement of Facts: The Fifth (All-Russian) Conference of the RSDLP', (*LCW* 15: 329); Lenin, [5 September 1909] 'The Liquidators Exposed', (*LCW* 16: 19).
79. Lenin, [5-17 January 1912] 'Resolutions of the Sixth (Prague) All-Russia Conference of the RSDLP', (*LCW* 17: 481); Lenin, [March 1911] 'The Social Structure of State Power, the Prospects and Liquidationism', (*LCW* 17: 163); Lenin, [2 August 1911] 'Introduction to the Pamphlet Two Parties', (*LCW* 17: 225).
80. Lenin, [5-17 January 1912] 'Resolutions of the Sixth (Prague) All-Russia Conference of the RSDLP', (*LCW* 17: 481).
81. Lenin, [July 1912] 'The Present Situation in the RSDLP', (*LCW* 18: 211); Lenin, [30 July 1912] 'On the Eve of the Elections to the Fourth Duma', (*LCW* 18: 240).
82. Lenin, [18 October 1911] 'The New Faction of Conciliators, or the Virtuous', (*LCW* 17: 25-77).
83. Alice Pate, 'The Party as Vanguard: The Role of the Russian Social Democratic Party in Strikes in St. Petersburg, 1912-1914', *Workers of the World: International Journal on Strikes and Social Conflicts*, 1, 1, (2012: 17).
84. Lenin, [1900] 'Draft of a Declaration of the Editorial Board of Iskra and Zarya', (*LCW* 4: 326); Lenin, [May 1901] 'Where to Begin?' (*LCW* 5: 21-22); Lenin, [March 1902] *What is to be Done?* (*LCW* 5: 502-03).
85. Lenin, [January 1913] 'On Bolshevism', (*LCW* 18: 485-486); Lenin, [22 April 1914] 'From the History of the Workers' Press in Russia', (*LCW* 20: 247-251).
86. Lenin, [24 July 1912] 'To the Editor of Nevskaya Zvezda', (*LCW* 35: 42-43).
87. Elwood, (2011: 37-55); Lenin, [29 March 1913] 'Letter to Kamenev', (*LCW* 35: 93).
88. Lenin, [April-May 1920] *Left Wing Communism*, (*LCW* 31: 61).
89. August Nimtz, *Lenin's Electoral Strategy from Marx and Engels through the Revolution of 1905*, (2014a); Nimtz, *Lenin's Electoral Strategy from 1907 to the October Revolution of 1917*, (2014b). Doug Jenness, *Lenin as Election Campaign Manager* (1971).
90. Marx, [1852] *The Eighteenth Brumaire of Louis Bonaparte*, (*MECW* 11: 161, 179); Lenin, [3 April 1908] *Marxism and Revisionism*, (*LCW* 15: 36-37).
91. Lenin, [11 September 1909] 'The Faction of Supporters of Otzovism and God-Building', (*LCW* 16: 33).

92. Lenin, [1894] 'Friends of the People', (*LCW* 1: 290).
93. Marx and Engels, [March 1850] 'Address to the Communist League', (*MECW* 10: 284); Engels, [1884] *Origin of the Family, Private Property and State*, (*MECW* 26: 272).
94. Lenin, [18 September 1912] 'The Successes of the American Workers', (*LCW* 18: 335).
95. Lenin, [12-14 July 1912] 'The Results of Six Months' Work', (*LCW* 18: 196-97).
96. Lenin, [April-May 1920] *Left Wing Communism*, (*LCW* 31: 65).
97. Lenin, [January 1912] 'Elections to the Fourth Duma: Sixth Conference of the RSDLP', (*LCW* 17: 468).
98. Nimtz, (2014a: 91).
99. Lenin, [13 September 1905] 'Friends Meet', (*LCW* 9: 258).
100. Lenin, [11 October 1905] 'Letter to Anatoli Lunacharsky', (*LCW* 34: 353).
101. Nimtz, (2014a: 128, 131); Lenin, [12 August 1906] 'The Boycott', (*LCW* 11: 141).
102. Lenin, [26 June 1907] 'Against Boycott', (*LCW* 13: 43).
103. Nimtz, (2014a: 167-168).
104. Le Blanc, (2015: 136).
105. Nimtz, (2014b: 41-42); Lenin, [November 1910] 'Historical Meaning of Inner-Party Struggle in Russia', (*LCW* 16: 390).
106. Nimtz, (2014b: 50-51); Lenin, [18 October 1911] 'The Election Campaign and the Election Platform', (*LCW* 17: 281-83); Engels, [18-29 June 1891] 'A Critique of the Draft Social-Democratic Programme of 1891', (*MECW* 27: 219).
107. Nimtz, (2014b: 68).
108. Lenin, [4 November 1906] 'A Dissenting Opinion Recorded at the All-Russian Conference of the RSDLP', (*LCW* 11: 300).
109. Nimtz, (2014a: 132-134); Lenin, [December 1911] 'Campaign for Elections to the Fourth Duma', (*LCW* 17: 378).
110. Lenin, [10 May 1906] 'The Workers' Group in the State Duma', (*LCW* 10: 402); Nimtz, (2014a: 104-05).
111. Nimtz, (2014a: 151); Nimtz, (2014b: 16).
112. Nimtz, (2014b: 46, 59).
113. Lenin, [28 January 1909] 'On the Road', (*LCW* 15: 352-53).
114. Lenin, [25 April 1906] 'Dissenting Opinion on the Composition of the Parliamentary Group of the RSDLP', (*LCW* 10: 303-04).
115. Lenin, [19 March 1908] 'On to the Straight Road', (*LCW* 15: 20-21).
116. Aleksei Badayev, *The Bolsheviks in the Tsarist Duma*, (1929).
117. Lenin, [24 June 1912] 'The Elections and the Opposition', (*LCW* 18: 132).
118. Lenin, [November 1912] 'Concerning Certain Speeches by Workers' Deputies', (*LCW* 18: 418).
119. Lenin, [1902] What is to be Done? (*LCW* 5: 375, 384-85).
120. Lih, (2008: 390, 625-26).
121. Lane, (1968: 143).
122. Lenin, [December 1910] 'Strike Statistics in Russia', (*LCW* 16: 395-421).
123. Michael Melancon, 'The Ninth Circle: The Lena Goldfield Workers and the Massacre of 4 April 1912', *Slavic Review*, 53, 3 (1994: 766, 789).
124. Kevin Murphy, 'The Pre-revolutionary Strike Movement in Russia, 1912-1916', *Workers of the World: International Journal on Strikes and Social Conflicts*, 1, 1, (2012: 19-20).
125. Lenin, [November 1912] 'Concerning the Event of November 15', (*LCW* 18: 425); Lenin, [February 1913] 'Resolutions of the Cracow Meeting of the Central Committee of the RSDLP and party functionaries', (*LCW* 18: 456).
126. Lenin, [12 January 1913] 'The Development of Revolutionary Strikes and Street Demonstrations', (*LCW* 18: 474, 476).
127. Nimtz, (2014b: 93-94).
128. Steve Smith, 'Craft Consciousness, Class Consciousness: Petrograd 1917', *History Workshop*, 11, (1981: 41-48).
129. Carl Schorske, *German Social Democracy, 1905-1917: The Development of the Great Schism*, (1955); Lenin, [April 1914] 'What should not be copied from the German Movement', (*LCW*

20: 257-58).
130. Paul Le Blanc, *Unfinished Leninism*, (2014: 108).
131. Lenin, [November 1900] 'The Urgent Tasks of Our Movement', (*LCW* 4: 370-71).

THE RUSSIAN REVOLUTION: WHEN WORKERS TOOK POWER

THE RUSSIAN REVOLUTION: WHEN WORKERS TOOK POWER

Lyubov Popova, 'Untitled Textile Design', 1924

In the aftermath of the revolution a group of "Productivist" artists argued that the distinction between "fine" and "applied" art should be erased, so all art could play a useful role in constructing the new society. They also argued that reproducible formats were preferable as they could be disseminated throughout the populace instead of being hoarded by wealthy individuals. Productivist artists applied their skills to a variety of different kinds of objects, including crockery, posters, buildings and textiles, the latter being represented in this example by Lyubov Popova.

4. Soviets, workers' democracy and workers' control

The Marxist worldview is well summed up in the rules of the First International, that "the emancipation of the working classes must be conquered by the working classes themselves". Working class self-liberation is the heart of socialism. Without the workingclass to drive trains, sew clothes, enter data, or look after the next generation of workers, capitalists cannot make profits. The working class has huge potential strength and strategic power in capitalist society. But to combat the enormous forces of the owners and managers of capital, capitalist states and the dominance of bourgeois ideology, the working class needs its own strong, political organisations.

Marx believed that the development of an organised labour movement was the crucial agency for affecting emancipatory socialist transformation. In the *Communist Manifesto*, he lauded the combination of workers into trade unions, "permanent associations in order to make provision beforehand for these occasional revolts" and the "organisation of the proletarians into a class and consequently into a political party". The task of workers' organisations are to ensure that "the working classes are bestriding the scene of history no longer as servile retainers, but as independent actors, conscious of their own responsibility".[1]

On the eve of 1917, some 2.6 million workers were employed in the Russian empire's manufacturing establishments, twice the figure of 1890. These establishments were concentrated in the west of the country. In addition, more than half the industrial workforce in Russia were employed in factories with more than 500 workers. Thousands of workers in a single factory was not uncommon. A number of factories employed more than 10,000 workers each. The Putilov metal works in Petersburg had 30,000 workers by the time the revolution broke out. These factors made a comparatively strong and dynamic working-class.

Workers displayed tremendous militancy. Workers' strikes toppled the tsar. On returning to their workbenches, workers proceeding to dismantle the autocratic structure of management in the factories. They demanded the "constitutional factory" in parallel with demands for liberty in politics as a whole. Workers set up soviets (councils) as alternative nodes of power, emanating from workplaces but taking over the functions of local and eventually central government. According, to historian Steve Smith, democratisation of factory relations assumed a variety of forms. Hated foreman and administrators fled or were expelled. At the Putilov works, "workers thrust the one-time leader of the factory Black Hundreds, Puzanov, into a wheelbarrow, poured red lead over his head, and trundled him off to a nearby canal, into which they threatened to deposit him in punishment for his past misdemeanours". Factory rule books, with their punitive fines and humiliating searches, were torn up. Most importantly, factory committees were created to represent the interests of workers to management.[2]

In 1917, working-class democracy flourished as never before. Different forms of workers' organisation thrived — soviets, factory committees, trade unions, political parties and other ad hoc arrangements. These forms, which had developed previously (particularly around the 1905 revolution), overlapped each other, combining political and economic fronts of the class struggle. They yielded strikes and other forms of workers' action, giving rise to debates about workers' control. These modes of organisation inspired other workers internationally and were copied widely decades after the Russian experience. A revived working class movement in the 21st century will need to assimilate the lessons of these struggles — they are essential to working class self-liberation.

Russian workers' organisation before 1917

The first attempts by Russian workers at self-organisation took two principal forms: strike committees and mutual-aid societies. In February 1885 a strike broke out in the Morozov textile plant in Tver. Management called on the workers to elect deputies to conduct negotiations. When the strike ended, most of the elected delegates were sacked. Similar incidents occurred ten years later during a textile workers strike in Ivanovo-Voznesensk. The strikers were asked to select spokespersons to present workers' demands to the governor. The twenty-five deputies included several women. Negotiations proved fruitless and some of the delegates were arrested.

Another form instigated by the police chief Zubatov were state-sponsored yellow unions. The autocracy allowed permanent delegations so that workers could negotiate legally with industrial managements and governmental factory inspectors. A law was passed in 1903 creating factory elders (*starosti*) in industry. Father Gapon's Union of Russian Factory and Mill Workers of St Petersburg, which instigated the demonstration in 1905 that was so savagely repressed, was one such organisation.³

Historian Oskar Anweiler chronicled the history of the soviets as part of these wider efforts by Russian workers to organise. The soviets are rightly synonymous with the Russian revolution. It was the soviets that became the basis of state power in place of the Provisional Government and the old tsarist state. "All power to the soviets" was the unifying demand the Bolsheviks popularised throughout much of 1917. It was the soviets that organised from workplaces up to government level. It was soviets that not only workers, but soldiers and peasants adopted, forming the most representative democratic bodies ever seen in history.

The soviets emerged out of the strike movement in 1905. The workers on their own initiative (though often influenced by Marxist activists) elected representatives who were increasingly recognised by management as the workers' representatives in charge of negotiations. These committees had various names: assembly of delegates or deputies, workers' commissions, commission of electors, council of factory elders, council of authorised representatives, strike committee, and the like — or simply deputies.

The first soviet of the Russian revolution appeared in mid-May 1905 in Ivanovo-Voznesensk, where the RSDLP was dominated by the Bolshevik faction. On 11 May, a party conference took place outside the town attended by factory and mill delegates. By the evening of 12 May, some 30,000 workers were on strike. They constituted the Ivanovo-Voznesensk council of representatives with the support of a factory inspector. The soviet numbered 110 deputies. The majority of representatives were under 25 and they included at least 28 women. The Bolsheviks took a leading role in the soviet, with about a third of the delegates. The soviet ran the strike for three weeks, before the military intervened. When the employers demanded a declaration from every worker that they would return to work under the old conditions, the strike dragged on until mid-July, when several leaders were arrested. Although the workers gained no material advantages, the Ivanovo-Voznesensk strike left a lasting impression on Russian public opinion by its unprecedented solidarity and its long duration.⁴

Strikes by printers and rail workers in September-October prompted the formation of the Petersburg soviet in October 1905. The first meeting took place at the Technological Institute with about 40 delegates involved. S Zborovski, a Menshevik, presided at the first session. The participants issued their appeal to Petersburg workers for election of delegates. As the soviet expanded representatives from the Mensheviks, Bolsheviks and Socialist Revolutionaries (SRs) were officially admitted. Pyotr Khrustalev (Nosar) was elected permanent chair of the soviet. The prestige and authority of the Petersburg soviet prompted the formation of workers' councils in Russia's larger and smaller industrial cities from October to December 1905. About fifty councils of workers' deputies have been traced, as well as several soldiers' and peasants' councils. On 27 November, the day after Khrustalev was arrested, Trotsky replaced him as chair of the Petersburg soviet. On 3 December, the executive committee and about 200 deputies were arrested.[v]

The attitude of some socialists to the first soviets was not good. On 26 and 27 October, the workers and deputies of a number of large concerns decided on their own initiative to introduce the eight-hour day. When the question was debated at a plenary of the Petersburg soviet, Viktor Chernov, leader of the SRs opposed the eight-hour day campaign as a "syndicalist deviation", declaring, "we are not yet done with absolutism, and you want to take on the bourgeoisie". Leading Mensheviks were little better. Martynov, put it quite plainly: "The co-existence of two independent proletarian organisations — a social democratic party organisation and another one that is officially non-partisan, though influenced by the social democrats — is an abnormal phenomenon that must disappear sooner or later. When we recommended the creation of organs of the revolutionary self-government of the proletariat, we considered this form of organisation as something provisional and temporary".

Bolshevik workers participated in the founding of the Petersburg soviet during the October strike. The party committee sent its official representatives to the executive committee; among them Bogdan Knuniants, Pyotr Krasikov and Dmitri Sverchkov. During the first few days of the soviet's existence, when it functioned as a strike committee, the Bolsheviks were supportive. This changed when after the October strike ended the soviet began developing into an instrument of political leadership for the metropolitan working class. The Bolsheviks got the joint committee representing both factions of the RSDLP to pass a resolution demanding that the soviet officially accept the social democratic programme. Knuniants wrote an article, 'Soviet or Party?' (1905) which posed the question, "which political party it recognises as leader and which political programme it follows". But Lenin intervened, perceiving the soviets as embryonic organs of workers' power and convincing the Bolsheviks to participate in building them. All social democratic factions henceforth agreed on the importance of participating in the soviets as militant working-class fighting organisations.⁶

The revival of soviets in 1917

As we saw in chapter 2, the soviets were revived in 1917 by social democratic activists, starting in Petrograd during the last days of the tsar. In the first weeks of its existence, the Petrograd soviet was a huge permanent assembly of workers and soldiers. The number of delegates exploded. In the first week of March 1917 it reached 1,200. By the second half of March it rose to almost 3,000. The executive committee, which consisted of 42 members, established a "bureau" of seven members in mid-March to deal with current business. After the all-Russian conference of soviets in late March and early April 1917, 16 provincial representatives were taken into the executive committee. The bureau was enlarged to 24 members and from then on it met daily, while the executive committee sat three times a week. The leadership of the Petrograd soviet was politically dominated by the Mensheviks and SRs. Borough soviets were also established, with the Bolsheviks stronger at this level.

Soviets again spread across Russia. At the Moscow district conference of soviets, held between 25-27 March, 70 workers' councils and 38 soldiers' councils were represented. The Moscow soviet of workers' deputies was the second largest in Russia. By 1 June, 700 deputies belonged to it. A conference held in the Donets Basin in mid-March numbered 48 soviets. In April, representatives of 80 soviets met at a district congress in Kiev. Since Mensheviks and Bolsheviks belonged to the same organisation in a number of cities until spring 1917, it was not until later that the Bolsheviks appeared as a separate faction in the soviets. Recent research by historian Nikolai Smirnov has estimated that by the end of March there were already more than 600 soviets of workers', soldiers', sailors', peasants' and Cossacks' deputies in operation. According to the incomplete data available, by October 1917 there were 1,429 soviets functioning in Russia. Of these, 706 involved workers and soldiers, 235 were united soviets of workers, soldiers and peasants, 455 were peasant, and 33 were soldiers' soviets.⁷

Soldiers' soviets were established in great numbers during 1917, often jointly with workers. On 1 March, Order No.1 of the Petrograd workers' and soldiers' council decreed the election of troop committees in the infantry companies, battalions, and regiments, and in equivalent units of other armed services, at militia headquarters, and on ships of the navy. Although the order was addressed only to soldiers in the Petrograd military district, and a few days later the wording of Order No.2 specifically restricted the first order to the capital, news about formation of independent soldiers' committees spread as rapidly as tidings of the revolution itself. Only a few days later, frontline units also began to elect their own soviets of soldiers' deputies.

On 6 March, at the instigation of the workers' soviet and the soldiers' soviet, delegates from nearby villages met in Moscow for a conference, and on 18 March formally established a soviet of peasants' deputies, after an appeal of the Moscow association of cooperatives. In mid-April, a council of peasants' deputies of the Petrograd garrison was established with 280 deputies elected by the soldiers. Typically, the first peasant councils were formed not at the lowest level in the villages, but in urban centres. Between March and May 1917, 20 provincial councils were established in the respective capitals. They emerged from conferences of peasants' deputies, intellectuals, and party people, especially SRs.

The first all-Russian congress of peasants' deputies, held in Petrograd from 4 to 28 March 1917, represented an important stage in the movement. However, the peasants' congress met before there were many peasant councils in the villages to speak of. The number of village soviets remained small, especially because the old village assemblies had survived. Peasants' soviets at various levels generally remained independent of workers' and soldiers' soviets that existed alongside them. Anweiler argues that "very rarely was a soviet of workers', soldiers', and peasants' deputies formed; more frequently the soviets met in joint congresses within the provinces or their executive committees held joint deliberations". The SRs, who predominated in the peasants' councils, "increasingly feared takeovers by more radical workers and soldiers' soviets, and therefore resisted mergers".[8]

In June, the first all-Russian congress of soviets of workers' and soldiers' deputies, and the first all-Russian congress of soviets of peasants convened. With 20 million represented, these were by far the most democratic gatherings in Russian history. The congresses created the central executive committee (CEC) of the soviets of workers' and soldiers' deputies, and the executive committee of the soviets of peasants' deputies, respectively. Until November 1917 these two leading soviet organs operated separately. At the congress of soviets of workers' and soldiers' deputies, more than a thousand delegates represented 305 workers' and soldiers' soviets, 53 regional soviets, and 21 army organisations. Politically, the SRs with 285 members and Mensheviks with 248 dominated, against 105 Bolsheviks and some members of several smaller socialist groups, and 73 non-affiliated delegates. The CEC, with more than 250 members, was composed of 104 Mensheviks, 100 Socialist Revolutionaries, 35 Bolsheviks and 18 members of other so-

SOVIETS, WORKERS' DEMOCRACY AND WORKERS' CONTROL

cialist parties. At its first meeting, the CEC elected a 9-person presidium (executive) with Nikolai Chkheidze chairing, and a 50-member bureau, also composed according to party parity.

As described in chapter two, the Bolsheviks were able to win majorities in a large number of soviets by the autumn of 1917. Hundreds of soviets passed resolutions calling for "Peace, Bread, and Land" and "All Power to the Soviets", replacing the original leaders with more militant revolutionaries prepared to take the power.

The subsequent success of the October insurrection depended on a preponderance of Bolsheviks in soviets winning political influence and holding strategic positions. In Kronstadt, where the soviet had achieved sole power as early as May, new elections secured the left's majority. In Finland, the Bolsheviks captured a majority in most soviets, notably in Helsinki and Vyborg, and came close to eliminating the Provisional Government's power as early as September. In Estonia the soviets newly elected in September in Reval (Tallinn), Dorpat (Tartu), and Wenden (Tsesis) also had a strong majority of Bolsheviks and Left SRs. The Centrobalt, the organisation of Baltic Fleet sailors, ignored all orders from Petrograd and dealt directly with the commanders concerning possible military operations. The fifth army, considered the best at the northern front, in mid-October elected a new army committee with a Bolshevik majority. Just before the October insurrection, Bolsheviks were elected leaders in the majority of the workers' soviets of most industrial cities and in most soldiers' soviets in garrison towns. Their strongholds were in Finland, Estonia, Petrograd and its environs, parts of the northern front, the fleet, the central industrial region around Moscow, the Ural region and Siberia. The Bolsheviks found allies among the Left SRs and some anarchists. In other soviets, SRs and Mensheviks continued to hold the balance of power.[9]

After the February revolution the Petrograd soviet, for all practical purposes, possessed sole power in the capital. It controlled the barracks and thus the revolution's armed force. The minister of war Guchkov wrote on 9 March to the military commander-in-chief, General Alekseev: "The Provisional Government has no real power. Its orders are followed only if endorsed by the soviet of workers and soldiers deputies. The soviet possesses the actual power, such as troops, railroads, and postal and telegraphic communications". Stated bluntly, "the Provisional Government exists only by the soviet permission. The military especially can issue only orders that do not openly contradict those from the soviet". Sukhanov rightly characterised the Petrograd soviet as "a state within the state".

However, the dominant parties, the Mensheviks and the SRs, saw the soviets as subordinate to the Provisional Government. The all-Russian conference of soviets held in March-April 1917 advocated support of the Provisional Government, with simultaneous control by the soviets. On the night of 1 May the executive committee of the Petrograd soviet passed a resolution favouring socialist participation in the government. Kerensky himself assured the British ambassador, Sir George Buchanan, as early as May, "the soviets will die a natural death".

The Bolsheviks enthusiastically advocated "All power to the soviets", even when they were in a minority. However, they were not soviet fetishists, tailing behind the Menshevik and SRs leaders who held sway in the soviets. After the July days and the crackdown on the Bolsheviks, Lenin rejected the slogan "All power to the soviets", accusing the moderates of depriving the soviets of power, transforming them into a "fig leaf of counterrevolution". The soviets had become "ciphers, puppets; the real power is not in them". Instead he looked towards the factory committees as an alternative. The sixth Bolshevik congress in July debated the issues and withdrew the formula for soviet power. However, after defeating the Kornilov revolt and winning majority support in a large number of soviets, the Bolsheviks again agitated for "All power to the soviets" and took power under that slogan in October.[10]

Factory committees

In 1917, workers created factory committees to abolish the autocracy of the factory and bring about the democratisation of factory life. As early as 5 March, the Petrograd soviet called for formation of such committees, and on 10 March the soviet and the employers agreed on introduction of the eight-hour day and formation of "elders' councils" in the factories. On 23 April the Provisional Government issued regulations for factory committees. It facilitated the setting up of committees to represent workers' interests vis-à-vis management on questions such as pay and hours, to settle disputes between workers, to represent workers before the government and public institutions, and to engage in educational and cultural work. The law thus defined the functions of the factory committees narrowly. The aim of the government was to institutionalise them. Even the Petrograd Society of Factory and Mill Owners (PSFMO) backed the law.

Until the spring and early summer, especially in the metal industries, Mensheviks and SRs tended to dominate the factory committees. However, the committees became more radical as strike action ensued. This enabled Bolsheviks to take the lead and raise more revolutionary demands, including on the war and equality for women. At the first conference of the Petrograd factory committees, (30 May-5 June 1917), 499 delegates met. The strongest group among them was 261 metalworkers from 172 factory committees. The final resolution, introduced by Zinoviev, called for workers' control in the central economic institutions of the government and in private industry. It passed by 297 votes in favour, 21 against and 44 abstaining. Bolsheviks also predominated in the central council elected by the conference.

At the second Petrograd municipal conference, 7-12 August, approval was given by 213 votes against 26 nays and 22 abstentions to the resolution on workers' control, which had been accepted by the Bolshevik sixth party congress. In Moscow, on the other hand, the Mensheviks were still in the majority at the city-wide conference of factory committees in July: of 682 delegates only 191 voted for the Bolshevik resolution.

The employers launched an offensive against the factory committees over the summer of 1917. The PSFMO demanded that Matvei Skobelev, the Menshevik minister of labour, take action to curb the committees. On 23 August Skobelev issued a circular affirming that the right to hire and fire belonged exclusively to the employers, and five days later he issued a second circular forbidding the committees to meet during working hours.

The result, as with the soviets, was a further shift of support towards the Bolsheviks. The first and only all-Russian conference of factory committees was held 12-17 October, just before the October revolution. Its composition reflected the victory of the left among metropolitan workers: among 167 delegates, there were 96 Bolsheviks, 24 Socialist Revolutionaries, 13 anarchists, seven Mensheviks, five Maximalists, one Menshevik-Internationalist, and 21 unaffiliated members.

The factory committees did not last long under the new workers' government. At the first all-Russian congress of trade unions (7-14 January 1918) the dissident Bolshevik David Riazanov called on the factory committees to "choose that form of suicide which would be most useful to the labour movement as a whole". The sixth and final conference of Petrograd factory committees was held 22-27 January 1918. Most delegates recognised the necessity for the factory committees to become the workplace cells of industrial unions and thus the structures were absorbed into the newly constituted independent labour movement within the workers' state.[11]

What is the balance sheet on the factory committees? Their strength lay in their democratic structures, close to the base of working class power and therefore able to impose constraints and even workers' control on employers. As such they acted like the best trade unions — unions without bureaucrats at the top, unions that took militant action to tip the balance of forces at work in favour of the workers, unions that were led by delegates who were accountable directly to the rank and file workers. They became vehicles for workers to improve their wages, cut their hours and, in places, to lift some of the pressure of exploitation from the necks of workers. They were simultaneously political bodies, with committees elected often on party slates, which discussed and connected plant level issues to wider politics. The Bolsheviks were able to fight on wider issues, such as equality, and for male workers to accept women as comrades and leaders.

Of course they could not completely shake off shop patriotism, parochialism, and other elements of craft consciousness that exist in all labour movements. For example, at the all-Russian conference of factory committees, Alexandra Kollontai admonished delegates that "in the provinces you are doing nothing, or at least not enough, to raise the class consciousness of the working women".[12] The factory committees did not all push on to workers' control or beyond this to workers' self-management, with takeovers during 1917 mostly being temporary measures to ward off employers' sabotage, rather than a positive introduction of public ownership. But these weaknesses do not detract from the importance of the factory committees' experiment, which gave voice to thousands of workers, and underpinned the drive of the Russian working class to bring consistent democracy to society from top to bottom.

Trade unions

The first real trade union founded in Russia was the Moscow printers' union, set up illegally in 1903.

However, trade unions as a legal form of worker organisation really only emerged in Russia in the aftermath of the 1905 revolution. Legalised by the law of 4 March 1906, trade unions quickly formed and spread in Russia's major economic centres. But after Stolypin's coup d'état in June 1907, unions and other forms of labour organisation were banned.

In February 1917, 11 unions maintained a shadowy existence in the Petrograd underground. But, following the overthrow of the tsar, unions were active in coordinating strikes in the first four months of the revolution. By May, the Bolsheviks commanded a majority on the

Petrograd council of trade unions, with the support of the Mezhraionka, Riazanov and some of the Menshevik Internationalists. By the middle of June 1917, 1,733 trade unions had organised 1.8 million workers in 30 industries, ranging from textiles (38 unions with 346,000 members) to metals (200 unions with 285,000 members), medical services (100 unions with 66,000 members) and mining (two unions with 32,000 members).

Labour departments of local soviets collaborated actively in establishing trade unions. The third all-Russian conference of trade unions, 20-28 June 1917, was arranged by the labour department of the Petrograd soviet and the central bureaus of the trade unions in Petrograd and Moscow. Some of their work consisted in settling major and minor labour disputes from the early months of the revolution. The conference elected a provisional all-Russian central council of trade unions.

Toward the end of the summer and into the autumn, however, trade unions more actively discouraged strike activity as economically and politically counterproductive, while a large number of strikes proceeded without union approval in this period. By October as many as 2,000 unions, with a membership of over two million, about 10% of wage-earners of all kinds, had been formed. By December 1917, thousands more had joined the labour movement, which then totalled 2,753,300 workers in more than 2,000 unions. Trade union membership continued to climb, reaching 3.5 million by the end of the following year.[13]

The anarchist turned Bolshevik Bill Shatov quipped at the first congress of trade unions in 1918 that the trade unions were "vestiges of capitalist society at best, or 'living corpses' at worst". But the workers' revolution opened up enormous possibilities for independent trade unions to organise and to become a material factor in workplaces and wider political life.

Strikes

One measure of the strength and development of the working-class movement in Russia during 1917 was the extent of strikes. The pattern of strikes has been mapped and dissected by historians Diane Koenker and William Rosenberg.

Strike activity as a whole in 1917 occurred in two distinct patterns, one related to strikes as single events, the other to the number of workers on strike. Strikes occurred in two broad clusters, in May-June, and again in late September-October. March and April witnessed relatively few strikes, and in early to mid-July, at the time of the military offensive and the July Days crisis, there were also relatively few strikes (although in Petrograd and elsewhere, there were a large number of demonstrations and protests of other sorts). The spring and autumn strike clusters were roughly equal in terms of the numbers of strikes which occurred, and there was certainly no dramatic increase from spring to autumn. In contrast, looking at the numbers of strikers rather than strikes, the growth in participation is stunning. There were a relative handful of strikers in April, increasing substantially in May, June and July, before escalating again quite dramatically in late September and October, when as many as half of a million workers walked off their jobs.

Over the eight-month span from March to October 1917, no less than 2.4 million workers went on strike to press claims for better wages, better working conditions, changes in work rules, dignified treatment and, less frequently, political change. Some 1,300 strikes have been recorded, which may well underestimate the extent of activity during these months. Koenker and Rosenberg argue that the strike movement played an important role in the evolution of both class formations and social identities during 1917 in several ways. For many workers, "the very act of participating in strikes was a means of identifying with a broader collective based on the relationship to the means of production. To be a 'worker' took on an important social and political meaning, even if one worked as a waiter in a Petrograd café or a cab driver in Piatigorsk".

The pages of the Bolshevik newspaper *Pravda* were full of long and attentive reports about strikes by a wide range of workers, including woodworkers, clerks, dyers and laundry workers, shop assistants and other service-sector employees. Strikes involving woman were prominently reported — notably the Petrograd laundry workers' dispute in May. Koenker and Rosenberg argue that Bolshevik strike reports were distinguished by "the apparent recognition that activist behaviour by generally 'dormant' workers like shop assistants and women laundry employees was itself a matter of real political import, worthy of extensive reporting largely one suspects as an example to others". Bolshevik papers portrayed the strike movement "in the grandest possible terms, encouraging diverse segments of the labour force to abandon their narrow interests and to identify with a working class that transcended the limits of manufacturing industries... A broad commonality of interest and an aggregate workers' 'class'".[14]

It is important to point out that the total number of strikes during 1917 in Russia was not that high by global and historical standards at the time or since. Strike activity played an important role in developing class consciousness, but lots of strikes do not equal revolution — and, equally, revolution is much more than just lots of strikes. Although there was a rising crescendo of strikers in September-October, other forms of economic struggle (such as workers' control and soviet democracy) as well as political action were more indicative of the rise in revolutionary understanding among the working class.

Workers' control

Alongside widespread strike activity during 1917, other forms of class struggle flourished. One of the most novel was the movement for "workers' control", which grew up from the workplace to become one of the first decrees passed by the new revolutionary workers' government.

Smith argues that the slogan of "workers' control" arose spontaneously among workers in Petrograd in the spring of 1917. Its roots appear to be more anarcho-syndicalist than social-democratic. But the movement for workers' control, "far from aiming at an anarchist utopia based on factory communes", was, in its initial stages at least, "concerned with the far more practical aim of limiting economic disruption, maintaining production and preserving jobs". The policy of workers' control of production was "first and foremost an attempt by factory committees to stem the tide of economic chaos... The impulse behind the movement, far from being ideological, was initially practical". In the majority of factories, the key concern of the committees in the early stages was to keep production going rather than establishing industrial democracy or workers' self-management.

However, the demand for workers' control evolved during 1917. Smith argues that in the eight months between February and October, "workers' control went from being reactive, defensive and observational to being active, offensive and interventionist. From being concerned essentially to supervise production, workers' control developed into an attempt to actively intervene in production and drastically limit the authority of capital". For example, some factory committees transcended the "normal" sphere of trade-union activity moving to the realm of "control" of hiring and firing workers. However, the extent of this activity should not be exaggerated: in Russian, control implies oversight, as distinct from administration.

By October 1917, 289,000 workers, or 74% of Petrograd's industrial workforce, worked in enterprises under some form of workers' control. There were 244 factory committees in Petrograd province by October, but only 39% operated under workers' control. Workers' control thus affected only large factories, and left the majority of smaller enterprises untouched. As historian David Mandel has documented, despite the popularity of the slogan of workers' control, "genuine control, in the sense of full access to documents and systematic monitoring of management, largely eluded the workers before October".[15]

Cold War western interpretations of workers' control of production posit a dichotomy between the Bolshevik party and the factory committee movement. This is particularly obtuse since most of the leading cadres in the factory committees advocating workers' control were also members of the Bolshevik party. Bolsheviks did not believe that workers' control and state organisation of the economy were incompatible; in fact, democratic control at work was a necessary condition for workers to rule politically. The Bolshevik attitude sharply contrasted with those of the majority of Mensheviks and SR leaders, who utterly rejected workers' control.[16]

At a national conference of factory committees on the eve of the October revolution, a Menshevik delegate argued that one could not discuss workers' control without first deciding the nature of the revolution, which "we say... is not a social but political but with a social leavening". An anarchist delegate was equally definite: "We are living through a social revolution." But the Bolshevik Nikolai Skrypnik insisted that "workers' control is not socialism. It is only one of the transitional measures that bring us nearer to socialism".[17]

Conclusion

Workers' democracy is an irreplaceable component of our vision of the class struggle that drives the fight for socialism. In just about every high point in working-class struggle, workers have taken over their workplaces and effectively posed the question of power. But clarity about the meaning of terms is important.

Workers' control means at least "dual power within a workplace" — a situation where the bosses may still formally own the plant, but workers have an effective veto over key decisions, extending beyond wage bargaining to other conditions, working practices, hiring and firing. Workers' control may go as far as establishing new social relations of production within a workplace, even where capitalist relations dominate for the economy as a whole. But workers' control is transitory, unstable. Either it leads to nationalisation, a workers' government taking over the industry in which that workplace is situated ,and the installing of workers' self-management of that industry, or it is inevitably driven back and workers lose control of the limited powers they have won.

Worker participation is something altogether different. It may mean having worker directors on the management board, it may involve formal channels of consultation, such as safety committees, staff meetings and working parties. But ownership and power still lie effectively with capitalists and their managers. Worker participation is often not a step towards workers' control but, at best, ameliorating exploitation — ultimately it is taking a hand in our own exploitation. In the words of one syndicalist-turned-communist from the time, "such methods force workers to undertake responsibility for the development of property which they do not own, and become part of an organisation which is pledged to prevent them from ever owning it".[18] It is a long way from workers' control — especially when the bourgeois state remains intact and workers have not formed their own mass workplace organisations.

Workers' self-management is different again. Self-management is about the running of workplaces under socialism, when workers also establish their own state, and are breaking down capitalist social relations between workplaces and replacing them with social relations of production based on needs. The starting point for these higher forms of social production is building a militant, democratic and independent labour movement in today's conditions. It means socialists organising in the workplaces, organising across workplaces and unions in rank-and-file movements and drawing on the experiences of the past to take power.

References

1. Karl Marx [October 1864] 'Provisional Rules of the Association, (*MECW* 20: 14); Marx [1848] *The Communist Manifesto*, (*MECW* 6: 493); Marx [12 May 1869] 'Address to the National Labor Union of the United States', (*MECW* 21: 54).
2. James Bater, 'St. Petersburg and Moscow on the eve of revolution'. In Daniel Kaiser, *The Workers' Revolution in Russia, 1917: The View from Below*, (1987 27); Steve Smith 'Petrograd in 1917: the view from below'. In *Kaiser*, (1987: 63).
3. Oskar Anweiler, [1958] *The Soviets: The Russian workers, peasants, and soldiers councils*, (1974: 23-25).
4. Anweiler, (1974: 37, 40-42); David Lane, *The Roots of Russian Communism*, (1968: 143).
5. Anweiler, (1974: 46-47, 59-60).
6. Anweiler, (1974: 56, 70, 76-78); Trotsky, [25 August 1921] 'Letter to Istpart' and Dmitrii Sverchkov, [1925] *At the Dawn of the Revolution*. In Pete Glatter, 'The Russian Revolution of 1905: Change through Struggle', *Revolutionary History*, 9, 1, (2005: 118-120); Lenin, [2-4 November 1905] 'Our Tasks and the Soviet of Workers' Deputies', (*LCW* 10: 21); Lenin, [July 1906] The Dissolution of the Duma and the Tasks of the Proletariat, (*LCW* 11: 124).
7. Anweiler, (1974: 106-09, 113-14); Nikolai Smirnov, 'The Soviets'. In Edward Acton, Vladimir Cherniaev and William Rosenberg, *Critical Companion to the Russian Revolution 1914-1921*, (2001: 432).
8. Anweiler, (1974: 117, 120-122).
9. Smirnov, (2001: 430-31); Anweiler, (1974: 123-24, 179, 184-85).
10. Anweiler, (1974: 128-136, 141, 170-72); Lenin, *Dissolution*, (*LCW* 11: 124).
11. David Mandel, *The Petrograd Workers and the Fall of the Old Regime*, (1983: 95). Anweiler, (1974: 125-126); Steve Smith, *Red Petrograd: Revolution in the Factories*, (1983: 79, 220-222); Smith, *The Russian Revolution: A Very Short Introduction*, (2001: 348-52); David Mandel, *The Petrograd Workers and the Soviet Seizure of Power*, (1984: 276).
12. Alix Holt, *Selected Writings of Alexandra Kollontai*, (1977: 115).
13. Smith, (1983: 103-04, 111-12, 152); Diane Koenker, 'The Trade Unions'. In Acton et al, (2001: 446-452); Anweiler, (1974: 135-36).
14. Koenker and Rosenberg, 'Skilled Workers and the Strike Movement in Revolutionary Russia', *Journal of Social History*, 19, 4, (1986: 609-11); Koenker and Rosenberg, 'Perceptions and realities of labour protest, March to October 1917'. In Edith Frankel et al, *Revolution in Russia: Reassessments of 1917*, (1992: 131, 134-35, 141-43).
15. Mandel, (1984: 276).
16. Smith, (1983: 142, 145-47, 149, 185).
17. David Mandel, 'The Factory Committee Movement in the Russian Revolution'. In Immanuel Ness and Dario Azzellini, *Ours to Master and to Own*, (2011: 105).
18. John Murphy [1918] 'Compromise or Independence'.

THE RUSSIAN REVOLUTION: WHEN WORKERS TOOK POWER

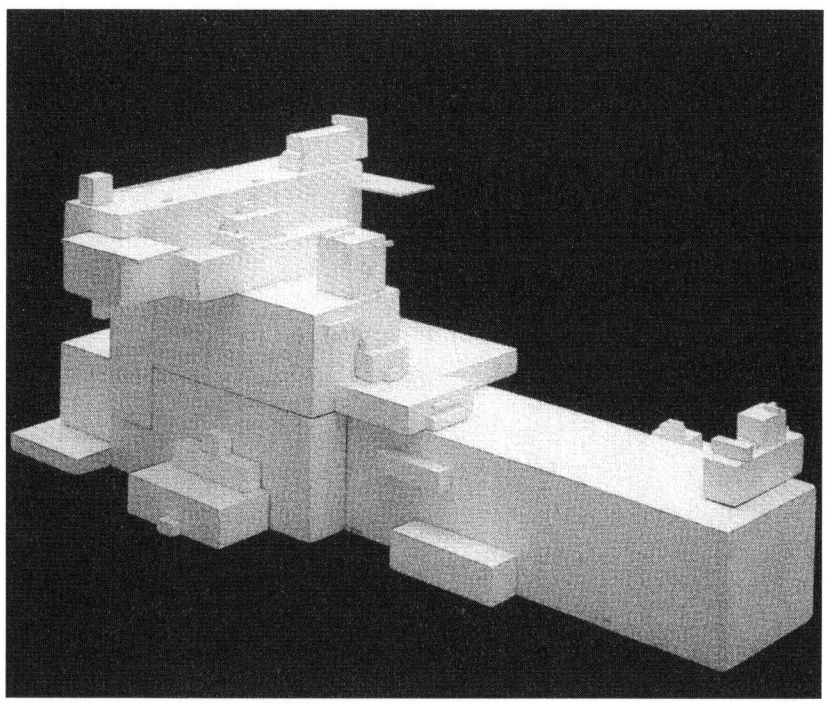

Kazimir Malevich, 'Architecton Beta', c.1920

Kazimir Malevich made a name for himself as an abstract painter in the 1910s. However his "Architectons" of the 1920s were table-top sculptures, with quasi-architectural compositions (though not specific functional intent), which were intended to show how the formal experiments of modernist art could provide inspiration for the socialist architecture of the future.

5. Permanent revolution

The central tenet of revolutionary Marxism is that socialism is the self-emancipation of the working class. But what are revolutionaries to do when the working class — the social group of men, women and children whose livelihoods to one degree or another depend on wages — is a small minority of the population? Or when the nascent working class movement — of unions, cultural groups and political organisations — is tiny? What are socialists to do when all of the plebeian and oppressed groups in society are suffering under the yoke of repressive autocracy, which refuses to permit democracy, agrarian reform, national freedom, or even basic liberties? That was the situation in Russia at the beginning of the twentieth century.

Historically, Marxists have used the concept of "permanent revolution" to grapple with these issues. The term permanent revolution probably dates back to the 1789-99 French Revolution when it meant a continuing or uninterrupted revolution to overthrow existing state power. The US Marxist Hal Draper detected at least three versions of permanent revolution in the early writings of Marx and Engels, which they drew from their participation in the 1848-49 revolutions. Their final version directly counterposed proletarian revolution to absolutism. Marx and Engels argued that the political revolution against the old power could not be made by the liberal bourgeoisie, or by the petty bourgeois democracy, but only under the hegemony of the proletariat. Marx summed up their view in the *Address of the Central Committee to the Communist League*, (1850): "[The workers] must do the utmost for their final victory by making it clear to themselves what their class interests are, by taking up their position as an independent party as soon as possible... Their battle cry must be: The revolution in permanence".[1]

The Marxist, social democratic parties (as they were known) that allied together in the Second International after 1889 also articulated the term, and a concept of permanent revolution. Prominent leaders — Franz Mehring, Karl Kautsky, Rosa Luxemburg, David Riazanov and Alexander Helphand (known as Parvus) — all contributed to the intellectual culture that encouraged Russian Marxists to form distinctive ideas of permanent revolution. Richard Day and Daniel Gaido's book, *Witnesses to Permanent Revolution* (2011) translates many of their innovative texts into English for the first time, showing the intellectual roots of permanent revolution as Russian Marxists would have encountered it at the beginning of the twentieth century.[2]

It was Leon Trotsky who, standing on the shoulders of other revolutionaries, analysed the situation in Russia most clearly and drew the sharpest conclusions. Trotsky's analysis of the 1905 revolution — what he later called uneven and combined development — as well as the political strategy he derived from it — known as permanent revolution — repay careful reading. Workers' Liberty believes Trotsky's conceptions are valid on their historical merits and for their methodological insights, which we can learn from today.

Russian social democracy in 1905

On Sunday 9 January 1905, Father Gapon led a peaceful demonstration to the Winter Palace to implore the tsar to provide food relief. The peaceful procession was fired on, killing a thousand people. This event became known as "Bloody Sunday", and it sparked a series of strikes and military mutinies that rocked the tsarist regime, culminating in a "hot autumn". In September, printers in Moscow and then St Petersburg came out on strike. In October they were followed by rail workers. By the middle of October militants had created the soviet of workers' deputies, designed to coordinate a general strike. Although the tsar managed to repress the revolutionary wave, the experience of the 1905 revolution provided Russian social democracy with enormous lessons, which would inform their activities during 1917. It also drew out significant political differences between the various factions of the Russian Social Democratic Labour Party (RSDLP), such as the Mensheviks, Bolsheviks, and others, like Trotsky, who was developing a permanent revolution perspective.

The Mensheviks in 1905

Whilst some Mensheviks played a prominent role in the events of 1905 (including in the soviets), the Menshevik theory on the character of the revolution was the scholastic, mechanical Marxism. They saw the bourgeois revolution and the socialist revolution as two distinct stages, divided by a long time period in between. They argued that the immediate task was to win political freedom by overthrowing the tsarist autocracy and that all else was subordinate. For the Mensheviks, the role of the working class was to (critically) support and ally with bourgeois liberals.

During the 1905 revolution, Georgi Plekhanov denounced all talk of "the seizure of power by the social-democrats during the now impending bourgeois revolution". Axelrod was even more emphatic, as the revolutionary tide ebbed. The immediate task of the party "consists not in organising the proletariat to overthrow bourgeois rule, but in destroying root and branch a social and political order which prevents the bourgeoisie from attaining unfettered power". Social relations in Russia "have not matured beyond the point of bourgeois revolution: history impels workers and revolutionaries more and more strongly towards bourgeois revolutionism". Owing to the absence of political rights, "there can be no question of a direct struggle of the proletariat with other classes for the attainment of political power". "We cannot, in absolutist Russia", he argued, "ignore the objective historical requirement for 'political cooperation' between the proletariat and the bourgeoisie". On the contrary, "the political crux of Russian social democracy consists precisely in the problem of organically and systematically uniting the cause of the proletariat with the claims of a broad democracy as they are determined by the social content of our revolution".[3]

Lenin and the 1905 revolution

Lenin and the Bolshevik faction accepted that the Russian revolution would begin as a bourgeois revolution, but beyond that they disagreed markedly with the Mensheviks. Lenin had no truck with the idea that the Russian bourgeoisie was capable of leading its own revolution to the end. From the beginning of the century, Lenin began sharply criticising the proposed alliance with the liberals, suggesting that at best they could be "utilised" by social democrats. However, as we will see, Lenin also held distinct views from Trotsky on the strategic direction of Russia after the overthrow of tsarism and the possibilities for immediate socialist rule. He also disagreed on how to relate to peasant organisation.

Lenin's first major assessment of 1905 was set out in the pamphlet, *Two Tactics of Social-Democracy in the Democratic Revolution*, (June-July 1905). This was primarily a polemic against the Menshevik view, expressed by Aleksandr Martynov in his pamphlet, *Two Dictatorships*. Lenin argued:

> *Marxists are absolutely convinced of the bourgeois character of the Russian revolution. What does this mean? It means that the democratic reforms in the political system and the social and economic reforms, which have become a necessity for Russia, do not in themselves imply the undermining of capitalism, the undermining of bourgeois rule; on the contrary, they will, for the first time, really clear the ground for a wide and rapid, European, and not Asiatic, development of capitalism; they will, for the first time, make it possible for the bourgeoisie to rule as a class.*

Lenin argued that the bourgeois revolution was in the interests of the working class in Russia. "A bourgeois revolution is a revolution that does not depart from the framework of the bourgeois i.e. capitalist, socio-economic system." He added: "In countries like Russia, the working class suffers not so much from capitalism as from the insufficient development of capitalism. The working class is therefore decidedly interested in the broadest, freest and most rapid development of capitalism." Lenin later spelt out that this meant the American model of capitalist development, which he believed would most rapidly develop the working class as the essential agent of socialism.[iv] Lenin advocated the formation of a "provisional revolutionary government", which social democrats would be willing to join even though they were in a minority. (The Mensheviks mocked Lenin for socialist ministerialism.)

Early in 1905, Lenin criticised Parvus' and Trotsky's call for a working-class government. In *Two Tactics*, Lenin discounted the prospect of a socialist seizure of power. He denounced "absurd and semi-anarchist ideas of giving immediate effect to the maximum programme and the conquest of power for a socialist revolution". He added, "but of course it will be a democratic, not a socialist dictatorship [Marxists commonly used "dictatorship" as a neutral synonym for "state power"]. It will be unable (without a series of intermediate stages of revolutionary development) to affect the foundation of capitalism".[5]

A key difference was Lenin's desire to cement a worker-peasant alliance. He argued that because the working class was a minority within Russian society it would have to rely on mass peasant action and organisation to break the autocracy. He wrote: "We shall bend every effort to help the entire peasantry achieve the democratic revolution, in order thereby to make it easier for us, the party of the proletariat, to pass on as quickly as possible to the new and higher task — the socialist revolution".[6] He therefore counterposed his formula, first articulated at the third congress of the RSDLP (in reality a Bolshevik-only conference, held in April 1905), the "revolutionary democratic dictatorship of the proletariat and the peasantry", against both the Mensheviks and Trotsky's position.

Trotsky in 1905 and after

Trotsky was just 25 when he secretly returned to Russia from exile in Europe in February 1905. Forced to flee again to Finland in May, he then returned to St Petersburg in October, becoming first vice-chair and then, in November, chair of the Petersburg soviet. He also edited newspapers such as *Nachalo*. On 2 December, the soviet leaders were arrested, and put on trial the following year. Trotsky's deep involvement in the events of 1905 sealed his reputation as a revolutionary and informed his assessment of the experience. Just prior to and during the 1905 revolution, he began to tentatively spell out the premises of uneven and combined development and the strategy of permanent revolution.

Trotsky developed his version of permanent revolution to answer an apparent paradox within Marxism. In his preface to the first edition of *Capital*, Marx had stated that "the industrially more developed country shows the less developed only the image of its own future".[7] Trotsky rejected the misreading of this passage "which nourishes itself on historical cliché and formal analogies and transforms historical epochs into a logical succession of inflexible social categories (feudalism, capitalism, socialism, autocracy, bourgeois republic, dictatorship of the proletariat)".[8] He believed it would be a mistake to identify the Russian revolution with the events of 1789-93 or 1848. "Historical analogies", he said, "cannot take the place of social analysis". For Trotsky, "Marxism is above all a method of analysis - not analysis of texts, but analysis of social relations".[9]

Trotsky's other methodological starting point was to understand the Russian revolution within the context of global capitalism. He argued that "Marxism takes its point of departure from world economy, not as a sum of national parts, but as a mighty and independent reality which has been created by the international division of labour and the world market, and which in our epoch imperiously dominates the national markets".[10]

Trotsky formulated his perspective on the conquest of power by the Russian workers during the summer of 1905. In his 'Introduction to Ferdinand Lassalle's Speech to the Jury' (July 1905), Trotsky argued that in the coming upheaval workers would be compelled to make their own socialist revolution, form their own government, and take socialist measures. He concluded:

> *It goes without saying that the proletariat must fulfil its mission, just as the bourgeoisie did in its own time, with the help of the peasantry and the petty bourgeoisie. It must lead the countryside, draw it into the movement, make it vitally interested in the success of its plans. But, inevitably, the proletariat remains the leader. This is not the "dictatorship of the proletariat and the peasantry", [i.e. Lenin's formula] it is the dictatorship of the proletariat supported by the peasantry. And the proletariat's work will not, of course, be confined within the limits of a single state. The very*

logic of its position will immediately throw it into the world arena.[11]

Trotsky first used the term "permanent revolution", or at least its semantic equivalent "uninterrupted revolution", in 'Social Democracy and Revolution' (25 November 1905). He wrote:

> *Uninterrupted revolution is becoming the law of self-preservation for the proletariat... The complete victory of the revolution signifies the victory of the proletariat.*
> *The latter, in turn, means further uninterrupted revolution. The proletariat is accomplishing the basic tasks of democracy, and at some moment the very logic of its struggle to consolidate its political rule places before it purely socialist problems. Revolutionary continuity is being established between the minimum and the maximum programme. It is not a question of a single "blow", a day, or a month, but of an entire historical epoch. It would be absurd to try to fix its duration in advance.*[12]

Trotsky summed up his conclusions with the expression "a revolution in permanenz" in 'Foreword to Karl Marx on the Paris Commune' (December 1905). By this he meant, "The proletariat is the sole force leading the revolution and the principal fighter on its behalf. The proletariat seizes the entire field and is never satisfied, nor will it ever be satisfied, by any concession; through every respite or temporary retreat, it will lead the revolution to the victory in which it will take power." Trotsky explicitly called on the Russian working class to take power in its own name. He wrote:

> *The first tasks that the proletariat will face immediately upon seizing power will be political ones: to fortify its position, to arm the revolution, to disarm the reaction, to extend the base of the revolution, and to rebuild the state... Abolition of the standing army and police, arming of the people, elimination of the bureaucratic mandarinate, introduction of elections for all public servants, equalisation of their salaries, and separation of the church from the state — these are the measures that must be implemented first, following the example of the [Paris] Commune.*[13]

After his arrest in December 1905, and during 15 months in prison, Trotsky was able to take the daring sweep and brilliance of these ideas, together with his direct, concrete experience of leading the revolution, to produce his first synthesis of permanent revolution, published as *Results and Prospects* (1906). He summed up the crucial question thus:

> *Here we are confronted by questions of tactics: should we consciously work towards a working-class government in proportion as the development of the revolution brings this stage nearer, or must we at that moment regard political power as a misfortune which the bourgeois revolution is ready to thrust upon the workers, and which it would be better to avoid?*
>
> *In the event of a decisive victory of the revolution, power will pass into the hands of that class which plays a leading role in the struggle — in other words, into the hands of the proletariat. Let us say at once that this by no means precludes revolutionary representatives of non-proletarian social groups entering the government. They can and should be in the government: a sound policy will compel the proletariat to call to power the influential leaders of the urban petty-bourgeoisie, of the intellectuals and of the peasantry. The whole problem consists in this: who will determine the content of the government's policy, who will form within it a solid majority?*
>
> *And when we speak of a workers' government, by this we reply that the hegemony should belong to the working class... When we speak of a workers' government we have in view a government in which the working-class representatives dominate and lead. The proletariat, in order to consolidate its power, cannot but widen the base of the revolution.*[14]

Trotsky's originality lay in the demand, not simply for a workers' government in Russia, but for the workers to go on to make a socialist revolution, overthrow the tsarist state and institute workers' self-rule. No other Marxist had painted permanent revolution in such bright colours and no other Marxist had previously taken this bold political conclusion in Russia.

Trotsky's response to critics after 1905

After the 1905 revolution Trotsky also reflected on the differences between his version of permanent revolution and the views of both the Bolsheviks and the Mensheviks. In *Results and Prospects* (1906), he tackled Lenin's position on the peasants and the worker-peasant alliance. Trotsky argued that the proletariat in power "will stand before the peasants as the class which has emancipated it". He did not accept that peasant organisation would compete with working class hegemony, arguing "historical experience shows that the peasantry are absolutely incapable of taking up an independent political role". As such he dismissed the revolutionary democratic dictatorship of the proletariat and the peasantry. He wrote: "It is not really a matter of whether we regard it as admissible in principle, whether 'we do or do not desire' such a form of political co-operation. We simply think that it is unrealisable — at least in a direct immediate sense".[15]

The Narodniks (Russian 19th century utopian socialists) had traditionally criticised Marxists for underestimating the peasantry. Such a charge was not true of Trotsky. At the height of 1905, when he chaired the Petersburg soviet, he co-signed a manifesto with representatives of the All-Russian Peasants' Union, setting out their demands, including for debt relief. In his book *1905*, written for a European socialist audience, he devoted a chapter to the peasantry and the agrarian question, and another to the peasant riots.

Trotsky believed that because Russia was a capitalist country, where wealth, public life and political experience were increasingly concentrated in the towns, "the peasantry cannot play a leading revolutionary role". He argued that "history cannot entrust the *muznik* [peasant] with the task of liberating a bourgeois nation from its bonds". Because of its "dispersion, political backwardness, and especially of its deep inner contradictions which cannot be resolved within the framework of a capitalist system", the peasantry can only "deal the old order some powerful blows from the rear, by spontaneous risings in the countryside, on the one hand, and by creating discontent within the army on the other". He noted that the 1905 revolution had been defeated by "the bayonets of the peasant army".[16]

In other respects, Trotsky's position was closer to Lenin's. There was evidently some rapprochment between the two, in light of the experience. In September 1905 Lenin stated that: "We stand for uninterrupted revolution. We shall not stop halfway". The advent of workers' soviets would have shifted Lenin's position — he characterised these workers' organisations as "the embryo of a provisional revolutionary government". Two years later he would describe the democratic dictatorship as "workers' governments in towns, peasant committees in the villages".[17]

Both Lenin and Trotsky hailed Kautsky's 'Driving Forces' essay in 1906 as vindication of their views. Both understood the Russian revolution as going beyond a bourgeois-democratic revolution, and saw working class leadership as central. At the RSDLP congress in 1907, Lenin noted a convergence in their positions. He wrote: "Trotsky acknowledged the permissibility and usefulness of a Left bloc [with the peasants] against the liberal bourgeoisie. These facts are sufficient to acknowledge that Trotsky has come closer to our views. Quite apart from the question of 'uninterrupted revolution', we have solidarity on fundamental points in the question of the attitude towards bourgeois parties".[18]

Permanent revolution in 1917

Trotsky spent the first years of the First World War in France. On 31 March 1916 he was deported to Spain, and then to the United States on 25 December 1916. He arrived in New York on 13 January 1917, where he resided at the outbreak of the February revolution. He left New York on 27 March, but his ship was intercepted by British authorities and he was interned in a prison camp for a month in Canada. Freed on 29 April, he reached Russia on 4 May.

Despite displacement, exile and imprisonment, Trotsky continued to promote permanent revolution. Up to 1917, he believed his views had been vindicated. During the First World War he argued that "the proletariat is the only independent force that can now exist in the revolutionary movement". Based on the experience of the 1905 Russian revolution and the period of reaction after it, "we can expect the peasantry to play a less independent, not to mention decisive, role in the development of revolutionary events than it did in 1905". The very factor that strengthened the Russian proletariat — the development of capitalism — was "leading to the final disappearance of urban bourgeois democracy as a political force and to the further social disintegration of the peasantry as an 'estate'". Trotsky concluded: "If a 'national' revolution could not be completed in 1905, then a second national revolution, that is, a revolution that unites "the nation" against the old regime, cannot even be posed".[19] In 'The Struggle for Power' (October 1915) he advocated "a revolutionary workers' government, the conquest of power by the Russian proletariat".[20]

At the beginning of 1917 Trotsky again hailed the leadership of the Russian workers over other classes. He wrote: "Russia's new history was opened... by the Russian proletariat through its struggle. This is a basic fact. We social-democrats build our conclusions and our tactics upon it." He continued to warn that "the interests of the different peasant layers are in themselves heterogeneous".[21]

Trotsky greeted news of the February revolution with joy and hope. "The Russian proletariat will fulfil its historic work at the head of the Russian people... Liberal fire extinguishers, it is too late." The Russian revolution "will not stop... it will sweep away the bourgeois liberals from its path". Trotsky predicted that "an open conflict between the forces of the revolution, led by the urban proletariat, and the anti-revolutionary liberal bourgeoisie which has temporarily come to power, is completely inevitable".[22] Trotsky believed permanent revolution was coming to pass. He wrote:

In this struggle the proletariat, uniting around itself the insurgent popular masses, must set as its direct objective the conquest of power. Only a revolutionary workers' government will have the volition and ability, even during the preparation for the Constituent Assembly, to conduct a radical democratic purge in the country, reconstruct the army from top to bottom. Turn it into a revolutionary militia, and in fact demonstrate to the peasant masses that their salvation lies only in support for a revolutionary workers' regime.

He reiterated the themes of working-class hegemony over the peasantry, and the international context for revolutionary success. The agrarian question "will depend on how quickly the liberal-imperialist government can be replaced by the revolutionary workers' government, based directly on the proletariat and the lower strata of the peasantry who ally themselves with it". The war had "turned the whole of Europe into a powder-keg of social revolution". The Russian proletariat was "now throwing a burning torch into this powder keg. To suppose that this torch will not set off an explosion, would be to reason against all the laws of historical logic and psychology".[23]

Upon his return to Russia, Trotsky put his energies entirely into organising and writing for the seizure of power. On the eve of the October revolution, in *What Next?* (September 1917), he set out a permanent revolution perspective:

Casting aside the chains of capitalist power, the revolution would have become permanent, that is, continuous it would have applied its state power, not to the perpetuation of the rule of capitalist exploitation, but, on the contrary, to its undoing. Its ultimate accomplishments on this field would have depended on the successes of the proletarian revolution in Europe. On the other hand, the Russian revolution might give an all the greater impetus to the revolution in Western Europe, the more resolutely and courageously it put down the opposition of its own bourgeoisie. Such was and such remains the sole and only actual prospect for the further development of the revolution... We have always pointed out that petty bourgeois democracy is incapable of solving this problem, and that the only power that can guide the revolution to its goal is the proletariat, drawing its strength from the masses of the people.

Trotsky described the struggle for power as "first and the foremost problem of the working class". The proletariat, "dragging with it the semi-proletarian masses and pushing aside its leaders of yesterday… will establish the regime of the workers' democracy". Crucially, the further successes of the proletariat "will then depend first and foremost on the European, particularly on the German revolution". In contrast, the Mensheviks looked upon the Russian revolution "from a narrow nationalistic standpoint" and reduced "the task of the revolution to that of creating a bourgeois democratic republic". The struggle for capturing power was not "merely the next step of a national democratic revolution". It was "the fulfilment of our international duty, the conquest of one of the most important positions on the whole front of the struggle against world imperialism". Trotsky's summary formula was "A permanent revolution or a permanent slaughter! That is the struggle in which the stake is the future of man".[24]

Uneven and combined development

Trotsky was in no doubt that the experience of 1917 had vindicated his conception of permanent revolution. Looking back from the vantage point of the early 1930s, he wrote that "it was exactly on the basis of this conception, that is, the theory of the permanent revolution, that the writer of these lines *foretold the inevitability* of the October Revolution, thirteen years before it took place".[25] After 1917, Trotsky continued to refine and develop permanent revolution. In particular, he elaborated the concepts of uneven and combined development to explain why apparently backward Russia was the first place where the working class could make a socialist revolution. In the first chapter of *The History of the Russian Revolution*, Trotsky wrote:

> *The fundamental and most stable feature of Russian history is the slow tempo of her development, with the economic backwardness, primitiveness of social forms and low level of culture resulting from it...*
>
> *Although compelled to follow after the advanced countries, a backward country does not take things in the same order. The privilege of historic backwardness — and such a privilege exists — permits, or rather compels, the adoption of whatever is ready in advance of any specified date, skipping a whole series of intermediate stages.*
>
> *The development of historically backward nations leads necessarily to a peculiar combination of different stages in the historic process. Their development as a whole acquires a planless, complex, combined character...*
>
> *The possibility of skipping over intermediate steps is of course by no means absolute. Its degree is determined in the long run by the economic and cultural capacities of the country. The backward nation, moreover, not infrequently debases the achievements borrowed from outside in the process of adapting them to its own more primitive culture. In this the very process of assimilation acquires a self-contradictory character. Thus*

the introduction of certain elements of Western technique and training, above all military and industrial, under Peter I, led to a strengthening of serfdom as the fundamental form of labour organisation. European armament and European loans — both indubitable products of a higher culture — led to a strengthening of tsarism, which delayed in its turn the development of the country.

The laws of history have nothing in common with a pedantic schematism. Unevenness, the most general law of the historic process, reveals itself most sharply and complexly in the destiny of the backward countries. Under the whip of external necessity their backward culture is compelled to make leaps. From the universal law of unevenness thus derives another law which, for the lack of a better name, we may call the law of combined development — by which we mean a drawing together of the different stages of the journey, a combining of the separate steps, an amalgam of archaic with more contemporary forms. Without this law, to be taken of course, in its whole material content, it is impossible to understand the history of Russia, and indeed of any country of the second, third or tenth cultural class. [26]

Trotsky reflected that "the collapse of Russian capitalism was a local avalanche in a universal social formation. We have attributed the October revolution in the last analysis not to the fact of Russia's backwardness, but to the law of combined development".[27] Russia was ripe for socialist revolution because of the particular interpenetration of its own forms with those of the capitalist world economy. Capitalist development had begun, but heavily financed by foreign loans. An atrophied state under pressure from more advanced competitors resisted elementary land reform, while promoting advanced industry. The result was a weak bourgeois class, while the small but savagely exploited working class, heavily concentrated in modern factories, was disproportionately strong. This was a powerful explanation for what had unfolded in Russia during the revolutionary period.

Did Lenin adopt permanent revolution in 1917?

Did Lenin come over to permanent revolution in 1917? Some have interpreted his *April Theses* and subsequent political evolution as a "conversion". Thus the historian Joel Carmichael argues that Lenin had "accepted" and even "embraced" Trotsky's theory of permanent revolution in the crucible of events in 1917, while Marcel Liebman argues that Lenin's strategy in 1917 had "a clearly 'Trotskyist' flavour to it".[28]

However, Trotsky did not argue that Lenin became a "Trotskyist" in 1917, and Lenin never publicly admitted to a conversion. Trotsky did argue that beneath the language there was an "identity" between their political assessments and conclusions in 1917. Elsewhere he suggested that permanent revolution "coincides entirely" with the fundamental strategic line of Bolshevism. But Trotsky was quite explicit that the Bolsheviks did not adopt permanent revolution in 1917. The differences were used by the Stalinists as a stick to beat Trotsky with after Lenin's death.[29]

At the outbreak of revolution, Lenin was marooned in Switzerland while Trotsky was mired in New York. Despite the geographical separation, there was a convergence of their different perspectives and significant agreement about political conclusions. At the very least their views were compatible and certainly dovetailed. It was Lenin who moved most from his pre-revolution assessments and closer to Trotsky's. However, Lenin did not simply adopt Trotsky's formulations.

Lenin's reassessment in 1917

Lenin began 1917 by giving a lecture on the lessons from the 1905 revolution. The peculiarity of the Russian revolution of 1905 was that "it was a bourgeois-democratic revolution in its social content, but a proletarian revolution in its methods of struggle". It was a bourgeois-democratic revolution "since its immediate aim… was a democratic republic, the eight-hour day and confiscation of the immense estates of the nobility". At the same time, "the Russian revolution was also a proletarian revolution, not only in the sense that the proletariat was the leading force, the vanguard of the movement, but also in the sense that a specifically proletarian weapon of struggle — the strike — was the principal means of bringing the masses into motion and the most characteristic phenomenon in the wave-like rise of decisive events". Lenin argued that "the inexorable trend of the Russian revolution was towards an armed, decisive battle between the tsarist government and the vanguard of the class-conscious proletariat". Lenin added that the Russian revolution, because of its proletarian character, was the prologue to the coming European socialist revolution.[30]

Lenin was swift to reflect on the significance of the tsar's overthrow, and the establishment of the Provisional Government. In unpublished draft theses he denounced the new government of liberal bourgeois, landlords, and supporters of the imperialist war, who "cannot give the peoples of Russia (and the nations tied to us by the war) either peace, bread, or full freedom". He was unequivocal — no support for the Provisional Government — and made tentative steps towards a new strategy. He stated that "only a workers' government that relies, first, on the overwhelming majority of the peasant population, the farm labourers and poor peasants, and, second, on an alliance with the revolutionary workers of all countries in the war, can give the people peace, bread and full freedom". The revolutionary proletariat could therefore "only regard the revolution of 1 March [date from old calendar] as its initial, and by no means complete, victory on its momentous path". The working class "cannot but set itself the task of continuing the fight for a democratic republic and socialism". Practically, this meant organising soviets of workers' deputies, arming the workers and an "ideologically and organisationally independent" revolutionary proletarian party.[31]

Letters from Afar

Lenin's sense of urgency was expressed in a series of 'Letters from Afar' (1917), sent from Switzerland to comrades in Russia, in which he championed the soviet of workers' deputies as "the embryo of a workers' government". If the Russian revolution was a bourgeois revolution, Marxists must open the eyes of the workers "to the deception practised by the bourgeois politicians, teach them to put no faith in words, to depend entirely on their own strength, their own organisation, their own unity, and their own weapons".

Who were the proletariat's allies in this revolution? First, "the broad mass of the semi-proletarian and partly also of the small-peasant population, who number scores of millions and constitute the overwhelming majority of the population of Russia". Second, "the ally of the Russian proletariat is the proletariat of all the belligerent countries and of all countries in general". Lenin referred to workers' soviets and a workers' government, while differentiating the peasant population, rather than regarding it as the workers' ally "as a whole". He reiterated these points in the second letter, arguing that "only a proletarian republic, backed by the rural workers and the poorest section of the peasants and town dwellers, can secure peace, provide bread, order and freedom".[32]

Lenin's fifth letter defined the immediate tasks of the revolutionary proletariat in Russia as finding the road to a second revolution. This meant transferring power to "a government of the workers and poorest peasants". This government had to "smash, completely eliminate, the old state machine, the army, the police force and bureaucracy" and base itself on the soviets and the workers' militias. Soviets of agricultural wage-workers, separate from peasant soviets, were necessary. This government would have to take "transitional measures" or steps towards socialism.[33]

Lenin was anxious to return to Russia to participate in the revolution. In a farewell letter to Swiss workers, he reiterated his *internationalist* perspective: that "in Russia, socialism cannot triumph directly and immediately". The Russian proletariat could not "bring the socialist revolution to a victorious conclusion". But it could give the Russian revolution "a mighty sweep that would create the most favourable conditions for a socialist revolution, and would, in a sense, start it". It could "facilitate the rise of a situation in which its chief, its most trustworthy and most reliable collaborator, the European and American socialist proletariat, could join the decisive battles".[34]

The April Theses

Lenin arrived in Russia on the night of 3 April 1917. The following day he presented his views to the Bolshevik fraction and then to a meeting of Bolsheviks and Mensheviks, during the soviet conference taking place in Petersburg. The 'April Theses' spelt out the orientation he had developed in recent months. The second thesis stated that the "the specific feature of the present situation in Russia is that the country is passing from the first stage of the revolution — which, owing to the insufficient class-consciousness and organisation of the proletariat, placed power in the hands of the bourgeoisie — to its second stage, which must place power in the hands of the proletariat and the poorest sections of the peasants". The third thesis insisted on "no support for the Provisional Government", which was "a government of capitalists", an "imperialist government". The eighth point stated: "It is not our immediate task to 'introduce' socialism, but only to bring social production and the distribution of products at once under the control of the soviets of workers' deputies." The practical tasks included changing the party's programme and name (to Communist Party), as well as taking the initiative for a new workers' international.[35]

In the party discussion on 4 April, Lenin condemned those Bolsheviks who had shown confidence in the Provisional Government, saying this was "the death of socialism", and threatening to split with them. He flayed Kamenev's article in *Pravda* which demanded the Provisional Government renounce annexations, calling it "nonsense" and a "flagrant mockery". Lenin criticised the manifesto of the soviet of workers' deputies as completely lacking class-consciousness. He warned that unification of the Bolsheviks with Menshevik defencists [i.e. having a pro-war position] would be "a betrayal of socialism" and that he would split from such an arrangement.³⁶

Lenin published the April Theses in *Pravda* and then a pamphlet, 'Letter on tactics', which came out in April 1917. His assessment was that "the power is in the hands of a different class, a new class, namely, the bourgeoisie" and that, to this extent, "the bourgeois, or the bourgeois-democratic, revolution in Russia is completed". In response to "old Bolsheviks" who said that the bourgeois-democratic revolution is completed only by the "revolutionary-democratic dictatorship of the proletariat and the peasantry" and that the agrarian revolution had not even started, he said "the Bolshevik slogans and ideas on the whole have been confirmed by history; but concretely things have worked out differently; they are more original, more peculiar, more variegated than anyone could have expected". He chastised old Bolsheviks for "reiterating formulas senselessly learned by rote instead of studying the specific features of the new and living reality". He said that the revolutionary-democratic dictatorship of the proletariat and the peasantry had already become a reality in the form of the soviet of workers' and soldiers' deputies. The formula was "already antiquated" and those who advocated it were "behind the times".

Lenin always emphasised concrete realities. Marxists must "take cognisance of real life", he said, "and not cling to a theory of yesterday". According to the old way of thinking, the rule of the bourgeoisie could and should be followed by the rule of the proletariat and the peasantry, by their dictatorship. In real life, "things have already turned out differently; there has been an extremely original, novel and unprecedented interlacing of the one with the other". Side by side, existing together, simultaneously, was the rule of the bourgeoisie (the Provisional Government) and a revolutionary-democratic dictatorship of the proletariat and the peasantry (the soviet). Lenin insisted that a Marxist must not "abandon the ground of careful analysis of class relations... But, in assessing a given situation, a Marxist must proceed not from what is possible, but from what is real".³⁷

But Lenin also anticipated the charge of "Trotskyism" and backtracked somewhat. He pointed to the danger of "wanting to arrive at the socialist revolution by 'skipping' the bourgeois-democratic revolution — which is not yet completed and has not yet exhausted the peasant movement". He rejected the slogan "No tsar, but a workers' government" (used by Parvus in the summer of 1905). He said that there can be no government (barring a bourgeois government) in Russia other than that of the soviets of workers', agricultural labourers', soldiers' and peasants' deputies. He claimed to have "absolutely ensured" himself against any playing at "seizure of power" by a workers' government by referring to the experience of the Paris Commune.[38] This rather missed the point that Marx and Engels regarded the Paris Commune as at least a workers' government, if not the dictatorship of the proletariat.

Lenin turned to Kamenev's disagreements with the April Theses, expressed in *Pravda*. Kamenev's first mistake, said Lenin, was that "the question of 'completion' of the bourgeois democratic revolution was stated wrongly". The question is put in an abstract, simple, one-colour, way, "to prevent oneself from seeing the exceedingly complex reality, which is at least two-coloured". The formula "the bourgeois-democratic revolution is not completed" was "obsolete". It was "no good at all. It is dead. And it is no use trying to revive it". Second, practically no-one knew whether it was still possible for a special "revolutionary-democratic dictatorship of the proletariat and the peasantry", detached from the bourgeois government, to emerge in Russia. Marxist tactics "cannot be based on the unknown".[39]

Lenin revisited these arguments in another pamphlet 'The Tasks of the Proletariat in Our Revolution: Draft Platform for the Proletarian Party', (April 1917). Here he reiterated that the bourgeois-democratic revolution in Russia was completed and no support or confidence could be given to the Provisional Government. The Petrograd and the other soviets constituted a revolutionary-democratic dictatorship of the proletariat and the peasantry, albeit not a "pure" form. Again Lenin made the crucial point of differentiating the peasantry, demanding that "without necessarily splitting the soviets of peasants' deputies at once, the party of the proletariat must explain the need for organising separate soviets of agricultural labourers' deputies and separate soviets of deputies from the poor (semi-proletarian) peasants, or, at least, for holding regular separate conferences of deputies of this class status in the shape of separate groups or parties within the general soviets of peasants' deputies".[40]

The Bolsheviks reorientate

Lenin tested his arguments in a series of Bolshevik party discussions during April 1917. The first was the Petrograd city conference of the RSDLP (Bolsheviks) held on 14-22 April 1917. Lenin told delegates that events had "created an entirely new situation". The chief mistake made by revolutionaries was that "they look backward at the old revolutions, whereas life gives us too many new things that have to be fitted into the general pattern of events". The soviet was "a dictatorship of the proletariat and the peasantry". But it had entered into an agreement with the bourgeoisie. And "this is where the 'old' Bolshevism needs revising. The situation that has arisen shows that the dictatorship of the proletariat and the peasantry is interlocked with the power of the bourgeoisie. An amazingly unique situation".

The past "contains no instances of a revolution where the representatives of the revolutionary proletariat and peasantry, though fully armed, concluded an alliance with the bourgeoisie, and though having the power, ceded it to the bourgeoisie". Lenin repeated his thinking on the Paris Commune. That experience, "furnished an example of a state of the soviet type, an example of direct power wielded by the organised and armed workers, an example of the dictatorship of workers and peasants". The interlocking of the soviet with the Provisional Government means "the next stage is the dictatorship of the proletariat". But "the proletariat is not yet sufficiently organised and enlightened; it must be enlightened". The answer was to organise "soviets of workers' and other deputies... all over the country".[41]

After a vigorous debate, Lenin concluded the discussion. He said "a new line follows from the policy of Bolshevism... We take as our point of departure conflicting class interests". "Old Bolshevism", he said, "should be discarded". He again characterised 'Trotskyism' by the slogan, "No tsar, but a workers' government", which he said was wrong. And he said "a petty bourgeoisie exists, and it cannot be dismissed. But it is in two parts. The poorer of the two is with the working class". The following day Lenin chastised Kamenev for Menshevism, stating that he was "shifting to the policy of Chkheidze and Steklov".[42]

Convened by the Bolsheviks, the seventh all-Russia conference of the RSDLP took place on 24-29 April. Once again Lenin gave the report on the current situation. He demanded "a precise class analysis of current events" and argued that "as far as the bourgeois revolution is concerned... that revolution is already completed". The Russian revolution had created the soviets. "No bourgeois country in the world has or can have such state institutions. No socialist revolution can be operative with any other state power than this". The soviets "must take power not for the purpose of building an ordinary bourgeois republic, nor for the purpose of making a direct transition to socialism". The soviets "must take power in order to make the first concrete steps towards this transition, steps that can and should be made". He stated: "We cannot be for 'introducing' socialism — this would be the height of absurdity". However, "we must preach socialism", including to the peasants, but concretely in terms of practical measures to enable them to improve their farming. Taking power was "the only practical measure and the only way out".[43]

Winding up the discussion, he stated that "our differences with Comrade Kamenev are not very great, because by agreeing with us he has changed his position". "We are at one with comrade Kamenev, except on the question of control. He views control as a political act... We will not accept control. People tell us that we have isolated ourselves, that, by uttering a lot of terrible words about communism, we have frightened the bourgeoisie into fits... Maybe! But it was not this that isolated us". Rykov said that socialism must come from other countries with a more developed industry. Lenin replied: "But that is not so. Nobody can say who will begin it and who will end it. That is not Marxism; it is a parody of Marxism". He again rejected the slogan "No tsar, but a dictatorship of the proletariat" because he said it would have meant "skipping over the petty bourgeoisie".[44]

Lenin argued that the Bolsheviks should amend their party programme to include the demand for a "democratic proletarian-peasant republic". He said other possibilities such as "a republic of soviets of workers', soldiers', and peasants' deputies" should be considered. The point was not what an institution is called, "but what its political character and structure is". The term "proletarian-peasant republic", indicated "its social content and political character". The Bolsheviks resolved to establish "separate and independent organisation of the agricultural proletariat", in the form of "soviets of agricultural labourers' deputies (as well as of separate soviets of deputies of the semi-proletarian peasantry) and in the form of proletarian groups or factions within the general soviets of peasants' deputies".[45]

Lenin was clear on opposing the bourgeoisie. Opponents of the Bolsheviks said it was "a bourgeois revolution", it was "useless to speak of socialism", Lenin said. But the Bolshevik would say the opposite: "Since the bourgeoisie cannot find a way out of the present situation, the revolution is bound to go on." Lenin said the revolutionaries "must not confine ourselves to democratic phrases; we must make the situation clear to the masses, and indicate a number of practical measures to them, namely, they must take over the syndicates — control them through the Soviets, etc. When all such measures are carried out, Russia will be standing with one foot in socialism".

The resolution stated that the Russian revolution was "only the first stage of the first of the proletarian revolutions which are the inevitable result of war". Operating as it did in one of the most backward countries of Europe, amidst a vast population of small peasants, "the proletariat of Russia cannot aim at immediately putting into effect socialist changes". But it would be a grave error "to infer from this that the working class must support the bourgeoisie, or that it must keep its activities within limits acceptable to the petty bourgeoisie, or that the proletariat must renounce its leading role in the matter of explaining to the people the urgency of taking a number of practical steps towards socialism for which the time is now ripe".[46]

The conference resolved to seek "closer relations and unity" with groups and trends that had adopted a real internationalist stand, such as the Mezhraionka (inter-district) group, which Trotsky belonged to. At the beginning of the year Lenin privately regarded Trotsky as a "scoundrel", and as late as March warned not to "get entangled in stupid 'unification' attempts... with the wobblers" such as Trotsky. Yet, in April, Lenin was publicly calling for his release from prison and return to Russia. On Trotsky's return he held formal discussions with the Bolsheviks. By the end of May, Lenin was publicly lauding an agreement with the Mezhraionka group "for getting comrade Trotsky to edit a popular organ".[47]

After months of close collaboration, the Mezhraionka joined the Bolshevik Party at the end of July 1917, and Trotsky was elected to the central committee. He was the Bolshevik nominee to chair the Petrograd soviet. By September, Lenin was praising Trotsky's tactic of boycott of the so-called Democratic Conference and recommending him for the party's list of candidates for the Constituent Assembly. Lenin registered their political convergence a week after the seizure of power, telling the central committee that since Trotsky had rejected conciliation with the Mensheviks and the SRs "from that time on there has been no better Bolshevik".[48]

Critiques of permanent revolution

There have been numerous efforts to champion Lenin's views in juxtaposition to Trotsky's, not least by Stalinists. Ironically, the most serious efforts among activists to elevate Lenin and downgrade Trotsky have come from ex-Trotskyists such as Doug Jenness (American Socialist Workers Party) and Doug Lorimer (Democratic Socialist Party Australia). In the early 1980s, Jenness debated veteran Trotskyist Ernest Mandel on the merits of permanent revolution, as part of the American SWP's uncritical adaptation to the Castro Stalinist government in Cuba. Junking the Trotskyist baggage of permanent revolution was a turning point in this party's degeneration.[49] A similar debate took place at the end of the 1990s between Lorimer and Phil Hearse (Socialist Resistance in Britain) as the DSP adapted to Stalinist politics in Asia.[50]

Jenness and Lorimer argue that Trotsky's permanent revolution strategy in 1905 and again in 1917, in so far as it differed from that of the Bolsheviks, was "wrong" and that had Trotsky's view prevailed, the Russian workers "would have gone down to defeat". They regard the April debates between Lenin and Kamenev as merely about tactics rather than strategy. [51] Further, they deny that the October 1917 revolution was a socialist revolution, dating this almost a year later. Instead, they regard the regime as a workers' and peasants government during its first year. [52]

A comparable and more substantial recent challenge to permanent revolution as the strategy of victory in 1917 has come from historian Lars Lih. In a series of academic papers and articles in the socialist press, he resolutely defends the "old Bolshevik" strategy, most notably associated with Kamenev and Stalin, as a better way to understand Bolshevik activity during 1917. Lih argues that the heart of old Bolshevism was a strategy for the goal of democratic revolution "to the end".[53] Lih's theoretical innovation is to introduce a third alternative, between the Menshevik position of support for the Provisional Government and Trotsky's perspective of socialist revolution. He calls old Bolshevism "the possibility of an insurrection against the Provisional Government in order to defend revolutionary goals and to carry out a thorough-going democratic transformation". He interprets Lenin's talk of a second stage or second revolution as meaning a *"narodnaia vlast"* that will put "the party of the proletariat" in power and carry out the democratic revolution to the end.

Lih accepts that Lenin introduced something new into Bolshevik politics in 1917, what he dubs "old Bolshevism plus".[54] He bases this on an interpretation of Lenin's first *Letter from Afar*, when Lenin goes beyond the old Bolshevik framework only when he talks of moving toward socialism in Russia itself, prior to and independent of international revolution. This new theme is summed up in the phrase: "steps toward socialism".[55] Lih argues that "the catalyst for Lenin's innovation was an article by Kautsky on the Russian revolution that appeared on 23 March 1917".[56] Contrary to "a widespread misconception", insistence on the "socialist character of the revolution" was not "a necessary condition for the project of replacing the Provisional Government with a *vlast* based on popular forces". Lih believes that Trotsky is "absolutely wrong" about the Bolshevik message in 1917. The Bolsheviks "did not preach socialist revolution in 1917".[57] By October, instead of rejecting old Bolshevism as outmoded, Lih believes that after it was "correspondingly modified" to fit the new situation, "old Bolshevism had been triumphantly vindicated".[58]

THE RUSSIAN REVOLUTION: WHEN WORKERS TOOK POWER

Lars Lih's assessment of the Russian workers' revolution in 1917 suffers from many of the same problems as the activist critiques, while adding theoretical errors that take him a long way from Marxism. First, Lih's methodology in assessing the realities of 1917 is woeful. He does not answer the fundamental question about October 1917: which class ruled? Historians, Marxist or otherwise, require clarity on the class nature of the new state the revolutionaries built after smashing the old institutions of the bourgeois state — its army, police, civil service, judiciary, and legislature. Clarity is required on the class character of the new government established after October 1917. And it is necessary to be clear about the kind of social relations of production that existed before 1917.

In the Trotskyist account, these answers are straightforward. The Provisional Government was a bourgeois government presiding over a capitalist state and capitalist relations of production, albeit with some residual pre-capitalist structures. The Bolsheviks were overwhelmingly a workers' party, which led the workers (and soldiers and peasants) to smash the old bourgeois state, and set up a workers' state, with its own forms of rule (the soviets), its own, new, army, militias, courts, and legislature. They formed a workers' government, initially alone, then briefly as the dominant partner in a coalition with the left SRs, before finally being forced to rule by themselves.

In contrast, Lih sees only "people's power" with no definite class character. Perhaps it is a two (or more) class state, or two class government. Lih does not precisely define what kind of social relations it sought to transform. In short, Lih's "second revolution" as people's power suffers from precisely the objection Trotsky raised against his critics after 1905: he proceeds on the basis of texts, not from an analysis of social relations. The fact that the texts are Bolshevik-authored makes no difference. Without an analysis of class structures, class formations, class relations and class organisations, Lih's assessment cannot stand as an alternative Marxist analysis of what happened in 1917.

Second, Lih's approach suffers from the related methodological problem of redefining terms that have a precise Marxist meaning, and the substitution of his own concepts. For example, he defines "soviet republic" as "the most advanced form of democratic republic". This is not Lenin's definition or even a recognisably Marxist understanding. His chief confusion here is over the nature of bourgeois and proletarian revolutions. A proletarian, working-class, revolution is simultaneously a socialist revolution because it is both the forcible seizure of power by the organised working class from the capitalist class and its agents, an act of destruction of bourgeois institutions, and an act of creation, namely of new structures of state and society.

Socialist revolution can also therefore be understood as a process, whereby the new workers' government uses the powers of the new workers' state to help the workers wrestle control over all aspects of society, thus transforming the social relations of production.

This is not socialism itself because the creation of socialist relations of production requires international integration. A transitional form of society may exist over a protracted period, as simultaneous workers' revolution in most states are unlikely. Lih rightly believes that the Bolsheviks were not building socialism in one country (in the sense of socialist relations of production), as Stalin later falsely claimed to be doing. That is impossible and Lenin, Trotsky and others fully recognised it as such. But when workers seize power this is socialist revolution, even in an isolated, backward country where workers face stiff limits on how far they can transform their society from top to bottom in the absence of other workers' revolutions globally.

Lih claims on the basis of popular leaflets published in Moscow during 1917 that the Bolsheviks hardly mentioned socialism. But this is to misconstrue the nature of Marxist agitation, which takes as its point of departure the needs and yearning of millions of Russian workers, soldiers and peasants. This agitation, aimed at a mass audience, is a means of rousing the readers to fight, to take action. This is not a representative sample of the Marxist programme or the wider educational nature of Marxist propaganda. A reading of Bolshevik newspapers, journals and books indicates that socialism, in the sense of working class self-emancipation, oozed from every pore of Bolshevik work during 1917.

Lih has stretched the conception of "democratic revolution to the end" to its *reductio ad absurdum*. Since 1848 Marxists have been clear that even during the classic bourgeois revolution (such as the French revolution of 1789-93), although wide layers of society had rebelled to overthrow the absolutist monarchy, it was the capitalist class that benefited most, in terms of the state, forms of government and social relations of production. Revolutionaries learned from the series of European revolutions of 1848. Then they hoped for thorough democratic transformations only to find the bourgeois parties tied to the old ruling classes and unwilling to carry through transformation for fear of the emerging workers' movement.

Early Russian Marxists who advocated support for the bourgeois parties (such as the Kadets) in the bourgeois revolution took the *Communist Manifesto* as their guide, forgetting that Marx and Engels had reassessed based on the experience of 1848-49 and come out for "permanent revolution", for the working-class to fight for its own independent interests in such events. Lih makes a similar mistake is seeing continuity in Lenin, when there was evolution in 1917.

Trotsky anticipated Lih's conception of "democratic revolution to the end" and its weaknesses. In his 1908 essay, 'Our Differences', Trotsky criticised the Mensheviks and Bolsheviks for fetishising "carrying the revolution to the end". Both sides "interpreted this in a purely formal sense, that is, in the sense that we had to achieve our minimum programme, after which would come an era of 'normal' capitalism in a democratic setting". However, "carrying the revolution to the end" presupposed "the overthrow of tsarism and the transfer of state power into the hands of a revolutionary public force". Trotsky asked: what force? The Mensheviks said: bourgeois democracy. The Bolsheviks said: the proletariat and the peasantry. For the Mensheviks, their abstract "carrying the revolution to the end" turned, in practice, into "supporting the Kadets nonetheless". Trotsky's conclusion remained: "only the proletariat in its class struggle, placing the peasant masses under its revolutionary leadership, can 'carry the revolution to the end'."

Trotsky also pointed to the flaw in the old Bolshevik conception of "carrying the revolution to the end". If the workers played the leading role in the revolution, what would be the point of "imposing a political limitation upon itself" once in power? As soon as the proletariat seizes power, "it is bound immediately, on the very first day, to be confronted with the problem of unemployment". "Self-limitation" by a workers' government "would mean nothing other than the betrayal of the interests of the unemployed and strikers — more, of the whole proletariat — in the name of the establishment of a republic". He posed the issues starkly:

> The workers' government will from the start be faced with the task of uniting its forces with those of the socialist proletariat of Western Europe. Only in this way will its temporary revolutionary hegemony become the prologue to a socialist dictatorship. Thus permanent revolution will become, for the Russian proletariat, a matter of class self-preservation. If the workers' party cannot show sufficient initiative for aggressive revolutionary tactics, if it limits itself to the frugal diet of a dictatorship that is merely national and merely democratic, the united reactionary forces of Europe will waste no time in making it clear that a working class, if it happens to be in power, must throw the whole of its strength into the struggle for a socialist revolution.[59]

Lih's also misreads Lenin's politics by suggesting that even into 1917 the focus was on fighting for democracy "to the end" more than socialism. Even in one of his earliest essays, 'What the "Friends of the People" Are and How they Fight the Social-Democrats' (1894), Lenin spelt out the connection between the workers' fight against absolutism and the fight for socialism. He wrote:

> *Accordingly, it is on the working class that the Social-Democrats concentrate all their attention and all their activities. When its advanced representatives have mastered the ideas of scientific socialism, the idea of the historical role of the Russian worker, when these ideas become widespread, and when stable organisations are formed among the workers to transform the workers' present sporadic economic war into conscious class struggle—then the Russian worker, rising at the head of all the democratic elements, will overthrow absolutism and lead the Russian proletariat (side by side with the proletariat of all countries) along the straight road of open political struggle to the victorious communist revolution.*[60]

Lenin's ideas began to evolve even before the February revolution took place in 1917. His lecture on 1905 and other writings (some not published until after his death) further indicate important changes in his outlook. He began to abandon the notion of the "revolutionary democratic dictatorship of the proletariat and the peasantry", which he had defended resolutely since 1905. Two revisions effectively destroyed the notion completely. First, he spoke of a "workers' government", implying that the workers' would imminently face the task of taking power in the forthcoming revolution. This was not an ultimatum: when and how workers could seize power was a matter of the balance of class forces and the extent of support for the Bolsheviks, matters of class consciousness that Lenin did not seek to ignore. However the strategic goal of a specifically workers' government rather than some sought of alliance with the peasantry was a new departure.

Second, the concomitant change in his attitude towards the peasantry took several forms. It was no longer about winning the peasantry "as a whole", but of concentration of the poorest peasants and the agricultural waged workers that was the crucial internal alliance the urban labour movement needed to make. Further, he no longer looked towards specifically peasant organisations such as the Trudoviks or the Peasant Union to ally with, largely because of their defencism during the war. This was incidentally before Kautsky published his article on Russia (23 March), which Lih claims is responsible for Lenin's "steps towards socialism". It is more accurate to see Lenin taking steps towards permanent revolution, even though differences of emphasis and language remained between him and Trotsky.

It is notable that when Lih crafts his most detailed expositions of the old Bolshevik scenario, he is forced to rely on the writings of Stalin and Kamenev. These writings may more or less sum up the Bolshevik perspective before 1917 — and in Stalin and Kamenev's cases, long into 1917. But they were not Lenin's views because Lenin had earlier changed his mind. Other Bolsheviks "came over to his position", as he put it at the end of the April debates. These were ideological struggles, about strategy and goals, not just tactical disputes.

Lih is also wrong to favour Lenin's "October 1915" theses over his April 1917 theses. In his theses of October 1915 and in a letter to Shliapnikov from the same period, Lenin was outlining a perspective for the Russian workers' movement that had been thrown backwards by the war and the betrayal of many socialists. Then, it was a matter of reviving the struggle against absolutism. Thus Lenin stated his opposition to the establishment of soviets at this time. The situation after the February revolution in 1917 was completely different and Lenin recognised this. The tsar had been overthrown. The soviets were a fact of working-class life. In such circumstances, the "old Bolshevism" was no longer relevant. It was behind the times and did not specify the new political tasks.

Historian John Marot has produced a detailed critique of Lih's views. Marot makes valuable points about the way Lih handles Marxist nomenclature and his habit of introducing Russian terms when translations are capable of conveying meaning and nuance to an English language audience. Marot draws out the contrast between Lenin's strategy in 1905 compared to 1917. In the earlier revolution, the Bolsheviks believed it was right not only to support a Provisional Government when the tsar was overthrown, but also to join that government, even as a minority party. That such a Provisional Government might be dominated by bourgeois liberal parties did not rule out the Bolshevik participation in principle — something for which they were taunted by Mensheviks, who resolved to support a Provisional Government from the outside as the "party of extreme opposition". However in 1917, Lenin's strategy rejected support for (never mind joining) the Provisional Government; in the changed conditions Lenin wanted to overthrow it at the earliest possible moment.

Marot points out that the Bolshevik position on the Provisional Government from 1905 never got to be applied because no such Provisional Government ever arose in 1905. In the April 1917 debates, Lenin called for the (eventual) overthrow of the actually existing Provisional Government. Neither he, nor the Bolsheviks nor the Mensheviks "could ever have contemplated such a call in 1905". There is "neither continuity nor discontinuity with the old 1905 Bolshevik position of participation in a Provisional Government here because that position was meant to respond to a Provisional Government that the Bolsheviks hoped would come into existence but never did". Now there is a new situation, which calls for a new position, not the application of the old one, as Lih thinks. Lenin has raised the discussion to an altogether different, superior plane. The political stakes were in 1917 much higher.

It is the appearance of soviets in 1917 from the beginning of the struggle, rather than towards the end as in 1905, that is crucial. These specifically working-class forms of organisations made it possible to conceive of an alternative government and even of an alternative workers' state, beyond the bounds of a Provisional Government that would prepare the ground for a Constituent Assembly and a bourgeois democratic republic. Without the appearance of the soviet, "any idea of destroying the Provisional Government and going beyond the bourgeois-democratic revolution was literally unthinkable". Trotsky grasped this potential in 1905 and make it the centre piece of his permanent revolution strategy. In 1917 Lenin caught up. At stake now, as Lenin saw it, was "what new goal the Bolsheviks should set themselves — not in relation to a no-longer-existing Tsarism but in relation to the actually existing Provisional Government, which has taken the place of Tsarism as the 'official' government".[61]

Lenin realised the old Bolshevik strategy in 1917 was a snare and convinced the party to reorientate. The new goal had practical consequences. It meant no unification with the Mensheviks, but clear demarcation from those soft on the Provisional Government. It meant renaming the social democratic party as a "communist party" (in 1918) to distinguish its goals from others cloaked in "socialist" clothes. Lenin's intervention was timely and essential. It set the Bolsheviks on the road to leading the workers to power in October 1917. Whether this perspective amounted to Trotsky's version of permanent revolution is a matter of historical comparison, not political significance, given their evident proximity. In 1917, they shared common assessments and political conclusions that were decisive in ensuring victory.

Conclusion

Trotsky was the most famous and brilliant proponent of permanent revolution. His perspective was not heretical or iconoclastic. Rather he drew on the assessments of some of the finest Marxists of the period to create a unique synthesis. Trotsky was the Marxist who foresaw more clearly than anyone else that the perspective of permanent revolution could frame the tasks of the Russian revolution in 1905 and again in 1917. His role as both seminal theorist and leading participant makes his contribution stand out among all others.

But Trotsky did not fetishise his perspective and was careful not to overstretch its importance. From the vantage point of the 1930s he reflected that "I am far from thinking that the theory of the permanent revolution has a 'finished' character or that it is a master key that unlocks all strategic problems". Rather the theory did not free Marxists "from the necessity of a concrete analysis of each new historic situation in each separate country"; on the contrary, it forced them to make such analyses. He argued that "to consider the theory of the permanent revolution as a suprahistorical dogma would contradict its very essence". Unfortunately many Trotskyists, those that did not reject the theory, would later make this very mistake — turning the theory into a dogma. Nonetheless Trotsky's writings on this subject give Marxists "a unique and correct starting point in the internal dynamic of each contemporary national revolution and in its uninterrupted connection with the international revolution".[62]

Trotsky's conception of uneven and combined development attempted to grapple with the impacts of the global expansion of capitalism, particularly on the system of states but also on classes within those states. His concepts such as the "whip of external necessity" and the "privilege of historical backwardness" were not confined to Russian conditions. Trotsky would fruitfully begin to apply these conceptions to explain the global political economy and international relations of his time, with regard to the emergence of the US as global hegemon, to the integration of China into the world economy and for developments in Latin America. Although individual states had their own national peculiarities, their mutual interdependence gave rise to contradictions and very different effects, with resultant impacts on class formation and class struggle. This international perspective has a far wider application, well beyond the original Russian context.

Trotsky thought through the implications of the fundamental Marxist proposition that socialism is the self-emancipation of the working class. The working class takes power only by making a socialist revolution. The working class is the revolutionary class in the modern world, even where it is a minority class. Working-class hegemony in any serious class struggle means a strong socialist labour movement can lead other oppressed social strata, resolving a universal, democratic and social tasks beyond its own immediate interests.

Most of all, he grasped the essence of a historical moment and drew out the central political conclusions — that the working class should make a socialist revolution to take power and form a workers' government, which would have to go beyond the bounds of a bourgeois democratic republic and implement its own class demands. Further, this would mean overthrowing the existing social relations and creating a workers' state, in advance of socialist revolutions in the rest of Europe.

References

1. Hal Draper, *Karl Marx's Theory of Revolution: Volume II: The Politics of Social Classes*, (1978: 201-04, 225, 238, 247-8, 251-52); Karl Marx and Frederick Engels, [March 1850] 'Address of the Central Committee to the Communist League', (*MECW* 10: 287).
2. Richard Day and Daniel Gaido, *Witnesses to Permanent Revolution*, (2011).
3. Plekhanov, [1905] 'On Engels' Ludwig Feuerbach', *SPW* 1, (1961: 507); Axelrod, Pavel (April-May 1906) 'Speech at the Fourth Party Congress', Abraham Ascher, *The Mensheviks in the Russian Revolution* (1976: 59-60).
4. Lenin, [June-July 1905] *Two Tactics of Social-Democracy in the Democratic Revolution*, (*LCW* 9: 48, 49-50).
5. Lenin, [April 1905] 'Social-Democracy and the Provisional Revolutionary Government', (*LCW* 8: 289, 291-92); Lenin, *Two Tactics*, (*LCW* 9: 28-29, 56-57).
6. Lenin, [1 September 1905] 'Social Democracy's Attitude toward the Peasant Movement', (*LCW* 9: 237).
7. Marx, [1867] *Preface to the first edition of Capital, volume 1*, (*MECW* 35: 9).
8. Trotsky, [28 June 1922], 'On the Special Features of Russia's Historical Development: A Reply to M N Pokrovsky', in *1905*, (1971: 331).
9. Trotsky, [1906], *Results and Prospects*, 1969: 36, 64
10. Trotsky, [1930], *The Permanent Revolution*, 1969: 146
11. Trotsky, [July 1905], 'Introduction to Ferdinand Lassalle's Speech to the Jury', Day and Gaido, (2011: 444).
12. Trotsky, [12 November 1905] 'Social Democracy and Revolution', Day and Gaido, (2011: 443-444, 455).
13. Trotsky, [December 1905] 'Foreword to Karl Marx, Parizhskaya Kommuna', Day and Gaido, (2011 511, 513, 514-517).
14. Trotsky, [1906], *Results and Prospects*, (1969: 67-70).
15. Trotsky, [1906], *Results and Prospects*, (1969: 71-73).
16. Trotsky, [1908] 'Our Differences: The Year 1905, the Reaction, and Revolutionary Prospects', in *1905*, (1971: 312, 263).
17. Lenin, 'Social Democracy's Attitude toward the Peasant Movement', (*LCW* 9: 237); Lenin, [2 November 1905] 'Our Tasks and the Soviet of Workers' Deputies', *LCW* 10: 21); Lenin, [November-December 1907], 'The Agrarian Programme of Social-Democracy in the First Russian Revolution, 1905-1907', (*LCW* 13: 392).
18. Lenin, [15-16 May 1907] 'Objections to Trotsky's Amendments to the Bolshevik Resolution on the Attitude towards Bourgeois Parties, Fifth Congress of the RSDLP', (*LCW* 12: 470).
19. Trotsky, [September 1915] 'The Social Forces in the Russian Revolution', John Riddell, *Lenin's Struggle for a Revolutionary International*, (1986: 387-88, 390).
20. Trotsky, [17 October 1915], 'The Struggle for Power', in *The Permanent Revolution*, (1969: 119, 121-122).
21. Trotsky, [20 January 1917], 'Lessons of the Great Year', *Journal of Trotsky Studies*, 1, 1993: 99, 101).
22. Trotsky, [16 March 1917], 'Revolution in Russia', *Journal of Trotsky Studies*, 1, (1993: 107-108); Trotsky, [17 March 1917], 'Two faces: The Internal Forces of the Russian revolution', *Journal of Trotsky Studies*, 1, (1993: 112); Trotsky, [19 March 1917], 'The Growing Conflict: The Internal Forces of the Russian revolution', *Journal of Trotsky Studies*, 1, (1993: 113).
23. Trotsky, [19 March 1917], 'The Growing Conflict: The Internal Forces of the Russian revolution', *Journal of Trotsky Studies*, 1, (1993: 114); Trotsky, [21 March 1917], 'How and from Whom to Defend the revolution', *Journal of Trotsky Studies*, 1, (1993: 120-121).
24. Trotsky, [1917] 'What Next?' In Louis Fraina, The Proletarian Revolution in Russia (1918). MIA
25. Trotsky, [1930] *The Permanent Revolution*, (1969: 151).
26. Trotsky, [1931] *The History of the Russian Revolution*, Vol.1, (1980: 1-6).
27. Trotsky, [1933] *The History of the Russian Revolution*, Vol.3, (1980: 379).

28. Joel Carmichael, 'Introduction', Nikolai Sukhanov, *The Russian Revolution 1917*, (1954: xxvii, xxviii); Joel Carmichael, *Trotsky: An Appreciation of his Life*, (1975: 156). Marcel Liebman, *Leninism under Lenin*, (1975: 180).
29. Trotsky, [23 May 1931] 'On Comrade Treint's declaration', in *Writings of Leon Trotsky* [1930-31], (1973: 277-78); Trotsky, [1923], 'The New Course', in *The Challenge of the Left Opposition* (1923-25), (1980: 101-102); Trotsky, [30 November 1924], 'Our Differences', in Challenge (1923-25), (1980: 278).
30. Lenin, [9 January 1917] 'Lecture on the 1905 revolution', (*LCW* 23: 239, 251-53).
31. Lenin, [4 March 1917] 'Draft Theses', (*LCW* 23: 287-90).
32. Lenin, [7 March 1917] 'Letters From Afar: First Letter: The First Stage of the First Revolution', (*LCW* 23: 304, 306-07); Lenin, [9 March 1917] 'Letters From Afar: Second Letter: The New Government and the Proletariat', (*LCW* 23: 310).
33. Lenin, [26 March 1917] 'Letters From Afar: Fifth Letter: The Tasks Involved in the Building of the Revolutionary Proletarian State', (*LCW* 23: 340-41).
34. Lenin, [26 March 1917] 'Farewell Letter to the Swiss Workers', (*LCW* 23: 371-372).
35. Lenin, [4 April 1917] 'The Tasks of the Proletariat in the Present Revolution (April theses)', (*LCW* 24: 22-24).
36. Lenin, [4 April 1917] 'The March 1917 Party Conference', in Trotsky, The Stalin School of Falsification, (1937: 293-94).
37. Lenin, [8-13 April 1917] 'Letters on Tactics: First Letter Assessment of the Present Situation', (*LCW* 24: 44-46).
38. Lenin, 'Letters on Tactics', (*LCW* 24: 48-49).
39. Lenin, 'Letters on Tactics', (*LCW* 24: 50-51).
40. Lenin, [10 April 1917] 'The Tasks of the Proletariat in Our Revolution: Draft Platform for the Proletarian Party', (*LCW* 24: 57-58, 60-61, 72).
41. Lenin, [14 April 1917] 'Report on the Present Situation and the Attitude towards the Provisional Government, (*LCW* 24: 141-42, 145-46).
42. Lenin, [14 April 1917] 'Concluding Remarks in the Debate Concerning the Report on the Present Situation', (*LCW* 24: 148-150); Lenin, [15 April 1917] 'Two Remarks during the Debate on the Resolution concerning the Attitude towards the Provisional Government', (*LCW* 24: 152).
43. Lenin, [24 April 1917] 'Report on the Current Situation', (*LCW* 24: 229-30, 241-43).
44. Lenin, [24 April 1917] 'Speech Winding up the Debate on the Report on the Current Situation', (*LCW* 24: 244-46).
45. Lenin, [28 April 1917] 'Report on the Question of Revising the Party Programme', (*LCW* 24: 248); Lenin, [28 April 1917] 'Resolution on the Agrarian Question', (*LCW* 24: 292).
46. Lenin, [29 April 1917] 'Speech in Favour of the Resolution on the Current Situation', (*LCW* 24: 302); Lenin, [29 April 1917] 'Resolution on the Current Situation', (*LCW* 24: 310-11).
47. Lenin, [28 April 1917] 'Resolution on Uniting the Internationalists against the Petty-Bourgeois Defencist Bloc', (*LCW* 24: 294); Lenin, [19 February 1917] 'Letter to Inessa Armand', (*LCW* 35: 288); Lenin, [17 March 1917] 'Letter to Alexandra Kollontai', (*LCW* 35: 298); Lenin, [10 April 1917] 'The Tasks of the Proletariat in Our Revolution Draft Platform for the Proletarian Party', (*LCW* 24: 83); Lenin, [30 May 1917] 'Speech Concerning an Organ of the Press for the Petrograd Committee', (*LCW* 24: 543).
48. Lenin, [22-24 September 1917 'From A Publicist's Diary: The Mistakes Of Our Party', (*LCW* 26: 57); Lenin, [29 September 1917] 'On the list of candidates for the Constituent Assembly', (*LCW* 41: 446-47); Lenin, [1 November 1917] 'The Lost Document', in Trotsky, *The Real Situation in Russia*, (1928: 226); Trotsky, *The Stalin School of Falsification*, (1937: 105).
49. Doug Jenness, [June 1982] 'Our Political Continuity with Bolshevism'; Jenness, [November 1981] 'How Lenin Saw the Russian Revolution'; Ernest Mandel, [April 1982] 'The Debate over the Character and Goals of the Russian Revolution'; Mandel, [12 December 1982] 'In Defense of Permanent Revolution: A Reply to Doug Jenness'. The texts are collected in In Steve Clark, *Bolshevism and the Russian Revolution: A Debate* (2013).
50. Doug Lorimer, [1998] *Trotsky's Theory of Permanent Revolution: A Leninist Critique*; Phil

Hearse, [1999] 'Permanent Revolution — A Reply to Doug Lorimer', *The Activist*, 9, 8; Lorimer, [1999] 'In Defence of Lenin's Marxist Policy of a Two-Stage, Uninterrupted Revolution', *The Activist*, 9, 8; Hearse, [2000] 'Either A 'Socialist Revolution Or A Make-Believe Revolution: A Rejoinder', *The Activist*, 10, 2; Lorimer, [2000] 'Imperialist Economism, Democracy and the Socialist Revolution', *The Activist*, 10, 2.

51. Jenness, [1982] in Clark (2013: 65, 47); Lorimer (1998: 24, 71-73).

52. Jenness, [1982] in Clark (2013: 48-50, 58); Lorimer [1999].

53. Lih, 'The ironic triumph of old Bolshevism: the debates of April 1917 in context', *Russian History*, 38, (2011: 201); Lih, 'The four wagers of Lenin in 1917', *Weekly Worker*, 785, 17 September (2009); Lih, 'April theses': myth and reality', *Weekly Worker*, 836, 7 October (2010: 6-7).

54. Lih, 'The ironic triumph' (2011: 202-208, 2010-11, 216-218).

55. Lih, 'Letter from Afar, Corrections from Up Close: The Bolshevik Consensus of March 1917', *Kritika*, 16, 4 (2015: 802, 806, 812, 816).

56. Lih, 'The ironic triumph' (2011: 220-21); Kautsky, [23 March 1917] 'Prospects of the Russian Revolution', *Weekly Worker*, 800, 14 January (2010).

57. Lih, 'The ironic triumph' (2011: 202, 218); Lih, 'Letter from Afar' (2015: 819); Lih, 'Agreementism (Soglashatelstvo): The Key Issue in the Politics of 1917: Talk given at Slavic Convention', Philadelphia, November (2015).

58. Lih, 'The ironic triumph' (2011: 227-28, 231, 234, 236, 239, 240, 241).

59. Trotsky, [1908] 'Our Differences: The Year 1905, the Reaction, and Revolutionary Prospects', in *1905*, (1971: 311-17).

60. Lenin, [1894] 'What the "Friends of the People" Are and How they Fight the Social-Democrats', (*LCW* 1: 300).

61. John Marot, 'Lenin, Bolshevism, and Social-Democratic political theory', *Historical Materialism*, 22, 2-3, (2014: 145, 148-49, 155, 163).

62. Trotsky, [22 September 1931] 'Another letter to Albert Treint', in *Writings of Leon Trotsky* [1930-31], (1973: 368).

El Lissitzky, 'Beat the White Circle With the Red Wedge', 1919

6. War and the myth of defeatism

The First World War (1914-18) was fought between two imperialist camps, wedded together by a series of agreements signed long before the outbreak of hostilities. The war was a hugely important turning point in world history and divided the socialist movement. How did those Marxist socialists who opposed the war orientate themselves? How did they articulate their opposition? They understood that the politics of war followed from their concrete assessment of the class dynamics of global capitalism. They identified with the dictum of the German military strategist Carl von Clausewitz that "war is the continuation of politics by other [violent] means". This method, adopted by Marx and Engels, was widely shared by revolutionary socialists before the conflict. It was well summed up by Lenin:

> *This famous aphorism ["war is the continuation of politics by other means"] was uttered by one of the profoundest writers on the problems of war, Clausewitz. Marxists have always rightly regarded this thesis as the theoretical basis of views concerning the significance of every given war…*
>
> *Apply this view to the present war. You will see that for decades, for almost half a century, the governments and the ruling classes of England, and France, and Germany, and Italy, and Austria, and Russia, pursued a policy of plundering colonies, of oppressing other nations, of suppressing the working-class movement. It is this, and only this, policy that is being continued in the present war. In particular, the policy of both Austria and Russia, peace-time as well as in war, is a policy of enslaving and not of liberating nations…*
>
> *It is sufficient to glance at the present war from the viewpoint that it is a continuation of the politics of the great powers, and of the principal classes within them, to see at once the howling anti-historicalness, falsity and hypocrisy of the view that the "defence of the fatherland" idea can be justified in the present war.*[1]

Anti-war Marxists were isolated and persecuted after hostilities began, but their fortitude paid dividends. As the conflict dragged on, the killing failed to abate, and military stalemate promised only more years of misery, mass opposition to the war revived. It fuelled the almighty wave of revolutionary fervour that helped bring the war to an end and reshape the post-war period. The First World War opened millions of workers and soldiers to socialist politics and socialist revolution. Nowhere was this more evident than in Russia, where opposition to the war formed the backdrop to the 1917 revolution.

The collapse of the Second International

On the eve of war the socialist parties of the world had a total membership of more than four million, and there were about 700 socialist deputies in the various parliaments. Socialists had an analysis of the period they were living through and the organisation to counter the war drive. At every juncture in the lead up to the cataclysm, socialists had demonstrated their opposition to war, not only with fine resolutions but with working-class mobilisations. Big demonstrations took place on 5 November 1911 — the day Italy announced the annexation of Tripoli. Mass demonstrations began on 20 October 1912, when in Berlin alone more than 250,000 workers were mobilised and protests continued to the end of the year. On 15 July 1914 an anti-war protest by 100,000 demonstrators took place in Unter den Linden, Berlin. Sixty thousand people took part in an impressive rally in Berlin on 27 July 1914 and demonstrations followed in the great industrial centres of Germany.[2]

Yet, in August 1914, the First World War became an accomplished fact. On 4 August 1914, the parliamentary fraction of the German SPD voted unanimously to finance the German state's war effort, repudiating socialist internationalism and giving their own ruling class a free pass to prosecute the war. British, French and Belgian socialist leaders also voted for war and the Socialist International collapsed. Only Serbian and Russian socialists pledged to oppose the conflict. Dragiša Lapčević and Triša Kaclerović of the Serbian Socialist party voted against war credits in their national parliament on 4 August, while four days later, the Bolshevik and Menshevik Duma fractions read a joint declaration refusing support for military appropriations and walked out of the assembly prior to the vote.[3]

Against the rising tide of chauvinism, small groups of revolutionary socialists immediately began to organise to oppose the war. In early August 1914, some SPD opponents of the war met in Rosa Luxemburg's apartment and decided to send telegrams to left-wing party officials, inviting them to discuss a collective response to the parliamentary betrayal. Clara Zetkin responded positively, but most made excuses and only a handful were prepared to meet. On 21 September, Karl Liebknecht told SPD leaders that the decision to support war credits was wrong. In December 1914 he would vote against further war spending in the Reichstag, a public stand that resounded across Europe. Exiled Bolsheviks met in Bern, Switzerland in early September 1914 and adopted Lenin's appeal, 'The Tasks of Revolutionary Social Democracy in the European War'. In October, Trotsky wrote the pamphlet *War and the International*, articulating his opposition.

On 26-28 March 1915, the first wartime international socialist conference convened, when 29 delegates from seven countries met in Bern. The conference originated with a proposal made by the exiled Russian Bolshevik Inessa Armand to Zetkin, still head of the socialist women's movement affiliated to the Second International. Zetkin organised the gathering and drafted its final statement. It concluded: "Down with capitalism, which sacrifices untold millions to the wealth and power of the propertied! Down with the war! Forward to socialism!" Zetkin focused on the goal of peace, and avoided mentioning the split among socialists. The Bolshevik delegates supported an alternative text that accused the leaderships of most socialist parties of the belligerent countries of committing "a real betrayal in respect of socialism, supplanting it with nationalism". Zetkin's text was approved by 21 votes to 6. The Bolsheviks and the Polish delegate (Anna Kamenska) voted against, but joined in editing the final text and in common work after the conference.

On 7 April 1915, socialist youth representatives met in Bern, adopting a manifesto against the war. The pre-war Socialist Youth International, formed in 1907, had campaigned actively against militarism, but when the war broke out it ceased to function. Youth organisations with 34,000 members were represented at the Bern meeting, with delegates from Norway, Denmark, the Netherlands, Germany, Switzerland, Italy, Poland, Bulgaria and Russia. A new international secretariat was established in Zürich, with Willi Münzenberg as secretary. A quarterly magazine was launched, called *Jugend-Internationale* (*Youth International*), which became an important instrument for discussion among anti-war socialists.[4]

The Zimmerwald conference, held in Switzerland on 5-8 September 1915, marked a turning point for the socialist anti-war movement. Some 42 delegates from 11 countries met at this international gathering of socialist currents opposed to the First World War. The modesty of the affair was captured by Trotsky's joke as delegates arrived that "half a century after the formation of the First International it was still possible to fit all the internationalists in Europe into four coaches". However, Trotsky's 'Zimmerwald Manifesto' carried by the conference helped inspire a movement of anti-war socialist activists across the warring countries of Europe. Trotsky wrote soon after that "the conference of Zimmerwald has saved the honour of Europe and the ideals of the conference will save Europe itself".

While delegates agreed on opposition to the war, they were divided over how to oppose it and on what practical steps would be necessary to renew international socialist organisation. The main conference organiser, Swiss socialist Robert Grimm, sought above all to revive the structures of the shattered Socialist International. By contrast, left-wing delegates, led by the Bolsheviks, wanted a new revolutionary international. On the first day of the conference, a letter from imprisoned Karl Liebknecht was read out to the conference with great enthusiasm. Liebknecht emphasised the need for class-struggle activity and to break socialists from the wartime alliance with capitalist states. He summed this up as: "civil war not civil peace". A minority resolution drafted by Karl Radek on behalf of delegates from Russia, Poland, Latvia, Germany, and Switzerland said workers should aim at "the overthrow of the capitalist government" and an end to capitalist power. Although Radek's resolution was rejected, it launched the Zimmerwald Left.

The second socialist anti-war conference was held on 24-30 April 1916 in the village of Kiental in Switzerland. Some 43 delegates and observers came from France, Germany, Italy, Poland, Portugal, Russia, Serbia, Switzerland and Britain. More than a dozen delegates, including Trotsky, were denied travel documents and could not take part. The conference united socialists who opposed the war effort of their respective ruling classes and worked for mass workers' action to end the slaughter. They agreed on immediate peace without annexations or indemnities. However, they were divided on how peace was to be achieved. While the majority of delegates favoured pressuring the governments to negotiate a peace agreement, the Bolshevik-led minority called on workers to struggle "for political power, for socialism and for the unification of the socialist peoples". They called on soldiers to "lower your weapons and turn them against our common enemy — the capitalist governments".

The delegates also disagreed on how to renew the socialist movement. The moderates wanted to persuade the old socialist leaders who had betrayed the International in 1914 to reconvene its leading bodies. However, the left, including Luxemburg and Liebknecht's Spartacus League, called on workers to "turn their backs on social patriotism and, through revolutionary struggle against war and imperialism, to create the theoretical and organisational preconditions for preparing the launching of a new International". The conference united around a compromise text that condemned the social-patriotic leaders, without stating how the International's collapse was to be remedied.[5]

These small gatherings were vital places to clarify the necessary political tasks and to draw the most coherent political conclusions. They provided the Marxist left with the right orientation to lead the growing anti-war sentiment, which soon manifested itself in outright rebellion. They helped socialists in their quest to coalesce the forces for a new workers' international, one shorn of the opportunism of the discredited Second International and capable of leading the post-war revolutionary wave across Europe. Many of the participants would play a role in subsequent anti-war agitation, as well as the Russian revolution and the subsequent founding of the Communist International.

Marxism, imperialism and the First World War

Marxist revolutionaries have always understood that war is a basic drive between states in class societies. This understanding was given new focus in the late nineteenth century, when a conjuncture of rapid capitalist development across the globe gave rise to tension between existing bourgeois states, especially in Europe, and made the outbreak of a generalised conflict highly probable.

Engels warned of the risks of a European war from the early 1880s, when the great powers were beginning to align themselves into the opposing camps that would play out in the First World War. Both camps were "preparing for a decisive battle, for a war, such as the world has not yet seen, in which 10 to 15 million armed combatants will stand face to face". He repeated these warnings as part of preparing the burgeoning socialist parties for the outbreak of hostilities.[6]

The Second International was pledged to international working-class solidarity from its inception. The Stuttgart congress on 18-24 August 1907 involved 884 delegates from 25 countries. The debate on the question of the great powers' drive to war lasted six days. There was agreement that wars between capitalist states were "the outcome of their competition on the world market, for each state seeks not only to secure its existing markets, but also to conquer new ones". Luxemburg and Lenin proposed an amendment, which pledged international socialists "to exert every effort in order to prevent the outbreak of war by the means they consider most effective, which naturally vary according to the sharpening of the class struggle and the sharpening of the general political situation". If war broke out anyway, it was the duty of socialists "to intervene for its speedy termination and to strive with all their power to utilise the economic and political crisis created by the war to rouse the masses and thereby hasten the downfall of capitalist class rule".

The Second International congress held in Copenhagen on 28 August-3 September 1910 confirmed the Stuttgart resolution. The extraordinary congress held in Basel on 24-25 November 1912 was called in connection with the Balkan conflict and the fear that it would detonate a European war. The Congress adopted a manifesto repeating the key passages from Stuttgart, emphasising the imperialist nature of the approaching world war, and called on the socialists of all countries to wage a vigorous struggle against it.[7]

From the turn of the twentieth century, Marxists developed an analysis of international relations and the great power rivalry that leads to war. Karl Kautsky pioneered the understanding of the new epoch as one of "wars and revolutions", originally discussed as "Weltpolitik" (world policy), notably Germany's naval race with Britain. The term "Imperialism", taken from usage in England, was not just the age-old drive by big powers to conquer or subjugate territories, but a specific new trend, dating from the turn of the century, characterised by the domination of big centres of monopoly capital and finance capital, their competitive drive to establish relatively economically-integrated "empires" of colonies and spheres of influence, and to redivide a world already more or less fully divided-up between them, through cartels, protectionism, and militarism. As early as the SPD's Mainz Congress in 1900, during the debates over a resolution on world policy, Anton Friedrich described imperialism as "perhaps the last stage of development of capitalism".

Other writers such as Heinrich Cunow, Parvus and Rudolf Hilferding fleshed out the connections between finance capital, states and military rivalry. Imperialism was so ubiquitous that even the heavily bureaucratised SPD, at its party congress at Chemnitz, (15-21 September 1912) recognised that capitalism had reached its "highest stage" and voted to condemn it. Lenin's book *Imperialism: the Highest Stage of Capitalism* (1916) was neither original nor innovative, but a popular outline of Marxist understanding on this issue before the outbreak of the carnage, a mirror held up to expose the betrayal of the common pre-war politics by the majority of socialist party leaders when war broke out.[8]

Explaining the First World War

Lenin's summing up in 1916 of the combined wisdom Marxists had accumulated had many virtues. It was a comprehensible synthesis of significant trends in the world economy, which went a long way to explaining the drives that led the major powers into imperialist war. It was superior to bourgeois explanations from the time and since, which have oscillated between the "primacy of foreign policy", and those that elevate domestic policy in order to explain the onset of world war. The mainstream bourgeois accounts of the period fail to integrate system-wide processes with national level factors to offer a coherent explanation of the war.

Lenin's *Imperialism* identified how the enemy (capital and its states) had behaved and would behave in the near future. It explained how self-defeating the war would be for the ruling classes and for those in the labour movement that backed them. It charted a course for the labour movement, to renew the ties of international solidarity and to organise itself afresh in a new international organisation built on sturdier principles than the Second International. In particular, he highlighted the type of internationalism required of labour movements in advanced capitalist states, especially championing the rights of colonial peoples and other nations to self-determination, as a means of weakening the ruling class of the West but also liberating powerful social forces across the globe.

Lenin's analysis was a more-or-less adequate assessment of the conjuncture. However, it was a popular outline in some respects flawed even for its time. Lenin alternately used "finance capital" as signifying bank capital heavily enmeshed in, and substantially directing, industry, but also as signifying rentier capital distanced from industry. He derived the drive of capital to export abroad from a supposed "glut" or absence of investment opportunities in the home country. His dichotomy of earlier free-trade, competitive capitalism with the later imperialist, monopoly capitalism was overdrawn. Lenin's conception of capitalist states along a single line ranging from bourgeois democracy in the USA to Prussian militarism-bureaucratism in Germany was misleading, although he rejected Bukharin's equation of more imperialism automatically meaning less democracy. Making imperialism the highest or last stage of capitalism could be misread as reaching absolute impasse, although Lenin never saw capitalism in this fashion. Finally, his conception of a "labour aristocracy" to explain the collapse of socialist parties into chauvinism, whilst rightly damning the labour bureaucracy, was refuted by the revolutionary activities of the more privileged layers of the working class in Russia and elsewhere in Europe at the end of the war.[9]

Alexander Anievas argues that Lenin's analysis did not adequately tease out the connections between capitals and states.

Bukharin's version was not an improvement, since state and capital were fused into a single unit through his conception of "state-capitalist trusts". Both treated all imperialist states as essentially the same, whereas the tendency to export capital was a main feature of earlier developers (Britain and France), while later-developing capitalist states (particularly Germany) were characterised by "high levels of vertical-horizontal business integration (economies of scale), oligopolistic markets (cartels and trusts), large-scale banking-industrial combinations ('finance capital'), protectionist trade policies, export combinations, and statist forms of industrialisation". Attempts to amalgamate this as "monopoly capitalism" are similarly flawed. Trotsky's term — the possibility of combined as well as uneven development causing inter-imperialist rivalries — never entered into Lenin's framework.[10]

Yet *Lenin's Imperialism, the Highest Stage of Capitalism* is still regarded as a sacrosanct text on the left. It became fetishised by the Stalinists to justify the twists and turns of their foreign and domestic policy, by extracting turns of phrase and polemical asides, taken out of context to justify their new ideas. Lenin's book, and in particular the one-sided notion wrenched from it of "uneven development" was used to justify Stalin's theory of socialism in one country in his terrible *Short Course* textbook (1938).

The Stalinist notion that capitalist development is simply hindered or (in the language of the time) "retarded" in the colonial and semi-colonial countries was laid down at the Sixth Comintern Congress in 1928, as part of a political answer to the defeat suffered in China at the hands of Stalinists (and justly criticised by Trotsky). Lenin had in fact argued that imperialism brought more rapid capitalist development. Lenin's *Imperialism*, when read critically, provides important insights rather than the last word or eternal truths.

More recently, some Marxists have sought to rework Trotsky's concept of uneven and combined development into a theory of inter-state conflict and war to explain the spread of global capitalism and the specific drives that culminated in the First World War. This is a fruitful departure beyond the stale debates around imperialism. Anievas argues that the theory of uneven and combined development identifies three socio-international mechanisms of social interaction and development: "the 'whip of external necessity' (the pressures generated by interstate competition), the 'privilege of historic backwardness' (the opportunities opened up to late-developing states to adopt the most advanced cutting edge technologies from the leading states in the international system) and the 'contradictions of sociological amalgamation' (the time-compressed character of these developments, taking inorganic, spasmodic, and destabilising forms, and unhinging traditional social structures)."

Britain's "privileges of priority", as the first major place to extensively develop capitalist social relations of production and form a capitalist state, included a huge global colonial empire and the preponderance of military power. Later developing states did not need to start from scratch in their industrialisation drives, but acquired the most advanced technologies and organisational forms pioneered by earlier developers.

Thus France (1830s), Germany (1850s), Russia (late 1880s), Japan (1890s), and Italy (late 1890s) underwent a series of causally interwoven industrialisations, characterised by an interactive "leapfrogging" process (Trotsky's "skipping of stages" accrued by the "privilege of historic backwardness") emanating from the "whips of external necessity". But Germany's "combination of modern capitalism and medieval barbarism', as Trotsky characterised it, was reflected in both its domestic class structure and the peculiarity of its international position as spectacularly rising economic power with a relatively limited formal empire.

Tsarist Russia, under the "external whip" of "near constant contact with the more economically and militarily advanced Western powers", was "compelled to internalise the ready-made technologies, weapons and ideologies from 'the West' in the process of adapting them to its own 'less developed' social structure". Russia reaped the "privilege of backwardness", making tiger-leaps in its own development. But the "combined" Russian social formation was characterised by "a rapidly growing and ideologically radicalised proletarianised peasantry ('snatched from the plough and hurled into the factory furnace') existing alongside an unreformed absolutist monarchy and a dominant landowning aristocracy". The result was the rapid rise of a highly class-conscious proletariat, which nearly overthrew tsarist power in the midst of a war-induced domestic crisis in 1905. The tsarist response was rapid rearmament, destabilising the European military equilibrium and stimulating the German high command to press for war before the "window of opportunity" for a fight on two fronts was closed.[11]

This type of analysis, utilising and expanding the concepts of uneven and combined development, provides a more adequate explanation for the outbreak of the First World War at the specific conjuncture of 1914. While borrowing significantly from the theories of imperialism developed at the time by a range of Marxists, this conceptualisation better captures the dynamics of capitalism a century ago and provides a solid foundation for updating analysis to reach up to contemporary times.

The myth of "revolutionary defeatism"

Within the anti-war Marxist left there was solid agreement on class-struggle opposition to the First World War. However, there were significant differences of method and approach, which the Stalinists later fetishised into a "Leninist orthodoxy", just as they did with "imperialism", in order to justify the policies of the Stalinist state. The diminution of Marxist politics on war to "revolutionary defeatism" from the 1920s has made the assessment of subsequent wars more difficult. The myth of Lenin's "revolutionary defeatism" was comprehensively deconstructed in the early 1950s by Hal Draper, writing in the third camp Trotskyist magazine, *New International*.[12] Draper's account built on earlier critiques, notably by Trotsky, Alfred Rosmer and Max Shachtman, and can be supplemented with other materials from the archives. The sheath of defeatism around the Marxist politics on war is incoherent and unnecessary. It should be discarded.

Lenin opposed the First World War from the outset. He regarded the conflict as reactionary on both sides and therefore was opposed to both camps. In the first draft theses to his comrades in Bern, circulated in September 1914, Lenin wrote that "the European and world war has the clearly defined character of a bourgeois, imperialist and dynastic war". The real content and significance of the war was "a struggle for markets and for freedom to loot foreign countries, a striving to suppress the revolutionary movement of the proletariat and democracy in the individual countries, a desire to deceive, disunite, and slaughter the proletarians of all countries by setting the wage slaves of one nation against those of another so as to benefit the bourgeoisie". However, in a subordinate place in the draft, Lenin expressed the first formulation of "revolutionary defeatism". He wrote:

> *From the point of view of the working class and the labouring masses of all the peoples of Russia, by far the lesser evil would be the defeat of the tsar's armies and the tsar's monarchy, which oppresses Poland, the Ukraine, and a number of other peoples of Russia, and which inflames national hatred in order to increase the pressure of Great-Russia over the other nationalities and in order to strengthen the reaction of the barbarous government of the tsar's monarchy.*[13]

For the First World War, this position was confined to Russian socialists, rather than for the international left as a whole. Lenin spelt this out in a letter to Shliapnikov. He argued that "in order that the struggle may proceed along a definite and clear line, one must have a slogan that summarises it". This slogan was: "For us Russians, from the point of view of the interests of the labouring masses and the working class of Russia, there cannot be the slightest doubt, absolutely no doubt whatever, that the lesser evil would be, here and now, the defeat of tsarism in the present war". Lenin argued that tsarism was "a hundred times worse than kaiserism", although he also stated that "we do not want to help kaiserism". As Draper pointed out, the slogan of defeat began as a special Russian position on the war, with roots in the Russian exceptionalist position derived from Marx and Engels, from the time before there was an independent Russian labour movement.[14]

Shliapnikov recounted in his memoirs that the defeat slogan provoked "perplexity" within Russia. The Geneva section of the Bolshevik émigrés also expressed their objection to "defeatism". A letter to Lenin by V A Karpinskii (27 September 1914) criticised the draft paragraph, arguing that it "should be changed in order not to give rise to a misinterpretation of this passage: that the Russian social-democrats wish for the victory of the Germans and the defeat of the Russians". The Geneva Bolsheviks interpreted the passage as meaning to wish for the victory of the enemy government. But if Russian Bolsheviks saw reason to wish this, why attack the German social democrats for wishing the very same thing? Other voices expressed disquiet. Trotsky protested sharply against "Russia's defeat the lesser evil" in his pamphlet, *The War and the International* (1914). He declared that Russian socialists "must not for a moment entertain the idea of purchasing the doubtful liberation of Russia by the certain destruction of the liberty of Belgium and France, and — what is more important still — thereby inoculating the German and Austrian proletariat with the virus of imperialism".[15]

When the Bolshevik central committee published the party's position in November 1914, the "lesser evil" formulation was retained, although reflecting some of the objections raised in the previous months. The manifesto stated that it was "impossible to determine from the standpoint of the international proletariat which is the lesser evil for socialism: the defeat of one or the defeat of the other group of belligerent nations". However, for Russian social-democrats, "there cannot exist the least doubt that from the standpoint of the working class and of the labouring masses of all the peoples of Russia, the lesser evil would be the defeat of the tsarist monarchy, the most reactionary and barbarous government oppressing the greatest number of nations and the greatest mass of the populations of Europe and Asia".

Lenin re-emphasised his position with a slightly different form of words. He argued that it was "impossible for the Great-Russians to 'defend the fatherland' otherwise than by wishing defeat for tsarism in every war, this being the lesser evil for nine-tenths of the population of Great-Russia".

However, this did not settle the question among the Bolsheviks. Memoirs relate that "defeatism" raised objections in Russia and that there was a tendency to eliminate the word defeat "as a very odious one". The Moscow organisation adopted the theses of November 1914 with the exception of the paragraph on defeat.[16]

Between 27 February and 4 March 1915, the Bolsheviks convened a conference of the foreign sections of the party in Bern. The Bolshevik group from Baugy (Switzerland) presented a document with a number of criticisms of the war thesis, particularly the formulation "wish defeat", more than at the "lesser evil" formula. The objections stated:

> *The group denounces positively any advancing of the so-called slogan "the defeat of Russia"... the defeat of Russia is described as being the "lesser evil", after an objective evaluation of the other issues of the war...*
>
> *Such a consideration of the question, in the judgment of the group, is not only devoid of practical sense but also introduces into the question an undesirable confusion. If a revolutionary is obliged merely to "desire" the defeat, then there is no use in writing leading articles about it in the central organ of the political party; but if he is obliged to do more than merely "to desire", then this would be not simply an objective evaluation but the preaching of an active participation [i.e., taking of sides] in the war...*
>
> *Still more unsatisfactory... when the desirability of the defeat is explained by the revolutionary uprisings which may follow. The absolute impossibility of practical agitation in this sense compels the rejection à limite of such agitation for the defeat. We record that in the article referred to, the boundary line between the objective, fully admissible, and correct evaluation of the situation and the agitation for the defeat has not been traced at all; the group believes that it is an urgent necessity to have all confusion and obscurity in this question removed in a most decisive manner.*[17]

In the face of the Baugy group criticism, Lenin dropped the formulation that they had attacked. The resolution adopted said absolutely nothing about "wish defeat". Instead, the Bern resolution, which Lenin wrote, stated that "the struggle against the government that conducts the imperialist war must not halt in any country before the possibility of that country's defeat in consequence of revolutionary propaganda". However, "the defeat of the governmental army weakens the government, aids the liberation of the nationalities oppressed by it, and makes civil war against the ruling classes easier". As Draper pointed out, "do not halt before the risk" implies that socialists do not wish defeat itself, but that "what we wish is a continuation of the class struggle to socialist victory, and that we pursue this in spite of the fact that it may have an objective effect on the military plane".[18]

By March 1915, Lenin had produced four formulas of "defeatism" in an attempt to deal with the insoluble contradictions of the term (though without solving them). These were:

No.1: The special Russian position: defeat of Russia by Germany is the "lesser evil".

No.2: The objective statement that "defeat facilitates revolution".

No.3: The slogan: wish defeat in every country.

No.4: Do not halt before the risk of defeat.

These are four different political ideas. Only three of them are meaningful for the international movement (2, 3 and 4). Only two of them involve any wish for defeat (1 and 3). Only one took the form of a slogan.[19]

The next phase of the debate around defeatism took place in the Russian socialist press. It was conducted while the various factions of the RSDLP were seeking regroupment of anti-war socialist forces. At the beginning of 1915 there were tentative efforts made between the *Nashe Slovo* group (including Martov and Trotsky) and Lenin to collaborate on anti-war propaganda. At the Bern conference, the Bolsheviks decided to launch a new magazine, to be called *Kommunist*. Lenin invited Trotsky to become a collaborator on the magazine. However, Trotsky declined, not on grounds of any political differences, but on "organisational" grounds, around the Bolsheviks' factional methods. In the form of an open letter (June 1915), Trotsky spelt out his disagreement of defeatism:

> *Under no conditions can I agree with your opinion, which is emphasised by a resolution, that Russia's defeat would be a 'lesser evil'. This opinion represents a fundamental concession to the political methodology of social-patriotism, a concession for which there is no reason or justifi-*

cation, and which substitutes an orientation (extremely arbitrary under present conditions) along the lines of a 'lesser evil' for the revolutionary struggle against war and the conditions which generate this war.

Draper is right that Trotsky hit the nail on the head when he highlighted Lenin's "fundamental concession to the political methodology of social-patriotism" made by the "lesser evil" formulation of defeatism. The defeatist concept was simply defencism turned inside-out.[20]

Lenin's response was to dig in his heels about defeatism. He published a bitter rebuke, 'The Defeat of One's Own Government in the Imperialist War' (July 1915), which added no further clarity to the debate. He claimed that "revolutionary action against one's own government undoubtedly and incontrovertibly means not only desiring its defeat but really facilitating defeat". He added that this did not mean "blowing up bridges", organising unsuccessful military strikes or "helping the government to inflict defeat upon revolutionaries". Lenin also falsely ascribes the slogan "neither victory nor defeat" to Trotsky (and to Rosa Luxemburg), when in fact it was the Mensheviks who had actually raised as their slogan "neither victors nor vanquished". In the pamphlet *Socialism and War* (August 1915), Lenin wrote that socialists must "see the connection between the government's military reverses and the increased opportunity for overthrowing it... the socialists of all the belligerent countries should express their wish that all 'their' governments be defeated". He would continue to promote defeatism in the Bolshevik press and in private correspondence for another year.[21]

Trotsky responded emphatically. He wrote that "it never occurred to us [before the war] to link our political hopes, reformist or revolutionary, to tsarism's military misfortunes". A defeat, other things being equal, "that shatters one state structure, implies the corresponding strengthening of that of its adversary". And socialists "do not know of any social or state organisation in Europe, that it would be in the interests of the European proletariat to strengthen". Defeat "disorganises and demoralises the ruling reaction, but at the same time the war disorganises the whole of social life, especially the working class". Finally, a revolution growing out of defeats "inherits an economic life completely disordered by war, depleted public finances and very strained international relations". In short, the link between defeat and revolution "does not have a mechanical, but dialectical character". It was a "childish delusion" to conclude, "on the basis of an incorrect interpretation of the 'Russo-Japanese' experience [in

WAR AND THE MYTH OF DEFEATISM

1905], that military defeats automatically have a revolutionary impact on the masses".[22]

Trotsky continued to press his point. In a series of articles entitled 'The Programme of Peace' (1915-16) he evaluated a whole series of assessments of the war, and the necessary slogans to reconstitute an authentic left. The articles applied his permanent revolution perspective to a range of questions, including the 'United States of Europe' slogan. Trotsky showed in detail how the total consequences of the defeat of either side would be reactionary from the viewpoint of the socialist aims. He posed three possibilities for the outcome of the war: "a decisive victory of one of the belligerent sides; a general exhaustion of the opponents without a decisive preponderance of one over the other; and the intervention of the revolutionary proletariat, which interrupts the 'normal' development of military events".

Trotsky argued that "only charlatans or hopeless simpletons are capable of linking up the question of the freedom of the small peoples with the victory of one side or the other". Exactly the same result would follow if the war ended in a draw: "The termination of the war without conquerors or conquered is by itself no guarantee for anybody". Social-patriotism proposed to direct the policy of the proletariat along the lines of the "lesser evil" by joining one of the warring groups. Trotsky argued that socialists rejected this method. Instead:

The line of direction to be followed by the international proletariat and its national detachments must not be determined by secondary political and national features nor by problematical advantages of military preponderance of either side (whereby these problematical advantages must be paid for in advance with absolute renunciation of the independent policy of the proletariat), but by the fundamental antagonism existing between the international proletariat and the capitalist regime as a whole.

Draper points out why it was easy for Trotsky to reject Lenin's "lesser evil" formula. Trotsky wished neither the victory nor the defeat of either of the war camps, because he rejected the disjunction that it posed.[23]

Lenin persisted throughout 1916 to push the "defeatist" argument, shifting between formulations. He had not insisted that defeatism was a condition of the anti-war left at the early conferences of women, youth and Zimmerwald. However, for the first time, Lenin put forward the "defeat" slogan for a vote before the internationalist left in his theses presented at Kiental. In the first draft of these theses, Lenin wrote that "if we call the masses to struggle against their governments 'independently of the military situation of a given country', we thereby not only deny in principle the admissibility of 'defence of the fatherland' in the given war, but we admit the desirability of the defeat of every bourgeois government, for the transformation of the defeat into a revolution". He added that "this must be said openly: the revolutionary mass struggle cannot become an international one unless its conscious representatives unite openly in the name of defeat and overthrow of all bourgeois governments". In the RSDLP central committee's final proposals, he said it was necessary to state clearly what is merely hinted at in the Zimmerwald manifesto, that "revolutionary action during the war is impossible unless 'one's own' government is threatened with defeat". It must be stated clearly that "every defeat of the government in a reactionary war facilitates revolution, which alone is capable of bringing about a lasting and democratic peace".[24]

But the redefinition of "defeatism" to mean carrying on the class struggle in wartime, regardless of the consequences for the military situation, was a significant concession to other anti-war Marxists. Still Trotsky was not convinced. In August 1916, in an article on the factional situation in the Russian movement, Trotsky devoted a couple of paragraphs to the errors in the Bolsheviks' war line. He stated that "the paradoxical and internally contradictory formula 'the defeat of Russia is the lesser evil' creates difficulties for our German co-thinkers and does not enrich but rather hampers our agitation. It has provided the social-patriotic demagogues with a most important weapon in their struggle against our common banner".[25]

Still Lenin persisted. In his reply to Rosa Luxemburg's *Junius pamphlet* (July 1916), Lenin rhetorically posed the question whether "defeats help the cause of the revolutionary class". In another article, 'The Military Programme of the Proletarian Revolution' (September 1916), he reaffirmed that the proletariat must not only oppose all wars waged by the imperialist great powers, "but it must also wish for the defeat of 'its' government in such wars and utilise its defeat for revolutionary insurrection". But this was the last statement of the "defeatism" thesis by Lenin in its "internationalised" form. The final statement of the narrower special Russian form appeared in the article, 'On Separate Peace' (November 1916). He wrote that "it will prove that the Russian social-democrats who said that the defeat of tsarism, the complete military defeat of tsarism, is 'at any rate' a lesser evil were right". Even if the workers of Europe should prove unable to advance to socialism during the war, at least "Eastern Europe and Asia can march with seven-league strides towards democracy only if tsarism meets with utter military defeat".[26]

The demise and revival of "defeatism"

The overthrow of the tsar in February 1917 impacted on the war as well as on government. If this was the consummation of the bourgeois revolution, then the special Russian position no longer applied. It is no surprise therefore that "defeatism" plays no role during 1917. In fact Lenin explicitly abandoned defeatism in this period. In March 1918, at the special congress of soviets called to ratify the Brest-Litovsk treaty of peace with Germany, the SRs were against peace and for continuation of the war in spite of the complete exhaustion of the country. In reply to a speech by the Left SR Boris Kamkov about disrupting the army, Lenin remarked in passing: "He [Kamkov] heard that we were defeatists, and he reminded himself of this when we have ceased to be defeatists ... We were defeatists under the tsar, but under Tseretelli and Chernov [i.e., under the Kerensky regime] we were not defeatists".[27]

Draper summed up the change of assessment and the reasons for jettisoning defeatism. Lenin dropped defeatism, "in the face of the realisation, made vivid to him for the first time, that the defeat-slogan broke all links between the sentiments and interests of the masses and the programme of the consistent revolutionaries". In this sense, it was "sectarian". Second, Lenin's change of line after March 1917 reflected the fact that "the defeat slogan had a meaning only in terms of a war by the tsarist feudal despotism against a progressive capitalist revolutionary force". The February revolution "erased the rock-bottom motive which had led to the defeat-slogan in the first place — the "special Russian" consideration of tsarism as the unique menace, the greatest evil".

During the six years following the Russian revolution (1917-23), the term "defeatism" hardly appears in any of the major documents of Lenin or of the communist movement. We do not find it in the journal *Communist International*. The principal programmatic texts in this period of the Bolshevik Party, as well as of the Communist International, were all drafted by Trotsky and were all adopted without amendment. They include the resolution of the eighth Communist Party congress (1919), the manifesto of the first Comintern congress (1919), the manifesto and programme of the second Comintern congress (1920), the theses of the third Comintern congress (1921) and the report on war at the fourth Comintern congress (1922) — all without mention of "revolutionary defeatism". Instead these texts centre on "transforming imperialist war into civil war" or Liebknecht's formula, "the main enemy is in our own country".[28]

But defeatism would be revived at the beginning of the Stalinist counter-revolution, specifically by Zinoviev, the president of the Comintern, and at the time Stalin's partner in the troika who took over the helm of the Russian Communist Party when Lenin was incapacitated. Defeatism was first dubbed a "principle of Leninism" in the very first issue of the Comintern magazine, *Communist International* (February 1924) published after the death of Lenin. The author was Martynov, a long-time economist and former Menshevik who became a Stalinist hatchet man. He wanted to utilise the wartime debates to counterpose Lenin's "defeatism" to Trotsky's stance. It was followed by Zinoviev's article, 'War and Leninism', in the June 1924 edition.

In 1928, "defeatism' was canonised in the resolution on 'Programme of the Communist International' at the sixth Comintern congress, dominated by the Stalinists. It stated: "The principal slogans of the Communist International in the fight against the war danger are: turn the imperialist war into civil war, defeat of one's 'own' imperialist government, defence of the Soviet Union and of the colonies, should imperialist war be made on them, with every possible means." Communists were henceforth required to seek the defeat of their own government in any foreign policy situation in which the USSR was on the opposing side.[29]

Trotsky's later views

The expulsion of Trotsky's supporters from the Comintern after 1928 meant that "revolutionary defeatism" became a formula for debate among the opponents of war and Stalinism. In 1934 Trotsky attempted to clarify his stance in a text, 'War and the Fourth International'. Historian Jean-Paul Joubert has clarified the debate around these theses. At the outset, Trotsky saw no necessity for using the term "revolutionary defeatism" in the document, despite its length and programmatic purpose for the Fourth International. The first draft of paragraph discussing "defeatism" (found in the Trotsky Archives at Harvard) stated:

> *Defeatism is not a mere practical slogan, around which we can mobilise the masses during the war. The defeat of one's own national army can be an aim only in a single case, that is when we have a capitalist army fighting against a workers' state or marching against a developing revolution. But in the case of a war between two capitalist powers, the proletariat of neither of them can set itself the defeat of its own national army as a task.*

WAR AND THE MYTH OF DEFEATISM

The leader of the German section of the Fourth International, Eugene Bauer (Erwin Ackerknecht), with the support of Alfonso Leonetti, criticised Trotsky for distancing himself too far from "revolutionary defeatism" in the name of the "defence of the Soviet Union", which they still saw as a degenerated form of workers' state. They proposed an amendment. There is also a letter from Trotsky to the International Secretariat (5 January 1934) which states:

> *I cannot accept the amendment on defeatism a) because it says that we must desire the defeat, without saying whether we must do anything and, if so, precisely what, in order to bring it about. The Social-Democrats in exile are full of zeal for someone to fight Hitler and to relieve them of the necessity of doing anything; b) because the defeatist formula of Lenin in 1914-1916 had nothing yet to do with war between capitalist states and a workers' state, and did not draw any of the theoretical consequences which flow from that. Under Kerensky, Lenin was already declaring: "We are no longer defeatists". But since the distinctions which I drew in the first sentence of para 51 disturb you, I strike them out completely, and we may perhaps succeed later in agreeing on the precise statements which we need.*

Trotsky stepped back in order to avoid pointless conflict. He agreed to use the term of "defeatism", while defining it more benignly and warning his comrades against using it carelessly. The revised text read:

> *Lenin's formula, "defeat is the lesser evil", means not defeat of one's country is the lesser evil compared with the defeat of the enemy country but that a military defeat resulting from the growth of the revolutionary movement is infinitely more beneficial to the proletariat and to the whole people than military victory assured by "civil peace". Karl Liebknecht gave an unsurpassed formula of proletarian policy in time of war. "The chief enemy of the people is in its own country" ... The transformation of imperialist war into civil war is that general strategic task to which the whole work of a proletarian party during war should be subordinated.*

Trotsky, under the pressure of the Stalinist campaign against his Bolshevik credentials, wanted to remain "orthodox" without committing to something that he did not believe. Of Lenin's four formulas, he sometimes paraphrases the one which is furthest away from "wishing defeat", namely, do not stop before the risk of defeat. But mostly he developed this ingenious formula of his own, which had the advantage of sounding like the "lesser evil" formulation, but had a different content.[30]

Trotsky stuck with this interpretation of "defeatism" throughout the 1930s, during debates over Spain, the transitional programme and with his Palestinian supporters. He argued that revolutionary defeatism signified only that "in its class struggle the proletarian party does not stop at any 'patriotic' considerations, since defeat of its own imperialist government, brought about, or hastened, by the revolutionary movement of the masses, is an incomparably lesser evil than victory gained at the price of national unity, that is, the political prostration of the proletariat". Another formulation defined defeatism as "conducting an irreconcilable revolutionary struggle against one's own bourgeoisie as the main enemy, without being deterred by the fact that this struggle may result in the defeat of one's own government: given a revolutionary movement, the defeat of one's own government is a lesser evil".[31]

Trotsky did not use the term "revolutionary defeatism" in his *Manifesto* for the emergency conference of the Fourth International in May 1940. In his last unfinished book, *Stalin*, he continued to define Lenin's theory of defeatism as "in every country the struggle with one's own government, which wages the imperialist war, must not stop short before the possibility of the defeat of that country in consequence of revolutionary agitation". Nothing was said about wishing for defeat, trying to facilitate defeat, or linking the fate of the working class to the military outcome of an imperialist war.[32]

By this time, the most rational voices in the Trotskyist movement had abandoned the formula of "revolutionary defeatism. Alfred Rosmer, who took part in the internationalist struggles from the First World War through the Comintern to the Fourth International, wrote in his *Le Mouvement ouvrier pendant la guerre mondiale* (1936): "'Defeatism', even followed by the adjective 'revolutionary', puts the emphasis on defeat, whereas we should put it on revolution". Trotsky admired Rosmer's book very much, and in his review of it, went so far as to declare that "the rule should be established: nobody in our ranks who has not studied Rosmer's work ought to be allowed to speak publicly on the question of war".[33]

A year after Trotsky's death, Max Shachtman recommended that "so much confusion has been introduced in the concept of defeatism that I doubt if we would be losing too much if we dropped the word out of our vocabulary". After his own exhaustive investigation, Draper came to the same conclusion and called on Marxists to bury the dead. Lenin's defeatism "was born in a political mistake in 1904-

05; it was revived in confusion in 1914, to be shelved without stocktaking in 1917; it was revived again in malice and reaction in 1924; it was turned into a hollow phrase by 'explaining away' in the thirties; it was ignored in the forties; and now in the fifties any war policy based on it can only be disorienting or worse". Draper concluded that 'defeatism could "only stand in the way of a clear, 'full', uncompromising Marxist anti-war position, the position of the third camp".[34]

Conclusion

From the First World War to the cusp of the Second World War, Trotsky articulated the most coherent methodology for assessing each war on its merits from a Marxist perspective and then drawing political conclusions from that analysis. The rudiments of that approach were expressed in countless texts, including those written towards the end of his life. The elementary rules of proletarian strategy towards war, shared by Lenin, Trotsky, and other revolutionary socialists, were derived from the famous German military theoretician, Clausewitz. His proposition that war is the continuation of politics by other means led "naturally to the conclusion that the struggle against war is but the continuation of the general proletarian struggle during peace-time".

Working-class policy on war was not "automatically derived from the policy of the bourgeoisie, bearing only the opposite sign — this would make every sectarian a master strategist". In "ninety cases out of a hundred the workers actually place a minus sign where the bourgeoisie places a plus sign". But in ten cases "they are forced to fix the same sign as the bourgeoisie but with their own seal, in which is expressed their mistrust of the bourgeoisie". Rather than a "hermetically sealed formula", revolutionary socialists "must each time orient itself independently in the internal as well as the external situation, arriving at those decisions which correspond best to the interests of the proletariat". To carry the class struggle to its highest form — civil war — this is the task of revolutionary workers. To carry on the class struggle without stopping at any "patriotic" considerations, that is the central task in wartime.[35]

Trotsky summarised the method of assessment succinctly. He wrote: "The objective historical meaning of the war is of decisive importance for the proletariat: What class is conducting it and for the sake of what? This is decisive, and not the subterfuges of diplomacy by means of which the enemy can always be successfully portrayed to the people as an aggressor." Because war is waged "by both imperialist camps not for the defence of the fatherland or democracy but for the redivision of the world and colonial enslavement, a socialist has no right to prefer one bandit camp to another".[36] The line of march is determined by the class character of the combatants, their aims, and the political consequences of the war, not from secondary military considerations. That is the principal lesson from the debates a century ago.

References

1. Lenin, [July-August 1915] *Socialism and War*, (*LCW* 21: 304).
2. Georges Haupt, *Socialism and the Great War*, (1972: 132, 62, 82, 211, 233).
3. Craig Nation, *War on War*, (2009: 46, 33).
4. John Riddell, *Lenin's Struggle for a Revolutionary International*, (1986: 276-83); Nation, (1989: 68-71).
5. Riddell, (1986: 276-322, 510-39); Nation, (2009: 85-95, 136-43).
6. Engels [13-14 September 1886] 'Letter to Bebel', (*MECW* 47: 486-487); Engels [25 October 1886] 'The Political Situation in Europe'. (*MECW* 26: 415); Engels [April-May 1890] 'Foreign Policy of Russian Tsardom'. (*MECW* 27: 46).
7. Olga Gankin and Harold Fisher, *The Bolsheviks and the World War*, (1940: 57-59; 72-73; 81-85); Riddell, (1986: 33-35; 69-70; 88-90).
8. Richard Day and Daniel Gaido, *Discovering Imperialism*, (2012: 19 N.61; 644, 673).
9. Martin Thomas, 'Marxism and imperialism', *Workers' Liberty* 1/28, (1996).
10. Alexander Anievas, 'Marxist Theory and the Origins of the First World War'. In Alexander Anievas, *Cataclysm 1914: The First World War and the Making of Modern World Politics*, (2015: 106, 108-09).
11. Anievas, (2015: 113-16, 124, 134-36).
12. Draper's study was first published in *New International*, theoretical journal of the US Independent Socialist League, as a 3-part series in September-October 1953, November-December 1953 and January-February 1954. An edited version, *War and Revolution: Lenin and the Myth of Revolutionary Defeatism* (1996). Substantial extracts were published in *Workers' Liberty* magazine, 2/1, September 2001 and 2/2, March 2002. See also Brian Pearce, 'Lenin and Trotsky on Pacifism and Defeatism', *Labour Review*, 6, 1, (1961: 29-38).
13. Lenin, [24 August 1914] 'The Tasks of Revolutionary Social-Democracy in the European War', (*LCW* 21: 15-16, 18).
14. Lenin, [17 October 1914] 'Letter to Shlyapnikov', (*LCW* 35: 162); Draper, (1996: 54).
15. Gankin and Fisher, (1940: 148); Draper, (1996: 57); Trotsky, [October 1914] 'The War and the International'. In Pete Dickenson, *Trotsky on World War One*, (2015: 12).
16. Lenin, [1 November 1914] 'The War and Russian Social-Democracy', (*LCW* 21: 32); Lenin, [December 1914] 'On the National Pride of the Great Russians', (*LCW* 21: 104); Gankin and Fisher, (1940: 151).
17. Baugy group, [February 1915] 'On the Tasks of the Party', Gankin and Fisher, (1940: 189-91).
18. Lenin, [29 March 1915] 'Conference of the Foreign Sections of the RSDLP', (*LCW* 21: 163).
19. Draper, (1996: 64-65).
20. Gankin and Fisher (1940: 170); Draper, (1996: 67-68).
21. Lenin, [26 July 1915] 'The Defeat of One's Own Government in the Imperialist War', (*LCW* 21, 275-280); Lenin, [August 1915] Socialism and War, (*LCW* 21: 315); Lenin, [23 August 1915] 'Letter to Shlyapnikov', (*LCW* 35: 204);
22. Trotsky, [September 1915] 'The Military Disaster and Political Perspectives'. In Dickenson, (2015: 106-07, 109-10).
23. Trotsky, [1915-16] 'The Programme of Peace', *Fourth International*, 48, September, (1944: 281, 285); Draper, (1996: 92-93).
24. Lenin, [February-March 1916] 'Initial variant of the RSDLP Central Committee Proposal', (*LCW* 41: 375); Lenin, [February-March 1916] 'Proposals Submitted by the Central Committee of the RSDLP to the Second Socialist Conference', (*LCW* 22: 177).
25. Trotsky, [August 1916] 'Groupings in Russian Social-Democracy', Riddell, (1986: 405); Draper, (1996: 93-94).
26. Lenin, [July 1916] 'The Junius Pamphlet', (*LCW* 22: 319); Lenin, [September 1916] 'The Military Programme of the Proletarian Revolution', (*LCW* 23: 85); Lenin, [6 November 1916] 'On Separate Peace', (*LCW* 23: 132-33); Pearce (1961).

27. Lenin, [March 1918] 'Concluding Speech on the Report on the Ratification of the Peace Agreement of March 15, at the 4th Extraordinary All-Russian Congress of Soviets', (*LCW* 27: 193).
28. Draper, (1996: 96-97, 108-109, 111); Jean-Paul Joubert, 'Revolutionary Defeatism', *Revolutionary History*, 1, 3, autumn, (1988).
29. Draper, (1996: 114-116); Jane Degras, *The Communist International 1919-1943*, Volume 2, (1960: 525).
30. Trotsky, [10 June 1934] 'War and the Fourth International', *Writings of Leon Trotsky, 1933-1934*, (1975: 320); Joubert (1988); Draper, (1996: 119-120).
31. Trotsky, [14 September 1937] 'Answers to Questions on the Spanish Situation', *The Spanish Revolution, 1931-39*, (1973: 282-5, 289); Trotsky, [April 1938] 'The Death Agony of Capitalism and the Tasks of the Fourth International', *The Transitional Programme for Socialist Revolution*, (1974: 91); Trotsky, [22 May 1938] 'Learn To Think', *Writings of Leon Trotsky 1937-38*, (1976: 333-34); Trotsky, [1939] 'A Step Towards Social Patriotism', *Writings of Leon Trotsky, 1938-39*, (1974: 209).
32. Trotsky, [May 1940] 'Manifesto of the Fourth International on the Imperialist War and the Proletarian World Revolution', *Writings of Leon Trotsky, 1939-40*, (1973: 183-222); Trotsky, [1940] Stalin, (2016: 212); Draper, (1996: 122-23).
33. Alfred Rosmer [1936] 'Conclusion'. In From Syndicalism to Trotskyism: Writings of Alfred and Marguerite Rosmer, *Revolutionary History*, 7, 4, Winter, (2000-2001: 56); Trotsky, [21 March 1936] 'Alfred Rosmer's Book', *Writings of Leon Trotsky, 1935-36*, (1974: 284).
34. Max Shachtman, [1 September 1941] 'A Letter to a Comrade: On Some Aspects of the Russian Question', *Labor Action*, 5, 35, (1941: 2); Draper, (1996: 127, 129).
35. Trotsky, [22 May 1938] 'Learn to Think', *Writings of Leon Trotsky, 1937-38*, (1976: 332-34).
36. Trotsky, [30 December 1938] 'Lenin and Imperialist War', *Writings of Leon Trotsky, 1938-39*, (1974: 166).

Gustav Klutsis, Design for a Loud Speaker No.2, 1922

7. Consistent democracy and the national question

The 1917 revolution proved in practice the essential connection between socialism and democracy. If democracy really meant majority self-rule, then the seizure of power by the working class and the poor peasantry in 1917 consummated the most democratic revolution in human history. That is why the workers' state established in October 1917 immediately passed legislation implementing the most widespread freedoms into every area of working and social life hitherto seen. If democracy meant workers' representatives accountable to their working class base, then the models of the RSDLP and the workers' government in 1917, where leaders were paid the average wage of a skilled worker and recallable by democratic conferences, exemplified how to organise for socialism.

Democracy is irreplaceable within the workers' movement. It is essential to the functioning of a workers' state. It is indispensable as an economic mechanism for planning. Lenin argued that "just as socialism cannot be victorious unless it introduces complete democracy, so the proletariat will be unable to prepare for victory over the bourgeoisie unless it wages a many-sided, consistent and revolutionary struggle for democracy".[1]

Perhaps the best metaphor used in the Marxist tradition, summing up the importance of democracy for the working class movement, is the comparison of "light and air" to human life. Without light and air, there is no life on earth: without democracy, there is no mass working-class movement and hence no prospect for socialism. Lenin argued that "without political liberty all forms of workers' representation will remain a miserable fraud, and the proletariat will remain in prison as hitherto, without light, without air, and without the elbow-room it needs for the struggle to attain its complete emancipation".[2] One of the heinous crimes of Stalinism was to sever the bond between liberty and socialism.

For Lenin, the national question was one aspect — albeit a very important one in Russian conditions — of this wider policy of consistent democracy. Cold War historian Richard Pipes argued that Lenin's politics on the national question, particularly his slogan of "the right of nations to self-determination", was nothing but bait to lure non-Russian peoples, "a tactical device intended to win over the minorities".³ This cynical interpretation of Lenin on the national question is nonsense. Lenin was influenced by the actual oppression in tsarist Russia. As with so much else, he inherited much from the earlier Marxist tradition, particularly Marx, Engels and Kautsky — and he substantially developed that tradition. Lenin was animated by the vigorous debates within the international socialist movement, notably with the Bund inside Russia, Rosa Luxemburg and the Austrian socialists. These discussions covered socialist principles alongside strategy and tactics. They are relevant today because the national question remains a live issue across the globe. Applying analysis and providing answers to all forms of national oppression is still vital to renewing the working-class movement.

Lenin on consistent democracy

Lenin's conception of consistent democracy was one of his greatest bequests to future generations of socialists, although it has been buried for decades under the morass of Stalinism. He described Marx and Engels as "the greatest representatives of consistent nineteenth century democracy, who became the teachers of the revolutionary proletariat". Where bourgeois and petty bourgeois forces are wavering, inconsistent and half-hearted democrats, the working class movement and especially the revolutionary socialists within it, should be the most committed, consistent and wholehearted democrats. Democratic demands are essential to the Marxist programme, but each democratic demand is not an absolute. The struggle for democratic demands is subordinate to the working class revolutionary struggle to overthrow of the bourgeoisie.⁴

Consistent democracy was the expression Lenin frequently used as a shorthand for demands he thought Russian Marxists should raise to rally the working class and wider layers of the population around the struggle against the tsarist state. He used the term in many of his major programmatic statements, such as at the second party congress in 1903, the unity congress in 1906, the fifth party congress in 1907, the election campaign in 1912 and the Poronin RSDLP conference in 1913. He used consistent democracy as a polemical weapon against rival organisations — who were not consistent democrats — such as bourgeois parties like the Kadets and petty bourgeois parties like the Trudoviks.

Lenin argued that "the class nature of our political programme and political demands is expressed precisely in the fact that they stand for complete and consistent democracy". During the 1905 revolution, he argued that "the working class is free of the cowardice, the hypocritical half-heartedness that is characteristic of the bourgeoisie as a class. The working class can and must be fully and consistently democratic". Lenin urged RSDLP members to "come forward before the whole of the people with the advanced democratic slogans. For us, for the proletariat, the democratic revolution is only the first step on the road to the complete emancipation of labour from all exploitation, to the great socialist goal".

These slogans included the demand for a Constituent Assembly, the eight-hour day and national freedom. He continued to argue that it was the duty of class-conscious workers "to explain the tasks of consistent democracy: a republic, the eight-hour day and the confiscation of all landed estates". Consistent democracy was also a means of distinguishing what he called the "third camp" of socialists from the monarchists and the liberals during election campaigning.[5]

Lenin on the national question

Marx and Engels wrote a great deal on concrete national questions during their decades of activity, while the Second International developed a solid body of empirical and theoretical literature on the subject. The cosmopolitanism of Marx and Engels is well summed up by the rallying cries of the *Communist Manifesto*: "Workers have no country" and "Workers of the world, unite". In championing the cause of Polish independence, Engels expressed the aphorism that "a nation cannot be free and at the same time continue to oppress other nations". In the 1850s they supported Indian freedom from the British empire, looking forward to the time when "the Hindoos themselves shall have grown strong enough to throw off the English yoke altogether". The First International resolved that workers should support "the right of every people to dispose of itself". The slogans sum up democratic working class internationalism, which flows from the global scope of capitalism and the primacy of class over nationality. The logic of the position was this: once the working class of a nation oppressed by another has thrown off the yoke of oppression, it is free to fight the class struggle.[6]

The Second International also debated the national questions of its time, expanding and in some cases correcting Marx and Engels (such as over the false dividing of peoples into "historic" and "non-historic").[7] Kautsky also pioneered the conception of consistent democracy on the national question and predicted at the turn of the century that the Slavs were "destined to be the tempest that will break the ice of reaction and irresistibly bring a new, blessed springtime for the peoples".⁸ The Second International congress in London (21 July-1 August 1896) declared that it stood for "the full right of all nations to self-determination", a pledge repeated at the Copenhagen congress (28 August-3 September 1910).⁹

It was the national question where Lenin's conception of consistent democracy proved most advanced. The tsarist empire was a vast "prison-house of nations", a multinational state in which Russians comprised less than half the population. Because national oppression was acute, Lenin believed national revolts would contribute to the democratic drive to overthrow the tsar. The task was to ensure the working class had a democratic programme to rally the array of nationalities across Russia. Lenin believed the national question was vital throughout his political life, but his position underwent development. In his first draft programme of Russian social democracy (1895-96), he added the explicit demand for "equality for all nationalities" that had not been spelt out in previous Russian Marxist programmes.

In his more mature writing on the national question, Lenin followed Kautsky closely. He argued that "the national state is the rule and the 'norm' of capitalism; the multi-national state represents backwardness, or is an exception". From the standpoint of national relations, "the best conditions for the development of capitalism are undoubtedly provided by the national state". This did not mean that such a state, based on bourgeois relations, could eliminate the exploitation and oppression of nations. Rather, "self-determination of nations" in the Marxists' programme meant simply "political self-determination, state independence, and the formation of a national state". At the same time Lenin defined tersely what consistent democracy really meant on the national question: "We fight against the privileges and violence of the oppressor nation, and *do not in any way condone strivings for privileges on the part of the oppressed nation*" (emphasis added).¹⁰

1903 and the debate with the Bund

In the lead up to the second congress of the RSDLP, Lenin clarified his understanding of the national question, particularly its place in the programme of the party and in relation to class considerations. Point 7 of his draft programme, worked out with Plekhanov, called for the "recognition of the right to self-determination for all nations forming part of the state". Lenin wrote a comprehensive article for *Iskra*, 'The National Question in Our Programme' (July 1903), just before the second congress, setting out his position. Social-democrats should "always combat every attempt to influence national self-determination from without by violence or by any injustice". However, "our unreserved recognition of the struggle for freedom of self-determination does not in any way commit us to supporting every demand for national self-determination". The "positive and principal task" was "to further the self-determination of the proletariat in each nationality rather than that of peoples or nations". Socialists "always and unreservedly work for the very closest unity of the proletariat of all nationalities, and it is only in isolated and exceptional cases that we can advance and actively support demands conducive to the establishment of a new class state or to the substitution of a looser federal unity, etc., for the complete political unity of a state".

Therefore recognition of the right of nations to self-determination did not mean socialists were "duty bound to demand national independence always and unreservedly". It depended on the circumstances — the most important being the interests of workers' struggles. Russian social-democrats fight "against all manifestations of national oppression in Russia; they include in their programme not only complete equality of status for all languages, nationalities, etc., but also recognition of every nation's right to determine its own destiny". Recognising this right, "we subordinate to the interests of the proletarian struggle our support of the demand for national independence". This stance, originally developed for Poland, was "wholly applicable to every other national question".[11]

At the second congress, there was some debate within the *Iskra* faction and with the delegates from the Bund over the national question. Lenin argued that "the question of our attitude to the nationalities in particular is a tactical question and constitutes an application of our general principles to practical activity". The commission dealing with the party programme decided that Article 3 should call for "extensive local and regional self-government". This was important in terms of democracy for dispersed nationalities within the Russian empire.

Lenin opposed the word "regional", as it was vague and might be interpreted to mean that the social-democrats wanted to split the whole state up into small regions. Martov moved an amendment to the resolution, proposing that Article 3 should read: "Extensive local self-government; regional self-government for those border districts which in respect of conditions of life and make-up of population differ from the strictly-Russian localities". Trotsky opposed Martov's amendment as "superfluous" as it was already covered by later points on the national question, while Martynov considered that "the word 'self-determination' could not be given a wide interpretation: it meant merely the right for a nation to secede and form a separate political entity, and not at all regional self-government". Martov's amendment passed and so became part of the party programme — and something Lenin and Trotsky accepted in subsequent years.

The congress discussed Article 8 of the programme, as edited by the commission, which read: "The right of self-determination for all nations included within the bounds of the state". This was backed by *Iskra* supporters, while Bundists sought to amend it to account for the situation of Jewish workers within Russia. Vladimir Medem wanted to add support for "the establishment of institutions ensuring their full freedom of cultural development". Another Bundist Mark Liber argued that the party "should guarantee to every nationality the right to cultural development within the bounds of the state". However, the Bundist amendment was heavily defeated.[12]

Lenin's conception of the national question was underdeveloped in 1903. The idea of "self-determination of the working class" was incoherent for tackling national oppression. The understanding of self-determination as principally about political democracy was at least embryonic. However, there were few answers for oppressed nations within multinational states that did not qualify for independence. One spur to Lenin's thinking on the different forms of consistent democracy was the Balkan question. Apart from the historic oppression by Austrian and Turkish imperialism, the region also included mixed populations, with some peoples not resident in compact or contiguous territories. In these circumstances, Balkan socialists, backed by the international social democrats, advocated a federation. Lenin's consistent democratic outlook accepted this view. He wrote that "the class-conscious workers of the Balkan countries are the first to put forward the slogan of a consistently democratic solution of the national problem in the Balkans. That slogan calls for a Balkan federal republic". In Western Europe, "the proletariat there is still more vigorously proclaiming the slogan: No intervention! The Balkans for the Balkan peoples!"[13]

Lenin's mature thought

Lenin's mature position on the national question was articulated in great depth in 1913. In a series of newspaper articles, speeches, theses, pamphlets, programmes and parliamentary bills, he propagated a coherent answer to the national question not only in Russia and the rest of Europe, but for the wider world as well. Lenin's original reason for foregrounding the national question was "the orgy of Black-Hundred nationalism, the growth of nationalist tendencies among the liberal bourgeoisie and the growth of nationalist tendencies among the upper classes of the oppressed nationalities" in Russia. However, he was also influenced by the growing threat of imperialist rivalry leading to war, and the need for the international labour movement to find allies not only in Europe among the oppressed nations but also among the millions straining under the colonial yoke. Finally, Lenin was obliged to react by the apparent growing influence of ideas around "cultural-national autonomy" among Russian social democrats. Lenin's best summary of consistent democracy on the national question was given in a resolution at the Poronin party conference in September-October 1913. The key paragraphs stated:

> *1. Insofar as national peace is in any way possible in a capitalist society based on exploitation, profit-making and strife, it is attainable only under a consistently and thoroughly democratic republican system of government which guarantees full equality of all nations and languages, which recognises no compulsory official language, which provides the people with schools where instruction is given in all the native languages, and the constitution of which contains a fundamental law that prohibits any privileges whatsoever to any one nation and any encroachment whatsoever upon the rights of a national minority. This particularly calls for wide regional autonomy and fully democratic local self-government, with the boundaries of the self-governing and autonomous regions determined by the local inhabitants themselves on the basis of their economic and social conditions, national make-up of the population, etc...*
>
> *4. As regards the right of the nations oppressed by the tsarist monarchy to self-determination, i.e., the right to secede and form independent states, the social-democratic party must unquestionably champion this right. This is dictated by the fundamental principles of international democracy in general, and specifically by the unprecedented national oppression of the majority of the inhabitants of Russia by the tsarist monarchy, which is a most reactionary and barbarous state compared with its neighbouring states in Europe and Asia.*
>
> *5. The right of nations to self-determination (i.e., the constitutional guarantee of an absolutely free and democratic method of deciding the question of secession) must under no circumstances be confused with the expediency of a given nation's secession. The social-democratic party must decide the latter question exclusively on its merits in each particular case in conformity with the interests of social development as a whole and with the interests of the proletarian class struggle for socialism.*[14]

These formulations encompass all forms of national oppression, whether taking place within the boundaries of existing states or involving the separation of an oppressed group of people on a given territory to form a new state. The class criteria of workers' unity takes precedence, but this unity is brought about by the recognition of national oppression and the remedy of self-government. In Lenin's formulation nations do not qualify for rights based on an objective list of attributes. Rather, nationality has a self-defining, *subjective* aspect to it. As Lenin put it to a comrade, "Why will you not understand the psychology that is so important in the national question and which, if the slightest coercion is applied, besmirches, soils, nullifies the undoubtedly progressive importance of centralisation, large states and a uniform language?"[15]

Lenin once again summed up consistent democracy on the national question in more pithy terms. He stated that it meant: "No privileges for any nation or any one language. Not even the slightest degree of oppression or the slightest injustice in respect of a national minority — such are the principles of working class democracy". The following month he said: "The unity of the workers of all nationalities coupled with the fullest equality for the nationalities and the most consistently democratic state system — that is our slogan, and it is the slogan of international revolutionary social-democracy".[16]

Lenin elaborated further on the rationale behind the demand for national self-determination. He explained that the right of nations to self-determination was the "one special demand" on the national question. It meant the right of political secession from the oppressing state to form a separate, independent state. This was a decision to be taken by the parliament or a referendum of the seceding minority, such as when Norway seceded from Sweden in 1905. The right to self-determination is a universal right, applicable to all nations. It is a misnomer to suggest it only applied to oppressed nations, to muddle the "right" with whether to advocate independence (which would generally apply in the case of oppression). Lenin's analogy was with divorce.

Socialists and consistent democrats support the right to divorce. However, we do not advocate divorce as the answer to every troubled relationship. Recognition of the right to self-determination "does not exclude either propaganda and agitation against separation or the exposure of bourgeois nationalism". But "the denial of the right to secede is 'playing into the hands' of the most thorough-paced reactionary Great-Russian nationalism".[17]

And consistent democracy was not simply about the right to secede. The national programme of working-class democracy is: "absolutely no privileges for any one nation or any one language". This meant the promulgation of a law for the whole state making any measure introducing "any privilege of any kind for one of the nations and militating against the equality of nations or the rights of a national minority" illegal and unconstitutional. Lenin drafted a Bill on the equality of nations and the safeguarding of the rights of national minorities for the Duma, promoting wide regional and local self-government.[18]

The national question after 1917

One of the first acts of the new workers' government after the October revolution was the *Declaration of the Rights of Peoples of Russia*, (2 November 1917). It stated:

> *The Council of People's Commissars has resolved to base its approach on the following principles concerning the question of nationalities:*
> *1. Equality and sovereignty of the Russian peoples;*
> *2. The right of the Russian peoples to self-determination, as far as separation and the constitution of an independent state;*
> *3. Suppression of all privileges and restrictions, national or religious;*
> *4. Free development of national minorities and ethnic groups living on Russian territory.*

The new government signalled its intention to implement consistent democracy on the national question by recognising Finland's independence in January 1918. It established the People's Commissariat of National Affairs, known as Narkomnats. Between 1917 and 1923 the workers' state recognised some 17 autonomous regions and republics within the Russian federation and five independent republics outside it. Even in the context of civil war, the regime took steps to massively expand education and to make provision for the education of national minorities in their own indigenous languages. By 1924, some 25 different languages were published in the USSR and by 1927 this had almost doubled. For all its problems, the early Russian workers' state deserved the epithet of an "affirmative action" regime.[19]

Why did the term "consistent democracy" fade?

There is no evidence that Lenin abandoned the method of approach to the national question he had developed by 1913 and which he defended resolutely during the First World War. However, he did cease to use the terms "consistent democracy" as well as "the right of nations to self-determination" during the war and in the first year of the revolutionary regime. This requires some explanation.

In the first place, he was challenged by left Bolsheviks such as Bukharin as well as supporters of Rosa Luxemburg, who were vociferous in their rejection of the term "self-determination". This pressure from the left escalated during the war and was evident in discussions about the revised Bolshevik programme in 1919. However, these "lefts" were not in principle opposed to the idea of oppressed peoples seceding from multinational empires and from colonies under imperialism. Therefore, while Lenin wanted to work with the "lefts", he did not make a fetish of the terms, as long as the substance was accepted. As he put it, "we do not want to haggle over words. If there is a party that says in its programme… that it is against annexations, against the forcible retention of oppressed nations within the frontiers of its state, we declare our complete agreement in principle with that party. It would be absurd to insist on the word 'self-determination'". And as he put it to fellow communists in 1920, "the solution of all colonial and national questions [is] to proceed not from abstract postulates but from concrete realities".

In addition, in the aftermath of the October revolution, much of the vocabulary of "democracy" was used by right-wing social democrats opposed to the revolution and the freedoms that it had brought as a stick with which to beat the Bolshevik-led government. Mensheviks and other centrists beat their chests and grasped at terms such as "equality", "universal suffrage", "democracy", "pure democracy", and "consistent democracy" to attack Bolshevik rule. As Lenin put it: "Filled with petty-bourgeois prejudices, forgetting the most important thing in the teachings of Marx about the state, the 'socialists' of the Second International regard state power as something holy, as an idol, or as the result of formal voting, the absolute of "consistent democracy" (or whatever else they call this nonsense)". In this context, it is no surprise that Lenin stopped using their vocabulary.[20] But he retained the substance of the consistent democracy approach to the end of his life, both within the USSR and for the wider international communist movement.

Lenin's critique of Luxemburg
The principal challenger to Lenin's approach to the national question on the left came from Rosa Luxemburg and other Marxists who followed her. Luxemburg opposed the demand for the right of nations

to self-determination. Her position was summed up in a series of articles entitled 'The National Question and Autonomy' (1908-09). Luxemburg argued that the formula was "an empty, noncommittal phrase", like the "right" to eat off gold plates. During the First World War she cursed the right of nations to self-determination as "nothing but hollow, petty-bourgeois phraseology and humbug".[21] Luxemburg's position was widely adopted across the anti-war Marxist left, including by Bolsheviks such as Radek, Bukharin and Piatakov.

Lenin answered Luxemburg's rejection of self-determination in a series of articles in 1914-16. He argued that Luxemburg had "substituted the question of economic independence of states for the question of the political self-determination of nations in bourgeois society, and of their independence as states". Lenin stated that "the focal point in the social-democratic programme must be that division of nations into oppressor and oppressed which forms the essence of imperialism". It was from this division that "our definition of the 'right of nations to self-determination' must follow, a definition that is consistently democratic, revolutionary, and in accord with the general task of the immediate struggle for socialism". It meant social democrats in the oppressor nations "must demand that the oppressed nations should have the right of secession", while social democrats of the oppressed nations "must attach prime significance to the unity and the merging of the workers of the oppressed nations with those of the oppressor nations". Without it, the metropolitan socialists would merely be empty phrase mongering, while in the oppressed nations they would become the allies of their own national bourgeoisie.

An important part of Lenin's argument was that politics does not mechanically follow economics. Even if the economic trend is towards big integrated empires and extinction of small states, towards heavily-bureaucratised state machines, etc., there are also "other" trends, including national revolts of small nations and the spread of democratic struggles in general. Hence it is wrong to deduce the "impossibility" of self-determination from the economic trends. Lenin said the views of the opponents of self-determination led to "the conclusion that the vitality of small nations oppressed by imperialism has already been sapped, that they cannot play any role against imperialism, that support of their purely national aspirations will lead to nothing". Small nations may be powerless as an independent factor in the struggle against imperialism, but "play a part as one of the ferments, one of the bacilli, which help the real anti-imperialist force, the socialist proletariat, to make its appearance on the scene".

Lenin also explained that working class socialists don't automatically offer uncritical blanket support for every force opposing the big powers: our stance also depends on the positive class content of those clashes. He argued that "it is not every struggle against imperialism that we should support". Socialists "will not support a struggle of the reactionary classes against imperialism; we will not support an uprising of the reactionary classes against imperialism and capitalism". Lenin stated that "a 'negative' slogan unconnected with a definite positive solution will not 'sharpen', but dull consciousness, for such a slogan is a hollow phrase, mere shouting, meaningless declamation". Therefore "consistent, i.e., socialist, democrats proclaim, formulate and will implement this right [to form a national state], without which there is no path to complete, voluntary rapprochement and merging of nations".[22]

Lenin's critique of cultural national autonomy

A century ago the Austrian-Hungarian empire stretched out across Europe, a multinational empire of 53 million people and 15 different nationalities. In September 1899 the Social Democratic Workers' Party of Austria (SDAPÖ) started a debate on the national question at its congress in Brünn (now Brno in the Czech Republic).[23] Karl Renner and, later, Otto Bauer propagated "cultural-national autonomy" as their answer to the national question in Austria-Hungary, rejecting the territorialist solution based on the right of nations to self-determination. Bauer explained that cultural-national autonomy meant "the national minorities within each self-governing territory are to be constituted as corporations under public law, which, with complete autonomy, provide for the education system of the national minority and which grant legal assistance to the members of their people in their dealings with the authorities and the courts".[24]

Lenin had previously criticised the Bund for supporting an Austro-Marxist culturalist conception, but was more animated by Menshevik support for cultural-national autonomy at the Vienna conference in August 1912. The root of the problem for Lenin was the elevation of "national culture", which made concessions to the nationalist perspective, whereas the working-class movement needed a democratic and internationalist culture. Lenin highlighted the way in which cultural-national autonomy would institute permanently segregated nationalities, while at the same time downgrading the consistently democratic task of transforming existing multinational states such as Austria and Russia.

Lenin was particularly scathing about the proposal to segregate schools along national lines, which would entrench divisions between peoples (just as religious schools did), rather than work towards workers' unity.

Instead, Lenin argued for the provision of different languages within mixed schools. Although much heat was generated by the debate, Renner's and Bauer's scheme of personal autonomy never became part of the official social democratic programme. Nor was it ever implemented in practice — although Renner ordered a study of it when he because president of Austria after the war. In reality cultural-national autonomy was an artificial and ultimately doomed attempt to maintain the integrity of an unviable empire. Neither the working class movement nor the oppressed nations held within its boundaries wanted to cling to this framework when the empire broke up after the war.[25]

Trotsky's defence of consistent democracy

Trotsky adopted the social democratic orthodoxy on the national question and was therefore close to Lenin's position of consistent democracy long before the October 1917 revolution. Trotsky would become the most resolute defender of consistent democracy and the Marxist who most developed the notion along Lenin's lines in the decades after the revolution. He argued that "the most important service [social democracy] can render to the cause of democracy consists in unappeasable and relentlessly distrustful criticism of all liberal parties, from the standpoint of consistent democratism".[26]

In 1903, Trotsky supported Lenin's position on the national question in the debate on the party programme and spoke against the Bund. In the First World War he upheld the traditional position of the RSDLP. He wrote that "recognition of every nation's right to self-determination" meant "recognition of each nation's right to state independence — and thus it obliges social democracy to oppose every regime that involves the compulsory cohabitation of nations or fragments of nations and, depending on circumstances of time and place, to assist the struggle of nations and national minorities against the yoke of a foreign nation".[27]

In his *History of the Russian Revolution*, Trotsky championed Lenin's policy on nationalities "as a most important constituent element into the October revolution". He wrote that "in the years before the war the Bolsheviks had described themselves in the legal press as 'consistent democrats'. This pseudonym was not accidentally chosen. The slogans of revolutionary democracy, Bolshevism and Bolshevism alone carried through to its logical conclusion". The war "proved conclusively that the programme of 'consistent democracy' could be no otherwise enacted than through a proletarian revolution".[28]

Similarly, in the last year of his life, he promoted Lenin's position on the national question in opposing past and contemporary opponents. For Trotsky, Lenin regarded nationality as "unseverably connected with territory, economy and class structure". However Lenin "refused at the same time to regard the historical state, the borders of which cut across the living body of the nations, as a sacrosanct and inviolate category". He demanded "recognition of the right to secession and independent existence for each national portion of the state". In so far as the various nationalities coexist within the borders of one state, "their cultural interests must find the highest possible satisfaction within the framework of the broadest regional (and consequently, territorial) autonomy, including statutory guarantees of the rights of each minority". At the same time, "Lenin deemed it the incontrovertible duty of all the workers of a given state, irrespective of nationality, to unite in one and the same class organisations".[29]

One unusual way in which Trotsky applied his commitment to consistent democracy was in attempting to extend it to the oppression faced by African Americans in the USA. He recognised that black people in the US principally suffered racial oppression and that black people in Africa did not constitute a unified nation. It was not a matter of socialists imposing nationhood on African Americans, but appreciating that national self-definition may develop from their oppression. If US blacks become a nation then "that is a question of their consciousness, that is, what they desire and what they strive for". Trotsky emphasised the all-important subjective element to nationality, citing Belgians and Swiss peoples as examples where simple linguistic criteria were not sufficient. He argued that "an abstract criterion is not decisive in this question, but much more decisive is the historical consciousness, their feelings and their impulses. But that also is not determined accidentally but rather by the general conditions". The example illustrates the sensitivity of Trotsky's thinking towards the subjective and emergent possibilities of national struggles, even though in this case the majority of African Americans did not self-define as a nation nor seek to form a separate black state in the south of the United States (in fact, many decided to move north).[30]

Lenin's differences with Stalin

It used to be a commonplace on the left that Stalin's only contribution to Bolshevik theory was the pamphlet, *Marxism and the National Ques-*

tion (1913). It was often thought that Lenin or Bukharin had directly supervised Stalin, or at least edited the manuscript to make it fit for publication. However, it appears the manuscript was mostly Stalin's own work — and all the worse for it. Stalin, whose background was Georgian, had taken an interest in the national question before he wrote the pamphlet. He concurred with Lenin on the critique of the Bund, the Mensheviks and the Austrian social democrats. However, there is much else about the pamphlet that is far from Lenin's conception of consistent democracy.

Stalin stated that: "A nation is a historically constituted, stable community of people, formed on the basis of a common language, territory, economic life, and psychological make-up manifested in a common culture". This dogmatic definition was an amalgam of terms derived from Kautsky, Bauer, Renner and Medem. But whereas their analyses were supple, Stalin's was a rigid, objective list of criteria, which he then used to classify various peoples as "nations" or "not nations". Stalin's novelty was to introduce the conception of nations as a "stable" community, suggesting a permanence to national identity that is missing from other Marxist writing on the national question.

Although Stalin formally defended the right of nations to self-determination, he did not provide consistently democratic answers for national minorities living within multinational states for whom independence is not a viable option. He also mangled the critique of the Austrian approach, misdating their adoption of cultural-national autonomy to the Brünn congress in 1899. Despite the apparent praise for the pamphlet, it is notable that Lenin spent a great deal of time during 1913-14 (and after Stalin's work was published), clarifying and developing his own ideas of consistent democracy. Nowhere did Stalin's innovations provide the starting point for Lenin's theorising.[31]

Marxism and the fight against anti-semitism

An important test of the utility of Marxist thinking on the national question is how it is applied to the oppression and exploitation of Jewish people in modern history. This is often called "the Jewish question" in the literature, but there are many embedded questions for socialists to tackle if they are serious about Jewish emancipation. At least three aspects stand out: the specific forms of anti-semitism suffered by Jewish people in recent centuries, the status of Jewish people as a collectivity and the assessment of Zionism as an expression of Jewish national identity. The classical Marxist tradition on these questions is highly contradictory, not least because the forms of Jewish oppression and the responses to it have evolved considerably over the last 100 years. But the tradition of consistent democracy articulated by Lenin and Trotsky provides the best framework for tackling this oppression in today's conditions.

Anti-semitism has taken many forms in history. Jewish people suffered oppression at the hands of ancient imperial powers. The persecution of Judaism as a religion has been rife for millennia, underpinning the exclusion of Jewish people from social relations across Europe and the Middle East during the feudal and early capitalist periods. Anti-semitism has taken the secularised form of stereotyping Jewish economic power, including through banking, government and the media, generalised into a supposed global conspiracy. Anti-semitism has taken a virulent racist form in the modern world, leading to Nazi genocidal practices that ultimately resulted in the holocaust. Anti-semitism has taken the form of uniquely denying the Israeli-Jewish people their collective self-definition as a nation, saying that they should not, like other peoples, exercise their own self-rule. Sadly, the labour and socialist movement has not been immune to these forms of anti-semitism, and indeed in the 40s and 50s the Stalinist USSR promoted a form of "left anti-semitism"; this has been adopted by some Trotskyists, anti-capitalists and radical campaigners in recent years.

Marx never grappled adequately with these forms of anti-semitism. As a young radical democrat he broke from those who expressed openly anti-semitic politics. His main public intervention, 'On the Jewish Question' (1843), contained a strong defence of Jewish emancipation, but was spoiled by his use of anti-Jewish economic stereotypes. Marx did not make a significant positive contribution on the issue of Jewish oppression and anti-semitism. Engels and German social democrats such as Bebel, Kautsky and Luxemburg were generally far clearer, openly condemning anti-semitism. However, they treated anti-semitism as a backward relic of past modes of production, rather than the product of modern capitalism.

Bebel condemned anti-semitism as "the socialism of fools" (the expression apparently originated with the Austrian democrat Ferdinand Kronawetter) and he took a very strong public stance against the anti-semitism that riddled German politics and society at the turn of the century. Nevertheless the problem with this phrase, as historian Lars Fischer points out, is that it accepts the "kernel of truth" approach, namely the view that anti-semites have a point about the role of Jewish people in modern capitalism, but have embraced the wrong solution, whereas socialists will resolve these problems with workers' power. The mistake is clear: accepting premises of anti-semites and even attributing some kind of misguided "socialism" to them makes huge concessions in principle to the racist worldview.[32]

A further mistake concerned a simplistic endorsement of "assimilation" — the view that Jewish people should be integrated into whatever society they live in with equal rights. This was a very common assumption among the best sections of the left at the beginning of twentieth century. Had the Jewish question simply been about religion or economic exclusion, this might have made sense. However, the growth of virulent racial anti-semitism during the 19th and early 20th centuries rendered the assimilationist perspective redundant.

Lenin inherited this somewhat ambiguous international socialist tradition of opposing anti-semitism when he joined the movement in the early 1890s. However, it is clear from his writings that Lenin always condemned anti-semitism in the most intransigent fashion. In 1903, he welcomed the Ekaterinoslav manifesto explaining the social-democratic attitude towards anti-semitism. During the wave of pogroms at the time (including the Kishinev massacre) he pointed to the example of Russian, Ukrainian and Jewish workers in Odessa who took joint action against the pogromists. To combat anti-semitic violence, Lenin proposed the creation of workers' self-defence militias. He unequivocally attributed responsibility for the pogroms to the tsarist government and its supporters. In 1914, he argued that anti-semitism was "striking ever deeper root among the propertied classes" and that "the Jewish workers are suffering under a double yoke, both as workers and as Jews". He wrote that it was "a question of honour for Russian workers" to support draft legislation against anti-semitic discrimination. In 1917 Lenin denounced the counter-revolutionary press, "which is fomenting anti-semitism, inciting the masses against the Jews".

Lenin's attitude towards anti-semitism remained resolutely hostile when he led the new soviet workers' state. At the height of the civil war he wrote a denouncement. "Anti-semitism", he wrote, "means spreading enmity towards the Jews". He condemned "the accursed tsarist monarchy", its police, landowners and capitalists, for organising pogroms against the Jews. In other countries too, "we often see the capitalists fomenting hatred against the Jews in order to blind the workers, to divert their attention from the real enemy of the working people, capital". Anti-semitism was "a survival of ancient feudal times, when the priests burned heretics at the stake, when the peasants lived in slavery, and when the people were crushed and inarticulate". "The Jews", he said, were not "the enemies of the working people". The majority of Jewish people were workers: "they are our brothers, who, like us, are oppressed by capital; they are our comrades in the struggle for socialism". He concluded: "Shame on those who foment hatred towards the Jews, who foment hatred towards other nations". Jewish socialist parties co-operated with the Bolsheviks and continued to operate openly during the early years of the regime. The Russian Communist Party established a Jewish section (the *Evsektsiia*) and a number of leading Bundists joined the party. Jewish socialists who did not belong to the party played a major role in Narkomnats.[33]

Lenin's attitude on anti-semitism was far more progressive than Stalin's. Writing to his Bolshevik comrades in Baku during the 1907 London congress of the RSDLP, Stalin wrote: "one of the Bolsheviks... jestingly remarked that the Mensheviks were a Jewish faction... and hence it would not be amiss for us Bolsheviks to instigate a pogrom in the party". In his treatise on the national question, Stalin failed to engage with the issue of anti-semitism. Instead he denounced the struggle for a sabbath holiday as an apology for the Jewish religion and the campaign for Yiddish as purely nationalist. As historian Enzo Traverso put it, "anti-semitism seemed almost non-existent for Stalin... [his study] showed a basic indifference towards anti-semitism". Stalin in power was worse. He encouraged anti-semitic tropes against Trotsky and other oppositionists and incited anti-semitic attacks to the end of his life. Stalin is no part of the Marxist tradition against anti-semitism.[34]

Although classical Marxism developed a solid body of literature and political practice against anti-semitism, it remained hamstrung by the assimilationist perspective carried over from nineteenth century radicalism. However, Trotsky made substantial steps forward in addressing every aspect of Jewish oppression, starting with the stance towards anti-semitism. Trotsky came from a Jewish background, attending a Yiddish-speaking religious school at the age of seven. He suffered anti-semitism as a child, losing a year at a Russian secondary school because of the quota limiting the number of Jewish students. He began his political life as an ardent assimilationist, denouncing the Bund at the second RSDLP congress in 1903 and telling one of its leaders Vladimir Medem that he regarded himself as "neither a Russian nor a Jew, but as a social democrat". Trotsky's initial reaction to the Kishinev pogrom of 1903 was to argue that there was no necessity for a specific struggle against anti-semitism. However, he denounced the pogroms that accompanied tsarism's desperate attempts to stay in power in 1905 and used the platform of his trial to indict the regime as "an automaton for mass murder". In 1913 Trotsky devoted an essay to the Beilis case in Russia and, as Balkans correspondent for the paper *Kievskaya Mysl*, wrote articles on anti-semitism in Romania. As head of the Red Army during the civil war, Trotsky employed Jewish battalions in the fight against the pogromists — and within the Red Army itself, which had its own problems with anti-semitism.[35]

Trotsky made two principal innovations in the last years of his life that are of seminal importance for the Marxist tradition against anti-semitism. First, he came to understand the connection between anti-semitism and the rise of the ruling Stalinist bureaucracy in the USSR. In a letter to Bukharin (4 March 1926), Trotsky protested against anti-Jewish undertones in the whispering campaign: "Is it true, is it possible, that in our party, in Moscow, in workers' cells, anti-semitic agitation should be carried on with impunity?!" Bukharin, although seriously astonished, did not reply. Trotsky later recalled anti-semitic cartoons in the official party press and the way Stalin's supporters reminded audiences that "don't forget that the leaders of the opposition are Jews". At the height of the Moscow trials, Trotsky reflected that the ruling elite, what he called the Thermidorian reaction, "has stirred up all that is low, dark and backward in this agglomeration of 170 million people". To reinforce its domination "the bureaucracy does not even hesitate to resort in a scarcely camouflaged manner to chauvinistic tendencies, above all to anti-semitic ones". The Stalinist leadership manipulated "an anti-semitic state of feeling" with "a cunning skill in order to canalise and to direct especially against the Jews the existing discontent against the bureaucracy". They "exploited systematically, even if covertly, anti-semitic prejudices in order to entrench its rule". By teasing out this peculiar new form of left anti-semitism, which would be extended during the Second World War and its aftermath, Trotsky was preparing the revolutionary left to resist it.[36]

Second, towards the end of the 1930s and in light of the Nazi's accession to power, Trotsky began to consider anti-semitism from a different angle. He reflected that during his youth, "I rather leaned toward the prognosis that the Jews of different countries would be assimilated and that the Jewish question would thus disappear in a quasi-automatic fashion". However, "the historical development of the last quarter of a century has not confirmed this perspective. Decaying capitalism has everywhere swung over to an exacerbated nationalism, one part of which is anti-semitism". The Jewish question "has loomed largest in the most highly developed capitalist country of Europe, in Germany". He began to understand that the Jews were the first victims of a rotting capitalist imperialism, which the ruling class was trying to preserve by plunging humanity into a bloodbath. Capitalism "befouls the world atmosphere with the poisonous vapours of national and race hatred". Anti-semitism was "one of the most malignant convulsions of capitalism's death agony". Revolutionary socialists have the duty of "an uncompromising disclosure of the roots of race prejudice and all forms and shades of national arrogance and chauvinism, particularly anti-semitism".[37]

He warned of the growing existential threat to Jewish people in Europe and in the United States. He noted that "the number of countries which expel the Jews grows without cease". At the same time "it is possible to imagine without difficulty what awaits the Jews at the mere outbreak of the future world war. But even without war the next development of world reaction signifies with certainty the physical extermination of the Jews". He called for the "audacious mobilisation of the workers against reaction, creation of workers' militia, direct physical resistance to the fascist gangs". He expressed "moral solidarity" with Herschel Grynszpan, the 17-year-old Polish Jew who shot and killed a Nazi official in November 1938. On the cusp of the invasion of France, Trotsky warned of "the monstrous intensification of chauvinism and especially of anti-semitism". Decaying capitalist society was "striving to squeeze the Jewish people from all its pores; seventeen million individuals out of the two billion populating the globe". Hitler had given anti-semitism "a zoological form".[38]

Trotsky had begun to formulate the most profound critique of anti-semitism of any Marxist since the previous century. He had captured the modern form of virulent, racial anti-semitism embodied in Nazism. Trotsky had also slowly come to realise that, in the light of Nazism, assimilation was no longer a valid answer to anti-semitism. In doing so, he also began to unpick earlier Marxist notions of Jewish nationality and the attitude towards Zionism. These developments also warrant close attention.[39]

Marxism and Jewish nationality

How classical Marxists perceived the national status of Jewish people underwent an evolution as anti-semitism burgeoned into the twentieth century. On the one hand the Bund developed an analysis of Jewish people in Eastern Europe in national terms. Vladimir Medem set out the Bundist position systematically in his article 'Social Democracy and the National Question' (1904). But much of the RSDLP dismissed this view, most notably Plekhanov, who quipped that

Bundists were "Zionists afraid of seasickness".[40] Kautsky took a different view, designating Jewish people in Eastern Europe as a "caste" rather than a nationality.[41]

Lenin's views on the status of Jewish people were shaped by his understanding of relations in Russia and rooted in the Marxist debates of the time. Traverso cynically comments that Lenin "tended to accept the idea of a Jewish nation during periods of collaboration with the Bund... and deny it in phases of conflict". In 1903, in the aftermath of the second RSDLP congress (when the Bund had walked out), he quoted Kautsky that "the Jews have ceased to be a nation, for a nation without a territory is unthinkable", falling back on the criteria of language and territory. He added that "the idea that the Jews form a separate nation is reactionary politically".[42]

In the course of his re-elaboration of the national question in 1913, Lenin described the Jewish people as "the most oppressed and persecuted nation". More than half of the Jews in the world lived in Galicia and Russia, "backward and semi-barbarous countries, where the Jews are forcibly kept in the status of a caste". The other half "lives in the civilised world, and there the Jews do not live as a segregated caste". However, Lenin concluded (following Kautsky and Bauer) that "the Jews in the civilised world are not a nation, they have in the main become assimilated". Yet only months later, Lenin drafted the National Equality Bill, which he motivated partly because "no nationality in Russia is so oppressed and persecuted as the Jewish". While highlighting aspects of national oppression and distinguishing the status of Jewish people in different places, Lenin did not decisively break with the social-democratic orthodoxy on Jewish nationality.[43]

Again, it was Trotsky who pushed Marxism forwards on the question of Jewish national status. Between 1934 and 1940 he openly recognised the historic bankruptcy of the assimilationist model, stressed the national character of the Eastern European Jewry and proposed a territorial solution to Jewish oppression. Trotsky was asked whether the anti-semitism of German fascism compelled a different approach to the Jewish question on the part of communists. He answered that, "I do not know whether Jewry will be built up again as a nation. However, there can be no doubt that the material conditions for the existence of Jewry as an independent nation could be brought about only by the proletarian revolution". He also argued that "a workers' government is duty bound to create for the Jews, as for any nation, the very best circumstances for cultural development". This meant "to provide those Jews who desire to have their own schools, their own press, their own theatre etc, a separate territory for self-administration and development". Three years later he went further, arguing that "the Jews of different countries have created their press and developed the Yiddish language as an instrument adapted to modern-culture. One must therefore reckon with the fact that the Jewish nation will maintain itself for an entire epoch to come". Trotsky followed through the relentless logic of his analysis of anti-semitism and Jewish nationality, to entertain the prospect of a territorial solution to Jewish oppression.[44]

Marxism and Zionism

The classical Marxist analysis of Zionism also underwent evolution and development. Bundists developed a sharp early critique of Zionism, defining it as the ideology of the Jewish capitalist class. In March 1899, the Bundist newspaper *Der yiddisher arbeyter* published a critique of Zionism by Chaim Zhitlovsky, which stated that "there can never be peace between socialism and Zionism".[45] Kautsky articulated similar opposition to Zionism. Although not opposed in principle to Jewish colonisation, he believed that the Zionist movement was interfering with the activity of the Bund and undermining the zeal of the Jewish proletariat to work toward a socialist revolution.[46]

The early Soviet government carried over the social democratic common sense into its initial policy towards Zionism, both internally and in foreign policy. Internally, many Russian socialist Zionists supported the Bolshevik regime and joined the Communist Party's Jewish section (*Evsektsiia*). Socialist Zionists fused in 1917 to form the United Jewish Workers Socialist Party. In 1919 they formed the Communist Alliance with the Bund and in 1921 merged with the *Evsektsiia*. Poale Zion militants organised a regiment in the Red Army that bore the name 'Borokhov'. Historian Jonathan Frankel argues that "it would be wrong to give the impression that the war on Zionism was a central concern of the Soviet regime in general". For the Soviet leadership "Zionism remained very much a peripheral issue". Poale Zion retained its legal and public existence until 1928. Again, the Zionist pioneer youth movement, Hehaluts, was able to survive and run its own training groups until 1926-27. Both Poale Zion and Hehaluts were permitted to bring out their own journals in the USSR. The Poale Zion publication, *Evreiskaia proletarskaia mysl*, persistently argued against the official Comintern line with regard to Palestine. Young Zionist activists condemned to prison and penal exile in Siberia were frequently given the opportunity to renounce Soviet citizenship and emigrate to Palestine instead of serving out their sentence — more than 1000 were allowed to leave between 1924 and 1934. In 1928, the Soviet government decided to settle a Jewish colony in Birobidzhan, a region of Siberia larger than Belgium. The departments of defence and agriculture made the decision, without consulting the Jewish population. Between 1928 and 1933, some 20,000 Jewish people migrated to Birobidzhan, although less than half stayed in the harsh climate.[47]

The Communist International discussed Zionism sporadically from its inception, within the context of international inter-state relations and with regard to building a Palestinian Communist Party (PCP). At the second Comintern congress in July 1920 Lenin's original draft theses did not mention Zionism. However, during the debate, Maria Frumkina, a former Bundist leader who had recently led a faction into the Russian Communist Party, proposed an addition to the theses criticising the Zionist colonisation of Palestine. Michael Kohn responded on behalf of the Socialist Workers Party of Palestine. The 'Theses on the National and Colonial Question' adopted by the congress stated that "the Palestine affair is a crass example of Entente imperialism and the bourgeoisie of the relevant country in question working together to swindle the working class of an oppressed nation". Under the cover of "the creation of a Jewish state in Palestine, Zionism in general actually delivers the Arab working population of Palestine, where the toiling Jews constitute only a small minority, to exploitation by Britain".[48]

Similarly contrasting assessments of the Zionist project, both support and critique, were expressed at the Congress of Peoples of the East, held in September 1920 in Baku.[49] The third Comintern congress (June-July 1921) did not reflect any further on the question of Zionism, although the PCP did submit a resolution condemning the repression of their comrades after the May Day demonstrations earlier that year. The main related controversy came when Radek announced that the credentials commission had given Communist Poale Zion a consultative vote, which was challenged from the floor of the congress by the Italian communist Umberto Terracini.[50]

Palestine was discussed briefly at the fourth Comintern congress in November-December 1922. The main reporter on the 'Eastern Question', Willem van Ravesteyn (Communist Party of the Netherlands), said that in Palestine, "the two dominant forces, Jewish and Arab, are both discontented... British rule has not been capable of achieving even a limited degree of peaceful collaboration between the nationalities in the new Palestine. He noted that "the country is now on the eve of elections for a sort of representative body", "but the Arabs have announced a boycott of these elections".[51] This was a realistic assessment. In fact the British mandate's policy in Palestine was to play divide and rule with the Arab and Jewish populations, and often favoured Arab leaders over the Zionists.

The first Comintern executive (ECCI) resolution on Palestine (10 May 1923) referred to Palestine as "a backward, semi-feudal country, subject to a unique form of Zionist colonisation, promoted by imperialism". The first practical task of the PCP outlined by the Comintern was "to intensify its activity among the urban Arab proletariat and peasantry", and help them organise and become effective in the fight against Zionism and imperialism". An ECCI commission on the Palestine question urged the young communist party to establish closer contact with the broad masses of Arabs "in order to transform the party from an organisation of Jewish workers, into a truly territorial party". It also declared that "the Communist Party must support the nationalist movement for freedom of the Arabian population against the British-Zionist occupation". As such, the Comintern provided both a socio-political analysis of relations between peoples in Palestine and a coherent programme of work for communists to build their forces.[52]

This would change drastically by the end of the 1920s, when under Stalin's misleadership the Communist International lurched towards an ultra-left sectarian approach, known as the "third period". The critical turning point was the Hebron massacre in August 1929, when 67 Jews were killed, homes and synagogues destroyed and survivors had to be evacuated after Arab attacks. The Stalinised PCP and the Comintern executive blamed the Jewish victims and demonised the "Zionist fascists" for the killings. They accused the Histadrut trade union of being "an appendage of Jewish fascism and the British imperialists". A PCP member recommended that "the best thing the Jewish workers could do would be to quit Palestine altogether". The subsequent ECCI resolution claimed that "the fighting that broke out in August was undoubtedly organised by British agents, provoked by the Zionist-fascist bourgeoisie, and arranged by the Arab-Mohammedan reaction". Another ECCI resolution argued that "the appraisal of the rising as a 'pogrom' and concealed resistance to Arabisation are manifestations of Zionist and imperialist influence on the communists. The eradication of these attitudes is essential for the further development of the party".[53]

The Hebron massacre marked the destruction of a rational communist policy towards Zionism. The shrill, manic hatred of Zionism on the left can be dated to this episode. After the Hebron pogrom, the first equation of Zionism with fascism had been made. The demonisation of Jewish people in general became Stalinist policy, spread throughout the labour movements of the world by the communist parties. (It is important to note that the Trotskyist movement opposed the Stalinist version of the Hebron massacre.)[54]

The rabid Stalinist attitude towards Zionism, coupled with the threat posed by the accession of the Nazis, led Trotsky to reconsider his views on Zionism. Trotsky had followed the social-democratic orthodoxy as a young revolutionary and was highly critical of Zionism in his youth. In his analysis of the sixth Zionist congress in Basle (August 1903), 'The Decomposition of Zionism and Its Possible Successors', (*Iskra*, January 1904), made a vituperative attack on Theodore Herzl for seeking "the aid of the princes of the world" on behalf of "his" people. In Trotsky's eyes, Herzl was a "repulsive figure" and a "shameless adventurer", while Zionism was "a reckless adventure doomed to defeat".

As late as the beginning of 1934 he was still claiming to be "opposed to Zionism and all such forms of self-isolation on the part of the Jewish workers". However, he conceded that "the establishment of a territorial base for Jewry in Palestine or any other country is conceivable only with the migrations of large human masses. Only a triumphant socialism can take upon itself such tasks". This may take place "either on the basis of a mutual understanding, or with the aid of a kind of international proletarian tribunal which should take up this question and solve it". The blind-alley experienced by German Jewry and "the blind-alley in which Zionism finds itself is inseparably bound up with the blind-alley of world capitalism". He argued that "Zionism draws away the workers from the class struggle by means of unrealisable hopes of a Jewish state under capitalist conditions". But "a workers' government is duty bound to create for the Jews, as for any nation, the very best circumstances for cultural development". The international proletariat "will behave in the same way when it will become the master of the whole globe". Trotsky did not believe the Birobidzhan Jewish colony in Siberia was a satisfactory solution. The Jewish question "cannot be settled by means of 'socialism in one country'". The so-called "friends of the USSR" were satisfied with the creation of Birobidzhan, but it "cannot help reflecting all the vices of bureaucratic despotism". Birobidzhan was "a bureaucratic farce".[55]

Trotsky's assessment of the efforts to create a Jewish national state in Palestine continued to evolve. By 1937 he accepted that Zionism sprang from "the fact that the Jewish nation will maintain itself for an entire epoch to come" and that "the nation cannot normally exist without a common territory". However, he argued that Zionism was "incapable of resolving the Jewish question", particularly because "the conflict between the Jews and Arabs in Palestine acquires a more and more tragic and more and more menacing character". He did not believe that the Jewish question "can be resolved within the framework of rotting capitalism and under the control of British imperialism". The Jewish colonisation of Palestine was "a palliative", "a two-edged blade" and "a tragic mirage". However, he accepted that Zionism was "utopian and reactionary" under decaying capitalism, nevertheless while "under the regime of a socialist federation", it could "take on real and salutary meaning". He asked "How could any Marxist or even any consistent democrat object to this?"

In the last months of his life, Trotsky urged his supporters in the United States to "elaborate a kind of platform for the Jewish question, a balance on the whole experience of Zionism with the simple conclusion that the Jewish people cannot save themselves except by socialist revolution". The attempt to solve the Jewish question through the migration of Jews to Palestine "can now be seen for what it is, a tragic mockery of the Jewish people". He chastised the British government for renouncing its promise to help them found their "own home" in a foreign land. He feared that "the future development of military events may well transform Palestine into a bloody trap for several hundred thousand Jews".[56]

Conclusion

The subsequent history of the national question has proven conclusively that Lenin and Trotsky's consistently democratic approach was correct. Luxemburg and the Austro-Marxists were proven wrong by the subsequent history of the next century. The international working-class movement would have to address national questions in Europe and of course many others across the globe. The forming of nation states in Europe and in the colonies has shown it is not a utopian project. Far from reactionary, national liberation movements were progressive and democratic when compared to the multinational empires from which they emerged. Far from being able to leave the national question until after the socialist revolution, Marxists have to formulate a democratic programme on the national question in order to cement the kind of working-class unity necessary to take on the capitalist states.

The classical Marxist legacy on anti-semitism, Jewish nationality and Zionism is a real life, often agonising, case study of the problem of national oppression, with all its knotty contradictions. Trotsky did most to develop a consistently democratic approach on these questions. Of course, he did not live to witness either the holocaust or the creation of the state of Israel. But his assessments were broadly accurate and his prognoses borne out by events. The new virulent form of anti-semitism in Nazi Germany was an existential threat to the Jewish people around the world. The vicious persecution of Jews in Stalinist Russia continued after the war. The result was the resurgence of a Jewish national consciousness, which crystallised into a territorial state in Palestine, created in war with the Arab peoples of the region. We cannot read off our assessment of twenty-first century anti-semitism and Zionism from Trotsky's views in the 1930s. But his method of approach — which developed Lenin's conception of consistent democracy on the national question — provides an unsurpassed anchor of principles and process.

References

1. Lenin, [February 1916] 'The Socialist Revolution and the Right of Nations to Self-Determination', (*LCW* 22: 144).
2. Lenin, [15 August 1903] 'An Era of Reforms', (*LCW* 6: 515).
3. Richard Pipes, *The Formation of the Soviet Union*, (1997: v).
4. Lenin, [12 December 1914] 'On the National Pride of the Great Russians', (*LCW* 21: 104); Lenin, [February 1916] 'The Socialist Revolution and the Right of Nations to Self-Determination', (*LCW* 22: 149).
5. Lenin, [April 1902] 'A Letter to the Northern League', (*LCW* 6: 163); Lenin, [27 June 1905] 'The Revolutionary Army and the Revolutionary Government', (*LCW* 8: 568); Lenin, [8 December 1911] 'The Slogans and Organisation of Social-Democratic Work Inside and Outside the Duma', (*LCW* 17: 341); Lenin, [8-9 May 1912] 'The Trudoviks and the Worker Democrats', (*LCW* 18: 42-43).
6. Marx, [1848] *The Communist Manifesto*, (*MECW* 6: 495, 497, 502-03, 519); Engels, [29 November 1847] 'Speech on Poland', (*MECW* 6: 389); Marx, [22 July 1853] *The Future Results of British Rule in India*, (*MECW* 12: 217-18, 221); Ian Cummins, *Marx, Engels and National Movements*, (1980: 94).
7. Roman Rosdolsky, Engels and the `Nonhistoric' Peoples: the National Question in the Revolution of 1848, *Critique*, (1987).
8. Karl Kautsky, [1899] 'Partikularismus and Sozialdemokratie', in Horace Davis, *The National Question — Selected Writings by Rosa Luxemburg*, (1976: 246); Kautsky, [1896] 'Introduction to Revolution and Counter-Revolution in Germany', in Jack Jacobs, *On Socialists and The Jewish Question after Marx*, (1992: 34); Kautsky, [1902] 'The Slavs and Revolution', in Day and Gaido, *Witnesses to Permanent Revolution*, (2011: 65).
9. Lenin, [February-May 1914] 'The Right of Nations to Self-Determination', (*LCW* 20: 430-431); Gankin and Fisher, *The Bolsheviks and the World War*, (1940: 73).
10. Lenin, [6 April 1914] 'On the Question of National Policy', *LCW* 20: 219); Lenin, [1895-96] 'Draft and Explanation of a Programme for the Social-Democratic Party', (*LCW* 2: 97); Lenin, [February-May 1914] 'The Right of Nations to Self-Determination', (*LCW* 20: 400, 411-412).
11. Lenin, [February 1902] 'Draft Programme of the Russian Social-Democratic Labour Party', (*LCW* 6: 28); Lenin, [15 July 1903] 'The National Question in Our Programme', (*LCW* 6: 452-53, 459-60).
12. Brian Pearce, *1903: Minutes of the Second Congress of the RSDLP*, (1978: 40, 221-223, 229-231).
13. Lenin, [21 October 1912] 'A Chapter of World History', (*LCW* 18: 368).
14. Lenin, [September 1913] 'Resolutions of the Summer 1913, Joint Conference of the Central Committee of the RSDLP and Party Officials', (*LCW* 19: 427-29).
15. Lenin, [23 November 1913] 'Letter to S. G. Shahumyan', (*LCW* 19: 499).
16. Lenin, [10 May 1913] 'The Working Class and the National Question', (*LCW* 19: 91-92); Lenin, [25 June 1913] 'Draft Platform for the Fourth Congress of Social-Democrats of the Latvian Area', (*LCW* 19: 116).
17. Lenin, [15 December 1913] 'The National Programme of the RSDLP, (*LCW* 19: 541-544).
18. Lenin, [December 1913] *Critical Remarks on the National Question*, (*LCW* 20: 22); Lenin, [6 May 1914] 'Bill on the Equality of Nations and the Safeguarding of the Rights of National Minorities', (*LCW* 20: 281).
19. Lenin and Stalin, [2 November 1917] 'Declaration of the Rights of Peoples of Russia'. In James Bunyan and Harold Fisher, *The Bolshevik Revolution, 1917-1918: Documents and Materials*, (1961: 283); Hélène Carrère d'Encausse, *The Great Challenge: Nationalities and the Bolshevik State*, (1992); Jeremy Smith, *The Bolsheviks and the National Question*, (1999); Terry Martin, *The Affirmative Action Empire* (2001).
20. Lenin, [July 1916] 'The Discussion on Self-Determination Summed Up', (*LCW* 22: 329); Lenin, [26 July 1920], 'Report of the Commission on the National and Colonial Questions',

CONSISTENT DEMOCRACY AND THE NATIONAL QUESTION

(*LCW* 31: 240); Lenin, [16 December 1919] 'The Constituent Assembly Elections and the Dictatorship of the Proletariat', (*LCW* 30: 257, 262-263).

21. Luxemburg, [July 1896], 'The Polish Question at the International Congress in London'. In Davis, (1976: 50, 56-58); Luxemburg, [1908-09] *The National Question*. In Davis, (1976: 110, 122-23, 135, 140); Luxemburg, [1915] *The Junius Pamphlet*. In Davis, (1976: 290); Luxemburg, [1918] *The Russian Revolution*. In Davis, (1976: 292-93).

22. Lenin, [February-May 1914] 'The Right of Nations to Self-Determination', (*LCW* 20: 399); Lenin, [16 October 1915] 'The Revolutionary Proletariat and the Right of Nations to Self-Determination', (*LCW* 21: 409); Lenin, [July 1916] 'The Discussion on Self-Determination Summed Up', (*LCW* 22: 353, 357); Lenin, [August-October 1916] 'A Caricature of Marxism and Imperialist Economism', (*LCW* 23: 63, 71, 75).

23. Arthur Kogan, 'The Social Democrats and the Conflict of Nationalities in the Habsburg Monarchy', *Journal of Modern History*, 21, 3, (1949: 206-13); Lenin, [December 1913] *Critical Remarks on the National Question*, (*LCW* 20: 39).

24. Karl Renner, [1899] 'State and Nation', in Ephraim Nimni, *National-Cultural Autonomy and its Contemporary Critics*, (2005); Otto Bauer, [1907] *The Question of Nationalities and Social Democracy*, (2000: 283).

25. Lenin, [June 1913] 'Theses on the National Question', (*LCW* 19: 246); Lenin, [28 November 1913] '"Cultural-National" Autonomy', (*LCW* 19: 503).

26. Trotsky, [1906], 'In Defence of the Party', *Journal of Trotsky Studies*, 2, (1994: 94).

27. Trotsky, [July 1915], 'The Nation and the Economy', in John Riddell, *Lenin's Struggle for a Revolutionary International*, (1986: 370).

28. Trotsky, [1930], *The History of the Russian Revolution, Vol.1*, (1980: 328); Trotsky, [1930], *HRR, Vol.3*, (1980: 139).

29. Trotsky, [1940], *Stalin*, (2016: 195-96).

30. Trotsky, [28 February 1933], 'The Negro Question in America', in *Leon Trotsky on Black Nationalism and Self-determination*, (1978: 24, 28); Richard Fraser, 'For the Materialist Conception of the Negro Question' (1955) on revolutionary integrationism.

31. Carrère d'Encausse, (1992: 35-38); Erik Van Ree, 'Stalin and the National Question', *Revolutionary Russia*, 7, 2, December 1994: 220-22); Stalin, [March-May 1913] 'Marxism and the National Question', Stalin, *Marxism and the National and Colonial Question*, (1936: 8).

32. Robert Fine, 'Rereading Marx on the "Jewish Question": Marx as a Critic of Antisemitism'. In Marcel Stoetzler, *Antisemitism and the Constitution of Sociology*, (2014: 144-45); Anderson, (2010: 52); Ronnie Gechtman, 'The Debates on the National and Jewish Questions in the Second International and the Jewish Labor Bund, 1889-1914'. In August Grabski, *Rebels Against Zion*, (2011); Lars Fischer, *The Socialist Response to Antisemitism in Imperial Germany*, (2007: 6).

33. Enzo Traverso, *The Marxists and the Jewish Question*, (1994: 134-34); Lenin, [15 February 1903] 'Does the Jewish Proletariat Need an "Independent Political Party"?' (*LCW* 6: 329); Lenin, [15 August 1903] 'The Latest Word in Bundist Nationalism', (*LCW* 6: 519); Lenin, [28 March 1914] 'The National Equality Bill', (*LCW* 20: 172); Lenin, [17 June 1917] 'How to Fight Counter-Revolution', (*LCW* 25: 97); Lenin, [March 1919] 'Anti-Jewish Pogroms', (*LCW* 29: 252-253); Carrère d'Encausse, (1992: 149-150): Smith, (1999: 113-15).

34. Trotsky, *Stalin*, (2016: 194; 577); Traverso, (1994: 135-36).

35. Trotsky, *My Life*, (1975: 37-39, 47); Robert Wistrich, *Revolutionary Jews from Marx to Trotsky*, (1976: 190-91, 195-96); Stephen Cohen, *Bukharin and the Bolshevik Revolution*, (1973: 239-40, 473)

36. Trotsky, [18 January 1937] 'Interview with the Jewish Telegraphic Agency'. In *Trotsky, On the Jewish Question*, (1970: 21); Trotsky, [22 February 1937] 'Thermidor and Anti-Semitism', *On the Jewish Question*, (1970: 28); Trotsky, [13 January 1938] 'Does the Soviet Government Still Follow the Principles Adopted Twenty Years Ago'? *In Writings 1937-38*, (1976: 131).

37. Trotsky, 'Interview with the Jewish Telegraphic Agency', *On the Jewish Question*, (1970: 21); Trotsky, [1938] 'The Death Agony of Capitalism and the Tasks of the Fourth International'. In *The Transitional Program for Socialist Revolution*, (1973: 93).

38. Trotsky, [22 December 1938] 'Letter to American Jews menaced by fascism and anti-Semitism', *On the Jewish Question*, (1970: 29); Trotsky, [14 February 1939], 'For Grynszpan', *Writings 1938-39*, (1974: 192); Trotsky, [May 1940], 'Manifesto of the Fourth International on Imperialist War and the Imperialist War', *Writings 1939-40*, (1973: 184, 193).
39. Traverso, (1994: 203-04); Wistrich, (1976: 205-207).
40. Traverso, (1994: 98-103, 123); Roni Gechtman, 'A "Museum of Bad Taste"?: The Jewish Labour Bund and the Bolshevik Position Regarding the National Question, 1903-1914', *Canadian Journal of History*, 43, 1, (2008: 37).
41. Kautsky, [31 August 1906] 'Letter to the Bund', Jacobs, (1992: 30-31).
42. Yoav Peled, 'Lenin on the Jewish Question', *Political Studies*, 35, (1987: 63-66); Traverso, (1994: 130); Lenin, [22 October 1903] 'The Position of the Bund in the Party', (*LCW* 7: 99-101).
43. Lenin, Critical Remarks, (*LCW* 20: 26, 29); Lenin, [28 March 1914] 'The National Equality Bill', (*LCW* 20: 172).
44. Traverso, (1994: 202); Trotsky, [February 1934] 'On the "Jewish Problem"'; Trotsky, [October 1934] 'Reply to a Question about Birobidjan'; Trotsky, [18 January 1937] 'Interview with the Jewish Telegraphic Agency', *On the Jewish Question*, (1970: 18-20).
45. Jack Jakobs, 'Bundist Anti-Zionism in Interwar Poland', in Grabski, (2011: 68).
46. Traverso, (1994: 86); Kautsky, [1921], *Are the Jews a Race?*
47. Traverso, (1994: 154, 157); Jonathan Frankel, 'The Soviet Regime and Anti-Zionism: An Analysis'. In Ezra Mendelsohn, *Essential Papers on Jews and the Left*, (1997: 443-44).
48. Riddell, *Workers of the World and Oppressed Peoples, Unite! Proceedings and Documents of the Second Congress of the Communist International, 1920*, (1991: 261-62, 266, 274-75, 289).
49. Riddell, *To See the Dawn: Baku, 1920 – First Congress of the Peoples of the East*, (1993: 226, 283-84, 286-87, 289-90).
50. Riddell, *To the Masses: Proceedings of the Third Congress of the Communist International, 1921*, (2015: 1196-97, 175, 321-22).
51. Riddell, *Toward the United Front: Proceedings of the Fourth Congress of the Communist International, 1922*, (2011: 676, 724, 440, 961).
52. Ran Greenstein, 'Class, Nation, and Political Organization: The Anti-Zionist Left in Israel/Palestine', *International Labor and Working-Class History*, 75, 1, (2009); ECCI, [5 May 1924] *From the Fourth to the Fifth World Congress*, (1924: 67).
53. 'The revolt in Palestine, Communiqué of the CC of the CP of Palestine', *Inprecor*, 9, 54, 27 September, (1929: 1163); 'The revolt in Palestine, Communiqué of the CC of the CP of Palestine', *Inprecor*, 9, 56, 4 October (1929: 1220-21); Bob (Jaffa), 'The Communist Party and the Arab Revolt', *Inprecor*, 9, 61, 25 October, (1929: 1322); ECCI, [16 October 1929] 'Resolution of the ECCI Political Secretariat on The Insurrection Movement In Arabistan', Jane Degras, *The Communist International, 1919-1943: Documents, Vol.3*, (1965: 76-77); ECCI, [26 November 1929] 'Resolution on the Insurrection Movement in Arabistan', Degras (1965: 83-84).
54. Max Shachtman, 'Palestine — Pogrom or Revolution?'
55. Wistrich, (1976: 195); Trotsky, [February 1934] 'On the "Jewish Problem"', *On the Jewish Question*, (1970: 17-18); Trotsky, [October 1934] 'Reply to a Question about Birobidjan', *On the Jewish Question*, (1970: 19); Trotsky, [28 January 1934] 'Letter to Kling', Writings Supplement, 1934-40, (1979: 444); Trotsky, [22 February 1937] 'Thermidor and Anti-Semitism', *On the Jewish Question*, (1970: 28); Trotsky, [22 December 1938] 'Letter to American Jews menaced by fascism and anti-Semitism', *On the Jewish Question*, (1970: 29-30).
56. Trotsky, [18 January 1937] 'Interview with the Jewish Telegraphic Agency', *On the Jewish Question*, (1970: 20-22); Trotsky, [22 December 1938] 'Letter to American Jews menaced by fascism and anti-Semitism', *On the Jewish Question*, (1970: 29-30); Trotsky, [(22 February 1937] 'Thermidor and Anti-Semitism', *On the Jewish Question*, (1970: 28); Trotsky, [15 June 1940], Discussions with Trotsky, in *Writings 1939-40*, p. 287); Trotsky, [July 1940], 'On the Jewish Problem', *Fourth International*, 6, 12, December, (1945: 379).

Alexandra Exter, 'Construction', 1922-3

8. Women's liberation and the Russian revolution

The Russian revolution advanced women's liberation more than any other event in modern history.

Women were makers of the Russian revolution. They were not revolutionary "brides" "handmaidens", "daughters", "midwives" or any other derogatory appellation found in many history books. They were active participants and *as a group* integral to the revolutionary process. As a woman Moscow textile worker recalled with pride: "We carried the revolution on our shoulders. And we didn't give in!" Aleksandra Kollontai, probably the most prominent woman socialist during the 1917 revolution, told a women's conference a year after the seizure of power: "The conclusion to the story is that women can do anything".[1]

Socialist feminists were central to leading the revolution. Strong, determined Bolshevik women, political activists and intellectuals in their own right, made a positive contribution to the revolution. In fact the RSDLP was the best place in Russian society where women could find emancipation from patriarchal traditions. Historians such as Barbara Evans Clements, Jane McDermid, Anna Hillyar and Katy Turton have demonstrated how these "Bolshevik feminists" fought for women's liberation as an integral part of their fight for socialism. Women such as Kollontai formulated a vibrant Marxist-feminist outlook, raising questions and seeking answers to matters that remain central in today's conditions.[2]

The role of women in the Russian revolution is an integral part of the whole story and every chapter of this book. But the considerable part played by Bolshevik feminists is explored in more detail in this chapter. It reiterates the irreplaceable role women played throughout 1917, describes some prominent women leaders, and examines how Bolshevik women ('*Bolshevichki*') organised, building on the tradition of organising working-class women established by the German SPD. It assesses the achievements and limits of the Bolshevik government in the realm of women's freedom. It evaluates the theoretical contribution of women revolutionaries — especially Kollontai — which speak to contemporary socialist feminist debates. The legacy of Bolshevik feminism is a vital resource for anyone fighting for women's liberation today.

Women — makers of the 1917 revolution

Conventional histories of the Russian revolution typically ignore or downplay the role of women. In an important book about the women's liberation movement in Russia, historian Richard Stites claims that during the revolutionary year of 1917, women acted only as the initiators of the February revolution and as defenders of the Provisional Government in October. He argues that women did not walk the corridors of power and were not therefore involved in the important decisions that changed the course of history. He concludes "there is no sense in trying to magnify the role played by the female half of the population [during 1917]".[3] Stalinist histories are little better, at best portraying women as "Lenin's little helpers", subordinates who merely carried out the will of the glorious leader. Yet women played an enormous part in making the Russian revolution the festival of the oppressed it was. It is worth reiterating events from previous chapters in more depth and adding some personal examples to emphasis this.

The proportion of women in the industrial workforce as a whole soared in Russia from 27% in 1914 to 43% in 1917. The numbers of women factory workers rose from 732,000 in 1914 to more than a million at the onset of revolution. By January 1917, around 130,000 women worked in Petrograd factories, while there were approximately 80,000 employed as domestic servants, 50,000 office workers and another 50,000 as shop workers. On the cusp of the revolution, women workers were also spending on average 40 hours a week simply queuing for food. As McDermid and Hillyar put it: "Women did not 'take to the streets' in 1917, they already spent much of the time there, travelling, working, socialising, on errands, queuing, scouring for provisions, looting, rioting and 'gossiping'".[4]

Women sparked the revolution that overthrew the tsar in February 1917 and it was social democratic women who took the lead. The RSDLP had established a Petrograd women's circle and it was this circle that decided that international women's day should be commemorated with an anti-war demonstration. Four years earlier, socialist women had celebrated international women's day for the first time in Russia and, in February 1915, a brief appeal was issued, signed by the "Organisation of Women Workers of the RSDLP", indicating the involvement of Bolshevik, Mezhraionka and other socialist women.

On 23 February 1917 (8 March in the western calendar), various factory meetings were organised across Petrograd. Revolutionary socialist agitators addressed those gatherings, calling on women workers to demonstrate. Female textile workers from the Vyborg district called for strikes, arguing that women carried an excessive workload while working in the factory and caring for children. They convinced male workers to join the strike and then rallied support by marching to other factories and calling out other workers.

Nina Agadzhanova, a member of the RSDLP since 1907 and with a decade of underground revolutionary activity, worked as a machine operator at Novyi Promet factory. Agadzhanova and Mariia Vydrina organised mass meetings at the factory and fought to bring the workers out to join the strikes. Anastasia Deviatkina, a Bolshevik since 1904, organised and led the demonstration of women workers and soldiers' wives on international women's day. Striking women workers from the Sampsonievskaia cotton-spinning mill brought out workers from the Ludwig Nobel factory. I M Gordienko, a male Bolshevik activist working there, remembered how "masses of militant women workers flooded the narrow street. Those who noticed us began to wave their hands and shouted, 'Come on out! Down your tools!' Snowballs were thrown through windows. We decided to join the demonstration. A short meeting took place at the main office by the gates, and the workers went out onto the street".

The strikers marched to the central district of Petrograd. Confronted by Cossacks, they surrounded them and described their miserable situation, exploited for profits while their men were slaughtered, pointing out that the Cossacks too had mothers, wives and sisters and children suffering from such privation. They convinced soldiers to refuse to fire on the crowds. A Bolshevik woman worker, Arishina Kruglova, described one encounter between her factory and soldiers: "A detachment of Cossacks bore down on us quickly. But we did not waver; we stood in a solid wall as though turned to stone... The soldiers... lowered their rifles... Someone at the rear yelled: 'Cossacks, you are our brothers, you can't shoot us'. And the Cossacks turned their horses around".[5] Through such courage, the tsarist state crumbled and the autocracy was ended.

But February was not the end of women's involvement. Many continued to organise, some becoming delegates to local and citywide soviets. Some took part in factory committees and participated in strikes. In May 1917, 40,000 Petrograd women laundry workers struck for increased wages, the eight-hour day and for more machinery to lighten their load. They were led by Sofia Goncharskaia, Bolshevik leader of the union of laundry workers. In May, women constituted a significant proportion of the participants in a prolonged strike of 350 workers in dye and dry clean premises along with around another 150 sales people from affiliated shops in Petrograd. In June, mostly women workers in the capital's teashops and restaurants also took strike action.[6]

The Bolshevik party had to catch up with the militancy shown by women workers in February 1917. On 19 March a demonstration sponsored by the bourgeois League for Women's Equality marched to the Tauride Palace to demand the Provisional Government support full civil rights for women. When Kollontai spoke at the rally, the crowd hooted down her criticism of bourgeois feminism. The Bolshevik Inessa Armand attended as an observer at a preparatory meeting in May 1917 for an all-Russian women's congress, proposed by the League for Women's Equality. She gave a speech claiming that proletarian women had nothing in common with bourgeois women and should have nothing to do with the proposed congress; Armand led a walkout of six other worker-representatives.

In 1917, the *Bolshevichki* engaged in all the activities that prepared the way for their party's seizure of power in October. As Clements has put it, "they made speeches, wrote newspaper articles, served as soviet and duma delegates, did clerical work, ran committees, and, in the autumn... built bombs and trained with pro-Bolshevik militia units, the Red Guards". As they had in the past, "*Bolshevichki* did what was needed, with little regard being given to their gender". The revolution "actually intensified the party's longstanding practice of engaging women in all its activities". In March 1917, the Petrograd committee of the party recognised the need and potential for systematic work among women. A bureau was set up and resumed publication of *Rabotnitsa* (*Woman Worker*) newspaper, which had first appeared before the war. It was, however, emphasised that no independent women's organisation was being formed. The women who edited and wrote for *Rabotnitsa* organised women workers and soldiers' wives throughout Petrograd, including a school to prepare women as agitators in their own workplaces. McDermid and Hillyar argue that "*Rabotnitsa* played a crucial role," reaching thousands of women and helping to "pressure male workers into recognising women as comrades in their struggle". A similar paper, *Zhizn rabotnitsy* (*The Women Workers' Life*), was established in Moscow.[7]

The Bolshevik party fought to have women represented on factory committees and acted within the metal workers' union to challenge patriarchal attitudes and tactics that discriminated against women. Bolshevik women participated in many of the great events of 1917. Liudmila Stal, who had joined the RSDLP in 1898, was a party agitator in Petrograd. From August 1917 Stal worked as an editor of *Pro-*

letarshoe delo, a Kronstadt newspaper, and as a member of the party executive committee. Liza Pylaeva, who had joined the Bolshevik party in February 1917, succeeded in smuggling Bolshevik party documents in a basket to evade soldiers during the repression of the July days. Pylaeva was the only female on the eight-member inter-district committee of the Socialist Union of Working Youth in Petrograd, which held a conference on 18 August. (Of the eight, four were Bolsheviks, two non-party and two anarchists.)

Traditional histories focus on Mariia Bochkareva, who led the women's battalion that defended the Provisional Government in its last days at the Winter Palace. Such histories, hostile to the revolution, focus on Bochkareva because she was not fighting for women's rights, but to continue the war effort. By contrast, thousands of Bolshevik women who took part in the seizure of power are often ignored. In the October revolution, Bolshevik women carried arms. Large numbers took part in the October revolution, fighting in the Red Guards, serving in their medical brigades and maintaining communications. Arishina Kruglova, who joined the RSDLP in 1905, organised Red Guards in her area and, during the October revolution, raided wealthier districts of the city in search of weapons and helped with local medical work. Mariia Avilova, who joined the party a year before the revolution, headed Red Guard units during October 1917. Elena Giliarova, who represented soldiers on the Petrograd soviet, ran first aid courses and trained female Bolsheviks and sympathisers to join the Red Guards. Evgeniia Adamovich and Feodosiia Drabkina, both RSDLP members since 1903, worked in the Petrograd military revolutionary committee, organising the actual seizure of power in October. Elena Rozmirovich, a party member since 1904, worked from Smolny.[8]

Perhaps the most graphic incident in 1917 involved the Bolshevik Evgeniia Bosh, who addressed the Keksgolm regiment of the second guard's corps (known as "the wild division") in central Ukraine when they were on leave from frontline duty. Bosh spent two hours haranguing a thousand battle-hardened soldiers about the evils of the Provisional Government and the necessity of replacing it with a soviet government. The men listened attentively and asked her questions for a further two hours. When Bosh finally told the soldiers that she had to leave, the company's musical band rushed off to find its instruments and the wild division escorted her to her car with hurrahs and music. They would later fight for the Bolsheviks under Bosh's leadership.[9]

What characterised the *Bolshevichki* in 1917? Clements argues that they adhered to the collective identity of the RSDLP and its Bolshevik faction. Russia's social democrats saw themselves as "a band of comrades armed with a powerful understanding of their world, whose purpose it was to educate the workers and provide them with leadership in the coming revolution". This collective identity consisted of, first, "a worldview that embraces a conception of the world as it really is and an alternative vision of what it might ideally become". A second element was "a conceptualisation of the movement itself that lays out the proper spheres of action for the movement and its goals and defines the proper character of members". The third element was "the movement's group memory, that is, shared interpretations of common experiences". In particular, the ethic that Bolshevik women valued most was *tverdaia*, which meant hard, firm, and steadfast. A *tverdaia* revolutionary woman was tough, durable and "hard-as-a-rock". But to be hard was "to think rationally, to examine facts and draw conclusions in a disciplined, logical way. It was also to be realistic, strong-willed and goal-orientated".[10]

This attitude and outlook is clear from the biographies of the most prominent Bolshevik women during the revolutionary period. A decade after the October revolution, Kollontai reflected on the women who had played a leading role in the revolution. Kollontai highlighted the roles of Nadezhda Krupskaia, Inessa Armand, Elena Stasova, Klavdiia Nikolaeva, Konkordiia Samoilova, Vera Slutskaia, Evgeniia Bosh, Varvara Iakovleva, Anna Elizarova and Mariia Ulianova.[11] Their biographies show how they forged their Marxist credentials through decades of shared revolutionary work, legal and underground, imprisonment and exile, writing and distributing publications, arguing, convincing and persuading workers to join the struggle — and, most of all, building the party.

What did the Russian revolution do for women?

What did the workers' state do for women? On the second anniversary of the October revolution, Lenin claimed that "in the course of two years of Soviet power in one of the most backward countries of Europe more has been done to emancipate women, to make her the equal of the 'strong' sex, than has been done during the past 130 years by all the advanced, enlightened, 'democratic' republics of the world taken together".[12] After the Bolsheviks took power, they scrapped old, reactionary laws. They legislated for full legal and political equality for women, including the right to divorce and the right to vote. The Bolsheviks wanted to liberate women from the burden of housework and tackle wartime shortages, so they established communal kitchens, laundries, schools and nurseries. They introduced rights such as two months paid maternity leave and paid nursing breaks for mothers at work to breastfeed their babies. They ran education campaigns against oppressive religious authorities, both Christian and Muslim.

In November 1917, a month after the revolution, two decrees established civil marriage and allowed for divorce at the request of either partner. The code on marriage, the family and guardianship, ratified in October 1918, established a new doctrine based on individual rights and the equality of the sexes. The new family code eliminated the distinction between "legitimate" and "illegitimate" children. It allowed women to claim child support from men, whether they were married to them or not. The code also established the right of each spouse to their own property and the right of all children to parental support until the age of 18. The Bolsheviks also abolished all laws against homosexual acts and other consensual sexual activity, with the new law based on the principle of "the absolute non-interference of the state and society into sexual matters, so long as nobody is injured, and no one's interests are encroached upon". The framers of the new law recognised that this was not socialist law as such, but rather transitional and preparatory for further improvements.

During the first months of soviet power decrees were passed aimed at improving the material conditions of life for working-class women. One decree ordered all lying-in hospitals and all centres, clinics and institutes of gynaecology and midwifery be transferred to the Department for the Protection of Mother and Child. Medical services for expectant mothers would be organised on the basis that medical assistance be available to all mothers in need, doctors be paid a state salary, and expectant and nursing mothers would be protected against being practised upon by unskilled midwives and medical students. The decree also replaced one-year midwifery courses with two-year courses. The same decree ordered the creation of a model Palace of Motherhood — the conversion of all the lying-in hospitals and children's homes in Moscow and Petrograd into one general institution and the renaming of children's homes. In November 1920, the Bolshevik government became the first in the world to legalise abortion, although it was motivated as a temporary necessity due to the perilous state of the country for raising children, rather than in terms of women's reproductive choice.[13]

Under the pressure of the dire economic and social circumstances of the civil war, the functions of the family were transferred to the state. The threat of starvation in the urban centres forced the government to establish control over food supplies and by 1920 hundreds of thousands of working-class families were eating in state canteens. At one point in 1921, over 90% of Moscow residents ate in public dining halls. Communal laundries were established in larger towns and nurseries and kindergartens were created to care for pre-school children. But the arrangements were not simply made by exigency: they fitted with the Bolsheviks' vision of a new, equalitarian society. For example, Trotsky advocated collective housekeeping units set up by the "most enterprising and progressive families" as a way out of the present deadlock, a way to jump from the "realm of necessity to the realm of freedom".[14]

The workers' government also used the power of the state to enforce equality in the face of religious opposition, against both Christian and Muslim authorities. On 17 December 1917, the soviet government abolished the existing legal system and established elected people's courts. In Turkestan, where the population was almost entirely Muslim, the Bolshevik government at first tried to abolish the old system of sharia law, but then retreated to allow its use as long as it did not contradict soviet law. The election of judges was brought in but removed in 1922, in part because it reinforced the power of religious authorities. From 1925, the sovietisation of central Asia led to rapid decline in religious courts. Between 1924 and 1928 customary practices such as the abduction of women and the payment of ransom were outlawed. Practices such as polygamy, the marriage of pre-pubescent girls and vendetta were forbidden, while women's right to testify as witnesses was enforced. Education in medressahs and cheders was attacked.

From 1926, the increasingly bureaucratised regime organised mass demonstrations where women were forcibly unveiled and weddings invaded to prevent arranged marriages. Communist Party women's sections were empowered to intrude into a person's private life, to carry out family hygiene campaigns and set up women's clubs. This was part of a pattern of retreat from the earlier emancipatory goals of revolution in many areas of gender relations.[15]

The Bolshevik government also made a qualitative step forward in the realm of sexual politics and more specifically, in increasing the freedom of lesbians and gay men. Historian Dan Healey has demonstrated how the early workers' government tore up the old, reactionary tsarist laws against sodomy that had been used to persecute gay men in Russia, and instead deliberately chose not to legislate in matters of sexual freedom, effectively legalising same sex relations.

The Bolsheviks did not make a specific theoretical contribution to the question of homosexual emancipation. However, they inherited the German social democratic tradition of practical support for sodomy decriminalisation. SPD leader August Bebel was among the first signatories to Magnus Hirschfeld's petition to repeal paragraph 175 of the German criminal code against male same-sex acts and the first politician to speak in the Reichstag in favour of this campaign in 1898.

Hence within weeks of coming to power the Bolsheviks began revising the criminal code. When this was finally revised and published in 1918, it omitted the previous references to sodomy found in tsarist law. In 1923 Nikolai Semashko, the commissar of health, visited Hirschfeld's Institute for Sex Research with a delegation of Russian doctors. The Institute's journal reported that Semashko stated how pleased he was that in the new Russia, the former penalty against homosexuals had been completely abolished. In 1925, the Bolshevik social hygienist Grigorii Batkis published *The Sexual Revolution in Russia*, which stated that in the USSR homosexuality was a private matter, to be treated like so-called "natural' intercourse". Batkis and other Soviet representatives contributed to Hirschfeld's World League for Sexual Reform and were praised for the decriminalisation of male homosexuality. Kollontai was a member of the League's international committee of directors.[16] Healey highlights a legal case of a woman who had lived as a man since the revolution and who had married another woman in 1922. As late as 1927, the courts recognised the marriage as legal because it was concluded by mutual consent. Without exaggerating these achievements or ignoring their limitations — given the conditions of conflict and social deprivation in the civil war that followed the revolution these measures were difficult to implement — it is important to recognise the practical steps made by the first workers' state.

How did Bolshevik women organise?

How and why did *Bolshevichki* organise in the way they did? Why were they apparently so implacably hostile to the feminists of their time? Above all else, Bolshevik women were inspired to organise by the model they had witnessed pioneered by the German SPD. Kollontai published a pamphlet, 'Women Workers Struggle for their Rights' (1919), which is a venerable eulogy of the German working-class women's movement. Without ambiguity, she argued the German example was the one Russian Bolsheviks should follow. In particular she was inspired by the SPD leader August Bebel's book *Woman and Socialism* and by Clara Zetkin's organisational work.

Zetkin edited the party's women's paper *Die Gleichheit* (*Equality*), supported women organisers, special women's conferences, and autonomous women's organisation within the party.[17]

Zetkin also convened international women's organisation, starting from a caucus at the Second International's congress in 1896. The first official international women's conference took place at the instigation of German SPD women at Stuttgart in 1907. Some 58 delegates from 15 countries discussed voting rights for women and the forms of international cooperation between socialist women's organisations throughout the world. The second international women's conference met at Copenhagen in 1910, with almost 100 representatives from 17 countries. The conference was notable for its resolution to introduce an international women's day. Although events and demonstrations had been held before, for example in the USA, international women's day was celebrated for the first time on 19 March 1911 in Austria, Denmark, Germany, and Switzerland. As more women from more countries joined in, 8 March became established as the international women's day. A third international women's conference was planned to coincide with the tenth international socialist congress, schedule for Vienna in August 1914. However, both foundered on the outbreak of the First World War.[18]

Bebel had referred to bourgeois feminists as "enemy sisters" and this was reinforced by the hostility they expressed towards the SPD. In 1903, Anita Augspurg, president of the German Union for Women's Suffrage, denounced the SPD, preferring to support the liberal People's Party and other bourgeois parties. However, Kollontai was aware of the growing bureaucratisation of the SPD, which she denounced in her book, *Around Workers' Europe* (1912). Although the SPD had around 175,000 women members by 1914, (around 16%), it had closed the women's bureau. Zetkin continued to insist that the socialist women's movement still required "a certain measure of independence and freedom of movement". Despite these reversals in Germany, the seeds of an autonomous working-class women's movement had been planted internationally.[19]

Kollontai explained the organisational lessons she had learned from the international experience in her *Social Basis of the Woman Question* (1909). She wrote that "we must ask ourselves whether a single united women's movement is possible in a society based on class contradictions". She argued that "the women who take part in the liberation movement do not represent one homogeneous mass". Rather, women are divided (like men) into two camps: "the interests and aspirations of one group of women bring it close to the bourgeois class, while the other group has close connections with the proletariat, and its claims for liberation encompass a full solution to the woman question". Although both camps called for women's liberation, "their aims and interests are different. Each of the groups unconsciously takes its starting point from the interests of its own class, which gives a specific class colouring to the targets and tasks it sets itself".

Kollontai's view was nuanced, recognising that they were living through a period where a broad social movement of women was taking place. She accepted that in certain circumstances short-term campaigns and demands made by women of all classes could coincide. However, "the final aims of the two camps, which in the long term determine the direction of the movement and the tactics to be used, differ sharply". While feminists believed that the achievement of equal rights with men within the framework of the contemporary capitalist world represents a sufficient end in itself, "equal rights at the present time are, for the proletarian women, only a means of advancing the struggle against the economic slavery of the working class". The feminists saw men as the main enemy, for men had "unjustly seized all rights and privileges for themselves, leaving women only chains and duties". Working class women had a different attitude. They did not see "men as the enemy and the oppressor; on the contrary, they think of men as their comrades, who share with them the drudgery of the daily round and fight with them for a better future". Kollontai accepted that "several specific aspects of the contemporary system lie with double weight upon women". However working-class woman and her male comrade "are enslaved by the same social conditions; the same hated chains of capitalism oppress their will and deprive them of the joys and charms of life". If that was true, then "a woman can possess equal rights and be truly free only in a world of socialised labour, of harmony and justice" — in other words, a socialist society. This final aim did not prevent working-class women from fighting "to improve their status even within the framework of the current bourgeois system". However, they also recognised these efforts are "constantly hindered by obstacles that derive from the very nature of capitalism". The feminists were "unwilling and incapable of understanding this". In such circumstances, unity with the feminists was not possible.[20]

However, Bolshevik women also faced opposition and indifference by their own male comrades towards their organising efforts. Again Kollontai confronted the attitudes of some working-class revolutionaries, who contested the need for a women's socialist movement. They asked: "What is a women workers' movement? What are its tasks, its aims? Why can't it merge with the general movement of the working class, why can't it be dissolved in the general movement, since the social democrats deny the existence of an independent women's question? Isn't it a hangover from bourgeois feminism?" Kollontai replied that "a woman worker is not only a member of the working class, but at the same time she is a representative of one entire half of the human race". Socialists, demanding equal rights for women in state and society, "do not shut their eyes to the fact that the woman's responsibilities towards the social collective society, will always be somewhat different to men's. The woman is not only an independent worker and citizen — at the same time she is a mother, a bearer of the future". Kollontai recognised that while working-class women were exploited in the same systematic way as working-class men (although frequently more savagely exploited), the role of the family and the state towards women, as well as bourgeois ideology, gave rise to specific forms of oppression. Separate women's organisation (through intra-party collectives, commissions, women workers' bureaux and so on) should carry out "special agitational work adapted to the level of the questions women want to have answered" so as to recruit women to revolutionary struggle, as well as putting forward demands that tackle the specific forms of oppression faced by women as women in capitalist society.[21]

The *Bolshevichki* almost certainly would have rejected the title "Bolshevik feminists", although in our time this label appears apposite. Bolshevik women may have baulked at the epithet not because they were opposed to women's liberation, but because the meaning of "feminism" in the epoch they grew up in was different to the modern connotation. In their time, there was no mass women's movement, of the kind that emerged in the 1960s and 1970s in many parts of the world. Feminism in the early twentieth century meant mostly the campaign by upper and ruling class women to gain equal rights for themselves — although many of the women from this social layer, suffering a lack of status in society, would be drawn into radical politics. However, the organisations of bourgeois feminists were implacably hostile to these social democratic parties, did not make alliances with them, nor seek to vote for them where they operated in conditions of legality. And the socialist movement that Bolshevik women were part of was very different from today's fragmented left. Therefore the hostility towards "feminism" and the scepticism about separate women's organisation have to be seen in that context. Bolshevik women also faced indifferent and at times hostile male socialists who dominated the parties they belonged to. The argument at the time was about the political independence of the mass working-class movement and the tactics of how a mass working-class political party with power foreseeable and in sight should relate to other organisations. They would not concede ground to those that opposed them organisationally, politically and ideologically. Bolshevik women had to navigate between the perils of bourgeois feminism and socialist "economism" to carve out their autonomous organisation. They came to their conclusions based on their own experience and the best international examples — notably from Germany.

In 1914, the Bolshevik faction decided to begin publication of the women's paper *Rabotnitsa*, on the initiative of Inessa Armand. The general upsurge in the strike movement after 1912 was reflected in greater militancy among working-class women. *Rabotnitsa* was designed to be a legal publication to help with the tasks of organising women workers. The editorial board was arrested on the eve of the first issue, but Anna Elizarova succeeded in editing and then printing 12,000 copies. The journal appeared seven times, between February and June 1914, before it was banned. The editorial of the first issue declared that women's place in society was determined by class divisions rather than sexual differences. Thus, the woman question centred on how to make women "comrades in the common struggle quickly. The solidarity between working men and women, the common cause, the common goals, and the common path to these goals: such is the resolution of the 'woman question' for the working class". But the journal also pointed to the double burden of women's work, being responsible for the housework as well as having a job outside the home. Although Armand was critical of the contents of the first issues and of the decision to print Menshevik reports, the paper was a breakthrough in putting the woman question on the party's agenda.[22]

Russian women's organisation during 1917

After the overthrow of the tsar, the Petrograd committee of the Bolshevik party decided to organise systematically among working women. The publication of the journal *Rabotnitsa* resumed, although local party leaders stressed that it was not an independent women's organisation. Liudmilla Stal noted that despite the German model, the women experienced some resistance from some male party workers. When Kollontai argued for a dedicated women's bureau at the April Bolshevik conference, the party prevailed on her to withdraw the resolution. As the economic situation worsened after June, with falling wages, spiralling inflation, and increasing unemployment, *Rabotnitsa* upbraided some factory committees that tried to force women workers whose husbands, brothers or fathers worked in the same factory to leave their jobs. According to McDermid, "the Bolsheviks argued in terms of class solidarity, wanting the men to treat the women as equal members of the working class". Krupskaya and Armand addressed women in special pamphlets and at meetings, as well as through the pages of *Rabotnitsa*, on the need for female involvement in the struggle against counter-revolution.

The editors of *Rabotnitsa* in Petrograd called a conference of working women for 25 October 1917, but it was postponed because of the seizure of power. The conference took place on 12 November when more than 500 women — many of them not belonging to the Bolshevik party — showed up to approve the Bolshevik regime. Armand attempted to call an all-Russian congress of working women in February 1918, but it was postponed until May and then downgraded to a Moscow city conference when only 130 attended. *Rabotnitsa* ceased publication in January 1918, so the Bolshevik women's movement did not have its own paper for two and half years. Instead it had to make do with special "women's pages" in the regular party press. However, the first all-Russian working women's conference convened in November 1918 was a great success, with more than 1,100 delegates arriving, when only 300 had been expected for accommodation.

In 1918, the party established the new central commission for agitation and propaganda among working women, chaired by Armand and assisted by Kollontai and Samoilova. In August 1919 the party leaders decided to replace the commission with a new women's section of the central committee (*zhenotdel*) and to make Armand its first director. In spring 1920, Armand prepared a new monthly publication, entitled *Kommunistka*. The first double issue of 30,000 copies came out in July 1920. During the civil war, *zhenotdel* concentrated on winning the support of women for the Red Army and the party. During the famine of 1921, it focused on relief work. McDermid argues that "*zhenotdel* was not simply a proletarian version of the pre-revolutionary feminist philanthropy".

It sought above all "to raise women's consciousness, to educate them and to make them active participants in their own right, and on a massive scale, in the knowledge that they had the full support of the state". *Zhenotdel* published simply-worded magazines addressed specifically to women. It also set up day-care and eating facilities, as well as organising consumer and producer cooperatives. By 1928 "*zhenotdel* had offices in every region of the Soviet Union. It had even penetrated the Soviet East where the opposition to the emancipation of women was fierce and often savage".[23] In the space of a decade, the Bolshevik feminists had built a vibrant working class-based women's movement within the ruling workers' party and within the Russian workers' state.

The communist women's movement

The *Bolshevichki* were internationalists to the core and their success in Russia meant they simultaneously helped to create the international communist women's movement. Armand and Kollontai had been instrumental in helping Zetkin to call the international women's conference in March 1915, the first official gathering to oppose the First World War. Hundreds of thousands of working-class women around the globe rallied to the Russian revolution and, despite the efforts of the great imperialist powers and the old tsarist army, the workers' state survived. The founding congress of the third, communist international in March 1919 passed a resolution written by Kollontai, which stated that "the dictatorship of the proletariat can be won and maintained only with the energetic and active participation of working-class women".[24]

The first international conference of communist women was held on 30 July-2 August 1920, during the second Comintern congress. Armand organised the conference, drawing up the agenda, drafting the resolutions and writing a background brochure for delegates. However, Elwood describes the event as a "small and undistinguished gathering in Moscow. Kollontai, Krupskaia, Balabanoff and Zetkin… were conspicuous by their absence". The 21 delegates who did attend the opening ceremony in the Bolshoi theatre "were outnumbered by the women factory workers observing the proceedings from the surrounding balconies". The theses 'For the communist women's movement' were drawn up for presentation to the world congress but were considered instead by the ECCI, which published them later in 1920. The appeal 'To the working women of the world' condemned the triple slavery faced by the majority of humanity, with women burdened "by the cares of housework, cooking and child rearing". It also praised the soviet republic for creating thousands of crèches, nurseries, children's homes, canteens and kindergartens. The 'Theses on the development of work among women of all countries', edited by Zetkin, argued that the communist international carried forward "on a higher historical plane" the work that "the Second International began but was unable to carry out consistently". Communist parties were instructed to take special measures and establish special institutions to reach women. These included women's agitation committees in branches (with men allowed to join), a women's page in every party newspaper, a national women's secretariat, a regular theoretical women's magazine and a national women's conference. An international women's secretariat was established and associated with the executive committee of the Comintern, with its own publication and structures.[25]

The second international conference of communist women was held in Moscow, on 9-15 June 1921, on the eve of the third Comintern congress. Zetkin made a report to the Comintern congress, explaining that 82 delegates from 28 countries had attended the women's gathering. She reiterated the arguments made at previous conferences: "There is no special communist women's organisation. There is only a movement, an organisation of communist women inside the communist party, together with the communist men"; "we do not in the slightest lose sight of the common interests and struggle of proletarian men and women"; "we welcome it when the women's committees include men, with their greater political experience and knowledge". She criticised the bureaucratic leaders of the socialist parties and trade unions, who had "triply betrayed the interests of employed women", by abandoning the struggle for 'equal pay for equal work', for approving the expulsion of women from employment after the war and for failing to struggle against the "crying injustice" of less unemployment compensation for women. Kollontai also spoke about women's distinctive role in society and pointed to the example of Soviet Russia, where the task was "training women to undertake active, creative work and placing them in responsible posts".

The third Comintern congress approved the 'Theses on methods and forms of work of the communist parties among women' on 8 July 1921. The main resolution stated that "there is no special women's question, nor should there be a special women's movement". Communism would be won "not by the united efforts of women of different classes, but by the united struggle of all the exploited". It continued that the Comintern "is strongly opposed to forming separate, special women's associations within the party or the trade unions, or in the form of a special women's organisation. However, it nonetheless recognised the need for the Communist parties to use special methods of work among women. It therefore recognises that it is appropriate to create special organs to carry out this work inside all Communist parties".[26] This seemed like a step back from previous modes of organisation.

The fourth Comintern congress discussion on women in 1922 was brief and did not raise any significant new theoretical questions. However, the speeches explained how the women's section's work was to be integrated with other party work. Zetkin spoke once again of the need for autonomous organisation, reflecting that "however much communist work among women must be firmly linked ideologically and organically to the life of each party, we nonetheless need special bodies to carry out this work". She argued that "every man is welcome to take part in the special communist work carried out among women. That applies to our committees as well as to our entire activity in its various expressions and arenas". Zetkin approved of the work of women comrades in Italy, who she lauded for having founded groups for "sympathising women". And she argued that it was vital for communist parties in colonial and semi-colonial countries to carry out this work.

The German communist Hertha Sturm gave a sober assessment of the unhappy state of the international's women's work. She told the congress, "we have a certain gauge in the number of women members in the communist parties... perhaps ten per cent". She advocated small party schools for women comrades and pointed to an extensive women's press in the International, mentioning *Communist Women's International*, the Dutch *De Voorbode* [*The Herald*], *Žena* [*Woman*] in Czechoslovakia, *L'Ouvrière* [*Woman Worker*] in France and *Compagna* [*Woman Comrade*] in Italy. Sturm urged delegates to carry out "the decisions of the women's conference last year and the world congress, women's supplements must be added to all party publications". Other speakers explained what women's organisations had done in Russia. Sofia Smidovich recalled the role of women's publications in 1917. The Russian Communist Party central committee was publishing two magazines for women workers. Varsenika Kasparova reminded delegates that women across the globe suffered from "particularly oppressive subjugation". She said the Comintern was about creating "an intelligentsia of revolutionary women" to fight for women's liberation and socialism.[27]

As historian John Riddell argues, the Comintern women's journal, *Communist Women's International*, "was a formidable educational tool that published 1,300 pages over its five years of existence. No advice on childcare here; no recipes. Each issue contained several articles on the women's movements and women's rights activity both within and without the communist international, as well as analysis of working-class politics as a whole". The work of the women's movement centred on two main world campaigns: to build international women's day, and to support International Workers' Aid for Soviet Russia, particularly its aid to Soviet women. Large numbers of women were recruited. The proportion of women among party members ranged from a high of 20% in Czechoslovakia and Norway down to about 2% in France and Italy. In Germany and Russia, it rose gradually in the 1920s to 17% and 14% respectively. The absolute numbers were high: more than a hundred thousand women were members of the communist international.[28]

The Comintern also directed how women should seek to organise in Asia, in societies at very different stages of development and where traditional patriarchal relations were particularly entrenched. At the third congress, the Comintern urged communist women's commissions to "conduct a vigorous struggle against all prejudices, customs, and religious practices that bear down on women. This agitation should also be addressed to men". However, the sections "must strictly avoid tactless, inappropriate, or rude attacks on religious beliefs or national traditions, while still resisting the influence of nationalism and religion". At the fourth congress, Zetkin was candid about the challenges faced. She argued: "In the countries of the East, women live and work overwhelmingly under patriarchal and pre-capitalist forms of social life, bending under prejudices grey with age, oppressed by social institutions, by religion, customs and habits".[29] Like the work of the *zhenotdel*, these steps were often tentative and fraught with contradictions and mistakes. But they nevertheless underlined the commitment to make women's work truly internationalist as well as liberationist in every part of the globe.

Theorising women's oppression

Kollontai contributed numerous books, articles and pamphlets spelling out her commitment to women's liberation, basing herself on a realistic assessment of the women's oppression at the time. She expanded Marxist theory in a number of important respects, building on the work of Marx and Engels, Bebel and Zetkin, notably on domestic labour, what she called women's "second shift" in the family and most of all in the realm of sexual politics. Kollontai articulated the co-constitution of a classless society and the liberation of women, when she argued that "If the emancipation of women is unthinkable without communism, then communism is unthinkable without the full emancipation of women". But Kollontai was no idle dreamer: she assessed the role of women at work and in the family under capitalism, how pregnancy and childbirth were managed and the significance of politics rights. She also highlighted the subordinate status women endured in sexual relations in general. Her views also evolved, spurred on by the experience of the Russian revolution, from the orthodox imitation of the German SPD model to a more libertarian Bolshevik stance. This was a gulf she described as "a whole geological shift in the field of social and economic relations". It was this originality, emerging out of the Marxist tradition, that makes Kollontai's Bolshevik feminism so relevant to subsequent feminist thought.[30]

Kollontai believed the growth of industry and the incorporation of masses of women into the labour force was itself revolutionary. Despite the horrors of industrialisation, Kollontai believed the enforced trend of women's work outside the home, as the only way to raise their consciousness and to make them independent. She argued that "It is the universal spread of female labour that has contributed most of all to the radical change in family life". Kollontai believed that women only became aware of their needs when they became an integral part of the labour force. However, it was her sharp assessment of the nexus of waged work and family life for women that gave Kollontai's analysis its resonance. Kollontai was explicit that "the woman is oppressed not only as a seller of her labour, but also as a mother, as a woman". Capitalism had placed a "crushing burden" on woman's shoulders: it has made her a wage-worker without having reduced her cares as housekeeper or mother. Woman "staggers beneath the weight of this triple load". She emphasised that "the modem family structure, to a lesser or greater extent, oppresses women of all classes and all layers of the population".[31]

Kollontai was incisive in her description of the realities of women under capitalism. She stated that "the ceremony of marriage, even among the working class, is a funeral service said over the corpse of dead feelings". The burden of housework was similarly disparaged. She wrote: "Even if a working woman were to live a thousand years... There would always be a new layer of dust to be removed from the mantelpiece, her husband would always come in hungry and her children bring in mud on their shoes". Lenin echoed these sentiments, arguing that even in Soviet Russia women continued to be a "domestic slave", because "petty housework crushes, strangles, stultifies and degrades her, chains her to the kitchen and the nursery, and she wastes her labour on barbarously unproductive, petty, nerve-wracking, stultifying and crushing drudgery". Kollontai was damning about the provision of services for pregnant women, pointing to the exceptional Swiss example, where eight weeks maternity leave for the working mother was made compulsory in 1878. Finally, Kollontai was also scathing about the way "the personality of a woman is judged almost exclusively in terms of her sexual life". She savaged the sexual harassment and abuse of women in the workplace, condemning "all those gentlemen owning and administering industrial enterprises who force women among their workforce and clerical staff to satisfy their sexual whims, using the threat of dismissal to achieve their ends" and those "masters of the house" who "rape their servants and throw them out pregnant on to the street".[32]

How did Kollontai break new ground theoretically? She demonstrated that women's oppression could not be reduced to economic factors alone, but rather was a function of a range of deep seated political, cultural and ideological practices. She made women's liberation an integral part of the revolutionary theory of Russian Marxism and posited the conception of a new woman with a new morality as a crucial part of that theory. This gave her Marxism a libertarian edge that went beyond the conventional personal politics of her contemporaries, even those from the socialist movement.

One of Kollontai's major contributions was her recognition that division of labour itself, rather than just private property as Engels saw it, carried the potential of women's oppression. Engels had painted a rosy picture of women's status prior to the emergence of private property, while Kollontai pointed to a tendency to devalue women's work even in traditional communal economies. She wrote that "many consider that the enslavement of women, her rightlessness, was born with the establishment of private property. Such an attitude is mistaken". The enslavement of women was "connected with the moment of the division of labour according to sex, when productive labour falls to the lot of men and secondary labour to the lot of women". As historian Karen Field argued, the recognition "permitted her a broader view of women's oppression than was available to most left theorists. It allowed her to recognise that it was not only the proletarian woman who was oppressed, but women everywhere… although quite differently in kind and degree".[33]

Kollontai also elevated the importance of the family in the Marxist theory of women's oppression. She argued that "for women, the solution of the family question is no less important than the achievement of political equality and economic independence". Kollontai recognised women's obligation under capitalism to take responsibility for the "second shift" of the household duties which must be done when their shift in the workplace is over. Although Engels and others had alluded to this double burden, Kollontai spelt it out. She wrote: "The woman who is wife, mother, and worker has to expend every ounce of energy to fulfil those roles". She has to work "the same hours as her husband in some factory, printing-house, or commercial establishment, and then on top of that she has to find the time to attend to her household and look after her children". But she also saw that the traditional family was changing, and most significantly, the dominant trend was "towards the transfer to the social collective (community) of those tasks and duties that hitherto were considered to be the inalienable functions of the members of individual families.[34]

However, perhaps the most significant theoretical breakthrough made by Kollontai concerned the realm of sexual relations. As the Bolshevik regime consolidated itself in the aftermath of the civil war, Kollontai argued that "the sexual act must be seen not as something shameful and sinful but as something which is as natural as the other needs of a healthy organism, such as hunger and thirst. Such phenomena cannot be judged as moral or immoral". This was very much a development of the advanced position held by Bebel, who stated that "how I eat, how I drink, how I sleep, and how I dress is my own personal business, just as my relations with the person of the opposite sex is also my own business". Kollontai celebrated sexual diversity, claiming that history had never seen such a variety of personal relationships as in Soviet Russia — "indissoluble marriage with its 'stable family', 'free unions', secret adultery; a girl living quite openly with her lover in so-called 'wild marriage'; pair marriage, marriage in threes and even the complicated marriage of four people — not to talk of the various forms of commercial prostitution". With these conceptions, she opened a wider vista for the exploration of sexual relations, connecting the fight for a workers' government with the fight for sexual freedom in a way scarcely conceived of by previous Marxists.[35]

Kollontai laid out a coherent vision of women's liberation. She argued that "with the change of economic conditions, with the evolution of the production relations, the inner physiognomy of woman also changes". The new woman could emerge as a type "only with the growth in the number of women who were earning their own livelihood". With workers' rule and evolving social relations of production, the social relations of the family would also change. She believed that "under the dictatorship of the proletariat, the material and economic considerations in which the family was grounded cease to exist". The economic dependence of women on men and the role of the family in the care of the younger generation would disappear, and with the obligation of all citizens to work, "woman has a value in the national economy which is independent of her family and marital status". The economic subjugation of women in marriage and the family is done away with and "responsibility for the care of the children and their physical and spiritual education is assumed by the social collective". And the changes would continue:

> Under communism everyone will be able to eat in the communal kitchens and dining-rooms. The working woman will not have to slave over the washtub any longer, or ruin her eyes in darning her stockings and mending her linen; she will simply take these things to the central laundries each week and collect the washed and ironed garments later. That will be another job less to do. Special clothes-mending centres will free the working woman from the hours spent on mending and give her the opportunity to devote her evenings to reading, attending meetings and concerts. Thus the four categories of housework are doomed to extinction with the victory of communism. And the working woman will surely have no cause to regret this. Communism liberates woman from her domestic slavery and makes her life richer and happier...
>
> Just as housework withers away, so the obligations of parents to their children wither away gradually until finally society assumes the full responsibility.[36]

In her futuristic vision, projecting forward from 1922 to 1970, she advocated a set of living arrangements in which "people do not live in families but in groups, according to their ages. Children have their 'palaces', the young people their smaller houses, adults live communally in the various ways that suit them, and the old people together in the 'houses'". "Those parents who wish to participate in the education of their children will by no means be prevented from doing so... the joys of parenthood will not be taken away from those who are capable of appreciating them". However, she foresaw social arrangements aimed specifically at lifting the difficulties surrounding pregnancy, childbirth and childcare that she understood were central to women's oppression in class societies. As a first step socialist society would guarantee "the possibility of giving birth to her child in healthy conditions, with the appropriate care for herself and her child, the possibility of looking after the child during the first weeks of its life, the possibility of feeding him herself without the risk of loss of pay". The state would provide "refuges for expectant and nursing women, to provide medical consultations for mother and child", as well as "a broad network of crèches, nursery schools and children's centres". Legislation would establish "a short working day, break periods for nursing mothers and a shortened day for young girls". The state would also guarantee sufficient material assistance to mothers during pregnancy, birth and the nursing period.[37]

Kollontai also had the vision to imagine very different sexual relations in the future socialist society. Even before the revolution, she posed the question of whether "free love" was possible. Her answer was that "only a whole number of fundamental reforms in the sphere of social relations — reforms transposing obligations from the family to society and the state — could create a situation where the principle of 'free love' might to some extent be fulfilled". By this she meant revolution, as "only the fundamental transformation of all productive relations could create the social prerequisites to protect women from the negative aspects of the 'free love' formula". Only when women were "relieved of all those material burdens which at the present time create a dual dependence, on capital and on the husband", can the principle of 'free love' be implemented". Crucially, as she made clear in countless interventions after the October revolution, women must be as free as men to initiate and enjoy sexual encounters.[38]

Altogether, these theoretical conceptions laid the basis for the Bolshevik workers' government policies in the spheres of waged labour, family relations of marriage and divorce, childcare, communal eating and living facilities, reproduction rights and greater sexual freedom. The Bolsheviks did not merely permit the revolution in women's lives because they had to out of necessity. They did so because they had theorised these changes in advance and, in the shape of Kollontai in particular, gone far further than other pioneers in extending the boundaries of women's freedom. The party leadership, both women and men, shared common assumptions about the importance of women's liberation to the socialist project and these conceptions informed their practice when they came to power.

The limits of Bolshevik feminism

Bolshevik feminism and the international communist women's movement flourished from 1917 until the early 1920s. The marginalisation of the *Bolshevichki* can be seen as an important early part of the communist party's retreat from its democratic commitments. They were truncated and finally extinguished by the rise of Stalinism. The autonomous women's movement inside and outside Russia was downgraded and then terminated. Stalin's victory over the various oppositions paved the way for a reactionary backlash, what Trotsky called, through an analogy with the decline of the French revolution, "Thermidor in the family".[39] The *zhenotdel* was shut down in 1930. The Comintern allowed the women's commissions to wither in communist parties. In France, for example, the Communists abandoned advocacy not only of women's reproductive rights but even of their right to vote.[40] By the middle of the 30s, however, Stalinism imposed a return to patriarchy in the USSR. In 1936, new laws made with no public discussion made divorce more difficult, increased penalties for non-payment of alimony, criminalised abortion, and recriminalised prostitution and homosexuality. The regime glorified the traditional family and bound women into the double burden that Kollontai once railed against.

Kollontai's personal fate epitomised the degeneration. An early oppositionist to the rising bureaucracy, Kollontai was still prepared as late as 1926 to praise Trotsky for his commitment to women's liberation. She was approached by the Left Opposition (the grouping which fought against the bureaucratisation of the Communist Party) but refused from her exile as an ambassador. As the Left Oppositionists were expelled in 1927, Kollontai openly condemned them in the pages of *Pravda*.[41] She would successively distance herself from her radicalism on women's liberation, parroting the traditional virtues during the Second World War. Kollontai would be the only survivor (other than Stalin the perpetrator) from the original central committee that decided on the October insurrection, to live beyond the purges.

Historian Elizabeth Wood argues that the transformation after October 1917 in Russia "was emphatically not a feminist revolution" and that the Bolsheviks always had a negative view of women, as the most conservative part of the working class, backward, passive and a brake on the revolution. Of course it is relatively easy to point to examples where Bolshevik practice was mistaken and just plain wrong, to cases of male obstruction and to the limitations of the practical measures enacted by the new workers' government. The litany of mistakes would include the 1905 cancelled meeting Kollontai recorded in her autobiography, in which some men put a sign on the door: "Meeting for women only called off — tomorrow a meeting for men only," And the Petersburg committee's proclamation that women workers should boycott the women's congress in 1908. In 1917, it was wrong for the Bolshevik men to undermine initial efforts to establish a department for work among women and for the April Bolshevik conference to bureaucratically withdraw the resolution on separate women's organisation. Women remained in a minority at the time of the revolution and afterwards, representing about 10% of the Bolshevik party's membership. Nevertheless, these objections can serve to erase the memory and importance of the cadre of serious, determined, committed and extremely capable women comrades who should take their place in the Bolshevik tradition. To say the Bolsheviks only turned to special work among women because of rivalry with Mensheviks and SRs ignores the fact that the Bolsheviks carried out this work more effectively and with more success than these competitors.[42]

It is possible to pick holes in the early practical efforts of the Bolshevik workers' government to tackle women's oppression, impeded as they were by so many material difficulties. Communal eating facilities did sometimes mean, as historian Sheila Rowbotham put it, the right to "eat shit collectively". True also that abortion rights were motivated by the problems of raising children, rather than concern for women's reproductive rights, but the establishment of abortion rights was a tremendous step forward. Cultural change was inevitably uneven. As Healey argues, in Soviet Russia, "same-sex relations could be harmless in some instances, dangerous in others. Homosexuals had an ambiguous status with both positive and negative political valences". The tolerance of same-sex relations also coexisted with notions of medical and educational interventions, as well as variable law enforcement.[43] In the context of civil war and imperialist intervention, never mind the economic backwardness and isolation of the workers' state, huge barriers were in the path of the Bolsheviks. The revolutionaries of 1917 believed they were in transition to socialism, not that they had already created a communist utopia. They were developing their ideas as the revolution unfolded — for example, their support for the German communists who advocated abortion rights in the 1920s under the slogan, "Your body belongs to you". However they recognised that without the material support from other workers' revolutions, their efforts would face insurmountable constraints. A more nuanced historical appraisal would be to compare the record of the Bolsheviks with the best bourgeois democratic regimes of the time and, in this respect, the Bolshevik regime compares very favourably.

Although some of the criticisms have force, it is important to resist anachronism when criticising Bolshevik feminism through the lens of subsequent feminist movements. Context matters. The "feminists" they railed against were not the leaders of mass movements, but mostly women able to function legally in a society that outlawed or heavily restricted the organising efforts of socialist women and men. These feminists were regarded as "bourgeois" not simply for their social origins but because of their politics. They backed bourgeois regimes and bourgeois parties; they explicitly opposed social democratic parties, despite the support these parties gave to women's liberation. Similarly, Bolshevik women did not advocate an autonomous women's movement, because they were already part of a great, mass labour movement that was the insurgent force against the ruling powers and capable of coming to power and enacting emancipatory measures in the near future. In those circumstances, separate bourgeois women's movements did not challenge the powers oppressing them, but weakened the principal forces — the socialists — standing against the ruling classes and for women's liberation.

Even the most advanced thinkers such as Kollontai had some of the theoretical weaknesses and made errors. It is possible to find assumptions of the "mother instinct" and the naturalising of other social attributes. Some Bolshevik writing did portray women as weaker or backward compared to men. Socialists of the time seemed to assume that women would do housework, whether it was women within a conventional family or women as part of a collective, communal (albeit more technological) arrangement. They did not challenge head on the necessity for male behaviour to change if women's liberation were to permeate all the way down. Kollontai was wrong when she called prostitutes in Soviet Russia "labour deserters" — an attitude we would certainly not endorse today. (At the same time, she did oppose criminalising the women involved.) Nor did the Bolsheviks examine the implicit heterosexual orientation behind their pronouncements on sexual freedom. Their language was an aberration and their theoretical development inevitably truncated. But the Bolsheviks had the right method of approach, the right starting point in assessing the many-sided realities of women's lives in the capitalism of their time, the makings of a systemic explanation for women's oppression, political strategies based on actual circumstances to tackle the root causes of that oppression and a vision of an alternative society where women's freedom could flourish.

Conclusion

The Bolshevik feminists constantly repeated the mantra that there was no special woman question, yet they developed both a political practice and an ideological theory that treated women's oppression as distinct and unique — this contradiction defines both the strengths and the weaknesses of their achievements. Yet the Bolsheviks did have an assessment of the specific oppression of women in capitalist society, which was not reducible to economic factors, or to class exploitation, or indeed simply to the bourgeois family. This was a multi-layered analysis of the subordination and domination of women, which took in political, cultural, sexual, personal and other social relations. The Bolshevichki developed a political strategy and programme for advancing women's freedom, derived from the German SPD model but adapted to Russian conditions, which they proceeded to implement after 1917. From this assessment and strategy flowed special methods of work among women, both as waged workers, but also as women subject to a whole range of social oppression.

The Bolshevik feminists continued the policy of earlier socialists (with Zetkin the most prominent living link), where mass parties included all kinds of sections and sub-organisations, and saw the women's movement as existing with limited organisational autonomy within the party. The Bolshevik perspective was for mass communist parties to build mass communist women's movements, in competition with bourgeois feminist movements. Today, in the absence of mass revolutionary parties and with very different global women's movements, to abstractly proclaim the need for a communist women's movement would be mistaken. On the other hand, to argue that there are "no special women questions" is also wrong — specific oppressions of all kinds outside of the capital-labour relationship exist and are important factors in the way we all experience social life.

A Marxist approach to the women's movement today is very different compared to the 1920s. Today small Marxist propaganda groups support and intervene in the existing amorphous women's movement, arguing for Marxist politics in women's movement campaigns and showing the class nature of "the women question". We fight for a women's movement that is led by class-conscious Marxists, but such a movement would have organisational autonomy from Marxist organisation. Alongside specific political demands, the main transitional demand for this conception is to fight for a mass working class-based women's movement, focusing on the need for the women's movement to orientate to working class women. However the Bolshevik emphasis on separate women's committees and fractions within the party (and by extension within labour movement organisations), women's papers, women's schools, and other measures to create a cadre of Marxist women, retain their full force.

References

1. Jane McDermid and Anna Hillyar, *Midwives of the Revolution*, (1999: 200); Barbara Evans Clements, *Bolshevik Feminist: Life of Alexandra Kollontai*, (1979: 156); McDermid, 'The Evolution of Soviet Attitudes towards Women and the Family', University of Glasgow PhD thesis, (1988).
2. McDermid and Hillyar, *Women and Work in Russia 1880-1930: A Study in Continuity through Change*, (1998); Barbara Evans Clements, *Bolshevik Women*, (1997); Katy Turton, *Forgotten Lives: The Role of Lenin's Sisters in the Russian Revolution, 1864-1937*, (2007); Carter Elwood, *Inessa Armand: Revolutionary and Feminist*, (1992).
3. Richard Stites, *The Women's Liberation Movement in Russia: Feminism, Nihilism, and Bolshevism, 1860-1930*, (1978: 289).
4. McDermid and Hillyar, (1998: 144-45, 149); McDermid and Hillyar (1999: 16).
5. Eduard Burdzhalov, *Russia's Second Revolution: The February 1917 Uprising in Petrograd*, (1987: 105, 114-15); McDermid and Hillyar, (1998: 152, 155); McDermid and Hillyar, (1999: 139).
6. McDermid and Hillyar, (1998: 165- 166).
7. Clements, (1979: 111); Elwood, (1992: 209); Clements, (1997: 125); McDermid and Hillyar, (1998: 158-59, 162, 164-65).
8. McDermid and Hillyar, (1999: 166-170).
9. Clements, (1997: 129).
10. Clements, (1997: 57-59, 61-62).
11. Alexandra Kollontai, [November 1927], 'Women Fighters in the Days of the Great October Revolution', *Alexandra Kollontai: Selected Articles and Speeches,* (1984: 126-130); Hillyar, 'Revolutionary Women in Russia, 1870-1917: a prosopographical study', University of Southampton PhD thesis, (1999: 172-185); Elwood, (1992); Turton, (2007).
12. Lenin, [6 November 1919] 'Soviet Power and the Status of Women', (*LCW* 30: 122).
13. Janine Booth, *Comrades and Sisters*, (1999); Jayne Evans, 'Women in the Russia Revolution', *Why Socialist Feminism*, (2016).
14. Elwood, (1992: 249); L Trotsky, [13 July 1923] 'From the Old Family to the New', *Women and the Family*, (1973: 26).
15. Hélène Carrère d'Encausse, *The Great Challenge: Nationalities and the Bolshevik State*, (1992: 162-69).
16. Dan Healey, *Homosexual Desire in Revolutionary Russia*, (2001: 100-126).
17. Kollontai, [1919] 'Women Workers Struggle for their Rights', (1971: 20-30).
18. Kollontai, [1907-1916] 'International Socialist Conferences of Women Workers', *Selected Articles*, (1984: 38-57); Richard Evans, *Comrades and Sisters*, (1987: 58).
19. Marie Kennedy and Chris Tilly, 'Socialism, Feminism and the Stillbirth of Socialist Feminism in Europe, 1890-1920', *Science & Society*, 51, 1 (1987: 13-14); Karen Honeycutt, 'Clara Zetkin: A Socialist Approach to the Problem of Woman's Oppression', *Feminist Studies*, 3, 3/4 (1976: 140); Jean Quataert, *Reluctant feminists in German Social Democracy 1885-1917*, (1979).
20. Kollontai, [1909] 'The Social Basis of the Woman Question', *Selected Writings of Alexandra Kollontai*, (1977: 59-61).
21. Kollontai, [1919] 'Women Workers Struggle for their Rights', (1971: 13, 16-17).
22. McDermid, (1988: 175-76); Elwood, (1992: 121-23).
23. McDermid, (1988: 187-90, 401-04); Elwood, (1992: 234-244, 251).
24. John Riddell, *Founding the Communist International*, (1987: 250).
25. Elwood, (1992: 258); Riddell, *Workers of the World and Oppressed Peoples, Unite*, (1991: 972-74, 985, 993-96).
26. Riddell, *To the Masses*, (2015: 784-87, 792, 1011-12, 1014).
27. Riddell, *Toward the United Front*, (2011: 838-39, 848, 852, 862-63, 867-70).
28. Riddell, 'The Communist Women's Movement, 1921–26', *International Socialist Review*, #87, (2013)

29. Riddell, (2015: 1020-21); Riddell, (2012: 844).
30. Clements, (1979: 155); Kollontai, [1919] 'Women Workers Struggle for their Rights', (1971: 12).
31. McDermid, (1988: 284-85); Kollontai, [1920] 'Communism and the Family', *Selected Writings*, (1977: 251-52); Kollontai [17 February 1913] 'Women's Day February 1913', *Alexandra Kollontai: Selected Articles*, (1984: 63); Kollontai, [1920] 'Communism and the Family', (1977: 252); Kollontai, [1909] 'The Social Basis of the Woman Question', *Selected Writings*, (1977: 65).
32. Kollontai, [1915] 'Preface to the Book Society and Motherhood', *Selected Articles*, (1984: 109); Kollontai, [1920] 'Communism and the Family', (1977: 255); Lenin, [28 June 1919] 'A Great Beginning', (*LCW* 29: 429); Kollontai, [1915] 'Preface to the Book Society and Motherhood', *Selected Articles*, (1984: 99); Kollontai, [1921] 'Sexual Relations and the Class Struggle', *Selected Writings*, (1977: 245); Kollontai, [1909] 'The Social Basis of the Woman Question', (1977: 66-67).
33. Karen Field, 'Alexandra Kollontai: Precursor of Eurofeminism', Dialectical Anthropology, 6, 3, (1982: 230); Kollontai [1928] 'The Labour of Women in the Evolution of the Economy', *Selected Writings*, (1977: 211).
34. Kollontai, [1909] 'The Social Basis of the Woman Question', (1977: 64); Kollontai, [1920] 'Communism and the Family', (1977: 252); Kollontai, [1915] 'Preface to the Book Society and Motherhood', (1984: 98-99).
35. Kollontai, [1921] 'Theses on Communist Morality in the Sphere of Marital Relations', *Selected Writings*, (1977: 229); Stites, (1978: 264); Kollontai, [1921] 'Sexual Relations and the Class Struggle', (1977: 241).
36. Kollontai [1918] '"New Woman" from The New Morality and the Working Class', *The Autobiography of a Sexually Emancipated Communist Woman*, (1971: 95); Kollontai, [1921] 'Theses on Communist Morality in the Sphere of Marital Relations', (1977: 226); Kollontai, [1920] 'Communism and the Family', (1977: 255-56).
37. Kollontai, '"Soon (In Forty-Eight Years' Time)', (1977: 233); Kollontai, [1915] 'Preface to the Book Society and Motherhood', (1984: 109-10).
38. Kollontai, [1909] 'The Social Basis of the Woman Question', (1977: 66-67).
39. Trotsky, [1937] *The Revolution Betrayed*, (1972: 145).
40. Clements, (1997: 13); Riddell, (2013).
41. Beatrice Farnsworth, 'Bolshevism, the Woman Question, and Aleksandra Kollontai', *American Historical Review*, 81, 2, (1976: 313-14).
42. Elizabeth Wood, *The Baba and the Comrade*, (2000: 2, 38-39).
43. Clements, (1979: 46, 62); McDermid and Hillyar, (1999: 164); Healey, (2001: 130).

THE RUSSIAN REVOLUTION: WHEN WORKERS TOOK POWER

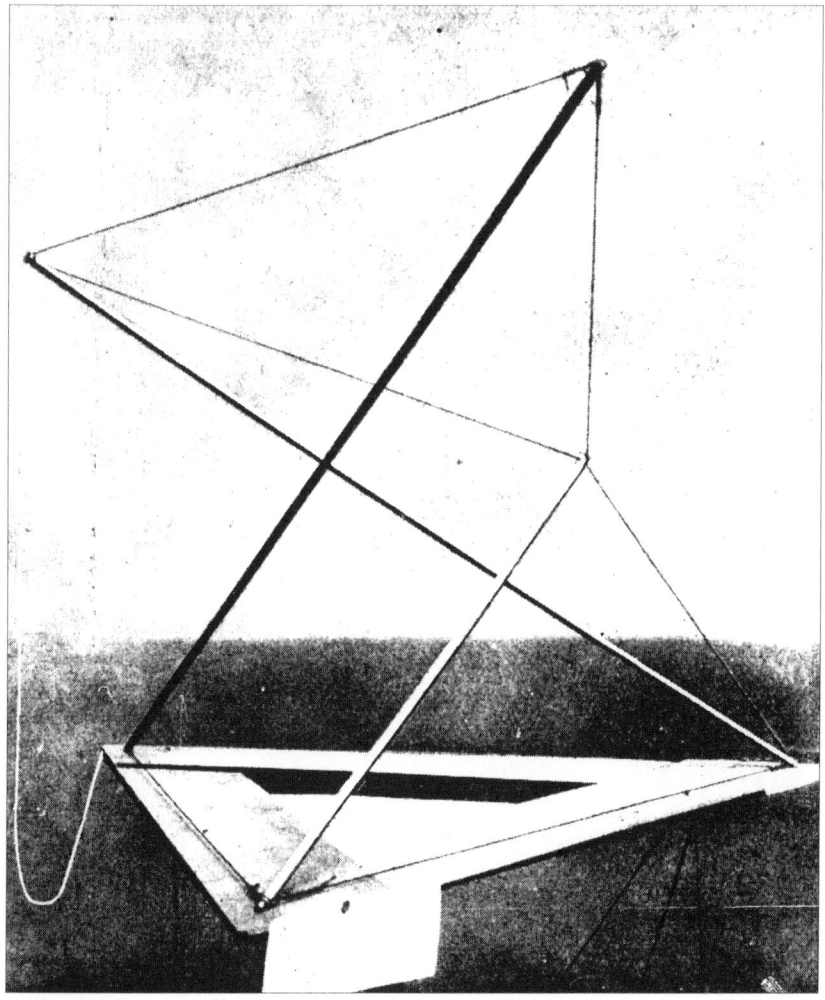

Karl Ioganson, 'Cold Structure IX', 1921

Karl Ioganson was one of a number of Constructivist artists who, in the early 1920s, were focussed not so much on creating objects as on experimentally working through design principles. Ioganson believed that artists could contribute to socialist society by adding creativity into the production process, rethinking both its material qualities and social capacities. His 'Cold Structures' pioneered what is now called "tensegrity" — a design principle in which the parts of a building hold each other up through their own weight. In the context of the civil war and a shortage of materials, this was intended as a way of building cheaply and easily, to aid a speedy construction of the new society.

9. The Communist International — school of strategy

By the beginning of the twentieth century capitalism had developed into a global economic and political system. Capital became globalised, even where it remained nationally-grounded, internally competitive and state-supported. Therefore the working class, on which the capitalist system depends, became an internationally interconnected, globally interdependent universal class, with the power and the interest to challenge the very social relations of production that create it. For these reasons internationalism is integral to the Marxist view of the world. And for these reasons, after 1917, the Russian revolutionaries knew that their new government of workers' liberty would be a beacon for workers across the globe. They also knew that workers' rule in Russia was doomed unless the working class in other major states took their opportunities to seize power and establish their own workers' states. International solidarity was not a pious wish but a burning necessity.

Lenin argued that the First International (1864-72) laid the foundation of an international organisation of the workers "for the preparation of their revolutionary attack on capital" and for the "proletarian, international struggle for socialism". The Second International (1889-1914) — a much larger organisation, including the mass socialist German SPD — "marked a period in which the soil was prepared for the broad, mass spread of the movement in a number of countries". The Second International was an international "whose growth proceeded in breadth, at the cost of a temporary drop in the revolutionary level, a temporary strengthening of opportunism, which in the end led to the disgraceful collapse of this International".[1]

The failure of most social democratic party leaders to oppose the First World War sounded the death knell of the Second International as a revolutionary working-class organisation. Hence the Marxists who coalesced around the Zimmerwald and Kiental conferences felt obliged to call for a new international (see chapter 7). This socialist anti-war movement and then the victorious workers' revolution in October 1917 created the basis for the founding of that new international. The Bolsheviks did not repudiate the best of the earlier internationals, but aimed to go beyond them.

The Communist International — known as the Comintern — was the Bolshevik-led attempt to spread the lessons of the Russian revolution and to create an international network of communist parties capable of leading the working class to power. The first four congresses of the Comintern (held between 1919 and 1922) were a concentrated school of revolutionary working-class strategy. It is now possible, for the first time in the English language, to read all the debates, thanks to the scholarship of John Riddell and his collaborators.[2]

The congress discussions refined and innovated important Marxist ideas. First, they made important assessments of the global political-economic situation, the balance of class forces and the conjuncture revolutionary Marxists found themselves in. Second, delegates learned how to transform small groups of followers into large and sometimes mass communist parties. They worked out ideas of how to build vibrant, disciplined communist parties, how to relate to other workers' parties, as well as how to work in trade unions and parliament. Third, the gatherings elaborated strategies to win the majority of workers, developing what became a Marxist "trinity" - the programme (including transitional demands), the united front and the crowning demand for a workers' government. Finally, the early congresses also sought hegemony for the workers' movement in all struggles of the oppressed and exploited — hence the discussions on women's liberation, the anti-imperialist united front and anti-racism. At the centre of all the debates was the necessity to wage the class struggle on all three fronts — the economic, the political and the ideological.

But the early Communist International would never have been able to achieve such depth of theoretical understanding without the events of the Russia revolution. The initiative to found the Comintern came from the Russian party. In fact the first four congresses can be considered as attempts to translate the rich lessons of the Russian revolution into languages that other international socialists could understand. However, these first meetings were collaborative ventures that were far from monolithic. They were seething with debate and sometimes conflict and the Russian comrades were not guaranteed to win everything they wanted. It was this shared experience of war and revolution, combined with open discussion of differences, that gave the final decisions such authority. The early Comintern was a high point in how internationalist revolutionary socialists should and could relate to each other.

The Comintern and the Russian party were above all animated by developments in Germany. The German revolution between 1918 and

1923 was the key to spreading the socialist revolution. A successful socialist revolution and the establishment of a workers' state in Germany would have unlocked possibilities across Europe. It would have broken the isolation the Russia regime faced and facilitated a leap forward in integrated economic planning. Pierre Broué's book, *The German Revolution, 1917-23*, explains the key events in Germany, including:

October 1918: Agitation in the navy; demonstration at Stuttgart
November 1918: Kiel sailors' mutiny; workers' and soldiers' councils; revolution in Berlin. SPD leader Friedrich Ebert becomes chancellor
January 1919: Founding of the German communist party (KPD). Murder of Rosa Luxemburg and Karl Liebknecht
During 1919: Short-lived local soviet republics established in Munich, Bremen and elsewhere.
March 1920: Right wing Kapp putsch met with a general strike
December 1920: Fusion of KPD with left wing of the USPD to form a mass communist party
March 1921: "March Action" by KPD is defeated
March 1923: Socialist government in Saxony with KPD support
August 1923: General strike against the Cuno government
October 1923: Workers' government in Thuringia.[3]

The first four congresses

Why was it called the *Communist International*? Marx and Engels had joined the first attempt to build a workers' international, in the form of the Communist League and had defined their politics in the *Communist Manifesto* (1848). Lenin had written in his April theses on his return to Russia in 1917 that the Bolshevik faction of the RSDLP should indicate its break with the reformists and warmongers by renaming themselves the communist party. Accordingly they renamed themselves the Russian Communist Party (Bolsheviks) in March 1918. At the end of 1918, as the war came to an end and as the Kaiser was toppled, the Spartacus League led by Rosa Luxemburg and Karl Liebknecht formed the Communist Party of Germany (KPD). This development spurred the Bolsheviks to propose a new international.

The first congress of the Comintern was delayed because although Luxemburg and Liebknecht had favoured forming a new international, they were not convinced about the timing. The KPD was immediately repressed after its formation — ironically by social democrats in government such as Gustav Noske. Luxemburg and

Liebknecht were murdered in January 1919, while other leaders arrested or driven into hiding. Even so it was by no means certain that the KPD would agree to support the founding of the new international. The KPD delegate to the first congress, Hugo Eberlein, arrived still opposed to it. The KPD's refusal may not have mortally wounded the project, but it would have damaged it, so the Bolsheviks had to proceed more slowly and diplomatically than they would have liked. Other delegates faced huge problems, including arrest, just to make their way to Russia, which was still in the midst of a bitter civil war.

Nevertheless the Communist International was founded at its first congress in Moscow on 2-6 March 1919. Some 51 delegates registered, representing 35 workers' organisations from 22 countries. In the main these revolutionaries were not leaders of mass parties but militants who opposed the war and who rallied to the Russian revolution. The first congress discussed the platform of the new international and Lenin's 'Theses on Bourgeois Democracy and Dictatorship of the Proletariat', which formed the basis of unity between participants. Delegates also discussed the international situation, made national reports and approved a manifesto drafted by Trotsky. The appeal to found a new international succeeded beyond expectations, with mass workers' organisations rallying to the Comintern.

The Comintern's second congress, held in Moscow from 19 July to 7 August 1920, was a much bigger and more ambitious affair. Some 218 delegates came from 37 countries, including 30 from Asia. Some represented parties with thousands of members and strong roots in their labour movements. However, many of the leaders of left-wing social democratic parties from France, Germany, and Italy were centrists, wavering between a revolutionary and a reformist politics. The second congress discussed the world political situation, the structure of communist parties — including the 21 conditions for admission to the Comintern — parliamentary work, trade unions and factory committees, the agrarian question, the national and colonial question, the communist women's movement and the communist youth movements. It also established an executive committee (the ECCI) and an apparatus to carry out the ongoing work.[4]

A month after the second congress finished, the Comintern convened a congress of peoples of the east in Baku. Some 2,050 delegates from 37 nationalities heard Zinoviev call for "a holy war for the liberation of the peoples of the East… To end the division of countries into advanced and backward, dependent and independent, metropolitan and colonial!" Communist parties were formed in Turkey,

Egypt, Iran, India (in exile), Korea, and Indonesia, and later China.[5]

The third congress took place in Moscow from 22 June to 12 July 1921. More than 600 delegates from 55 countries attended. The gathering discussed the world situation, tactics and strategy, the situation in Germany, Italy and Russia, the trade unions, the communist women's movement, the communist youth movement and the colonial question. It registered a change in the international situation — the fact that the communist parties developing within capitalist states across the globe did not have the support of the majority of their working classes. The main instruction therefore was to "attain the majority and reach the masses".[6]

The fourth congress took place in Moscow from 5 November to 5 December 1922. Some 350 full delegates from parties in 61 countries met to hammer out global socialist strategy. Among these parties, three had more than 100,000 members (Czechoslovakia, Germany and Russia); nine other parties in Europe had memberships of 10,000-100,000. It was perhaps the greatest ever gathering of Marxists. Present were Lenin, Trotsky, Radek, Zinoviev, Krupskaia, Bukharin, Evgeni Preobrazhenskii, Julien Marchlewski and others from the Russian party. They debated with Zetkin, Antonio Gramsci, Alfred Rosmer, Victor Serge, Boris Souvarine, Ernst Meyer, Andreu Nin, August Thalheimer, Pietro Tresso, Hugo Eberlein and Jack Murphy from European communist parties, James Cannon and Arne Swabeck from the US, as well as Asian Marxists such as Katayama Sen, Chen Duxiu, Tan Malaka, Liu Renjing and Manabendra Nath Roy. The clash of ideas was evident throughout, with "left" criticism from Bela Kun, Eugen Varga, Amadeo Bordiga, Ruth Fischer and Hugo Urbahns pitched against the sober realism of the Bolsheviks.[7]

The watchword of the early Comintern congresses was clarity. At the second congress, Zinoviev exclaimed: "We need clarity, clarity and once more clarity". At the fourth congress, Clara Zetkin would repeat the mantra, "Clarity, clarity and again clarity!" The sentiment was echoed by the youth leader Richard Schüller, who recalled the old slogan: "First clarity, then majority".[8] It was a goal to strive for and a measure of their success fighting the ideological front of the class struggle.

Assessments of the international situation

The Russian revolutionaries won in 1917 because throughout their lives they adhered to the Marxist dictum, often attributed to Lassalle, to always state boldly what is. The starting point for political policy was an assessment of the current reality and would always involve telling the truth to the workers about the situation, no matter how bitter. Trotsky articulated this method of analysis emphatically within the Comintern. After the founding conference, he argued that "the awakening masses demand that things be said out loud, that things be called by their real names, that there be no indefinite half-tones but clear and precise demarcations in politics, that the traitors be boycotted and hounded, that their places be taken by revolutionists devoted body and soul to the cause". Later in the manifesto he wrote after the third congress, he wrote that "the Communist International bases its policies on a calm and objective examination of the world situation. Only by carefully observing the field of battle, only through sober understanding, can the proletariat achieve victory".[9]

At the first and second congresses, the delegates believed the situation was imminently revolutionary. Zinoviev put this particularly bluntly at the second congress, arguing that "the epoch in which we live is that of open civil wars".[10] At the second congress, Lenin presented the 'Theses on the International Situation and the Fundamental Tasks of the Communist International', painting an analysis of the global conjuncture similar to the view he had developed during the war. He argued that "the economic relations of imperialism form the basis of the international situation as it now presents itself. In the course of the twentieth century a new, highest and final stage of capitalism has taken shape". However, he also sounded a note of caution on the existential crisis facing capitalism and the basis of revolutionary activity. He highlighted two widely-held errors. On the one hand, the "bourgeois economists always present this crisis, in the elegant English phrase, as mere 'unrest'". The situation in 1920 was a real revolutionary opportunity for the working class to take power. However, on the other hand "revolutionaries sometimes try to prove that there is absolutely no way out of the crisis". "This", he said, "is a mistake. There is no such thing as an absolutely hopeless situation". If the revolutionary could not rise to the occasion, then the bourgeoisie would recover. It was a prescient warning, since nowhere were revolutionary socialists able to repeat the Bolshevik experience and lead the workers to power. Capitalism tottered, workers' movements organised, but capital managed still to stabilise its rule.[11]

The change in the balance of class forces and between states was the subject of heated debate at the third congress in 1921. Trotsky delivered the 'Report on World Economic Crisis', urging delegates to "recognise that the bourgeoisie today still feels strong. In the past it was perhaps stronger, but at the very least it feels much stronger now than it did in 1919". The capitalist recovery was exemplified by the "fact of world-historical significance", namely that "the economic centre of gravity is no longer in Europe but in the United States". After the post-war economic crisis, there had been a capitalist recovery in 1921.

Trotsky posed the question that had exercised revolutionaries: must we conclude that when a boom begins after attempted or failed revolutions, this signifies that the revolution is finished? He chided those comrades who "base themselves on the notion that crisis is the mother of revolution, and that prosperity is, so to speak, the gravedigger of revolution". Trotsky denied any such mechanical association. "For there is simply no automatic linkage between the revolutionary working-class movement and crisis. Rather than an automatic linkage, what we have is a dialectical interaction". But he warned that the revolutionary upsurge could now be a matter of years, rather than months as they had previously believed.[12]

The discussion of the international political situation at the fourth congress took place on the same ground as laid down by the third. The basic assessment made by Trotsky was that the post-war revolutionary wave had ebbed, capitalism had temporarily stabilised, the working class was on the defensive and the communist parties were in a minority. Karl Radek tersely told the congress: "The conquest of power is not on the agenda as an immediate task". There were some differences of emphasis. Zinoviev argued that "what we are now experiencing is not one of capitalism's periodic crises but the crisis of capitalism, its twilight, its disintegration". However, Trotsky warned that "if the capitalist world lasts another several decades, well that would be a sentence of death for socialist Russia", and Radek stated that the policies of the Communist International "embrace a perspective for an entire epoch, but must still be cut to the shape of the next immediate period". The early Comintern therefore did not engage in panoramic crystal ball gazing or overblown catastrophism. Tight, short-term realist assessments were the order of the day.[13]

Party building

The Comintern's assessments of the international situation were aimed at orientating the burgeoning world communist movement and helping these parties to grapple with the tasks of winning power. The early Comintern was a series of attempts to help revolutionaries of different stripes, schooled in very different labour movements outside Russia, to assimilate the lessons of 1917. In the event, the Russians' advice on party building had to navigate between the opportunism of the reformists and centrists drawn to the Communist

International, and the sectarianism of various "lefts", including syndicalists, semi-anarchists and council communists.

Lenin's attempt to explain the RSDLP's approach was *Left-Wing Communism: an Infantile Disorder*. Written in April-May 1920, and published in time for delegates at the second congress, the book has many virtues, especially in the realm of strategy and tactics. One point Lenin makes, which is often overlooked, is the argument that the Bolshevik faction took its cue from the SPD model in Germany. He wrote that "history, incidentally, has now confirmed on a vast and worldwide scale the opinion we have always advocated, namely, that German revolutionary social-democracy… came closest to being the party the revolutionary proletariat needs in order to achieve victory!" Lenin's point was that the Bolsheviks did not invent their own special theory of the party, but borrowed and applied in Russian conditions the best methods they could observe in the international movement.

Lenin went on to map the stages in the evolution of the Bolshevik faction from its origins to the seizure of power. Unfortunately, he did not explain the first 20 years of efforts to found the RSDLP or indeed the founding conference in 1898, which have led many readers to equate the history of the party solely with the Bolshevik faction. On this point Lenin's words were ambiguous, stating that "as a current of political thought and as a political party, Bolshevism has existed since 1903". As a faction, the Bolsheviks did indeed originate from the split within the RSDLP. However, Lenin did not argue at the time nor subsequently that the Bolsheviks immediately became a definitively separate political party. He would of course have known the Bolshevik faction had reunified with the rest of the RSDLP in 1906 and only broke organisational ties again in 1912, and even, for many cells inside Russia, as late as 1917. However, Lenin did helpfully divide the history of the Bolshevik faction into its stages: the years of preparation for revolution (1903-05), the years of revolution (1905-07), the years of reaction (1907-10), the years of revival (1910-14), the First World War (1914-17) and the second revolution in Russia (February to October 1917). Lenin was trying to establish the historical context for subsequent discussions on party-building, crucial debates at the second congress of the Comintern.[14]

The second Comintern congress on party building
Zinoviev was the main reporter on the 'Theses on the Role of the Communist Party in the Proletarian Revolution' at the second congress. The resolution laid down in plain language what a genuine communist party ought to look like. The theses stated that commu-

nist parties should be "the most advanced, most class-conscious and therefore its most revolutionary part" of the working class. The party was "the organisational and political lever" to move the whole class, although "the concept of the party and that of the class must be kept strictly separate". Communist parties "must be organised on the basis of democratic centralism", which he defined as "election of the higher party cells by the lowest, the fact that all instructions by a superior body are unconditionally and necessarily binding on lower ones, and the existence of a strong central party leadership whose authority… is universally accepted".[15]

Zinoviev took on the arguments of those opposed to organising a party at all. He tackled Anton Pannekoek, whose pamphlet *World Revolution and Communist Tactics* was published and distributed at the congress. Zinoviev summed up the necessity of a proletarian party with an analogy. He argued that "you cannot counterpose the head to the torso. You cannot counterpose his right hand to his body. And the point is precisely that the party is the head of the working class. Organisation is the right hand of the proletariat in its struggle for emancipation". His strongest argument was to point to the immense power of the bourgeoisie lined up against the working class, arguing that without leadership the workers would not be able to make a successful revolution against the combined forces of the ruling class. He also alluded to the importance of bourgeois ideology in dividing the working class, implying a heterogeneity of ideas between workers that could only be united if the most advanced sections of the class organised and clarified the interests of the class as a whole. He acknowledged that the revolutionary syndicalists wanted to fight against the dictatorship of the bourgeoisie, "but do not know how". He dismissed "amorphous workers' unions living from hand to mouth" as inadequate for the task of seizing power, proposing instead "a party that encompasses the best of the working class, is built over decades, and is a firm nucleus".

Zinoviev went on to pose the question, what kind of party? His answer was that "we do not need a party like those of the Second International or some of those parties of the centre today. Such parties play an objectively reactionary role". His point was that the Comintern had become fantastically popular, attracting social democratic leaders who had played a treacherous role during the war and in the class struggle in their own countries, who now apparently sought to embrace communism, but only to keep control of their organisations as rank-and-file members moved left. Hence the second congress drew up the 21 conditions, imposing strict protocols for admission to the new international. Lenin explained this more clearly than Zinoviev a year later. He argued that the first step was "to create a real communist party so as to know whom we were talking to and whom we could fully trust". That meant "a clean break with the centrists and semi-centrists, whom in Russia we call Mensheviks". The conditions were only a preparatory step, but a necessary first step other parties had to follow.

Zinoviev made a rather one sided attempt to tackle the arguments of those revolutionaries who "agree a party is needed but not a centralised party with iron discipline". He argued that the most important experience of the Russian revolution was that "had we not had a centralised party built along military lines, with iron discipline, organised over the course of twenty years, by now we doubtless would have been defeated twenty times over". He stated that "to make use of the experiences of the Russian revolution, we must embrace one central idea above all others: we need a communist party — a centralised party with iron discipline". He believed "the best thing that we instilled in the Russian worker is love for the party". Zinoviev's concentration on the disciplinary aspect of the revolutionary party was understandable in the context of the swirl of amorphous ideas during 1920. But his failure to draw out the essential and complementary democratic essence of Bolshevism did not help the lefts to overcome their shortcomings and laid the ground for misunderstanding and distortion on these questions in later debates.[16] It was also left to Trotsky to spell out the kind of morality that should pervade a good communist party member in a leadership role:

> *In all their work whether as leader of a revolutionary strike, or as organiser of underground groups, or as secretary of a trade union, or as agitator at mass meetings, whether as deputy, cooperative worker or barricade fighter, the communist always remains true to themselves as a disciplined member of the communist party, a zealous fighter, a mortal enemy of capitalist society, its economic foundation, its state forms, its democratic lies, its religion and its morality. S/he is a self-sacrificing soldier of the proletarian revolution and an indefatigable herald of the new society.*[17]

The third Comintern congress on party building
The third congress returned to the question of party building, laying down detailed guidelines for how communist parties ought to function. The 'Theses on the Organisational Structure of the Communist Parties' were written by the Finnish communist Otto Kuusinen and the motivating speech was made by the German communist Wilhelm

Koenen. However, letters written before the congress indicate that Lenin made a series of amendments and additions to their work.

The theses affirmed the previous conclusion that a communist party "aims to be the vanguard of the proletariat, its leading contingent, in every phase of its revolutionary class struggle". However there is "no immutable, absolutely correct structure for communist parties". The theses stated that democratic centralism in a communist party "should be a true synthesis and fusion of centralism and proletarian democracy. This fusion can be achieved only on the foundation of constant and common activity and struggle by the entire party". It was not enough for a party to adopt a communist programme, particularly if most members' party work remained passive. The theses laid strong emphasis on the necessity of a "genuinely active membership", in which "everyone in its ranks... commit their energy and time to the party, to the extent possible under given circumstances, and to always do their best in its service".

The Comintern highlighted the importance of the formalities of party organisation. Membership of the communist party normally involves formal registration, initially as a candidate and later as a full member. It requires the regular payment of fixed dues, a subscription to the party newspaper, and, most importantly, the participation of every member in daily party work. Each member "should, as a rule, belong to a small working group, be it a committee, collective, fraction, or cell. This is the only way that party work can be properly allocated, led, and carried out". Leading party committees were obligated "to exert constant, inexhaustible, and direct leadership of the party's work". Members should make propaganda for communist ideas by doing "door-to-door agitation... specially organised street agitation, utilising posters and leaflets... and regular person-to-person agitation at workplaces, linked to distribution of written materials".

However, the only purpose of these internal party norms was to enable communists to better lead the workers "in an ongoing guerrilla war against the attacks of capital". Communists "must take part in all elemental working-class struggles and movements and lead the workers in every battle with the capitalists over hours and wages, working conditions, and the like". Special emphasis was laid on workplace cells and fractions, whose job it was to "strike these blows systematically". Communists were warned not to exempt "the lower level trade-union bureaucracy", whose "intentions are often good, they hide their weakness behind union by-laws and decisions and instructions of the union top leadership". Communist intervention in trade-union meetings and conferences "needs to be carefully prepared by the fractions and working groups".

The theses strongly emphasised the importance of the communist press. All party publications, including magazines, books, pamphlets and so on, had to be under the supervision of the party. The focus was more on the quality of newspapers than on their number, although the minimum expectation was to produce "a strong central organ, appearing if possible on a daily basis". The paper was the central tool for guiding the work of communists. The paper is the "daily weapon, which must be steeled and sharpened anew each day in order to be usable. The communist newspaper can be sustained only by ongoing and substantial material and financial contributions". What distinguished a communist newspaper was "direct involvement in campaigns led by the party".

Finally, and importantly, the theses spelt out more clearly than previously the relationship between democracy and centralism. They stated that "every party unit and committee and every single member has the right to express their wishes and make proposals, comments, and complaints at any time directly to the party central leadership or the International". Party members are "obligated always to conduct themselves, in all their public activity, as disciplined members of a combat organisation". When disagreements arise over a course of action, "these should, if possible, be settled within the party before acting". (The right to form factions was not spelt out explicitly but would have been obvious to all communists of that day. They also took rights of dissent and debate in the party press for granted). However, in order to ensure that every party decision will be carried out energetically by all party units and members, "the broadest possible range of members should be involved in considering and deciding every question". Above all, "the highest duty of every member is to defend the communist party and, above all, the Communist International, against all enemies of communism".[18] As such, the third congress provided the emerging communist parties with a manual to guide their organisational regime and make them a force to be reckoned with on all fronts of the class struggle.

The fourth Comintern congress on party building

Communist parties continued to develop in the year after the third congress, but there were fissures to the left, with some anarchist and syndicalist-influenced tendencies breaking away from the international. The leaders of the Russian party continued to intervene, spurred by the fifth anniversary of the October revolution and the impending fourth Comintern congress at the end of 1922. Trotsky reminded supporters that the communist party is "the organisation of the proletarian vanguard for the ideological fructification of the labour movement and the assumption of leadership in all spheres". He contrasted the success of the Bolsheviks in 1917 with the missed opportunities elsewhere in 1919 and 1920, posing the question: what was lacking? He answered, "lacking was the political premise, the subjective premise, i.e., cognisance of the situation by the proletariat. Lacking was an organisation at the head of the proletariat, capable of utilising the situation for nothing else but the direct organisational and technical preparation of an uprising, of the overturn, the seizure of power, and so forth. This is what was lacking".[19] Hence the fourth congress would also revisit the party question.

At the fourth congress in November-December 1922, Lenin made some of his last public interventions on the party question, despite suffering with ill health. His only speech to the congress referred back to the party organisation resolution at the third congress and could be regarded as his last testament to the international communist movement. His reflections repay careful reading, as they show the unfinished project of explaining the Russian experience to other international socialists. Lenin argued that the third congress resolution "is an excellent one, but it is almost entirely Russian, that is to say, everything in it is based on Russian experience. This is its good point, but it is also its failing. It is its failing because I am sure that no foreigner can read it". He argued that the resolution was too long, too "thoroughly imbued with the Russian spirit" and could not be carried out.

Lenin said that he had "the impression that we made a big mistake with this resolution, namely, that we blocked our own road to further success". The resolution was "excellently drafted" and he was "prepared to subscribe to every one of its fifty or more points". However, he was still critical of the Russian party for not learning "how to present our Russian experience to foreigners". Fellow revolutionaries "need something more advanced: first of all, they must learn to understand what we have written about the organisational structure of the communist parties, which the foreign comrades have signed without reading and understanding. This must be their first task". But in carrying out the resolution, foreign communists "cannot be content with hanging it in a corner like an icon and praying to it. Nothing will be achieved that way. They must assimilate part of the Russian experience".[20] Lenin urged delegates above all to study. He meant to study the situation they were in and study the states and labour movements in which they lived, and draw on, rather than mechanically apply, the methods and lessons of the Russian experience. Lenin also meant to study the real history of the RSDLP with all its twists and turns and false starts. There could be no blueprint, no definitive history to explain this history; it had to be thought about and argued over. The Bolsheviks gathered a great deal of historical material on Russian party history, including documents and testimony during the 1920s. Tragically, the Stalinisation of the Comintern would cut across these efforts and, apart from Trotsky's works, no further authentic party-building guidance was produced.

Strategy and tactics

Marxist strategy and tactics were not invented by the Comintern. The Communist League had discussed strategy before, during and after the 1848 revolutions, and the First International had vital strategic and tactical debates — for example, on the trade union question. Since Marxist strategy is essentially about combining the immediate struggle for reforms with the longer-term struggle for revolution, the Second International and its sections also engaged in frequent debates on these matters. The most prominent debate was with Bernstein and his revisionist current at the end of the nineteenth century — an attempt to remove the strategic goal from the movement. Luxemburg and Kautsky debated the mass strike prior to the First World War, with Kautsky drawing a rigid distinction between the "strategy of attrition" and the "strategy of overthrow". Trotsky criticised even the best Marxists of the Second International for confining themselves "solely to the conception of social democratic tactics... parliamentary tactics, trade union tactics, municipal tactics, cooperative tactics, and so on". Strategy — "the question of combining all forces and resources... to obtain victory over the enemy was really never raised... insofar as the practical task of the struggle for power was not raised". It was the 1905 revolution that "first posed, after a long interval, the fundamental or strategical questions of proletarian struggle". This gave the Russian Marxists "immense advantages" when the "great epoch of revolutionary strategy" began in 1917 for Russia and the rest of Europe.[21]

What are strategy and tactics?

The early Comintern discussion elaborated on the distinction between strategy and tactics, as well as applying these concepts to the realities the revolutionaries were in. Trotsky explained that these concepts took root only in the post-war years and were derived from military terminology. Tactics were understood as "the system of measures that serves a single current task or a single branch of the class struggle", whereas revolutionary strategy "embraces a combined system of actions which by their association, consistency, and growth must lead the proletariat to the conquest of power". The Comintern held a more flexible conception of strategy, allowing for "a strategy of manoeuvre, a strategy of position, or a strategy combining both elements".[22] In summary:

> By tactics in politics we understand, using the analogy of military science, the art of conducting isolated operations. By strategy, we understand the art of conquest, i.e., the seizure of power. Prior to the war we did not, as a rule, make this distinction...
> Strategy, of course, does not do away with tactics. The questions of the trade union movement, of parliamentary activity, and so on, do not disappear, but they now become invested with a new meaning as subordinate methods of a combined struggle for power. Tactics are subordinated to strategy.[23]

The first manual of strategy produced by the Comintern was Lenin's *Left-Wing Communism* (1920), to inform the second congress. Lenin demanded that communists "must absolutely work wherever the masses are to be found". Their job was to "seek out, investigate, predict, and grasp that which is nationally specific and nationally distinctive, in the concrete manner in which each country should tackle a single international task", namely, winning a majority among the workers and leading them to power. It was not sufficient to win the vanguard of the working class but to win support among the majority of the class. Strategy meant it was "necessary to link the strictest devotion to the ideas of communism with the ability to effect all the necessary practical compromises, tacks, conciliatory manoeuvres, zigzags, retreats and so on". Communists had to learn how to champion the interests of the workers' revolution (by propaganda, agitation and organisation) "in non-revolutionary bodies, and quite often in downright reactionary bodies, in a non-revolutionary situation, among the masses who are incapable of immediately appreciating the need for revolutionary methods of action". As such Lenin believed that Marxist politics was "more like algebra than elementary arithmetic, and still more like higher than elementary mathematics". Lenin explained that "tactics must be based on a sober and strictly objective appraisal of all the class forces in a particular state (and of the states that surround it, and of all states the world over) as well as of the experience of revolutionary movements". He emphasised that communist parties could not be built on "stereotyped, mechanically equated, and identical tactical rules of struggle". However, there were broad principles and these were demonstrated by communist work in bourgeois parliaments, the trade unions, and in other workers' organisations.[24]

Lenin warned the "lefts" who regarded parliamentarianism as politically obsolete that they had "mistaken their desire, their politico-ideological attitude, for objective reality". Of course, bourgeois democratic forms were inferior to working-class democratic forms such as soviets. But for millions of workers parliamentarianism was not obsolete: they still looked to the elected representatives in bourgeois legislatures to improve their lives. Parliamentary democracy was not obsolete to masses of the working class. Communists are "duty bound to call their bourgeois-democratic and parliamentary prejudices what they are — prejudices". But at the same time communists "must soberly follow the actual state of the class-consciousness and preparedness of the entire class (not only of its communist vanguard)". This meant communists standing for election to bourgeois legislatures, using parliament when elected as a platform for communist propaganda, proposing reforms and thereby demonstrating in practice the limitations of these organs (see chapter 4).

Lenin also warned against the attitude of the "lefts" towards the trade unions. Of course, many trade unions were (and still are) led by traitors to the working class, people who have accommodated to bourgeois politics. But the answer was not to withdraw from these workers' organisations and set up pure communist trade unions. Lenin reminded readers that the trade unions were "a tremendous step forward for the working class in the early days of capitalist development, inasmuch as they marked a transition from the workers' disunity and helplessness to the rudiments of class organisation". Even when the highest form of proletarian class organisation, the revolutionary party, had been formed, "the development of the proletariat did not, and could not, proceed anywhere in the world otherwise than through the trade unions, through reciprocal action between them and the party of the working class". Trade unions "are and will long remain an indispensable 'school of communism' and a preparatory school that trains proletarians to exercise their dictatorship, an indispensable organisation of the workers for the gradual transfer of the management of the whole economic life of the country to the working class". Organised fractions within the existing unions was the normal strategy for communists.[25]

The Second Comintern congress on strategy and tactics

When Lenin wrote *Left Wing Communism* in early 1920, there was an ongoing tactical debate among British comrades about whether their about-to-be formed communist party should affiliate to the Labour Party. In the pamphlet, Lenin confessed he had not yet made up his mind on the question of affiliation, although he acknowledged the "unique character" of the party, based on the trade unions, "whose very structure is so unlike that of the political parties usual in the European continent".[26]

By the time of the second congress, Lenin was advocating British communists affiliate to the Labour party. He stated that "I have come to the conclusion that the decision to remain within the Labour Party is the only correct tactic". He motivated his position on two grounds: first, the Marxists already inside the party, including members of the British Socialist Party (BSP), had freedom to criticise the leadership. Second, "members of the Labour Party are all members of trade unions. It has a very unusual structure, to be found in no other country. It is an organisation that embraces four million workers out of the six or seven million organised in trade unions". However, he conceded that some British communists such as Sylvia Pankhurst and Willie Gallagher disagreed and therefore proposed a special commission to examine the question.[27] After two days of debate in the commission and further contributions on the floor of the congress, delegates voted strongly in favour of affiliation. The resolution stated:

> *The Second Congress of the Third International should declare in favour of communist groups and organisations, or groups and organisations sympathising with communism, joining the Labour Party in Great Britain, despite its membership in the Second International. As long as this party ensures its affiliated organisations their present freedom of criticism and freedom to carry on work of propaganda, agitation and organisation in favour of the dictatorship of the proletariat and Soviet government, and as long as this party preserves the character of a federation of all trade union organisations of the working class, it is imperative for communists to do everything and to make certain compromises in order to be able to exercise their influence on the broadest masses of the workers, to expose their opportunist leaders from a higher tribune, that is in fuller view of the masses, and to hasten the transfer of political power from the direct representatives of the bourgeoisie to the 'labour lieutenants of the capitalist class', so that the masses may be more quickly weaned away from their last illusions on this score.*[28]

Both Pankhurst and Gallagher were given time to articulate their views to the whole congress. Lenin argued for clarity on the Labour Party question. Although he agreed with the BSP position, he nevertheless criticised its representative William McLaine, who called the Labour Party the political organisation of the trade union movement. Lenin said that he had "met the same view several times in the paper of the British Socialist Party. It is erroneous, and is partly the cause of the opposition, fully justified in some measure, coming from the British revolutionary workers". The concepts "political department of the trade unions" or "political expression" of the trade union movement, "are erroneous". Of course, most of the Labour Party's members were workers. However, "whether or not a party is really a political party of the workers does not depend solely upon a membership of workers but also upon those that lead it, and the content of its actions and its political tactics. Only this latter determines whether we really have before us a political party of the proletariat". Regarded from this point of view, he said "the Labour Party is a thoroughly bourgeois party, because, although made up of workers, it is led by reactionaries, and the worst kind of reactionaries at that, who act quite in the spirit of the bourgeoisie". It is an organisation of the bourgeoisie, which exists to systematically dupe the workers".

But that did not settle the question. Lenin argued that "the British Labour Party is in a very special position: it is a highly original type of party, or rather, it is not at all a party in the ordinary sense of the word". It was "made up of members of all trade unions, and has a membership of about four million, and allows sufficient freedom to all affiliated political parties". It included "a vast number of British workers who follow the lead of the worst bourgeois elements, the social-traitors". At the same time, the Labour Party had let the BSP into its ranks, "permitting it to have its own press organs, in which members of the self-same Labour Party can freely and openly declare that the party leaders are social-traitors". Lenin's forensic characterisation of the Labour Party as a bourgeois workers' party meant that tactically, it made sense for British communists to join it, seek affiliation to it and fight within it for their ideas. But to underline the tactical nature of the intervention, Lenin admitted that if the Labour leaders expelled British communists for "acting in a revolutionary manner in the Labour Party", then that would be "a great victory for the communist and revolutionary working class movement in Britain".[29]

The third Comintern congress on tactics and strategy
The third Comintern congress in 1921 reviewed and extended the

conceptions of tactics and strategy developed a year earlier at the second congress. Zinoviev gave the executive's report, in which he recalled the question of the British comrades' participation in the Labour Party. He reiterated that communists had "a great responsibility to take part in the mass organisation that embraces hundreds of thousands and millions of proletarians, to organise our forces there, form cells, and in this way win influence in it". The second congress gave a clear directive "to take part in these mass organisations and to oblige all our new communist groups to take part in formations like the Labour Party and in the trade unions". The Comintern told the comrades, "You have to organise there and struggle within the trade unions against the trade union bureaucracy and reform-socialist politics. You must succeed in winning influence in these organisations for communism". Zinoviev added, "I believe the British comrades will now admit that it was not they but the Second Congress that was right in this matter when it said: Not out of the Labour Party, but into it, in order to struggle for communism and expose the traitorous leaders from the inside".[30]

However, more important events prompted a further review of strategy and tactics. Lefts within the Comintern had promoted the so-called "theory of the offensive", which involved the voluntaristic pushing on with revolutionary actions in spite of adverse political conditions. In March 1921 the KPD suffered a huge defeat, which in part was of its own making, although some Comintern functionaries (notably Bela Kun) were also complicit. In an atmosphere of crisis, on 16 March, a social democratic security chief ordered police to occupy the mining district of Mansfeld, with the objective of disarming striking workers. After exchanges of gun fire, police occupied the district, only to be met by a local general strike. On 24 March the KPD central committee called for a general strike but it was not followed. A week later the KPD rescinded the strike order but the party was still made illegal. A number of its leaders, including Paul Levi, denounced the adventurist policies and were expelled. The German party lost a hundred thousand members, including many trade union cadres. This was the immediate background to the Comintern's discussions. The congress decided to describe the KPD's March action as a "forward step", while at the same time condemning the theory of "the offensive at all costs" which its supporters had put forward.

Karl Radek was the principal spokesperson for the Comintern's report. He began with an important methodological point, asserting that "the question of the Communist International's tactics and strategy cannot be separated from the facts regarding the period of time in which it is functioning. In determining its tactics, the Communist International must begin with a specific analysis of the present epoch". He therefore rightly regarded the strategy and tactics resolution as following from Trotsky's assessment of the political and economic situation provided earlier at the congress.

Radek argued that the main task the Comintern posed from its inception for the new communist groups and parties was "to win the broad masses of the proletariat for the goals of communism and to assemble the working-class forces that play a decisive role in social and political life". He added that "no matter how small a communist party may be, it has the task of marching at the head of the mass movement in its country".[31]

A sign of the polarisation between the Russian leadership, highly critical of the March escapade, and the German leaders, was the duration of the debate — over three days. Lenin summed up the mood of the Bolsheviks by insisting "not a single letter in the theses be altered". In fact they were amended, though no concessions were made to the German leadership. Bukharin harked back to examples in the Russian party's history to show that "the tactical line is something that is not fixed but is absolutely in motion, always determined by the specific position and the specific conditions". Trotsky also weighed in, arguing that "it is sometimes forgotten that we learn the art of strategy, precisely and soberly estimate the enemy's power, and analyse the situation, rather than rushing into battle to break the wall of passivity or, in the words of another comrade, 'to activate the party'".[32]

As John Riddell rightly highlights, there was a shift in strategy set in motion at the third congress. This involved: (1) the adoption of the united front policy (December 1921); (2) the elaboration of this policy with respect to positions on transitional demands and workers' governments and on anti-imperialist struggles (December 1922); (3) development of a policy for united resistance to fascism (May 1923). Although the Third Congress decisions were "a working compromise among a still very divided body of delegates, agreement was achieved around a strategic course of going 'to the masses', taking part in their daily struggles, and seeking to win their majority to a revolutionary course, as a precondition for achieving workers' power. The congress manifesto called on workers to join in a "single unified front'"[33] Reviewing these discussions reveals the methods of work communists can develop in today's conditions.

Programmes and transitional demands

Before the Communist International, Marxist programmes had included the *Communist Manifesto* (1848), the *Erfurt Programme* (1891), the Russian social democratic programme (1903) and the *Spartacus programme* (1918). One weakness of previous programmes was on the link between the minimum, immediate demands for reform and the maximum goal of socialism. One of the great gains of the third Comintern congress discussion and resolution on tactics and strategy was the codification of what became known as transitional demands. Radek's theses elaborated a conception of "partial demands", which would reshape the way communists fought alongside other workers still tied to reformist ideas and organisations. The key passages stated:

> *The communist parties do not propose a minimum programme for these struggles, one designed to reinforce and improve the rickety structure of capitalism. Instead, destruction of this structure remains their guiding goal and their immediate task. But to achieve this task, the communist parties have to advance demands whose achievement meets an immediate, urgent need of the working class, and fight for these demands regardless of whether they are compatible with the capitalist profit system...*
>
> *In place of the minimum programme of the centrists and reformists, the Communist International offers a struggle for the specific demands of the proletariat, as part of a system of demands that, in their totality, undermine the power of the bourgeoisie, organise the proletariat, and mark out the different stages of the struggle for proletarian dictatorship. Each of these demands gives expression to the needs of the broad masses, even when they do not yet consciously take a stand for proletarian dictatorship.*[34]

Radek explained that the task was "to work out clearly the differences between the minimum programme of social democracy, the action programme of the centrists, and the slogans of the Communist International". Previous minimum programmes of social democracy "advanced demands that could be realised within capitalist society. Their revolutionary effect arose from the fact that even these demands, which were realisable and essential to the working class, were rejected again and again by capitalist society". The Comintern's approach was that "rather than worrying that we may be reforming the capitalist state, we should focus instead on the fact that we are helping the worker in this struggle, and we will lead him beyond this struggle to other, heightened struggles". Radek said this approach did not fetishise particular slogans, as these "arise from the struggle itself".

Rather communists "must make the struggles of the masses for their immediate needs more acute and broaden them, teaching the workers to develop a greater need — the need to take possession of power".[35]

At the Fourth Comintern congress, August Thalheimer, who along with Heinrich Brandler had been utilising transitional demands to build united fronts between the KPD and other workers' organisations, confessed that he had "a sharp disagreement with Comrade Bukharin... [over] the question of transitional demands, demands for stages, and the minimum programme". He argued that "the specific disagreement between us and the reform-socialists is not the fact that we put demands for reforms, demands for a stage, or whatever you want to call them in a chambre séparée and keep them outside our programme. Rather, the difference is that we link transitional demands and slogans very tightly with our principles and goals. This linkage is, of course, no guarantee in itself, any more than having a good map guarantees that I will not lose my way". The matter was discussed at a meeting of five Russian communist party central committee members (Lenin, Trotsky, Zinoviev, Radek, Bukharin) on 20 November 1922 in favour of Thalheimer's proposal. The resolution vindicated the use of transitional slogans and was adopted unanimously. It stated:

> *3) The programmes of the national sections must motivate clearly and decisively the need to struggle for transitional demands, with the appropriate proviso that these demands are derived from the specific conditions of place and time;*
> *4) The overall programme must definitely provide a theoretical framework for all transitional and immediate demands. At the same time, the Fourth Congress strongly condemns efforts to portray as opportunism the inclusion of transitional demands in the programme.*[36]

The United Front

Another conception codified by the early Comintern that still resonates in the Marxist lexicon is the united front. It broadly concerns the way in which revolutionary socialists work with and alongside reformist workers for action around specific goals. It is premised on the fact that revolutionaries are in the minority, but can fight for reforms alongside other workers in order to develop the class struggle in a socialist direction. The fourth Comintern congress is important because it was the largest meeting to discuss how to implement the united front tactic.

The united front was the product of the experience of revolutionary workers, particularly in Germany, working out how to operate in the post-war circumstances they found themselves in. In November 1920, KPD activists in Stuttgart, led by Clara Zetkin, decided to launch a campaign for workers' unity in action. The Stuttgart communists made a proposal in the local metal workers' union to petition the union's national leadership and other unions for united action. The Stuttgart metal workers' leadership adopted five demands reflecting workers' most urgent needs, demands "held in common by all workers": reduce prices for necessities of life; produce at full capacity and increase unemployment benefits; reduce taxes paid by workers and raise taxes on the great private fortunes; establish workers' control of supply and distribution of raw materials and foodstuffs; and disarm reactionary gangs and arm the workers.[37]

The Stuttgart initiative got a good response, so the KPD central leadership (Zentrale) decided on 29 December 1920 to initiate a wider movement for united working-class action. Paul Levi and Radek drafted an open letter, published 8 January 1921. Although the KPD initiative was rebuffed by the SPD and USPD, the idea was propagated at the third Comintern congress in 1921. Lenin argued that "the open letter is a model" and this was stated in the theses on tactics and strategy. He said it was a model because "it is the first step in a practical method to win over the majority of the working class. In Europe, where almost all the proletarians are organised, we must win the majority of the working class". Trotsky's manifesto at the end of the third congress picked up on this conception, even using the expression that would later become ubiquitous. He argued that the bourgeoisie would be defeated by communists "taking up the questions of bread, of wages, of the workers' clothing and the workers' housing... This is a struggle to seize the enemy fortresses planted in our own camp. It is a struggle to form a front of struggle against which world capitalism can only fail". Only in the struggle for the most basic essentials of life of the working masses could communists "establish the unified front of the proletariat against the bourgeoisie and end the splintering of the proletariat". This proletarian front would be "strong and militant only if it is held together by communist parties, unified and strong in spirit and iron in their discipline". The third world congress "turns to communists everywhere with the call, 'To the masses!' and 'Establish the unified proletarian front!'"[38]

The Comintern executive did not try to force member parties to apply this policy. However, through a succession of discussions and experiences in the national sections, acceptance of the united front policy widened. At the fourth congress, debate focused on how, not whether, to apply it. Zinoviev explained what the united front meant in his executive report at the beginning of the congress. He said that "the united front is established by the overall situation of capitalism, by its economic and world political situation, and by the situation inside the workers' movement". The united front tactic was "the most effective means to win this majority of the working class. It must be stated clearly that the united front tactic is no mere episode in our struggle. It is a tactic that will endure for an entire period, perhaps an entire epoch". He added: "We are against reformism, but not against bettering the lives of the working class... We can only organise the working class if we fight for its partial demands".

Radek argued that workers must "unite at least for the struggle for bare existence, for a crust of bread". Communists should "conduct a struggle around questions that have the greatest immediate relevance to the broad working masses: questions of wages, hours of work, housing, defence against white danger, against the war danger, and all the issues of working people's daily life... Only by broadening, deepening and heightening these struggles will a struggle for [proletarian] dictatorship arise". However the Italian communist Amadeo Bordiga continued to oppose the tactic, arguing that "the danger exists of the united front degenerating into a communist revisionism".[39] Radek also explained what it meant in practice. He told the congress that the Communist Party of Great Britain would apply its united front tactic by seeking to affiliate to the Labour Party, and in the next election: "Vote for it and prepare for struggle against it". Solomon Lozovskii argued that the struggle for a united front of the trade union movement was the most important issue before the communist parties of every country.[40]

The Workers' Government
Probably the most wide-ranging and rancorous discussion at the fourth Comintern congress concerned the transitional slogan of a workers' government. Again, it was the German experience that loomed largest.

On 13 March 1920 a right-wing military putsch led by Wolfgang Kapp and General von Lüttwitz ousted the government in Berlin. The SPD-led trade unions (ADGB) called for a general strike to defend the republic. By 14 March the strike was solid across the country. Workers formed local strike committees, demonstrated and formed militias. On 17 March the putschists capitulated and fled. The general strike continued as workers demanded a new government and decisive action against the militarist threat. Trade union leader Carl

Legien proposed that the SPD's coalition with bourgeois parties be replaced by a workers' government formed by the SPD, the USPD and the trade unions. The KPD leadership eventually expressed support for this proposal and promised, subject to certain conditions, to act towards such a government as a "loyal opposition". The USPD refused to participate, which effectively finished the proposal.[41]

However, the debate continued to rage, particularly in state elections where the combination of SPD, USPD and KPD votes gave the workers' organisations a majority. The KPD called for a workers' republic based on councils like the Russian soviets. But in 1921 such councils did not exist in Germany or elsewhere. The KPD's leadership and Radek tried to formulate a governmental demand that related to Germany's existing political institutions, while pointing towards the goal of workers' power and came up with the "workers' government".

When the fourth Comintern congress opened in November 1922, Zinoviev, as well as ultra-left leaders such as Bordiga, held that the term "workers' government" referred only to a regime of the type established in Russia — a dictatorship of the proletariat. The German communist Ernst Meyer disagreed, arguing that it was important to differentiate between a social-democratic and a workers' government. He said: "We have seen social-democratic governments in Germany, in Saxony and Thuringia, and earlier also in Gotha, governments that we must support but that have nothing in common with what we understand to be a workers' government". He said that the workers' government "differs fundamentally from a social-democratic government, in that it does not merely carry the label of a socialist policy but actually carried out a socialist-communist policy in life". A workers' government will therefore not be parliamentary in character, or will be parliamentary only in a subordinate sense. It was "not a necessary occurrence, but rather a historical possibility".[42]

Radek criticised Zinoviev for defining the workers' government as merely a synonym for the dictatorship of the proletariat. Instead, the workers' government was "one of the possible points of transition to the dictatorship of the proletariat". The German, Norwegian, Czechoslovak workers could take a stand of "no coalition with the bourgeoisie, but rather a coalition with the workers' parties that can secure our eight-hour day, give us a bit more bread, and so on". That could lead to "the establishment of such a workers' government, whether through preliminary struggles or on the basis of a parliamentary combination". It was "nonsense to reject in doctrinaire fashion the possibility of such a situation".

Radek accepted some of Zinoviev's concerns and reservations. The workers' government would be "worthless unless the workers stand behind it, taking up arms and building factory councils that push this government and do not allow it to make compromises with the right". But if that were done, "the workers' government will be the starting point of a struggle for the dictatorship of the proletariat". For example, in Britain, "a parliamentary victory for the Labour Party is quite possible, and then the question will arise, what is this workers' government? Is it nothing more than a new edition of the bourgeois-liberal government". Radek's approach was transitional, taking the demands from the united front to their logical conclusion. But he did not argue that a workers' government was the only, indeed, the necessary or even likely road to power. This he summed up with a rather pithy joke. He told the congress: "It would be entirely wrong to present a picture that the evolution of humanity from ape to people's commissar necessarily passes through a phase of workers' government".[43]

Radek did not leave matters there. In his speech on the capitalist offensive three days later, he returned to his critique. He said: "Zinoviev offered an abstract classification of the possible forms of a workers' government. I agree with this attempt at classification... It is important for us here to replace the abstract classification with the question: 'What do the working masses — not just the communists — think when they talk of a workers' government?'... In Britain, they think of the Labour Party... The idea of a workers' government has the same meaning for the working masses: they think of a government of all workers' parties".

Radek accepted some caveats and acknowledged the nuances between different speakers. He said that "the workers' government is not inevitable, but possible. Or, following comrade Zinoviev, we can say paradoxically that it is not inevitable but is likely the most improbable road". The question to decide when going to the masses was "whether or not we are prepared to struggle for a workers' coalition government and create the preconditions for it". In his opinion, "in our struggle for the united front, we should say frankly that if the social democratic worker masses force their leaders to break with the bourgeoisie, we are ready to take part in a workers' government, provided this government is a vehicle for class struggle". The workers' government slogan "conceives of the united front as a unified political goal".[44]

Soon after the congress, Zetkin wrote an article 'The Workers' Government', summing up the importance of these discussions. She wrote: "In easily the majority of countries under capitalist domination, the workers' government appears as the crowning summit of the tactic of the united front, as the propaganda and rallying slogan of the hour".[45] Overall, Radek, Zetkin and Meyer's arguments on the workers' government slogan appear insightful and innovative. The approach would have helped communist parties to develop their influence within the labour movement, had they not been neutered by the rise of Stalinism. But the method was not forgotten: it was renewed and developed by the left opposition forces around Trotsky into the 1930s.

Black liberation in the United States

Comintern discussions in the early 1920s completely transformed conceptions of anti-racism and black liberation held by communists across the globe and in the communist party in the United States in particular. Historian Jacob Zumoff has produced a new history of the American communist party in the 1920s. He describes "the combination of the intervention of the Communist International — which forced the (white) party leadership to address black oppression — and the efforts of the early black communists to make the party assimilate the Comintern's directives". The change in the US party's politics on black oppression "offers the clearest example of the positive role of Comintern intervention in 'Americanising' the party".[46]

Before the Comintern, American socialist propaganda revealed little about the oppression of black people, despite the prevalence of racism since the civil war and the abolition of slavery. Some right-wing socialists such as Victor Berger were "openly racist, supporting segregation and opposing Asian immigration". Most left-wing socialists were "colour-blind": "they opposed racism, but did not see black oppression as central to maintaining American capitalism". Eugene Debs is the best example of the latter. He saw blacks as suffering from extreme class exploitation, but not racial oppression. In a 1903 article in *International Socialist Review*, he wrote that "there is no Negro question outside of the labour question". He stated, "The class struggle is colourless". Thus, the socialist party had "nothing special to offer to the Negro, and... cannot make separate appeals to all the races". In practice, this attitude towards racial oppression meant that the socialist party never attempted to fight for black liberation and tolerated racists such as Berger. Although the founders of the US communist party spoke out against anti-black racism in the shadow of lynch-mob terror, they continued the colour-blind approach and had nothing to offer apart from anti-racist appeals.[47]

The first Comintern intervention concerning racial oppression in the US took place at the second congress in 1920. The 'Theses on the National and Colonial Questions' mentioned "the Negroes in America" as one of the "nations that are dependent and do not have equal rights". In the lead-up to the congress, John Reed wrote a five-page summary of the history and condition of black people in the US. Lenin urged Reed to deliver a short presentation on the situation facing American black people. When Reed expressed reluctance, Lenin insisted that the report was absolutely necessary. Reed's speech broke no new ground and echoed the colour-blind position. He argued that the "only proper policy for the American communist to follow is to consider the Negro first of all as a labourer". Nonetheless, this was the first time an American communist noted the unique features of black oppression.[48]

The Comintern established a "Negro commission" at the third congress in 1921. Within the US, the Communist Party's first breakthrough in recruiting black cadres was the African Blood Brotherhood (ABB). The ABB was organised by Cyril Briggs and included Grace Campbell, Lovett Fort-Whiteman, Otto Huiswoud and Claude McKay among its members. At the fourth Comintern congress, a commission chaired by Huiswoud drafted theses on the black question. Claude McKay told a plenary session that the "black race at present has a special position in the economic life of the world". McKay condemned the traditional left-wing position, noting that there were "still strong prejudices of this kind among the American socialists and communists".[49] The commission made clear that fighting black oppression must be a key task of communists in the US. Zumoff argues that the fourth congress resolution, "whatever its limitations, was a turning point in the communist appreciation of the links between black oppression and capitalism. It also solidified the Comintern's reputation as a tribune of black concerns within the international movement".[50]

After the congress, Trotsky commissioned McKay to write a study of the black question. The book, published (in Russian) as *The Negroes in America*, argued that "the whole American nation", including white workers, were "possessed by a Negro neurosis". McKay was highly critical of the US Communist Party leadership. A measure of their indifference is the history of the book. Trotsky, not the American communists, commissioned McKay to write it and the US Communist Party never translated, published or distributed the book.[51]

James Cannon recalled how American communists broke with the socialist and radical tradition, which had no special programme on the black question. It was considered simply as an economic problem, part of the struggle between the workers and the capitalists. Cannon wrote: "The American communists in the early days, under the influence and pressure of the Russians in the Comintern, were slowly and painfully learning to change their attitude; to assimilate the new theory of the Negro question as a special question of doubly-exploited second-class citizens, requiring a programme of special demands as part of the overall programme — and to start doing something about it". Cannon registered the change of attitude. He wrote: "The influence of Lenin and the Russian Revolution... and then filtered through the activities of the communist party in the United States, contributed more than any other influence from any source to the recognition, and more or less general acceptance, of the Negro question as a special problem of American society—a problem which cannot be simply subsumed under the general heading of the conflict between capital and labour, as it was in the pre-communist radical movement".[52]

Conclusion

The lessons of the early Comintern were successively ignored and dismantled as Stalinism consumed and finally destroyed the Russian workers' state, the ruling party and the international itself, events which are outlined in the next chapter. The Comintern ceased to assess the realities of the international situation, abandoning the rational strategy and tactics of the early years. At the fifth congress of the Comintern in the summer of 1924 a programme of "Bolshevisation" of the communist parties was declared; inexperienced and capable leaders were replaced by proto-bureaucrats and careerists, factions were banned, internal debate was drowned in demagogy and heresy-hunting. The sectarian lurch at the sixth congress (17 July to 1 September 1928), known as the "third period", detached the communist parties from the labour movements that they sought to lead.

The Comintern conception of transitional demands was never further developed within the international. Although Thalheimer continued to defend transitional demands, Bukharin had succeeded in suppressing the policy by the time of the sixth congress in 1928. The programme adopted at that congress eschewed the transitional approach. Similarly, the sixth congress was a turning point in the communist approach to the black question. A resolution passed shortly after the congress established that the American black population in the so-called southern "Black Belt" was an oppressed nation with the right to self-determination up to independence from the US. Although others may have favoured the self-determination slogan, its Stalinist origins are clear. In particular, it was derivative of Stalin's two-stage theory of revolution, putting off socialism to the distant future.

The conceptions of the early Comintern would have proven extremely valuable in trying to prevent the rise of Hitler, although sadly both the social democrats and the communists ignored appeals based on these ideas when proposed by Trotsky. Before Hitler came to power, Trotsky advocated a policy of the united front. In 1930, he argued that "the policy of a united front of the workers against fascism flows from this situation".[53] Trotsky repeatedly argued for a united front as the threat grew, but his warnings went unheeded and the German labour movement was smashed. The united front tactic was the right policy and could have stopped the Nazis.

Yet the degeneration wrought by Stalinism could not completely eliminate the teachings of the first four Comintern congresses. Trotsky continued to develop conceptions of strategy and tactics, with the concomitant notions of transitional demands, the united front, and the workers' government, notably in his *Action Programme for France* (1934) and the *Death Agony of Capitalism and the Tasks of the Fourth International* (1938). Despite the misuse of these conceptions by many post-Trotsky Trotskyists, they are part of a priceless heritage from the early Comintern. Applied and adapted to current realities, they retain their vitality for our politics.

References

1. Lenin, [15 April 1919] 'The Third International and its Place in History', (*LCW* 29: 306-07).
2. John Riddell, *Founding the Communist International*, (1987); Riddell, *Workers of the World and Oppressed Peoples, Unite*, (1991); Riddell, *To the Masses: Proceedings of the Third Congress of the Communist International, 1921*, (2015); Riddell, *Toward the United Front: Proceedings of the Fourth Congress of the Communist International, 1922*, (2011).
3. Pierre Broué, *The German Revolution, 1917-23*, (2005: 920-32).
4. Riddell, 'Comintern: Revolutionary Internationalism in Lenin's Time', (2008: 11-12); Riddell, (1991: 8).
5. Riddell, *To See the Dawn: Baku Congress of the Peoples of the East, 1920*, (1993).
6. Riddell, (2015: 232).
7. Riddell, (2011: 55).
8. Zinoviev, [19 July 1920] 'Opening Address', Riddell, (1991: 103); Riddell, (2011: 851; 784).
9. Trotsky, [20 November 1919] 'French Socialism on the Eve of Revolution', *The First Five Years of the Communist International, Vol. 1* (1972: 70); Trotsky, [1921] 'Forward to New Work and New Struggles', Riddell, (2015: 1035).
10. Zinoviev, [23 July 1920] 'Report on the Role and Structure of the Communist Party', Riddell, (1991: 154-155, 190).
11. Lenin, [19 July 1920] 'Theses on the International Situation and the Fundamental Tasks of the Communist International', Riddell, (1991: 118).
12. Trotsky, [23 June 1921] 'Report on World Economic Crisis', Riddell, (2015: 103, 115, 119-120, 127, 133).
13. Riddell, (2011: 392-93, 120, 1150, 366, 474).
14. Lenin, [April-May 1920] *Left-Wing Communism: an Infantile Disorder*, (*LCW* 31: 33-34, 24, 26-29).
15. Zinoviev, [24 July 1920] 'Theses on the Role of the Communist Party in the Proletarian Revolution', Riddell, (1991: 191-200).
16. Zinoviev, [23 July 1920] 'Report on the Role and Structure of the Communist Party', Riddell, (1991: 144-48); Lenin, [1 July 1921] 'Tactics and Strategy – Discussion', Riddell, (2015: 470).
17. Trotsky, [August 1920] 'Manifesto of the Second World Congress', *First Five Years 1*, (1972: 132).
18. Kuusinen, [10 July 1921] 'Theses on the Organisational Structure of the Communist Parties', Riddell, (2015: 978-1002).
19. Trotsky, [2 March 1922] 'On the United Front', *First Five Years 2*, (1972: 108); Trotsky, [20 October 1922] 'The Fifth Anniversary of the October Revolution and the Fourth World Congress of the Communist International', *First Five Years 2*, (1972: 194).
20. Lenin, [13 November 1922] 'Five Years of the Russian Revolution and Perspectives for the World-Revolution', Riddell, (2011: 304-05).
21. Marcello Musto, *Workers Unite!: The International 150 Years Later*, (2014); Trotsky, [25 March 1931] 'The Question of Trade Union Unity', *Trotsky, Trade Unions in the Epoch of Imperialist Decay*, (1990: 63); Henry Tudor and J M Tudor, *Marxism and Social Democracy: The Revisionist Debate, 1896-1898* (1988); forerunners of Workers' Liberty published the first English translation of the Luxemburg-Kautsky debates, translated by Bruce Robinson in *Workers' Action* newspaper 143-153, June-September 1979; Trotsky, [15 September 1924] 'The Lessons of October', *Challenge of the Left Opposition*, (1975: 204).
22. Riddell, (2015: 924); Trotsky, [28 June 1928] 'Strategy and tactics in the imperialist epoch', *The Third International after Lenin*, (1970: 75); Trotsky, [1 April 1922] 'Report and Concluding Remarks at the Meeting of Military Delegates to the Eleventh Congress of the Russian Communist Party', *Military Writings and Speeches of Leon Trotsky, Vol. 5*, (1981: 379); Trotsky, [28 June 1928] 'Strategy and tactics in the imperialist epoch', *The Third International after Lenin*, (1970: 134-135).
23. Trotsky, [15 September 1924] 'The Lessons of October', (1975: 204).

24. Lenin, *Left-Wing Communism*, (*LCW* 31: 53, 92, 95, 97, 102, 63, 92).
25. Lenin, *Left-Wing Communism*, (*LCW* 31: 58, 50-51).
26. Lenin, *Left-Wing Communism*, (*LCW* 31: 78, 89); Lenin, [30 June 1920] 'Theses on Fundamental Tasks of the Second Congress of the Communist International', (*LCW* 31: 199).
27. Lenin, [23 July 1920] 'Role and Structure of the Communist Party', Riddell, (1991: 169-71).
28. Lenin, [30 June 1920] 'Theses on Fundamental Tasks of the Second Congress of the Communist International', (*LCW* 31: 199); Riddell, (1991: 760-61).
29. Lenin, [6 August 1920] 'Speech on Affiliation to the British Labour Party', (*LCW* 31: 257-263); Riddell, (1991: 738-744).
30. Zinoviev, [25 June 1921] 'Executive Committee Report', (Riddell 2015: 181-82, 184).
31. Radek, [30 June 1921] 'Tactics and Strategy – Report', Riddell, (2015: 406, 412, 415).
32. Lenin, [1 July 1921] 'Tactics and Strategy – Discussion', Riddell, (2015: 468); Bukharin, [1 July 1921] 'Tactics and Strategy – Discussion', Riddell, (2015: 509); Trotsky, [2 July 1921] 'Tactics and Strategy – Discussion', Riddell, (2015: 579).
33. Trotsky, [14 July 1921] 'Report on "The Balance Sheet" of the Third Congress of the Communist International', *First Five Years 1*, (1972: 297); Riddell, (2015: 45).
34. Trotsky, [14 July 1921] 'Report on "The Balance Sheet" of the Third Congress of the Communist International', *First Five Years 1*, (1972: 297); Riddell, (2015: 45).
35. Radek, [30 June 1921] 'Tactics and Strategy – Report', Riddell, (2015: 436-37, 440-41).
36. Riddell, (2011: 509-10, 632).
37. Broué, (2005: 469).
38. Lenin, [1 July 1921] 'Tactics and Strategy – Discussion', Riddell, (2015: 467); Trotsky, [17 July 1921] 'Forward to New Work and New Struggles', Riddell, (2015: 1037).
39. Riddell, (2011: 126, 129, 146, 393, 182, 457).
40. Riddell, (2011: 473, 552, 1038-9).
41. Broué, (2005: 369, 385).
42. Riddell, (2011: 129-130, 139-140).
43. Riddell, (2011: 167-68).
44. Riddell, (2011: 267-70, 399-401)..
45. Clara Zetkin, [1922] 'The Workers' Government', AWL website.
46. Jacob Zumoff, *The Communist International and US Communism, 1919–1929*, (2014: 287-88).
47. Zumoff, (2014: 289).
48. Zumoff, (2014: 293-94).
49. Zumoff, (2014: 299-307); Riddell, (2011: 806, 950).
50. Zumoff, (2014: 308).
51. Zumoff, (2014: 308-11).
52. James Cannon [1959] 'The Russian Revolution and the Black Struggle in the United States', *First Ten Years of American Communism*, (1962: 232, 238).
53. Trotsky, [26 September 1930] 'The Turn in the Communist International and the German Situation', *The Struggle against Fascism in Germany*, (1971: 70-73); Trotsky, [14 September 1932] 'The Only Road', *Struggle against Fascism*, (1971: 290); Trotsky, [23 February 1933] 'The United Front for Defence: A Letter to a Social Democratic Worker', *Struggle against Fascism*, (1971: 350-51).

THE RUSSIAN REVOLUTION: WHEN WORKERS TOOK POWER

Vera Mukhina, 'Worker and Kolkhoz Woman', 1937

From 1932 onwards the Stalinist state prescribed its official aesthetic. This was to be realist and triumphalist, with representational images celebrating the healthy bodies of Soviet workers and the nation's marvellous "progress". Modernist artists — including those who sought to democratise artistic formats and help rethink the basis of production — were barred from all state institutions and thus effectively purged. Many were exiled, killed and imprisoned.

10. Stalin's counter-revolution

In October 1917, the Russian working class led by the Bolshevik party, made its own authentic revolution, took power, smashed the old state and proceeded to build a new state based on workers' democracy. This tremendous socialist political and social revolution showed that working-class power is possible and that working class self-emancipation is also an enormous democratic festival of the oppressed. It is the only hope for human liberation.

Many on the left concede that 1917 was a wonderful flourishing of human freedom, but point to the eventual consequences of the revolution, and question whether it was misconceived from the start. Wasn't the revolution bound to be a hopeless adventure? After all, the October revolution was almost immediately followed by armed attacks on the new government, leading to three years of bitter civil war. Others say the Bolshevik leadership were seekers after power for themselves, not the Russian working class. The new regime dismissed the Constituent Assembly, set up its own secret police and suppressed protests. The democratic organs of the soviets, factory committees and trade unions would be subordinated and eventually destroyed. These subversions of democracy would become much worse, after Lenin died. The monstrous regime of Stalin was a totalitarian nightmare, with forced march industrialisation and collectivisation, millions sent to labour camps (the gulag) and the obliteration of the working-class movement.

The point is existential: anyone who seriously believes there is continuity between the programme and activities of the Bolsheviks and Stalinism will find it difficult to remain a revolutionary socialist. If such a working-class revolution is doomed to lead to Stalinist totalitarianism, then it is not a goal worth fighting for. If even the most politically conscious working-class revolutionary party cannot lead a successful socialist revolution and hold power without inevitably degenerating into Stalinism, then such a revolution is not an ambition worth pursuing, even on working-class democratic grounds.

Cold War histories of the Russian revolution strongly emphasise the "continuity thesis" ("Leninism led to Stalinism"). Histories written from this perspective seek the roots of Stalinism in some original sin within Bolshevik history, particularly in its mode of party organisation. And Stalinist histories mirror the Cold War approach, also asserting continuity between Lenin and Stalin, only this is said to be a virtue rather than a fault. Stalinist accounts also read back the terrible anti-democratic practices of the Stalinists into the early history of the Bolsheviks before the revolution. Both accounts are wrong historically and ruinous politically. A literal river of blood separates actual Leninism, a body of subtle Marxist ideas, from Stalinism. In fact Stalinism killed off the genuine followers of Leninism in Russia and internationally, notably the opposition around Trotsky, in order to kill off working-class rule in Russia after 1928.

This chapter explains how working-class rule in Russia after 1917 was dismantled. It defends the view that Russia remained a workers' state for most the 1920s, until the Stalinist bureaucracy became the ruling class after 1928. It addresses some serious problems with the early years of Bolshevik rule, seeking to put them in their historical context. It shows how the state bureaucracy strangled the organs of working class power, including the Bolshevik party itself. But it shows this process was not inevitable and that opportunities were missed to maintain working-class democracy. The chapter demonstrates that the oppositional movement around Trotsky was a real alternative to Stalinism in its time. Trotskyism fought Stalinism, but was ultimately shattered by the Stalinists. However, Trotsky in exile preserved the best of Leninism, provided the basis for understanding Stalinism, and harvested political ideas that can renew socialism after Stalinism.

Class and the Russian revolution

Working-class rule is a collective act: it can only be victorious when the majority of working-class people within a given state decide together to take power into their own hands. As such, working-class rule is a conscious, democratic act: workers have to decide for themselves through their collective, democratic organs of struggle to take power in their own interests. Working-class rule is also a revolutionary act: the workers make a conscious socialist revolution by overthrowing the existing bourgeois state, smashing the pillars of bourgeois rule and erecting their own state in its place. Workers can only rule through their own democratic organisations, which replace the blind workings of the free market with conscious planning and destructive production for profit with conscious production for need. Working-class political rule is the prerequisite of establishing its economic and social rule: without political power, workers cannot run society.

Working-class socialist revolution is qualitatively different from previous, bourgeois revolutions because workers must take and hold power consciously in their own interests. Whereas all sorts of political formations have made bourgeois revolutions in the past, only the working class can make socialism. A century ago socialist revolutionaries lived by this truth: Marxists today cannot renew the working-class movement without re-establishing this principle.

For Marxists, class societies are distinguished by the way in which the social surplus product is generated, controlled and distributed. This fundamental insight is at the heart of Marxist political economy and is the key to understanding class societies as exploitative systems. In *Capital*, Marx wrote that:

> *The specific economic form, in which unpaid surplus labour is pumped out of direct producers, determines the relationship of rulers and ruled... it is always the direct relationship of the owners of the conditions of production to the direct producers... which reveals the innermost secret, the hidden basis of the entire social structure, and with it the political form of the relation of sovereignty and dependence, in short, the corresponding specific form of the state.*[i]

In 1917, the Russian working class and its Bolshevik party held the levers of the social surplus for the first time. Workers had democratic control over the production and distribution of the surplus product. This was the basis for transforming social relations of production and thus other social relations. The process was cruelly cut short by the backwardness and isolation of the Russian workers' state after 1917, and the invasion of Russia by hostile armies, and further strangled by the rising bureaucracy inside Russia from the early 1920s. Stalinism from 1928 meant the definitive end to workers' rule and any possibility of reviving it. Stalinism meant the resumption of exploitation of Russian workers and peasants, in hitherto unforeseen and unprecedented ways, accompanied by the most terrible and naked coercion. After 1990 and the collapse of the Stalinist state, Russia returned to capitalism, in an authoritarian and bastardised form.

What did workers' rule mean in 1917?
The October revolution transferred power to a government that enjoyed the support of the majority of the working class.[2] The Bolshevik regime was a workers' government because the goals, programme, strategy, tactics and social composition served and represented the working-class. This combination of what the party was together with the ideology it espoused made the Bolshevik party a genuine class conscious vanguard of the working class.

The Bolshevik regime was also a workers' government because of the wide range of pro-working class measures that it passed immediately upon taking power. 116 different decrees in its first two months, issued not as administrative measures but as political instruments to build a new state. Russia became a workers' state because the workers shattered the old bourgeois state and replaced it with specifically working-class institutional forms of democracy — principally the soviets.[3] It was these democratic controls over the state — and through it over the surplus product — which made it a workers' state.

On 25 October 1917, the second soviet congress unanimously voted to form a coalition government of parties represented in the soviets. The congress created the council of peoples' commissars (Sovnarkom) as the day-to-day government, with Lenin as chair. Trotsky coined the name, to distinguish commissars from bourgeois cabinet ministers. On 29 October, the railworkers' union issued an ultimatum to the soviet government — form a coalition government or face a general strike across the rail network. The Bolsheviks enlarged the central executive committee (CEC) of the soviets to include the parties that had walked out, on the basis of proportional representation. The new CEC consisted of 62 Bolsheviks, 29 left SRs, six United Social-Democratic Internationalists (Mensheviks), three Ukrainian Socialists and one SR Maksimalist.[4] However, the moderates argued for the inclusion of bourgeois representatives from the Petrograd and Moscow municipal councils and the exclusion of Lenin and Trotsky. Only the left SRs were willing to come into the government. Therefore the Bolshevik-led workers' government was tentative and insecure. It took five days to recruit Sovnarkom's first staff member and another four days before a typist was found.[5]

On 14 December 1917, Lenin signed the first decree officially nationalising 81 businesses, a large majority of which employed more than a thousand persons. Factory committees were not responsible for the management of the enterprises.[6] Overall, between November 1917 and March 1918, 836 enterprises were nationalised, some forced through by action from below. On 28 June 1918, the government took some 2,000 joint-stock companies into state ownership.[7] The decree of nationalisation gave one-third of the places in management to the elected representatives of the workers, while giving effective control to the two-thirds appointed by Sovnarkom.[8] These measures gave the new regime effective control over the main levers of the economy. They successively expropriated the capitalist class in Russia and established new property relations, which formed the basis of the workers' state.

One important feature of the early soviet workers' state was its accountability to the all-Russian congress of soviets, where delegates were elected by local soviets of workers, peasants and soldiers. Initially at least, Lenin anticipated some degree of political pluralism in the soviets. In January 1918 he stated that "if the working people are dissatisfied with their party they can elect other delegates, hand power to another party and change the government without any revolution at all".[9] The third all-Russian soviet congress took place in January 1918 and ratified the dissolution of the Constituent Assembly. The congress elected a new CEC, comprising 162 Bolsheviks, 122 left SRs, and 21 members of other parties.[10] The fourth all-Russia congress of soviets (14-16 March 1918) ratified the Brest-Litovsk treaty, after a widespread and very public debate between and within parties. The soviet form of state also spread across Russia. Effectively, the soviets took the place of previous organs of municipal government. By February 1918, 86% of towns had created soviets as an alternative to the old forms of local government, though these were not always dominated by Bolsheviks and left SRs.[11]

How was workers' rule dismantled?

Workers' democracy immediately after the October insurrection was inevitably chaotic, with many workers' organisations overlapping in their functions. But the most important form of workers' rule was the soviets and these formed the basis of the new government and the new state. Workers also held power through their factory committees and trade unions. The early phases of the new regime saw efforts to integrate these forms of workers' democracy. The economic chaos inherited by the new government, coupled with the onset of civil war damaged and dampened working class democratic organisation and reduced the levers of workers' power largely to the party.

The decline of the working-class democracy is explained mainly by the political and economic situation the Bolsheviks faced — the dreadful economic inheritance, the terrible terms of peace with Germany, the behaviour of the opposition parties, which meant the Bolsheviks lacked reliable domestic allies and, from quite early on, armed opposition from domestic and foreign bourgeois forces. The officer-cadets guarding the Winter Palace were released after the October insurrection, but a few days later the same men organised an armed rising in the capital, supported by the Kadets. General Krasnov, who led the forces charged with retaking Petrograd, was also released, only to join the counter-revolutionaries in the south. The first counter-revolutionary army in the Don region was formed in late November 1917.

The international context and foreign intervention were vital forces driving on the civil war. Historian Evan Mawdsley argues that the "military operations of the central powers from February to May 1918 were the most important foreign intervention in the civil war. Hundreds of thousands of German, Austrian and Turkish troops were involved; 17 Russian provinces (as well as Poland) were occupied".[12] The British and French governments poured money, supplies and eventually troops into Russia to help build up "white armies" which wanted to overthrow the Bolshevik government and get Russia back into the First World War. Some 21 armies from 14 countries — including soldiers from France, Britain, the United States, Italy, Japan, Germany, Poland, Czechoslovakia, Finland and the Baltic states — took part in efforts to smash the first workers' state.

The other supposedly left parties within Russia rapidly came to play a counter-revolutionary role. The day after the seizure of power in October 1917, the majority of the SR central committee voted to undertake armed action against the Bolsheviks. In November 1917 the SR military commission planned to kidnap Lenin and Trotsky, entrusting the scheme to a group of officers. In spring 1918 the SRs hatched a plot to assassinate Lenin. At the Menshevik party congress in December 1917, the rightists led by Liber called on the party to join in a "fighting alliance of all anti-Bolshevik forces". In May 1918 the Mensheviks held an official and open conference at which they demanded the Constituent Assembly be called. But when the Czech legion clashed with the Bolsheviks, the Mensheviks' central committee said the attitude should be "friendly to the Czechs and hostile to the Bolsheviks".[13]

The left SRs joined the soviet government in December 1917 and supported the suppression of the Constituent Assembly. However, the left SRs deserted in March 1918 over the signing of the treaty of Brest-Litovsk (a treaty with Germany ceding territory and committing Russia to paying the victors billions). The treaty was harsh but it ended the war as the government had promised. In July 1918, left SRs assassinated the German ambassador in the hope of restarting war between Russia and Germany, while launching a revolt in the streets of the capital. Among the anarchists, adventurers, criminals and counter-revolutionaries thrived. Some anarchists took part in this rising. In September 1919, anarchists blew up the Moscow communist headquarters, killing 12 Bolshevik leaders and wounding 50, including Bukharin.[14]

One of the first decrees of the new soviet government was on workers' control, written in "a spirit of libertarianism".[15] However the Bolsheviks soon proposed to integrate the factory committees with the trade unions. There was debate within the committees and within the party about the merits of the proposals. Most of the leading cadres of the committees were also Bolsheviks. Most decided it was consistent with working-class democracy.[16] The trade unions were strengthened by the incorporation of the factory committees at the beginning of 1918. As early as January 1918 the first trade-union congress rejected Menshevik demands that the unions remain "independent", contending that in a workers' state their chief function was to "organise production and restore the battered productive forces of the country".[17]

One measure of the slippage in working-class democracy was fewer meetings of soviet bodies. Altogether Sovnarkom convened 203 times in 1918 and only 97 times in 1919. There were 69 meetings in 1920 and 51 in 1921. Another was the weakness of the CEC. After June 1918 CEC meetings fell from about two a week to one a fortnight, and in the course of 1919 these apparently ceased altogether. From June 1918 to 1921 the CEC consisted almost entirely of communists.[18]

There were also delays and interference in local soviet elections. Historian Alexander Rabinowitch has documented how the Bolsheviks contrived a majority in the new Petrograd soviet in June 1918. He concedes that "judging by official tabulations, the Bolsheviks had most success in direct elections at the workplace, electing 127 of 260 factory delegates". However, he also raises "the nagging question of how many Bolshevik deputies from factories were elected instead of the opposition because of press restrictions, voter intimidation, vote fraud, or the short duration of the campaign".[19]

The growing disenchantment of Petrograd workers with Bolshevik-led soviet power in the spring of 1918 was reflected in the formation of the Extraordinary Assembly of Delegates from Petrograd Factories and Plants (EAD). For Rabinowitch, the emergence of the EAD "was also stimulated by the widespread view that trade unions, factory committees and soviets, perhaps especially district soviets, were no longer representative, democratically-run working class institutions; instead they had been transformed into arbitrary, bureaucratic government agencies". However, the Bolsheviks suppressed the EAD to head off its planned general strike set for 2 July. By August, the soviets had become mostly a political rally than a decision-making body.[20]

Residual elements of workers' power persisted, alongside emergency administrative measures to restart production. By the autumn of 1918, 212 factories in Petrograd province had control-commissions.[21] In 1919, one-in-nine of enterprises in the country were under one-man management. In March 1920, 69% of Petrograd factories employing more than 200 workers were still run by a collegial board.[22] However, from December 1920 one-man management increased dramatically and other more collectivist forms of management diminished.

Trade union independence was not completely curtailed during the civil war. The Russian Communist Party's (RCP) eighth congress in March 1919 proposed a large self-managing role for the trade unions.[23] In June 1920, Sovnarkom issued a decree on the payment of bonuses in kind that gave the all-Russian trade-union council control of the bonus system. Unions also resisted attempts by the lesser state bodies to interfere with the setting of money wages. At the Moscow metalworkers' conference of February 1921, a Bolshevik trade union leader said the unions would go to court if necessary against administrators who ignored their pay rates.[24]

The role of the trade unions in a workers' state became the subject of intense party debate towards the end of the civil war. More than 100 papers were submitted to the "militarisation debate" (the emergency measures Trotsky proposed that would have militarised key industries and trade unions in order to jump-start production). On 19 January 1921, 3,500 communist sailors heard Zinoviev and Trotsky debate the issues.[25] Whatever the merits or faults with Trotsky's position, it was comprehensively defeated at the party's tenth congress in March 1921.

The tenth party congress made the unions responsible for mobilising workers for production tasks. In practice this was reduced mainly to campaigning for labour discipline. According to historian Simon Pirani, the unions' political dependence on the party manifested itself in two linked respects: "firstly, they helped to discipline workers who went outside the proscribed negotiating procedure and used the strike weapon to bargain". Secondly, "their apparatus became organisationally and financially more closely integrated with the state's. In industrial disputes, the unions almost always acted as, and were perceived by workers as, industrial managers' allies".[26]

At the Moscow province conference of soviets (15-17 December 1920), Kamenev acknowledged that the soviets had been emptied of their democratic functions.[27] However, in April 1921 new soviet elections were called, the first after the civil war. In Moscow the Bolsheviks had a majority, but only because they won seats in small workplaces and among office workers. The non-party socialists heavily defeated the Bolsheviks in all the large factories, and out of 2,000 delegates they had 500 seats. When the soviet convened, the Bolsheviks ignored appeals by the non-party socialists to work together on the soviet executive. It turned the soviet into "an empty talking-shop", representing a lost chance to revive workers' democracy.[28] Similarly, the role of the unions was tightly proscribed after the end of the civil war. According to Pirani, just as the soviet's function was redefined in 1921-22 as an organ of municipal administration, so the unions were allocated a new, subordinate role, implementing policies elaborated and supervised by party bodies. After the 1917 revolution, "trade union apparatuses had been established, financed from government funds. Although everyone in the Bolshevik party agreed that this was an undesirable state of affairs, and that the unions should be financed and run independently, they never were". In 1922 a campaign was run to ensure that workers contributed their subscriptions to shop-floor activists, instead of having them deducted in advance from their wages. But the campaign failed. "The unions grew as an apparatus, closely linked to the state apparatus".[29]

Pirani argues that by 1922, "bureaucratised unions routinely opposed strikes; had more unelected officials than elected ones; worked together with party and government to discipline and punish strike organisers; and became, despite some Bolsheviks' efforts to avoid it, heavily reliant on state funding". He concluded that "unions had become dependent on the state and factory committees were getting integrated into management". The idea that factory-level organisations would participate in political decisions about the republic's future, or even strategic management decisions, was abandoned. On industrial issues, "while workers could indeed use official procedures to change some things at factory level, they were largely deprived of the crucial weapons of striking, solidarity action and independent union organisation".[30]

Other recent research is less categorical. Historian Diane Koenker found that even after the civil war, "soviet printers often exercised their right (through their union) to approve the appointment of managerial personnel, and they could act energetically to remove or discipline managers and foremen who violated workers' sense of appropriate relations. Workers and their representatives likewise shared the disciplinary functions of management". Soviet printers, through their factory committees, production councils and shop floor meetings "acquired formal and informal power to intervene in the work process in ways that could protect their own interests and preferences".[31]

An honest reckoning with reality would conclude that soviet democracy had ceased to function by 1921. Even before the civil war had ended, direct workers' democracy had been substantially eroded. By 1922 the shift away from collegiality had been fully implemented. However, the forms of working-class democracy had not been abolished, nor had they been replaced by other bodies. The possibility of their regeneration still existed.

The Kronstadt rebellion

Leftist critics of Bolshevik rule often argue that the suppression of a rebellion of sailors at Kronstadt in March 1921 is proof that workers' rule was effectively dead after the civil war. They often ignore the destruction of the material basis of production wrought by years of armed conflict. Trotsky summed it up as "Russia — looted, weakened, exhausted, falling apart… our position is in the highest degree tragic". The transport system verged on utter collapse. Industry had no goods to trade with the peasants for grain. Inflation had destroyed the financial system. Disease, hunger and cold stalked the land.[32]

The Kronstadt sailors said they wanted equal rations instead of privileges for soviet bureaucrats, and concessions to the peasantry similar to those the government would introduce shortly after with its New Economic Policy. The Petropavlovsk sailors' resolution opposed the demand for a Constituent Assembly. However, the SR-Maximalists slogan "Power to the soviets and not to parties" was used on the masthead of the *Kronstadt Izvestia* newspaper and in the first radio broadcast.

Yet, looking beneath these slogans, it is clear this rebellion was militarily opposing Bolshevik party rule. The Kronstadt revolt was not a coherent democratic workers' movement and, having failed to placate or convince the rebels, the workers' government had no choice but to suppress rebellion in the naval base which dominated the country's second city.

The Kronstadt sailors distanced their revolt from the White Guards, and subsequent investigations have found few substantial links with right-wing forces or imperialist governments before the rebel leaders had fled (through several links soon after). Far from being denuded of revolutionary workers and composed mainly of fractious peasants, around 90% of the sailors had joined the navy before the civil war and half before the 1917 revolution. Three-quarters of the mutineers' revolutionary committee had served through the revolution and the civil war on the Bolshevik side.[33]

Perhaps if agrarian reform had been implemented earlier, or the government had taken a more diplomatic approach at the beginning of the revolt, the bloodshed might have been spared. The officials sent to negotiate with the sailors were bureaucratic and impatient, probably overwrought after countless missions. Afterwards, the government was overzealous in slandering the sailors and too harsh in repressing the mutineers. These are important matters, but secondary. The fundamental reason to suppress the revolt remains entirely valid. Faced with an armed revolt so soon after the civil war in a strategically important naval base close to Petrograd, with other cities simmering and armed rebellions in the south, the Bolshevik government ultimately had no option than to use force.

As Trotsky put it, "what the soviet government did reluctantly at Kronstadt was a tragic necessity". Earlier he had written that the revolt "could bring nothing but a victory of counter-revolution, entirely independent of the ideas the sailors had in their heads...since the insurgents took possession of the arms in the forts they could only be crushed with the aid of arms". Had the uprising triumphed, it would have been what Lenin called a "stepping stone" — perhaps with a short interregnum — the precursor for the whites and the capitalist powers to restart the civil war.[34]

Historian Paul Avrich's thorough account of Kronstadt criticises many of the arguments traditionally used by Trotskyists against the sailors. However, he concludes that "the historian can sympathise with the rebels and still concede that the Bolsheviks were justified in subduing them".[35] Victor Serge is often held up as a libertarian revolutionary critic of the Bolsheviks' suppression of the Kronstadt rebellion. A year after the revolt, Serge articulated tersely the bottom line justification for its suppression:

> Let us suppose briefly that the Kronstadt mutiny had turned out to be victorious. Its results would have been immediate chaos, the terrible kindling of a civil war in which this time the party of the revolutionary proletariat and the broad peasant masses would have been locked in combat. Within a short time a handful of liberal lawyers and Tsarist generals, fortified by the sympathies of the whole bourgeois world, would have drenched their hands in the blood of the Russian people in order to pick up the abandoned power. Thermidor would have come.[36]

Serge was certainly more critical towards the end of his life, but he did not abandon this basic defence of the Bolshevik government's action.[37] If Russia in 1921 was still some kind of workers' state (albeit, by that point, having bureaucratic deformations), then one has to conclude that the suppression of the mutiny was a "tragic necessity" in order to prevent even the tenuous forms of workers' self-rule from fully unravelling.

How did the state bureaucracy emerge?

In *The State and Revolution* (1917), Lenin wrote that the two institutions most characteristic of the bourgeois state machine were the bureaucracy and the standing army. The destruction of the bureaucratic-military state machine was "the precondition for every real people's revolution". Although abolishing the bureaucracy "at once, everywhere and completely", was out of the question, "to smash the old bureaucratic machine at once and to begin immediately to construct a new one that will make possible the gradual abolition of all bureaucracy" was possible. The socialist revolution would "reduce the role of state officials to that of simply carrying out our instructions as responsible, revocable, modestly paid 'foremen and accountants'". A new apparatus where officials are elected and recallable at any time, paid the average worker's wage, and subject to workers' control would ensure that "all may become 'bureaucrats' for a time and that, therefore, nobody may be able to become a 'bureaucrat'".[38] The early Bolshevik government required an administration simply to carry out decisions. What developed later was a bureaucracy that involved privileges and power for the administrators.[39]

Immediately after the soviet government was set up, the new regime was met with "a wall of hostility and non-cooperation". The old tsarist officials rejected the legitimacy of the workers' and peasants' government and refused to work for it. In one instance the saboteurs went so far as to remove the nibs from pens and pour away all the ink. In early December 1917 a nationwide strike of government officials took place. Within three weeks the back of the rebellion was broken. According to historian Harry Rigby, the sacking and arrest of the more intransigent senior civil servants decapitated the resistance and intimidated others.[40]

Rabinowitch argues that work stoppages by civil servants petered out, "not because they were smashed or replaced by freshly trained representatives of the revolutionary masses but because ultimately most of them were dependent on wages for survival".[41] Although a few senior officials were ready to collaborate, it was at first mainly the guards, cleaners, office messengers and so on who remained at their posts. The workers' state took steps to militate against bureaucratisation. For example, the salaries of the people's commissars were fixed at 500 rubles a month — not much higher than was earned by a skilled worker. In March 1918, the soviet government transferred to Moscow. It was there that the new rulers fused with the old staff in the face of new crises to create a distinct bureaucratic layer.[42]

The state atrophied in the face of economic collapse and civil war. In 1918, the extensive nationalisation of industry, creation of new economic coordinating agencies, intensified direction of local government bodies, and the exceptional organs, necessitated the recruitment of many thousands of new central government officials, including bourgeois specialists in the army. Rigby's research indicates that "over half the officials in the central offices of the commissariats, and perhaps 90% of the upper-echelon officials, had worked in some kind of administrative position before October 1917". Communists comprised only 10% of the main commissariats, (but made up half the Cheka).[43]

Moscow became dominated by a bureaucratic apparatus. The 231,000 people employed in offices in August 1918 represented 14% of the total population and 30% of the workforce.[44] Not only was carry-over high (50% to 80%) in the upper and middle reaches of the central government commissariats, but the social origins and occupation of these men and women clearly placed them within the lower-middle strata.[45] The situation was widely perceived as out of control by the end of the civil war. Bukharin joked that the history of humanity could be divided into three great periods: the matriarchate, the patriarchate and — the secretariat.[46]

The 1921 census revealed that almost a quarter of all senior soviet officials in the provinces who had acquired a definite occupational affiliation by 1914 stated that they were in more or less senior posts in governmental or private bureaucracies. While it is unlikely that many of these had been in high-level jobs, this represented some elements of continuity between the old elite and the new.[47] The old tsarist hierarchy had not held on intact in any meaningful sense. By 1922, the central administration was controlled by a generation more or less free of the presence of persons who had held high positions in the tsarist administration. Rather, as historian Dan Rowney shows, "the 1922 cohort of top administrators included a majority of persons who had been associated with the pre-revolutionary government and its institutions as teachers, physicians, soldiers, students, and of course bureaucrats — sometimes even as high-level bureaucrats if their skills were rare enough". The Bolsheviks who complained of the presence of too many "*chinovniki*" were not paranoid but "simply trying to face up to a problem that would not go away as fast as they had hoped it would".[48]

Lenin saw the threat more clearly than other leaders. From 1920 he railed against "the huge bureaucratic machine", "bureaucratic ulcer", "puffed-up commissars", the "rotten bureaucratic swamp", and the bureaucracy "throttling us". By 1921 he was prepared to define the new state sociologically as "a workers' state with bureaucratic distortions".[49] He urged Gleb Krzhizhanovskii at the state planning commission to reduce soviet office staff by a quarter or even half. He wrote in December 1921: "We don't know how to conduct a public trial for rotten bureaucracy; for this all of us... should be hung on stinking ropes. And I have not yet lost all hope that we shall be hung for this, and deservedly so."[50]

Lenin told the party's eleventh congress in March 1922: "If we take Moscow with its 4,700 communists in responsible positions, and if we take that huge bureaucratic machine, that gigantic heap, we must ask: who is directing whom? I doubt very much whether it can truthfully be said that the communists are directing that heap. To tell the truth they are not directing, they are being directed".[51] He told the fourth Comintern congress in November 1922:

> We took over the old machinery of state, and that was our misfortune. Very often this machinery operates against us. In 1917, after we seized power, the government officials sabotaged us. This frightened us very much and we pleaded: 'Please come back'. They all came back, but that was our misfortune. We now have a vast army of government employees, but lack sufficiently educated forces to exercise real control over them. In practice it often happens that here at the top, where we exercise political power, the machine functions somehow; but down below government employees have arbitrary control and they often exercise it in such a way as to counteract our measures. At the top, we have, I don't know how many, but at all events, I think, no more than a few thousand, at the outside several tens of thousands of our own people. Down below, however, there are hundreds of thousands of old officials whom we got from the tsar and from bourgeois society and who, partly deliberately and partly unwittingly, work against us.[52]

How did the party degenerate?

Academic histories tend to neglect the study of soviet government institutions in favour of accounts privileging the role of the party. But that is to project the later degeneration of the workers' state and the rise of the Stalinist bureaucracy onto the original revolution. At the beginning, neither the Bolshevik party central committee nor the Politburo (formed in 1919) functioned as the government. Lenin's cabinet was Sovnarkom and neither Lenin nor Trotsky occupied any post in the party machine.[53]

The party remained the principal agency of workers' rule throughout the civil war and in the early 1920s, essentially the only remaining democratic channel through which the working class still exercised its power. But the party was subjected to the pressure of the state bureaucracy and suffered its own forms of degeneration. Tracing the ways in which the party was subordinated to the bureaucracy is crucial to explaining how workers lost power and how the Stalinists ultimately triumphed.

The first year of the new regime was tumultuous for the party. It did not have a pre-existing bureaucratic apparatus at the time of the October revolution and it had to improve during the civil war. In February 1918, the staff of the RCP central committee consisted of 10 people.[54] The central committee secretariat's staff grew from 30 in February 1919 to 150 in March 1920 and 602 in the year up to March 1921.[55] In 1918, membership of the party dwindled in Petrograd, going from 30,000 in February to 13,472 in June, to about 6,000 in September, less than 2% of organised factory workers in the city.[56] Some of these losses were due to communists going off to fight in the civil war or join the administration of the new state elsewhere. Others left for the countryside to avoid hunger and disease.

Despite civil war losses, the party still retained about 12,000 "undergrounders" in 1922 and over three times that number who had joined between the February and October revolutions. Pre-October Bolsheviks monopolised the upper levels of the regime in the first two years of the new regime. Between 1919 and 1921, however, their numbers were heavily diluted with newcomers.[57] A survey of the Moscow regional party's members in October 1920 showed that a third joined between October 1917 and August 1919, and another half since then. Only a tiny minority (5%, some 1,763 members) had joined the party before 1917, while another 10% had joined in 1917 before October.[58]

Academic historiography has made the party the focal, integrating mechanism in the whole system of government, reserving for itself all the major decisions, directing, supervising and coordinating their operation and sorting out all problems and conflicts. Rigby argues that such an assumption is mistaken. In the first year or so after the revolution, "there was no evidence that leading Bolsheviks believed the party should perform such a role, there was no attempt to equip them to do so, and it did not in fact do so". However, between 1919 and 1921, "the relationship between party and state in Soviet Russia underwent a profound change and in the process Sovnarkom became increasingly dependent on the party central committee and its inner bodies in a variety of ways: for policy guidance, for resolution of important and disputed matters, for information necessary to effective executive action, for getting its programmes implemented in the provinces, for choosing its members and for staffing its offices".[59] The rot had begun to set in at the heart of the vanguard.

One-party rule

By the end of the civil war, Russia was a one-party state. A central reason for this was the implacable behaviour of the other parties during the civil war.[60] The process was not automatic, and proceeded in stages as the new regime developed. The Mensheviks and right SRs who had opposed soviet power in the first place remained legal in the early months of the new government. These parties were excluded from the national soviets in June 1918 (though they remained in local bodies), in the context of the burgeoning civil war and foreign intervention. Some anarchists had already turned against the regime in April 1918 and had been repressed. Most spectacular was the Left SRs' mid July 1918 attempt to incite an uprising and restart the war with Germany, which ended with an attempt to assassinate Lenin.

Nevertheless some political liberty persisted. Until the middle of 1918, the Kadet newspaper *Svoboda Rossii* was still published and an extensive Menshevik party press still existed.[61] The Mensheviks were briefly reinstated in the soviets on 30 November 1918. The newspaper of the Menshevik central committee resumed publication on 22 January 1919. This paper was so successful — it printed 100,000 copies — that after the fourth issue it came out daily. However, it was closed down again on 26 February 1919. In 1920 the Mensheviks had party offices and a club in Moscow, holding open party conferences. However, the Cheka raided their premises, sealed them up, confiscated papers, and arrested those assembled.

The SRs not allied with the counterrevolution were reinstated in the soviets in February 1919. A group of left SRs around Isaac Steinberg was briefly allowed in 1920 to publish a periodical called *Znamia*. Two different groups of right SRs published newspapers in 1919. Some, though not all, anarchist periodicals continued to appear until the last ones were closed down after the Kronstadt uprising. When Kropotkin died in February 1921, some anarchists were released from prison for his funeral and a 20,000 strong procession.[62]

In early 1920, repression was concentrated on the anarchists that had organised the bombing of a Moscow party meeting. The Moscow party bureau, rather than any soviet body, discussed in July 1920 a formal appeal for legalisation by the Moscow left SRs. It decided that given "the complexities of the current situation" the request could not be granted. The Cheka also kept an eye on the left SR Internationalist Group, 11 members of which were arrested and then released in September 1920.[63]

On 17 April 1921, Lenin criticised a Cheka report recommending that certain groups within the Menshevik, SR and anarchist parties should be legalised, and that individual Mensheviks and SRs should be released to take part in elections to the Moscow soviets.[64] There were non-Bolshevik deputies in the Moscow soviet up to 1923, although they did not threaten the Bolsheviks' majority.[65]

Was the party dead by 1921?
If the Bolshevik party was the central means through which a measure of working-class rule could be exercised in post-revolutionary Russia, then the various democratic oppositions to the party leadership are significant. The Bolshevik party had a history of debate, up to and including the October revolution, as discussed in previous chapters. The party leadership was divided in the immediate period after seizure of power over the composition of the new government. A substantial left communist opposition developed within the party against the signing of the Brest-Litovsk peace treaty, with the faction publishing its own journal *Kommunist* in early 1918. The Democratic Centralist group, led by Timofei Sapronov and Vladimir Smirnov, was formed at the eighth party congress in March-April 1919 around a critique of state and party democracy.

The Workers' Opposition, led by Aleksandr Shliapnikov and Aleksandra Kollontai, emerged in 1920. The Workers' Opposition platform was published in *Pravda* and also issued in 250,000 copies as a pamphlet. Kollontai complained that "The harm in bureaucracy… lies in the solution of all problems, not by means of an open exchange of opinions or by the immediate efforts of all concerned, but by means of formal decisions handed down from the central institutions… Some third person decides your fate: this is the whole essence of bureaucracy".[66]

In 1920 the Democratic Centralists and Workers' Oppositions were included in the commission charged with reorganising the party. The tenth party congress on 8-16 March 1921 condemned oppositions and temporarily banned factions within the party, but Lenin allowed for platforms, and oppositionists were still able to publish. Gavril Miasnikov agitated for workers' democracy and the free press, until he was expelled from the party in February 1922. He formed the Workers' Group the following year. Another opposition, the Workers' Truth group published *Rabochaya Pravda*, beginning in September 1921 and were expelled only in December 1923.[67]

After the civil war, there were a number of dissident workers who defined themselves as "non-party". It is arguable that the label "non-party" was simply a cover for opposition socialist activity by workers who previously associated with banned parties such as the Mensheviks and SRs. However, their ranks included previously loyal but now disillusioned Bolshevik militants. Kamenev criticised non-party workers because they were "brought together exactly by the fact that they do not have a worked-out programme and do not answer for each other". The criticism was essentially right. Even historians like Pirani who have championed the non-party militants acknowledge that these opposition groups were not a political alternative to the ruling party.[68]

The year 1922 was a turning point for the party. At the eleventh party congress in March 1922, Stalin became RCP general secretary and consolidated his grip on the apparatus. In May 1922, Lenin suffered a stroke, which would incapacitate him severely until his death in January 1924. During his brief recovery in late 1922-early 1923, Lenin waged his last struggle by forming a bloc with Trotsky to fight Stalin and the growing bureaucratism. However, the party and state machine in the hands of the "troika" (Zinoviev, Kamenev and Stalin) moved against Trotsky. In October 1922, Lenin chastised as "the height of absurdity" the troika's proposal to expel Trotsky from the central committee.[69] The sheer persistence of opposition shows that there was life left in the party and hence in the possibility that the workers could reimpose control through the party to reform the state.

The fusion of state and party bureaucracies

The bureaucracy was not born of the one-party state. Nor did it arise simply from the rule of the Bolshevik party. Administration is a necessary function of any state, but precisely because of its role in allocating, dividing up and distributing the surplus product, it carries the risk of developing into a bureaucratic layer with its own distinct interests. In backward Russia, such a bureaucracy composed of residue elements of the old ruling class was able to wrap its tentacles around the organs of workers' power from the beginning. The state bureaucracy — the industrial managers, military specialists and state functionaries — fused, combined, amalgamated and interpenetrated with a party apparatus increasingly controlled by Stalin after 1922, and which constituted the new ruling elite.[70] Failure to register this process is to treat the party and the state as reified historical actors, set apart from society.[71]

When whites threatened Petrograd in 1919, distinctions between party and soviet often appeared to break down altogether.[72] This bureaucratic social layer was not yet a ruling class. It had not made itself the sole master of the surplus product. But Stalin's secretariat strengthened its grip on party organisation. Even before the eleventh party congress of March-April 1922, "there were 7,000 national- and regional-level officials reporting directly to the secretariat's record and assignment department"; by the time of the congress, "this department had collated lists of 33,000 officials and set about taking charge of them". In late 1923 the first lists (*nomenklatury*) of party and state appointments that required central approval were drawn up. In 1924, record and assignment departments, responsible to their central parent body, were put into all the main branches of the state apparatus. The Moscow regional party's record and assignment department, set up in July 1922, appointed in its first seven months 5,863 party members (about one-fifth of the Moscow membership) to positions, mostly into central or local party or soviet bodies. "Appointism" — that is, the appointment rather than election of party and state officials that had begun during the civil war — now predominated. The tenth party congress had condemned it, but it became widespread by 1924-25.[73]

This bureaucratic layer gave itself material privileges that further differentiated it from the working class. The elite often had good living quarters, better meals, a car, a dacha, fine clothes and the freedom to travel. In late 1923, when the trade unions were protesting vociferously about industrial managers being overpaid, they pointed to the "doubtful specialists" who benefited. The Hungarian communist Bela Kun, living in exile in Moscow, received at least 25 times the minimum salary. Then there were non-cash benefits, such as the housing, education and healthcare, or the gold watches presented to party members in industrial management. In 1924, a trade union statistician was scandalised to discover that some *sluzhashchie* (service sector workers) admitted to earning more than 30 times the minimum wage.[74]

Communist industrial managers began to organise politically. They lobbied to secure their own position within the state bureaucracy. In December 1922, they launched a permanent council of industrialists and began to publish a journal. In 1923, a Moscow "Red directors" club was established as part of the national grouping, with

146 members. Significantly, the communist managers' lobbying was stiffly resisted by communist trade union leaders.[75]

Government service personnel in 1924 totalled about 1.8m. By 1926, the figure had increased to more than 2.3 million. The hypertrophy of the state was matched by the growth of the party. By 1924, only 14% of all commissars, deputies, department heads, and collegiums members in central agencies were registered as party members or candidates.[76] Of a total party membership of about a million in 1927, some 439,000 were employed by the state directly in the state apparatus or indirectly in such 'social' or 'economic' institutions.[77]

A degenerated workers' state until 1928?

The already backward state of the country coupled with international isolation severely limited the possibilities for the new workers' government. Similarly, the absence of reliable allies made the descent to one-party rule difficult to arrest. The onset of the civil war and foreign intervention only compounded these tendencies. In such circumstances, the emergence of a bureaucratic layer within the new state was inevitable. However, whether it would triumph was not a foregone conclusion: there was a struggle to preserve the forms of working class rule. Is the characterisation of Russia until 1928 as a degenerated workers' state therefore coherent? This designation only makes sense as long as it was possible for the Russian working class to still rule politically in some real or potential sense — that it still had channels, levers and institutions through which, if used, it could control the surplus product.

Pirani provides much colourful detail about Moscow after the civil war, including on the strength of bureaucracy and on the state of workers' organisation. However, by attributing the malaise to the party, he understates the role of the state bureaucracy, which had developed as a social force earlier and had already begun to usurp and subvert the party. Pirani also misconceives class relations. He argues that "despite this absence of a ruling class, exploitative social relationships based on alienated labour reappeared".[78] The slippage here is two-fold.

First, it is at least a minimal criterion for a Marxist analysis to define who the ruling class are in any situation. The issue is not whether socialist, non-exploitative relations had begun to emerge. In any case the immediate abolition of alienated labour was not possible in a backward, isolated economy. The critical question when social relations were in flux must be focused on the nature of the state. The question of "who ruled" is at least answered by the qualified "workers' state" formula.

Could things have been different? Pirani is remarkably fatalist. He accepts that the lack of democracy alone did not cause the degeneration of the revolution after 1921. Rather, "there were mountainous obstacles — principally, Russia's economic backwardness, and the failure of the revolution to spread — that anyway might not have been overcome". In the long run, he accepts that different choices would not have greatly altered the course of Russian history.[79]

Socialist historian Sam Farber argues that the Leninist regime (1917-24) "harmed workers' democracy for reasons that could not be simply reduced to 'objective necessity' and seriously weakened the possibilities of successful resistance to Stalinism". He believes the regime "politically disarmed the working class and the peasantry and made them unable to resist the onslaught of Stalinism".[80] Both Farber and Pirani are right to criticise those who over-exaggerate objective circumstances, structures and contexts during this transition period, to the exclusion of agency. However, they do not present a strategic alternative to Lenin and Trotsky's perspective of fighting to reform the party in order to combat the bureaucracy.

The Bolshevik leaders believed that the agents for any kind of socialist transformation in Russia in the early 1920s were the vanguard workers within the ruling party. These forces, some forged by decades of activity and others tempered by revolution and civil war, were the principal agents that could also fight the burgeoning bureaucracy. Hence their orientation to changing the party in order to oppose the bureaucracy.

It is still coherent to regard Russia for most of the 1920s as some sort of a workers' state. Not a socialist mode of production, but one in which the working class was still the ruling class, through the Bolshevik party. Certainly it was a heavily bureaucratised state where the institutions of working-class democracy had withered and faded. Undoubtedly there was an increasingly bureaucratised party within which the apparatus was strangling the healthy forces. But still a party where those who had made the revolution in 1917 held some weight. Vicarious abandonment of the Russian workers' state before it was finally lost serves neither our understanding of history nor our ability to learn the lessons, including the negative lessons, of the post-1917 period for contemporary politics.

How did the left opposition resist Stalinism?

The year 1923 represented a watershed in the development of the bureaucracy and in the growth of opposition to it inside the USSR. A battle for the hearts and minds of the working-class militants within the party, the backbone of the workers' state, began. The status of working-class rule was now represented only by worker-cadres within the revolutionary party, a tenuous thread connecting state and class. The outcome of the conflict within the party would determine the nature of the regime.

Trotsky had previously railed against "bureaucracy" almost entirely in terms of inefficiency. He had coined the term *glavkokratiia* in 1920, which became a popular by-word, but in the main, he utilised the term "bureaucracy" as a swear word against his opponents. But in April 1923, Trotsky went much deeper into the political alienation that defines bureaucracy, outlining the "principles that maintain and nourish bureaucratism [*biurokratizm*]."[81]

On 8 October 1923, Trotsky delivered a letter to the central committee launching his attack on the regime developing inside the party and the mistakes of Kamenev, Zinoviev and Stalin. A week later, a group of prominent Bolsheviks, including Preobrazhenskii, Antonov-Ovseenko, Smirnov, Piatakov, Muralov, Sapronov, Bosh, Iakovleva and Bubnov, submitted what became known as 'The Platform of the 46' to the Politburo, demanding a special conference of the central committee and leaders of the opposition to settle the differences. The 46 who signed the statement had apparently no direct contact with Trotsky at this time, but their views largely coincided with his. Trotsky made his concerns public in *Pravda* on 11 December 1923, later published as a pamphlet, *The New Course* (1924). Despite the limitations of his position, the critique sparked an important discussion, which shone the light on the emerging bureaucratic leadership. For a month, several pages in *Pravda* were occupied by articles, materials and resolutions of the party organisations devoted to the discussion.[82] However, in January 1924, just days before Lenin's death, Stalin defeated the opposition at the thirteenth RCP conference. His control of the apparatus ensured few opposition delegates attended. Stalin's report attacked Trotsky's ideas and accused him of elevating himself into a "superman" standing above the central committee. Stalin concluded by threatening to use the disciplinary procedure passed at the tenth congress to suppress the opposition.

The conflict within the ruling party continued to rage after Lenin's death. Krupskaia made "Lenin's testament", a document which included a call for the removal of Stalin, available to the central committee, with the intention that it be published for the thirteenth party congress (23-31 May 1924). Although the contents were revealed, the testament was partly suppressed, which allowed Stalin to maintain his position as general secretary. Trotsky published *The Lessons of October* (October 1924), savagely indicting Zinoviev and Kamenev for their failings in 1917. At the end of 1924, Stalin propagated his doctrine of "socialism in one country", to justify his internal and external political zigzags.

When the central committee met in January 1925, Zinoviev and Kamenev, stung by Trotsky's criticism, proposed his expulsion from the party — or at least from the Politburo. The majority, including Stalin, rejected this, although they accepted Trotsky's resignation as Commissar of War. In September 1925, Zinoviev began to raise objections to Stalin's theory of "socialism in one country". However, Zinoviev's "Leningrad opposition" was defeated at the fourteenth party congress (18-31 December 1925). Trotsky remained silent, but began to see the struggle in a new light. In May 1926, Trotsky, Zinoviev and Kamenev began to unite their factions.[83] The United Opposition criticised the majority's international policies (particularly its failure to break with the trade union leaders during the British general strike and with the Guomindang nationalists in China), which were informed by Stalin's doctrine of "socialism in one country". The United Opposition also condemned the continuing decline of democracy in soviet political institutions. It called for a return of the soviets, trade unions, and the party to the principle of "workers' democracy" as defined by the tenth party congress and the "new course" resolution. It demanded an end to the repression of oppositionists. The United Opposition called for the election of all officials, further proletarianisation of the party and its apparatus, and the assignment of more members of the party to work in industry. In addition, the opposition demanded the restoration of collective leadership and the removal of Stalin from the post of general secretary.[84]

Although the United Opposition was quickly joined by remnants of the Workers' Opposition and the Democratic Centralists, it still had few supporters. Serge estimated that Zinoviev had several thousand adherents in Leningrad, while Trotsky had 600 supporters in Moscow and several hundred in Kharkov, as well as some international co-thinkers. But the opposition, based on a cadre of old and experienced party leaders, conquered some fairly significant positions, according to historian Michel Reiman. It consolidated its influence in Leningrad, Ukraine, Transcaucasia, and the Urals region, in the universities, in some of the central government offices, in a number of factories of Moscow and the central industrial region, and among command staff of the army and navy. Organisers went out to party cells, with clandestine meetings held in workers' apartments or on the outskirts of town.[85]

When oppositionists tried to address party gatherings, they were shouted down. Their meetings were broken up violently by gangs organised by the party leadership. Leading oppositionists were removed from key party bodies, while rank and file oppositionists were threatened with exile, expulsion from the party, or loss of jobs. Faced with defeat and the prospect of reprisals, the United Opposition petitioned for a truce. Stalin agreed, but dictated severe terms — and then promptly resumed the factional battle. Embittered, Trotsky denounced Stalin as "the gravedigger of the revolution".[86]

In the spring of 1927 the struggle resumed with even greater intensity over developments in China. Stalin had pursued an alliance with the Guomindang nationalists led by Chiang Kai-shek, even making him an honorary member of the Communist International. The fledgling Chinese Communist Party had joined the Guomindang soon after it was formed on Comintern advice and had grown. Stalin insisted the Chinese communists remain inside the Guomindang, despite signs of fissure as the class struggle intensified. Trotsky warned in 1926 that the Chinese communists should break with the Guomindang. In April 1927, Chiang Kai-shek's forces occupied Shanghai and proceeded to massacre the Chinese communists. Instead of fighting for power, the Chinese communists had to fight for their lives. It was further proof of the folly of Stalin's socialism in one country and his misleadership of the Communist International.

Stalin's response was to intensify his attacks on the opposition. In June 1927 Stalin attempted to remove Trotsky and Zinoviev from the central committee. Yet the opposition persevered. In June and July 1927, "opposition activity was spreading like a river in flood". The opposition organised mass meetings of industrial workers in Ivanovo-Voznesensk, Leningrad, and Moscow. At a chemical plant in Moscow shouts were heard: 'Down with Stalin's dictatorship! Down with the Politburo!' In a secret report, the central committee's information department noted: "At several workplaces [the opposition] were successful, mobilising a significant group of workers. In some cases they took the lead at factory mass meetings, where their representatives took the chair". Oppositionists were able to tap into widespread labour discontent at food shortages, wage cuts and work intensification.[87]

On the tenth anniversary of the October revolution, the regime organised a demonstration in Moscow. Demonstrators filed past the main body of officials, but, recognising Trotsky and Zinoviev on a separate reviewing stand, thousands gathered around them, waving and shouting greetings. However, Stalin finally succeeded in expelling Trotsky and Zinoviev from the central committee in November 1927. The following day Adolf Ioffe, one of Trotsky's closest collaborators, committed suicide. Ioffe's funeral was the occasion for the last public demonstration of the opposition and Trotsky's final public speech in the USSR.[88]

At the fifteenth party congress (2-19 December 1927), there were no oppositionists among almost 1,700 delegates, representing a party of 1.2 million members. In 1927-28, about 8,000 oppositionists were expelled from the party and their leaders exiled. In January 1928, Trotsky was forcibly deported to Alma Ata, in a remote part of soviet central Asia.[89] The left opposition had lost the battle for the party and hence for the heart of the workers' state. But the only strategic path to resuscitating genuine workers' democracy had been to fight within the party. Therein lay the real value of the Left Opposition.

By early 1928 the opposition was decisively defeated. This was a signal for the party leadership to initiate a dramatic policy change — perceived by Trotsky and most of the opposition as a shift to the left, partly it was an attempt to mimic some of the tone, if not the real substance, of the opposition's platform. It began the forced industrialisation and collectivisation of agriculture of the USSR, which would catapult the country forward economically, but only through the savage exploitation of workers and peasants. Stalin's revolution from above precipitated a crisis within the Left Opposition. Two prominent oppositionists, Piatakov and Antonov-Ovseenko, capitulated, justifying their recantation on the grounds that Stalin was carrying out the opposition's programme. Others followed after Trotsky was expelled to Turkey in February 1929. In July, Preobrazhenskii, Radek and Smilga signed a document with 400 other exiles, renouncing the opposition and appealing for reinstatement in the party. In August, Khristian Rakovskii and others submitted their own counter-declaration, signed by approximately 500 oppositionists. On 3 November 1929, a statement of surrender signed by Smirnov and hundreds of other oppositionists appeared in *Pravda*.[90]

At the same time Stalin moved against the Right Opposition around Bukharin. Throughout 1929 the ambitious goals for industrialisation were repeatedly revised upwards. Then, at the sixteenth party congress in June 1930, Stalin demanded to "carry out the five-year plan in four years". The secret police sent hundreds of thousands of prisoners to work digging canals, building roads, felling timber and labouring in coal mines. A comparable revolution took place in agriculture. Between October 1929 and March 1930, the number of peasant households collectivised rose from under 8% to over 57%. On 27 December 1930 Stalin called for a policy of *"eliminating* the kulaks as a class". At the same time, the ruling apparatus was transformed. From January 1928 until January 1933 party membership climbed from 1.3 million to more than 3.5 million. Trotsky castigated this drive as "nothing less than the dissolution of the party into the class, that is, the abolition of the party". In 1932 Stalin's bureaucracy officially abandoned the traditional Bolshevik principle limiting the income of all party members to the level of a skilled worker.[91] The bureaucracy held power and privilege.

Trotsky's theories of the bureaucracy: a critique

Trotsky led the intransigent fight against the Stalinist bureaucracy from 1923 until his death in August 1940. Even those oppositionists who recanted in the late 1920s would be murdered, while Trotsky himself was assassinated by Stalin's agents.[92] Trotsky left a precious legacy of analyses of the bureaucracy, providing an evolving assessment of its development and drawing stark political conclusions. Socialist historian Thomas Twiss recently re-examined this analysis as far as 1936.

Twiss argues that Trotsky's analysis of bureaucracy can be divided into three phases. In the first phase, during 1918-22, Trotsky "did not address the problem of soviet bureaucracy in terms of a Marxist analysis of political alienation". He did not "define it in terms of the tendency of a political apparatus to stand over and dominate society; nor did he see it as related to the influence of exploitative classes on the soviet state". This was in contrast to the oppositionists and indeed to Lenin's analysis.

The second phase was Trotsky's analysis from 1923 to 1927, when he led the Left Opposition's fight against Stalinism inside the USSR. Twiss argues that, although Trotsky's analysis was persuasive, and rightly grounded in a strategy of reforming the ruling communist party in order to regenerate workers' rule, the analysis also had major shortcomings, which ultimately weakened the opposition's fight against Stalinism. Trotsky grappled with some of these contradictions and was able to produce a third, mature analysis of Stalinism by the mid-1930s, which led him to develop the perspective of political revolution to overthrow the Stalinist bureaucracy.[93]

Trotsky's second phase analysis grasped the authoritarian, centralising aspects of bureaucracy in strangling workers' power (such as the soviets), but did not foreground criticism of one-party rule and the ban on party factions. These were the crucial political reforms that would have helped to reinvigorate the political activity of the working class. Worse, Trotsky wrongly attributed this mostly to the influence of capitalist elements inside and outside the USSR. Of course the external threat of military intervention and competition from the capitalist world market were important. In 1926-27 Trotsky's most basic explanation for the growth of bureaucratism was the change he believed had occurred in the relative strength of social classes within the USSR. But what Trotsky underestimated was the extent of autonomy the bureaucracy had to follow its own path, which was neither forward to socialism nor backward to capitalism. He predicted that counter-revolution could come through either "a decisive and sharp overturn (with or without intervention) or... several successive shifts [to the right on the part of the party]", something he described by analogy with the French revolution as the danger of a soviet Thermidor.[94]

The closest the Left Opposition came to coherently explaining the bureaucracy as an autonomous force, as effectively a proto-ruling class in the making, came on the cusp of their own defeat. In May 1927, Trotsky began to suggest that the state and party apparatus had fused and used its power to fight the working-class forces of the Left Opposition. He wrote that the "whole official apparatus, both party and soviet, was striking out at the left wing of the party". However, Trotsky would not develop this insight further until the 1930s. This was the germ of his idea that the bureaucracy was a substitution for the working class, acting as a locum but in fact stripping the working class of the political levers to control its own state.

The oppositionist who did develop this line of reasoning was Rakovskii. In his famous 'Letter to Valentinov' (8 August 1928), Rakovskii traced the emergence of a single "soviet-party bureaucracy" or "party-soviet bureaucracy" in Russia after the revolution. Rakovskii agreed with Trotsky that these developments were related to factors such as the shifting balance of class forces and Russia's international isolation. However, he argued that such explanations were inadequate, for the same "difficulties would continue to exist up to a certain point, even if we allowed, for a moment, that the country was inhabited only by proletarian masses and the exterior was made up solely of proletarian states". Rather, the root of the problem was that "any new directing class" encounters "inherent difficulties" that could be described as "the 'professional dangers' of power". For Rakovskii, the reaction started when "the power began to pass both formally and effectively into the hands of an increasingly restricted number of citizens". The same differentiation had occurred in the party, leading to the creation of a combined party-state apparatus that was so autonomous that the "bureaucracy of the soviets and of the party constitutes a new order". The differentiation "at first only functional… later became social".[95]

During the years 1928-29 Trotsky's theory of bureaucracy entered a period of crisis. Repeatedly, events contradicted his expectations and predictions derived from the theory he had developed during the mid-1920s. After the defeat of the opposition, reality seemed to run directly counter to the path mapped by Trotsky's theory. Unfortunately, he continued to insist that the USSR remained a workers' state based on three criteria: "that the soviet state still defended the nationalisation of production and the state monopoly of foreign trade established by the October revolution; that a counterrevolutionary civil war had not yet occurred; and that the party and state could still be reformed by the proletariat".[96]

Trotsky should have heeded the analysis made by the Democratic Centralist Borodai in October 1928, who argued that the dictatorship of the proletariat had ceased to exist and that what had occurred was "Thermidor with a dry guillotine". As historian Robert Wistrich noted, Trotsky "seriously underestimated the power of the bureaucracy and its autonomy, the degree to which it had created its own social support, independent of other class forces which it kept fragmented and powerless through terror and repression". Trotsky failed to recognise that the bureaucracy had become an independent social force with its own material interests, in other words, a ruling class.[97]

After 1933, Trotsky began to articulate a fundamentally new theory of soviet bureaucracy. More than previously, he stressed the autonomy of the bureaucracy. Trotsky revised his use of the Thermidor and Bonapartism analogies, developed the concept of "bureaucratic caste" and abandoned the perspective of reform in the USSR. In February 1935, Trotsky designated Russia a "degenerated workers' state". Finally, at the beginning of 1936, he argued that a political revolution was necessary to topple the bureaucracy.[98]

Trotsky at last saw the restriction on party democracy as hampering the fight against the bureaucracy. As early as 1934 he suggested that the bureaucratisation of the soviets was a "result of the political monopoly of a single party". In 1936 Trotsky argued that "it is absolutely indisputable that the domination of a single party served as the juridical point of departure for the Stalinist totalitarian system". A year later he wrote that "the prohibition of oppositional parties brought after it the prohibition of factions. The prohibition of factions ended in a prohibition to think otherwise than the infallible leaders". He added that "the police-manufactured monolithism of the party resulted in a bureaucratic impunity which has become the source of all kinds of wantonness and corruption". In July 1939 Trotsky proclaimed, *"Whoever prohibits factions thereby liquidates party democracy and takes the first step toward a totalitarian regime"*.[99]

Trotsky's new theory of bureaucracy received its most complete expression in his book, *The Revolution Betrayed* (1937). He recognised that the ruling stratum was actually "something more than a bureaucracy". It was "in the full sense of the word the sole privileged and commanding stratum in the soviet society". This was because "the means of production belong to the state", but "the state, so to speak, 'belongs' to the bureaucracy". He argued that "if these as yet wholly new relations should solidify, become the norm and be legalised, whether with or without resistance from the workers, they would, in the long run, lead to a complete liquidation of the social conquests of the proletarian revolution".[100]

The sole criterion remaining for the USSR as a workers' state was the state property inherited from the 1917 revolution. Sean Matgamna has called this assessment "totalitarian economism", the fetishising of nationalised property over and above the actual realities of working-class disenfranchisement. Trotsky had steadily dropped other criteria defining Russia as a workers' state, crucially, the possibility of reform of the ruling party. However, in the last year of his life, Trotsky admitted that the existing property forms in the USSR could support a new ruling class. This was the final straw that broke the back of his characterisation of the USSR as a workers' state. Trotsky accepted that the working class had lost all levers to control the Russian state since the late 1920s. If the bureaucracy had its own property forms and made itself master of the surplus product, then this was effectively an admission that the Russian workers and peasants were exploited by the bureaucracy.[101] Although Trotsky never drew this conclusion before he was killed, the deduction was inescapable — and was recognised by Shachtman and his comrades. The workers' state created by the 1917 revolution was dead. It had died in 1928 when the possibility of regenerating the party was destroyed. The fate of the Russian revolution was sealed.

Conclusion

The process of formation of the bureaucratic ruling class was well underway by 1921, but still far from complete. In particular, the party itself had not been decisively subverted. Workers retained some levers, through the soviets and trade unions, for what might be called partial or negative control of production. Traditions of working-class organisation and a Marxist cadre had survived the civil war. The party had begun to degenerate but was far from dead. The proletarian vanguard that had made the revolution was not completely exhausted, although by the early 1920s it was severely weakened. The correct strategy flowing from this situation was, as both Lenin proposed early on and the Trotskyist opposition and the best of other oppositions, such as the Democratic Centralists, continued, to fight for working-class democracy, starting from within the party.

Was the Russian communist party in the mid-1920s a model for today? No. It was a degenerated, heavily bureaucratised party, shorn of basic democratic structures was no basis on which to make and sustain workers' revolutions at that time. However, the party that led the 1917 revolution is still an inspiration. This was the party that could take on and defeat all enemies, internal and external and survive the civil war. This was the party that would rancorously debate out its differences in public and with great sharpness, in order to clarify the assessment and to draw out the political conclusions.

That party along with the tradition it embodied was not finished after the civil war. Having made such a tremendous, irreplaceable contribution to the Russian working class over decades, it was entirely right for those who wanted to save the Russian revolution to seek to revive whatever could be salvaged from its ranks. There were no other forces, no other agents capable of turning the tables on the bureaucracy and on Stalin's machine at that time than the old guard of militant worker-Bolsheviks.

Could the opposition have done more and earlier? Undoubtedly. The revolutionaries should have opposed the ban on factions within the party and fought for the revival of the soviets. They could have opened up elections to the soviets and tried to collaborate with the best of the "non-party" groups in Moscow in 1921. They could have championed trade union independence from the state, and other basic freedoms to organise, publish and dissent. The working class still required the "light and air" of its democracy to control the surplus they created and take part in shaping the precarious, yet precious, workers' state.

Some historians and activists date the political expropriation of the working class to 1921 or 1924. The Democratic Centralists argued from 1926 that Russia was now ruled by the 'bureaucratic dictatorship of the secretariat' — hence a new party and a new revolution were necessary. But this is burying the revolution while it was still alive, while the fight within the party was still possible. However, after the defeat of the left opposition in 1927-28 and the closing off once and for all of the party as a channel for working class rule, it is correct to identify a qualitative shift in the situation.

After 1928 and with the onset of Stalin's forced march industrialisation and collectivisation, the working class no longer ruled politically in any sense and therefore it did not rule socially or economically either. The nationalised property relations were not sufficient. After 1928 the description of Russia as a degenerated workers' state is undoubtedly incoherent. If workers do not rule politically, then they cannot rule at all. That was the great truth that fundamentally undermines Trotsky's later theories of Stalinism.

If those on the left who want to abandon the Russian workers' state too early are mistaken, then so too are those who believe the workers' state persisted beyond the 1920s and even as far as 1990. For example, writing at the turn of this century, the British Trotskyist Alan Woods asserted that Trotsky's analysis of Stalinism, "with a delay of 60 years", had been "completely vindicated by history".[102] This makes a frozen dogma of Trotsky's words and ignores his own dynamic method. Trotsky insisted that if the USSR survived the Second World War then its class character would have to be reassessed. After 1945 the USSR did not collapse, but survived and expanded, creating its own empire in Eastern Europe. It reproduced the same nationalised property relations that Trotsky had long believed were unique to the 1917 revolution — and it did so while simultaneously crushing independent working class movements and savagely exploiting working classes. When Stalinism collapsed in the late 1980s, workers did not rise to defend "their" state: most were glad to be rid of their bureaucratic oppressors.

To say workers' states can be created without the active intervention of the working class makes a nonsense of working-class socialism. If there are substitute social agents for making socialism — including terrible tyrannies and totalitarian police states — then socialism will never become the goal of millions of workers. The association of Stalinism with socialism was for decades the millstone around the necks of those who sought workers' liberty. Trotsky's degenerated workers' state theory was broadly accurate in the 1920s as long as it remained possible to revive the Bolshevik party and renew workers' power. Once the Stalinist bureaucracy eliminated the Left Opposition and consolidated its own social base, it became the ruling class and Russia was no longer any sort of workers' state. To revive authentic working class socialism today — including the tremendous tradition of the 1917 revolution — it is essential to recognise the defeat and understand subsequent history in light of this assessment.

References

1. Marx, *Capital, Vol.3*, (*MECW* 37: 777-78).
2. Steve Smith, *Red Petrograd: Revolution in the Factories, 1917-1918*, (1983: 230).
3. Smith, *The Russian Revolution: A Very Short Introduction*, (2002: 40).
4. Alexander Rabinowitch, *The Bolsheviks in Power*, (2007: 12).
5. Harry Rigby, *Lenin's Government: Sovnarkom, 1917-1922*, (1979: 14, 31, 33).
6. Victor Serge, *Year One of the Russian Revolution*, (1992: 235-237).
7. Smith, (2002: 73).
8. Sam Farber, *Before Stalinism: the rise and fall of Soviet democracy*, (1990: 67).
9. Lenin, [13 January 1918] 'Replies to Notes: Extraordinary All-Russia Railwaymen's Congress', (*LCW* 26: 498).
10. Rigby, (1979: 166).
11. Smith, (2002: 45).
12. Evan Mawdsley, *The Russian Civil War*, (1987: 43).
13. Marcel Liebman, *Leninism under Lenin*, (1975: 312, 233, 244-48).
14. Marcel Liebman, *Leninism under Lenin*, (1975: 312, 233, 244-48).
15. Smith, (1983: 209-210).
16. Smith, (2002: 73); Smith, (1983: 150-151).
17. Smith, (2002: 74).
18. Rigby, (1979: 65, 169).
19. Rabinowitch, (2007: 251).
20. Rabinowitch, (2007: 223-224, 254, 324).
21. Smith, (1983: 231).
22. Farber, (1990: 69).
23. Farber, (1990: 84).
24. Pirani, 'Class Clashes With Party: Politics in Moscow between the Civil War and the New Economic Policy', *Historical Materialism*, 11, 2, (2003: 87).
25. Yoshimasa Tsuji, 'The Debate on the Trade Unions, 1920–21', *Revolutionary Russia*, 2, 1, (1989: 31, 87).
26. Pirani, 'Mass Mobilization versus Participatory Democracy: Moscow Workers and the Bolshevik Expropriation of Political Power'. In Don Filtzer, Wendy Goldman, Gijs Kessler and Simon Pirani, *A Dream Deferred: New Studies in Russian and Soviet Labour History*, (2009: 116-117).
27. Farber, (1990: 172).
28. Simon Pirani, *The Russian Revolution in Retreat, 1920-1924*, (2008: 98, 106).
29. Pirani, 'The Russian Workers and the Bolshevik Party in Power'. A talk to the Iranian Socialist Forum, a web discussion run by Iranian activists in exile, September, (2006).
30. Pirani, 'Socialism in the 21st century and the Russian Revolution', *International Socialism*, 128, (2010).
31. Diane Koenker, *Republic of Labor: Russian Printers and Soviet Socialism, 1918-1930*, (2005: 141).
32. Lars Lih '"Our Position is in the Highest Degree Tragic": Bolshevik 'Euphoria' in 1920', Mike Haynes and Jim Wolfreys, *History and Revolution*, (2007: 118).
33. Israel Getzler, *Kronstadt, 1917-1921: The Fate of a Soviet Democracy*, (1983: 231-32); Getzler, 'The Communist Leaders' Role in the Kronstadt Tragedy of 1921 in the Light of Recently Published Archival Documents', *Revolutionary Russia*, 15, 1, (2002).
34. Trotsky, [1940] 'Stalin', *Lenin and Trotsky, Kronstadt*, (1979: 123); Trotsky, [6 July 1937] 'The questions of Wendelin Thomas', *Kronstadt*, (1979: 100).
35. Paul Avrich, *Kronstadt 1921*, (1970: 6).
36. Serge, [21 March 1922] 'The Tragic Face of Revolution', David Cotterill, *The Serge-Trotsky Papers*, (1994: 19).
37. Serge, [10 September 1937] 'Fiction or Fact: Kronstadt', Cotterill, (1994: 165).
38. Lenin, [1917] *The State and Revolution*, (*LCW* 25: 407, 416, 425-26, 486).
39. Russell Block, *Lenin's Fight against Stalinism*, (1975: 11).

40. Rigby, (1979: 43-47).
41. Rabinowitch, (2007: 57).
42. Rigby, (1979: 46, 58).
43. Rigby, (1979: 61, 62, 64).
44. Richard Sakwa, 'Soviet communists in power: a study of Moscow during the Civil War, 1918-21', (1987: 191-192).
45. Daniel Orlovsky, 'State building in the civil war era'. Koenker, Rosenberg and Suny, (1989: 192).
46. Max Shachtman, *The New Course and the Struggle for the New Course*, (1965: 153-154).
47. Rigby, (1971: 434).
48. Don Rowney, *Transition to Technocracy: The Structural Origins of the Soviet Administrative State*, (1989: 118-119).
49. Lenin, [19 January 1921] 'The Party Crisis', (*LCW* 32: 48).
50. Lenin, [14 May 1921] 'To Comrade Krzhizhanovsky', (*LCW* 32: 372); Lenin, [23 December 1921] 'To P. A. Bogdanov', (*LCW* 36: 557).
51. Lenin, [27 March 1922] 'Political Report of the Central Committee of the RCP(B)', (*LCW* 33: 288).
52. Lenin, [13 November 1922] 'Five Years of the Russian Revolution and the Prospects of the World Revolution', (*LCW* 33: 428-429).
53. Rigby, (1979: xi).
54. Marcel Liebman, *Leninism under Lenin*, (1975: 279).
55. Pirani, (2008: 57).
56. Rabinowitch, (2007: 248, 343).
57. Rigby, 'The Soviet Political Elite', *British Journal of Political Science*, 1, 4, (1971: 418).
58. Pirani, (2008: 44).
59. Rigby, (1979: 176, 185-186).
60. Sakwa, (1987: 167).
61. Farber, (1990: 96).
62. Farber, (1990: 99, 124-127).
63. Pirani, (2003: 111, 112).
64. Farber, (1990: 197).
65. Sakwa, (1987: 168).
66. Alexandra Kollontai, [25 January 1921] 'The Workers' Opposition', *Selected Writings*, (1977: 191-92).
67. Liebman, (1975: 291-98); Farber, (1990: 76, 99-103).
68. Pirani, (2008: 95, 104, 237).
69. Valentina Vilkova, *The Struggle for Power*, (1996: 18).
70. Block, (1975: 22).
71. Orlovsky, (1989: 191).
72. Rabinowitch, (1989: 145).
73. Pirani, (2008: 170).
74. Pirani, (2008: 58, 174-75).
75. Pirani, (2008: 179).
76. Stephen Sternheimer, (1980) 'Administration for Development: The Emerging Bureaucratic Elite, 1920–1930'. Walter Pintner, and Don Rowney, *Russian Officialdom: The Bureaucratization of Russian Society from the Seventeenth to the Twentieth Century*, (1980: 324-325, 337).
77. Rowney 1989: 154, 162).
78. Pirani, (2008: 6).
79. Pirani 2008: 240).
80. Farber, 'The Russian Revolution in Retreat — review of Pirani', *Against the Current*, 136, (2008).
81. Thomas Twiss, *Trotsky and the Problem of Soviet Bureaucracy*, (2014: 93, 109); Trotsky, [3 April 1923] 'Civility and Politeness as a Necessary Lubricant in Daily Relations', *Problems of Everyday Life*, (1973: 50).

82. Vilkova, (1996: 30-31).
83. Twiss, (2014: 139-145).
84. Twiss, (2014: 148-150).
85. Victor Serge and Natalia Sedova, [1946-47] *The Life and Death of Leon Trotsky*, (2015: 137); Michel Reiman, *The Birth of Stalinism*, (1987: 19-20); Twiss, (2014: 150).
86. Twiss, (2014: 149, 152).
87. Twiss, (2014: 157); Reiman, (1987: 22); Alexei Gusev, 'The "Bolshevik-Leninist" Opposition and the Working Class, 1928-1929'. Filtzer et al, (2009: 153, 159).
88. Twiss, (2014: 190- 191).
89. Twiss, (2014: 191-92); Gusev, (2009: 153).
90. Twiss, (2014: 219, 232-33).
91. Twiss, (2014: 257-261, 298); Trotsky, *Writings 1930*, (1975: 144).
92. Bertrand Patenaude, *Trotsky: Downfall of a Revolutionary*, (2010).
93. Twiss, (2014: 72, 440-42).
94. Twiss, (2014: 167-68, 135-36, 153, 173); Trotsky, *Challenge of the Left Opposition, 1926–27*, (1980: 68).
95. Twiss, (2014: 162, 239-43); Trotsky, [May 1927] 'Declaration of the Eighty-Four', *Challenge of the Left Opposition, 1926-27*, (1980: 231); Rakovsky, *Selected Writings on Opposition in the USSR 1923–30*, (1980: 125-32).
96. Twiss, (2014: 196-97, 320); Trotsky, [4 October 1930] 'To the Bulgarian comrades', *Writings 1930–31*, (1973: 52-53).
97. Twiss, (2014: 245, 254-55); Robert Wistrich, *Trotsky: Fate of a Revolutionary*, (1979: 161).
98. Twiss, (2014: 331, 340, 352, 367-68); Trotsky, [20 July 1933] 'It Is Impossible to Remain in the Same International with Stalin, Manuilsky, Lozovsky and Company', *Writings 1933-34*, (1972: 20); Trotsky, [28 December 1934] 'The Stalinist bureaucracy and the Kirov assassination', *Writings 1934-35*, (1974: 196-97); Trotsky, [1 February 1935] 'The Workers' State, Thermidor and Bonapartism', *Writings 1934-35*, (1974: 237-242); Trotsky, [1 January 1936] 'The Class Nature of the Soviet State', *Writings 1935-36*, (1977: 224-25).
99. Twiss, (2014: 409-10, 447); Trotsky, [17 August 1934] 'If America should go Communist', *Writings 1934-35*, (1974: 121); Trotsky, [29 August 1936] 'Stalinism and Bolshevism', *Writings 1936-37*, (1978: 426); Trotsky, *On France*, (1979: 228).
100. Twiss, (2014: 405, 419); Trotsky, [1937] *The Revolution Betrayed*, (1972: 248-49).
101. Sean Matgamna, *The Fate of the Russian Revolution, Vol.1*, (1998: 110-14); Twiss, (2014: 455); Trotsky, [25 September 1939] 'The USSR in War', *In Defence of Marxism*, (1942: 9); Trotsky, *Stalin*, (2016: 718). Unfortunately Twiss doesn't assess the changes to Trotsky's analysis in the final four years of his life.
102. Alan Woods, 'The Revolution Betrayed – a Marxist Masterpiece', *In Defence of Marxism*, (2001).

THE RUSSIAN REVOLUTION: WHEN WORKERS TOOK POWER

THE RUSSIAN REVOLUTION: WHEN WORKERS TOOK POWER

Alexsandr Deineka, 'We Will See Who is Right', 1932

11. Why is the Russian revolution relevant today?

This book has set out, retell the story of the Russian Revolution in all its complexity and, in so doing, uncover some of the lies, half-truths and myths about the revolution's historical and contemporary detractors. At the heart of that task is defending the record of the Bolsheviks and their leading theorists and activists, in particular, Lenin and Trotsky. This book has therefore also told the story of that organisation, their historical origins, the kind of Marxism they developed in the Russian context and the controversies they debated.

To their detractors the Bolsheviks were coup makers and, ultimately, the founders of Stalinist totalitarianism. In fact, as this book has argued, fundamentally the Bolsheviks based themselves on the political compass of a democratically-organised workers' movement, the will of a millions-strong popular movement. Those deep roots in the Russian working class ensured that wide reaching socialist measures were the first acts of the Russian Revolution. Those acts sparked revolts around the world and refounded a mass Marxist, revolutionary socialist movement after the devastating impacts of the First World War.

It was only the exceptional difficulties of civil war, and the failure of further workers' revolutions in Europe, that fundamentally caused the revolution to go off course. Where mistakes were made, Lenin, Trotsky and others tried to rectify them, but alas too late. In a situation of isolation and scarcity. Stalin and his bureaucratic cohorts were able opportunistically to use these conditions to organise a counter-revolution.

The Russian revolution therefore represents the high point in working-class history so far. The Russian revolutionaries furnished a method of assessing modern capitalism, a socialist alternative and the party-political means for changing the world. Digested, updated and restated, these lessons can help Marxists to renew the socialist project in today's conditions.

The Russian revolution enriched **socialism**. The workers' state established by the revolution prioritised implementing a shorter working day, not only to reduce exploitation, but to free time for workers to govern. Reducing necessary labour time, so as to make more free-time for human endeavour, is the heart of socialist liberation.

The Russian Marxists were **consistent democrats**. They believed that democracy is a defining principle of socialism. Without democracy, genuinely socialist collective ownership is impossible. The Bolsheviks believed that a socialist who is not for democratic self-rule and liberty in relation to the state and society is not a socialist. The opposite is also true. The anti-socialist who is against extending democracy to the economic conditions governing people's lives is not really a democrat.

The socialist criticism of parliamentary democracy is not an opposition to democracy or a rejection of it. Socialists want the democratisation of every aspect of life. Pluto-democracy — the money-soaked, bourgeois democracy we have now under capitalism — is a shallow, impoverished version of democracy. Marxists defend even the limited forms of parliamentary democracy under threat by populists and fascists. The Bolsheviks stood for a republic, for a single assembly elected annually, with MPs paid a workers' wage and subject to recall by their constituents. A more generous democracy would facilitate the struggle for workers' power.

The Russian revolution vindicates **working class politics**. The working class was a minority in tsarist Russia, yet workers overthrew the autocracy and then went on to establish their own forms of democratic self-rule. The working class has the power and the interest to overthrow capitalist exploitation and replace it with global socialist relations of production. On this basis, society can be organised to meet our many-sided needs. Today the working class across the globe is billions-strong. More of the world's direct producers now do waged work than do peasant agriculture. Globally the social weight of the working class has never been greater.

Socialism means liberty

The Russian revolutionaries fought for **universal human liberation**. Even when their immediate goal was the overthrow of tsarism, they never forgot to champion the oppressed against the oppressors. The primary goal of the Russian revolutionaries was the establishment of working class rule, but they always saw this regime as the stepping stone to wider human emancipation.

The Bolsheviks understood that women's oppression is part of capitalism, directly part of the system of exploitation. **Women's liberation** is not possible while society continues to serve profit rather than need. Socialism will end exploitation. Through democratic economic planning, the world's rich resources could be released to serve people's needs. There are enough resources and technology in the world to provide food, housing, education and health care for everyone. A socialist society would reorganise domestic work on a collective basis.[1]

The Russian revolutionaries were **cosmopolitan internationalists**. They were fierce opponents of racist, colonialist and imperialist ideas. They fought against oppression on racial, national, religious and any other grounds. They were among the first opponents (and the first victims) of fascist reaction. A socialist society would cut the roots of all forms of oppression, putting all peoples on an equal footing. **Solidarity** is our answer to oppression.

Liberty is at the heart of socialism. It is a society committed to human flourishing — freedom to live, work and play. Socialism would facilitate the enormous expansion of political and economic liberty, sexual and personal freedom, cultural expression — for the whole of humanity. A socialist society is the only rational way to organise human affairs in the twenty-first century. Socialism is no utopia — it is a burning necessity.

The actuality of revolution

October 1917 demonstrated the **actuality of revolution**. The events in Russia during 1917 show that revolution is both possible and necessary: opposition to war and preparations for international women's day; agitation in the factories and in the streets for basic needs; publication of illegal newspapers and organising demonstrations. But the revolution did not cease with the overthrow of the tsar: dual power between the Provisional Government and the soviets; the "socialists" who became the last line of defence for the bourgeoisie; the reassessment of tasks by the Bolshevik intransigents; the clarity of purpose in demanding peace, bread and land; the proliferation of workers' democracy at every level; the mobilisation of millions; the debates on strategy and tactics; the winning of the majority of the working class to soviet rule; the preparation for insurrection and the implementation of revolutionary ideas.

The Russian revolution was the precursor of a century of mass working class mobilisation. The twentieth century witnessed revolutions where the working class played a crucial role: Germany (1918-23), Hungary (1919), China (1925-27), Spain (1936-39), Hungary (1956), France (1968), Chile (1973), Portugal (1974-75) and Poland (1980). In cases such as Iran (1978-79), and Eastern Europe (1989) the working class played a key role in overthrowing the old regime, even where the political balance of forces meant it could not impose its own forms. Events in China (1989), Indonesia (1998) and more recently during the Arab Spring (2011) contained elements of permanent revolution, where the working class played a leading role.

Workers succeeded in shaking and in some cases threatening the existing bourgeois (or Stalinist) states. Powerful mass organisations of workers' councils (or cordónes or shoras) were created. Mass strikes spread and new militant unions were formed. But in all these revolutions the working class lacked its own Marxist leadership capable of charting a strategy for self-emancipation. Ultimately, that is why they failed. The Russian revolution had the missing link — the revolutionary party.

The revolutionary party

The Russian revolutionaries conceived of socialism as the **conscious** act of the working class. They also understood that the working class in capitalist society is not a blank page: inevitably, it is pervaded with the ideas of the ruling class. Ideological chains buttress and tighten the economic shackles that exploit the working class.

The Bolsheviks understood that the struggle to fuse the spontaneous movement of the working class with the ideology that represents its long-term interests must take the form of a political party. The party organises the advanced layers of the working class into a force that is acutely class-conscious and ideologically clear.

The revolutionary party must be scientifically conscious and permanently organised for the working class struggle. It must be militant on all **three fronts of the class struggle**: the economic, political and the ideological. It must defend revolutionary Marxism and combat the ideology that springs up in the working class movement under bourgeois influence. The revolutionary party must be so organised and disciplined that it can fulfil its role of skeletal structure of the proletarian class in all its struggles, linking and co-ordinating the various aspects of the struggle. If it is to fulfil its tasks this party must fight continuously, consciously, to perfect itself, subordinating its organisational form to the tasks rigorously imposed by the nature and course of the struggle. This party will conduct the struggle of the proletariat in a campaign spirit — to win.

The experience of the working class in Russia — and later negatively in aborted revolutions elsewhere — led the Bolsheviks and the early Communist International to declare that only the construction of **revolutionary parties**, fully grounded on the theory and practice of Marxism could lead the working class to power. They denounced those who said there could be an absolute maturity of the working class, which could lead to an automatic transition to power. Magnificent risings had been led to defeat by the conservative apparatus of existing labour movements. The fight therefore was to overcome the 'crisis of leadership' in the working class — to create parties that would embody the historical interests of the working class.

The Russian revolutionaries organised on the basis of **democratic centralism**, an organic fusion into a higher unity. Each party member is a cell, and there can be no dead, inactive cells. This is absolutely vital both for centralised activity and for full democracy. A combat party, strongly centralised, can have no dead-wood; its function is to prepare, organise and fight the class struggle; it is an army on the march (Lenin's "column of steel"); its measure must be its will and ability to respond to events decisively and sharply.

The central leadership, democratically elected and controlled, must be in position to give directives that are binding. To do this effectively, it must know exactly what resources are available. Unless it knows as near as possible what forces it can muster, Bolshevik-type activity is not possible. Centralism demands an active membership.

Democracy also demands an active membership. Inactive members, dead cells, poison a living organism. Only an organisation with a fully active membership can be fully and consistently democratic. No democracy equals no unanimity of action, no confidence in the directives of the leadership. Trotsky compared democracy to oxygen, a functional need for an organic party. Party democracy, in decisions, in equality of rights for majorities and minorities. in the "neutrality" of the party machine in face of internal differences, play the vital function of allowing the party to live and grow and adapt and change aspects of its line where necessary.

Minority rights prevent monolithism. The leadership isn't divinely-appointed, functioning with papal pretensions to infallibility. The centre's positions are submitted to experience; the leaders' abilities to practical demonstration. Minorities are loyally active dissenting factions with potential alternatives: reserves, accepted and preserved by the party as a whole.

Only those who seriously devote their lives to socialism, who organise their lives around the single purpose of fighting for and with the working class can be revolutionary socialists of the vanguard. It is a hard logic — but one imposed by an equally hard reality. And it is this reality, with its tremendous pressures, dragging us down to accommodation, which we must rise above and overcome.

Lenin's point that the **ideological front is decisive** is borne out by the decades-long activity of the British working class, which has resulted in few basic political gains and economic victories built on shifting sand. The British working class, left to spontaneity through a peculiar combination of historical circumstances, has been utterly defeated ideologically. And this has conditioned everything else.[2]

At present there is no authoritative working class party in any state across the globe. There is no workers' international, nor even the embryo of such a centre. But there are Marxists everywhere and Marxist politics are universal. Marxist ideas are published, debated and argued over. And workers fight. The struggle never ceases. Therein lies our hope.

Strategy and tactics

What is the relevance of the Bolshevik and early Communist International discussions today, when circumstances in the world and in labour movements are so different? It is a mistake to dismiss the early Comintern as merely the work of "dead Russians" or matters of a bygone age. The early Comintern codified the lessons from the highest level of working class struggle seen so far in history. Embryonic and unfinished discussions around **transitional demands**, the **united front** and the **workers' government** provide fertile lines for Marxists engaged in workers' struggles today.

These lessons are irreplaceable for winning the majority of the working class to socialism. They are not restricted only to situations where Marxists have already organised mass parties. Revolutionary socialist parties cannot be built unless the revolutionaries struggle alongside reformist workers and convince them. Nor are they restricted only to pre-revolutionary situations when the fight for power may soon be on the agenda.

The misuse of transitional demands, the united front and the workers' government by sections of the left does not destroy their importance. The workers' government slogan is a bold tactical compromise. Although conditions today are very different, making propaganda for a workers' government answers the vital question of who should rule — for example, when the Labour Party campaigns for power or after the financial crisis. It has more agitational purchase in circumstances like Greece in 2015, when bourgeois states are destabilised. The demand plays a pivotal role in the transitional programme, linking day-to-day struggles within the present political system to the struggle to disrupt, overthrow and replace the existing state.

Anyone who wants to change the world today should stand on the shoulders of the early Comintern giants. During and immediately after the Russian revolution they saw much further than most of their epigones.

Imperialism and war

The Russian revolutionaries a century ago assessed global capitalism in terms of imperialist rivalry leading to world war. This was a powerful analysis, helping to orientate Marxists in an epoch of wars and revolutions. But to mechanically transpose Lenin's conjunctural assessment of empires and colonies a century ago onto subsequent history is to misunderstand the last century.

Today capitalist social relations of production dominate across the planet. Capitalist forms of exploitation undergird the world economy. Since 1945, global capitalism has undergone an epoch of the **"imperialism of free trade"**, radically distinct from the imperialism of 1900 or 1916. It is broadly a world of capitalist states, which act to make the conditions for capital accumulation. This regime is superintended by the US hyperpower, which has overwhelming military superiority and uses military force to police global capitalism. US hegemony persists, despite its setbacks. Trump, Brexit and the rise of populism may usher in a new era of fragmentation and protectionism.

Capitalist development has been and will always be highly uneven, but recent decades have seen significant **combined development**, particularly, the creation of new centres of accumulation with sub-imperialist states and, crucially, the growth of the industrial working class, which has renewed and expanded the objective basis for international socialism. It is on these tendencies that a revived labour movement can arise.

Contradictions between imperial powers exist. Despite the crises of the 1970s and more recently since 2007-08, a recrudescence of inter-imperial rivalry on the scale that led to the First World War has not emerged. Modern barbarous capitalist wars have to be understood concretely on the basis of today's real relations between states, in the context of the uneven and combined development of global capitalism.

The experience of wars during the 1980s and 1990s convinced Workers' Liberty that "revolutionary defeatism" was not adequate to understand modern wars. The wars in Afghanistan, the Falklands, the Iran-Iraq war, the first Gulf war and the wars in the former Yugoslavia were pivotal to unravelling the formula of "defeatism" in the modern world. We have seen the disorientation of those such as *Militant*, who welcomed the Russian attempt to subjugate Afghanistan, or those within the Mandelite "Fourth International", who backed the Argentine junta in its invasion of the Falklands, to those including the British SWP who flipped from backing Iran against Iraq to backing Saddam against the US-UK over Kuwait. "Defeatism" became incoherent with the Serb-revanchist assault on Bosnian and Kosovar peoples, justified by sections of the left in the name of "anti-imperialism".[3]

At no point did Workers' Liberty support the British or other bourgeois governments in their wars. But neither did we back their opponents in the name of "defeatism". Instead, we utilised the best of the method outlined by Trotsky to make an independent appraisal of each war and then draw political conclusions from that assessment.

The national question

The purpose of Lenin's policy of **consistent democracy** was to unite the international working class, so as to facilitate the fight for socialism. The overall Bolshevik policy on national minorities is more far-reaching and therefore more adequate than any solutions offered at the time or since. Most of the left has completely lost its bearings on the national question. However, the contribution of Lenin and Trotsky a century ago is still relevant, especially when pruned of the various excrescences and misinterpretations that have blighted the tradition.

Two contrary temptations haunt the revolutionary left on the national question. The first is to deny the legitimacy of national movements, condemning them as "petty bourgeois" and divisive, only to abstractly proclaim workers' unity. The second is to espouse uncritically the nationalist ideology of these movements and condemn the dominant nations en bloc as reactionary. The answer to continuing national oppression — such as the Kurds face today — is the politics of consistent democracy: the right of all nations to self-determination, the rights of minorities to maximum autonomy, no privileges for any people over another.

Israeli Jews are a nation and they should have the right of self-determination today like any other nation. To believe otherwise is to retreat to notions of "non-historic" and "bad" peoples. The conception of a "democratic secular state" in Israel-Palestine satisfies the national aspirations of neither people: Jews already have their own state and want to keep it; the Palestinians want their own state and are denied it. The answer is for the Palestinians to have their own state, alongside Israel, on the territories where they are (and were before they were driven out) a majority. This is the only programme that addresses the desires of both nations, and which can unite Jewish and Arab workers to fight together for socialism.

Similarly, only the demand for a federal united Ireland, with guarantees for the Protestants, satisfies the aspirations of the Catholics of the North whilst addressing the potential for oppression of the Protestants in future if the present relationship of forces were reversed. In each case, the policy of consistent democracy can be applied to the concrete situation and yield a programme to overcome national oppression on the basis of the equality of nations, and heal the divisions within the working class.[4]

Stalinism

Stalinism was the gravedigger of the Russian revolution. After 1928, Stalinist rule obliterated the remnants of workers' power in Russia, creating its own form of class society, where the bureaucracy exploited the workers and peasants. **Trotskyism** was the irreplaceable movement against Stalinism, originating among the finest militants from the Russian revolution. The pioneering Trotskyists were titans, political giants who stood against the tide of Stalinism and mostly paid for their principled politics with their lives.

Trotsky's strategy of **permanent revolution** was a great innovation for the Russian revolution and vindicated by the 1917 seizure of power. His generalisation of permanent revolution to China and Latin America expanded the essential Marxist principle of working class hegemony to societies where the workers were a small minority. Trotsky's concepts of uneven and combined development, on which the permanent revolution strategy rests, were brilliant generalisations, with wide applicability in his time and to contemporary capitalism.

Trotsky's theory of Russia as a degenerated workers' state was adequate as long as the ruling Communist party could be reformed. But after Stalin's bureaucracy became the sole master of the USSR, Trotsky's theory became increasingly incoherent. Once the working class had no prospect of holding power politically, it also lost power economically. Without political power the working class cannot be the ruling class in any sense. The bureaucracy was sole master of the surplus product.

Trotsky's theory couldn't explain the forced march industrialisation and collectivisation that began in 1928, savagely exploiting both the working class and the peasantry. Worse, the theory failed to explain the expansion of Stalinism, starting with the invasion of Poland, the Baltic States, Finland and Romania in 1939-40. It made no sense to argue that new workers' states were being created without the active intervention of the working class — created over the bones of that class.

The USSR expanded and emerged from the Second World War as the imperial power across Eastern Europe. Stalinist states were created under the umbrella of Stalinist armies. In Yugoslavia, China, Vietnam and Cuba, Stalinist party-armies created Stalinist states without the Russian army. But their social relations of production and their totalitarian states were identical in form. These Stalinist states mostly collapsed in 1989-91, reverting rapidly or more slowly into market capitalist states and integrating into the global capitalist economy.

The Stalinist states were no sort of socialist society, or even any form of workers' state. They were class societies, exploiting economies, essentially parallel to market capitalism as regards the development of the forces of production. Understanding the dynamics of Stalinism and its place in history are paramount for the renewal of working class socialism.[5]

Post-Trotsky Trotskyism

After Trotsky's death, most of his followers repeated his words, published his writings, but largely forgot his method. Post-Trotsky Trotskyism foundered because it was incapable of assessing the evolving nature of capitalism, failed to understand the nature of Stalinism and was unable to map an independent working class strategy.

Post-Trotsky Trotskyism — Mandel, Grant, Cliff, Healy and others (Lambert, Moreno, Lora) — failed to explain the growth, development and decline of Stalinism, principally in Russia but also in China, Cuba and other Stalinist states. The "deformed and degenerated workers' state" theories made the Stalinist states more progressive than capitalism and made the Trotskyists satellites of Stalinist states.

Post-Trotsky Trotskyism mangled permanent revolution, transforming it into a justification for the victorious Maoist-Stalinist party-army in 1949. The remnants of the Fourth International made the overturns that occurred in Russia, Yugoslavia, China, Vietnam and Cuba into socialist revolutions and the regimes they created into "workers' states".[6] They turned permanent revolution into a theory of substitutes for the working class, undermining the raison d'etre of Trotskyism.

If "orthodox" Trotskyism was wrong about Stalinism, those who changed the label fared little better. Tony Cliff's so-called state capitalism was neither a theory nor recognisably capitalism. Cliff did not proceed from the reality of the Stalinist states, but described a new form of class society, attaching the well-worn "state capitalist" label for political convenience. Cliff did not capture the dynamics of the

Stalinist states (at first treating them as a more progressive variant of capitalism), but instead distorted the Marxist political economy of capitalism. The SWP's "state capitalism" was neither authentically Marxist nor consistent with the facts.[7]

The mangling of anti-imperialism and permanent revolution has left most post-Trotsky Trotskyists as apologists for reactionaries, ranging from Castro in Cuba, Chávez in Venezuela, Assad in Syria, or various political Islamist currents. Thus the SWP's variant of "anti-imperialism" aligns with every state or movement, however regressive, in conflict with "imperialism", which it identifies solely with advanced capitalism, especially the USA. This is all a long way from Trotsky's original theory, which was premised on working class political independence.

Conclusion

Leon Trotsky salvaged much of the best traditions of the Russian revolution when he fought the rise of Stalinism, the growth of fascism and the great depression during the 1930s. Summing up the watchwords for revolutionary working class socialists, he instructed his supporters:

> *To face reality squarely; not to seek the line of least resistance; to call things by their right names; to speak the truth to the masses, no matter how bitter it may be; not to fear obstacles; to be true in little things as in big ones; to base one's programme on the logic of the class struggle; to be bold when the hour for action arrives — these are the rules of the Fourth International.*[8]

Every line reached back into the storehouse of knowledge Marxist revolutionaries had learned from their own hard-won experience in the early years of the twentieth century. This is a precious heritage, encapsulated in the Russian revolution. Working class socialists today do not start from scratch. We are inspired by our forebears and our tradition. We have the world to win.

The twenty-first century is already defined by global, epochal crises. Capitalism careers on, but its contradictions exact an ever greater toll on humanity and the planet. Marxists have long recognised that it will be socialism or the common ruin of contending classes. In a world of capitalist barbarism, economic turmoil, right-wing populist resurgence, of climate-wrecking planetary change, of continued exploitation and oppression — socialism is the goal well worth fighting for.

References

1. Janine Booth, *Comrades and Sisters*, (2004).
2. Rachel Lever, Phil Semp and Sean Matgamna, 'What We Are And What We Must Become', (July 1966).
3. Sean Matgamna, [March 1981] 'The Left and Afghanistan: 'Militant' on the Russian Occupation', *Workers' Action*, 182, 27-31; Sean Matgamna, [September 1982] 'The texts and the method', *Workers' Socialist Review*, 2, 16-21; Clive Bradley, [1988] 'Marxism and War, Is the SWP an Alternative?', 24-27; Sean Matgamna, [25 January 1991] *War in the Gulf*; Sean Matgamna, [April 1999] 'Who will save the Kosovars?'
4. Martin Thomas, 'Democracy and the Right to Secede', *New Politics*, (Summer 1993).
5. Sean Matgamna, 'Editorial: Reassessing the Eastern Bloc', *Socialist Organiser*, 371, (15 September 1988).
6. Michael Löwy, *The Politics of Combined and Uneven Development: The Theory of Permanent Revolution* (2010). Original edition published by Verso in 1981.
7. Marcel van der Linden, *Western Marxism and the Soviet Union* (2009).
8. Trotsky, [1938] *The Transitional Program for Socialist Revolution*, (1973: 108).

THE RUSSIAN REVOLUTION: WHEN WORKERS TOOK POWER

Aleksandr Rodchenko, 'Design for a Workers' Club', 1925

This design for a workers' club was presented at the Paris Expo in 1925 and included a tribute to Lenin who had died in the previous year. The design centered on educational activities, with space for reading and storage of socialist literature, as well as a slide projector for talks and a chess board with chairs. Whereas the Stalinist state commemorated Lenin by deifying him and making him the figurehead of a repressive state, Rodchenko honoured him with a design for a club where labourers could educate themselves and each other, working for their own emancipation.

Recommended reading

There are scores of books on the Russian revolution, many of very limited value for working class socialists. However some publications repay careful reading and re-reading. The following suggestions are in English and generally available, either to buy or through libraries. Many of the texts are also available through the Marxist Internet Archive, www.marxists.org.

Workers' Liberty's website includes a huge amount of material on the Russian revolution and its fate, www.workersliberty.org

Primary Marxist collections
Marx and Engels, *Collected Works* (*MECW*), 50 volumes
V I Lenin, *Collected Works* (*LCW*), 45 volumes
Leon Trotsky, *Writings of Leon Trotsky*, 14 volumes
Rosa Luxemburg, *The Complete Works of Rosa Luxemburg*, 14 volumes (projected)
Georgi Plekhanov, *Selected Philosophical Works* (*SPW*), 5 volumes
Antonio Gramsci, *Prison Notebooks*, 3 volumes so far.

How did the workers take power? The story of 1917
The best, most politically astute and highly readable account is Leon Trotsky, [1931-33] *The History of the Russian Revolution*, (1980). Trotsky combines analytical insight with rich prose and striking empirical detail. This is a great work, written by a key participant ,written to preserve the lessons of history from Stalinism.

The best academic account of the revolution in Petrograd is: Alexander Rabinowitch, [1968] *Prelude to Revolution*, (1991) and Alexander Rabinowitch, [1976] *Bolsheviks Come to Power: The Revolution of 1917 in Petrograd*, (2004). Both volumes explain the leading role of the workers and the important role played by the fractious and hugely effective Bolshevik party. Rex Wade, *The Russian Revolution, 1917*, (2005) draws out some important wider contextual matters. Steve Smith, *The Russian Revolution: A Very Short Introduction*, (2002) is brief but useful for beginners.

The most detailed accounts of the February revolution are Eduard Burdzhalov, *Russia's Second Revolution: The February 1917 Uprising in Petrograd*, (1987) and Tsuyoshi Hasegawa, *The February Revolution. Petrograd 1917*, (1981). William Chamberlin, [1935] *The Russian Revolution, Volume I: 1917-1918*, (1987) accessed important documents and pre-dates the Stalinist and Cold War histories. Paul Avrich, *The Anarchists in the Russian Revolution* (1973) explains the strengths and weaknesses of the anarchists' role in 1917. James White, *The Russian Revolution 1917-1921: A Short History*, (1994) is idiosyncratic, but does reveal some previously unexplored angles. There are numerous eyewitness accounts published subsequently. Nikolai Sukhanov, [1918-21] *The Russian Revolution 1917*, (abridged in English 1984) is among the most perceptive. Fedor Raskolnikov, [1925] *Kronstadt and Petrograd in 1917*, (1982) is also useful.

The party of victory
The history of the Narodnik populists, including their engagement with workers' struggles, is elegantly told in Franco Venturi, *Roots of Revolution*, (1960). Many documents from the early Russian workers' movement are translated into English in Neil Harding, *Marxism in Russia*, (1983).

Richard Mullin, *The Russian Social-Democratic Labour Party, 1899–1904: Documents of the 'Economist' Opposition to Iskra and Early Menshevism*, (2016) has a range of important texts with commentary for the founding period of the RSDLP. Lars Lih, *Lenin Rediscovered: 'What is to be Done' in Context*, (2008) provides a perceptive interpretation of Lenin's pamphlet and its significance within wider social democratic thought. The minutes of the second RSDLP congress are translated in Brian Pearce, *1903 — Second Congress of the Russian Social-democratic Labour Party*, (1978). David Lane, *The Roots of Russian Communism*, (1968) contains important data on the early RSDLP.

Paul Le Blanc, [1993] *Lenin and the Revolutionary Party*, (2015) and his *Unfinished Leninism* (2014) provide very useful and readable overviews of the development of Lenin's politics in relation to the RSDLP. Brian Pearce, 'Building the Bolshevik Party: Some Organisational Aspects', *Labour Review*, (February 1960) is a concise overview of how the Bolshevik faction became a party. August Nimtz, *Lenin's Electoral Strategy from Marx and Engels through the Revolution of 1905*, (2014a) and his *Lenin's Electoral Strategy from 1907 to the October Revolution of 1917*, (2014b) provide a comprehensive account of Lenin's parliamentary politics, bringing new insights to how the RSDLP developed. Georges Haupt, and Jean-Jacques Marie, *Makers of the Russian Revolution* (1974) translates the biographies of Bolshevik leaders written in the 1920s. Pierre Broué's, *Le Parti Bolchévique* (1971) has yet to find an English translator.

From Workers' Liberty, key texts are: Sean Matgamna, 'The Roots of Bolshevism', *Solidarity* (2003-04), Andrew Hornung and John

RECOMMENDED READING

O'Mahony, 'Lenin and the Russian Revolution', *Workers' Liberty* 3/28, (2010). And AWL, 'The history of Bolshevism', *Workers' Liberty* 3/0, (2005).

Soviets, workers' democracy and workers' control
The best accounts of workers' democracy and workers' control in 1917 are Steve Smith, *Red Petrograd: Revolution in the Factories*, (1983); David Mandel, *The Petrograd Workers and the Fall of the Old Regime*, (1983) and David Mandel, *The Petrograd Workers and the Soviet Seizure of Power*, (1984). Daniel Kaiser's collection, *The Workers' Revolution in Russia 1917*, (1987) contains valuable essays on workers' activity. Oskar Anweiler, [1958] *The Soviets: The Russian workers, peasants, and soldiers councils*, (1974) is dated, but readable. Pete Glatter, *The Russian Revolution of 1905: Change through Struggle, Revolutionary History*, 9, 1, (2005) contains original material and translations.

From Workers' Liberty, read: 'Factory bulletins from the early communist movement', *Workers' Liberty* 3/3, (2005).

Permanent revolution
The best sources are Trotsky's original essays, notably *Results and Prospects* (1906) and *Permanent Revolution* (1930), often published together. Arguably more expansive is Trotsky's other early book, *1905*, (1971). The articles collected by Louis Fraina, *The Proletarian Revolution in Russia* (1918) are also valuable. More recently, the historical roots have been explored in Richard Day and Daniel Gaido, *Witnesses to Permanent Revolution*, (2011). In recent debates about permanent revolution, the most pugnacious defence has been John Marot, 'Lenin, Bolshevism, and Social-Democratic political theory', *Historical Materialism*, 22, 2-3, (2014).

From Workers' Liberty the following are relevant: Clive Bradley, 'Sandinism and Permanent Revolution', *Workers' Liberty* 1/4, (1986), Clive Bradley, 'Permanent Revolution after Trotsky', *Workers' Liberty* 1/7, (1987) and Paul Hampton, 'Trotsky and Permanent Revolution', *Solidarity* 219, (5 October 2011).

War and the myth of defeatism
The most comprehensive account of the collapse of the Second International is Georges Haupt, *Socialism and the Great War*, (1972). The best collection of documents on the anti-war opposition are Olga Gankin and Harold Fisher, *The Bolsheviks and the World War*, (1940) and John Riddell, *Lenin's Struggle for a Revolutionary International*, (1986). R Craig Nation, *War on War*, (2009) provides a detailed account

of the debates among the left during the First World War. Alexander Anievas, *Cataclysm 1914: The First World War and the Making of Modern World Politics*, (2015) is a valuable collection of essays, containing Marxist explanations for the war.

Hal Draper, *War and Revolution: Lenin and the Myth of Revolutionary Defeatism* (1996), originally published in the early 1950s, is the best deconstruction of the anti-war debates on "defeatism". Jean-Paul Joubert, 'Revolutionary Defeatism', *Revolutionary History*, 1, 3, autumn, (1988) and 'Syndicalism to Trotskyism: Writings of Alfred and Marguerite Rosmer', *Revolutionary History*, 7, 4, Winter, (2000-2001) expand on Trotsky's thinking.

Workers' Liberty has published the following: Martin Thomas, 'Marxism and imperialism', *Workers' Liberty* 1/28, (1996) and 'Two critiques: 'Empire' and 'new imperialism', *Workers' Liberty*, 2/1, (2001), Colin Foster, 'The USA as hyperpower', *Workers' Liberty*, 2/1, (2001), Sean Matgamna, 'Apparatus Marxism in the Balkan war', *Workers' Liberty*, 2/1, (2001) and 'Dossier: Socialists and Wars', *Workers' Liberty*, 2/3, (2002).

Consistent democracy — the national question

There is no comprehensive account of Marxist politics on the national question. Probably the best on Marx is Kevin Anderson, *Marx at the Margins* (2010). Roman Rosdolsky, 'Engels and the "Nonhistoric" Peoples: the National Question in the Revolution of 1848', in *Critique*, (1987) is right about Engels' mistakes. Andreja Živkovič and Dragan Plavšič, 'The Balkan Socialist Tradition', *Revolutionary History*, 8, 3, (2003) is useful on the Second International debates.

No single book adequately discusses Lenin and Trotsky's politics on the national question. Consulting their own writings remains the best approach. Jeremy Smith, *The Bolsheviks and the National Question*, (1999) discusses the early soviet government. The best books on Marxists and Jewish oppression are Jack Jacobs, *On Socialists and The Jewish Question after Marx*, (1992) and Enzo Traverso, *The Marxists and the Jewish Question*, (1994).

Martin Thomas, 'Democracy and the Right to Secede', *New Politics*, (Summer 1993) explains Workers' Liberty's stance on consistent democracy in the context of Ireland and Israel-Palestine.

Women's liberation and the Russian revolution

The best overall accounts of Bolshevik women before, during and after 1917 are Barbara Evans Clements, *Bolshevik Women*, (1997) and Jane McDermid and Anna Hillyar, *Midwives of the Revolution*, (1999:

200). The best biographies are Barbara Evans Clements, *Bolshevik Feminist: Life of Alexandra Kollontai*, (1979), Katy Turton, *Forgotten Lives: The Role of Lenin's Sisters in the Russian Revolution, 1864-1937*, (2007) and Ralph Carter Elwood, *Inessa Armand: Revolutionary and Feminist*, (1992). Also useful is McDermid and Hillyar, *Women and Work in Russia 1880-1930: A Study in Continuity through Change*, (1998). Their PhD theses, which are online, include more detailed discussion not published in their books. There are two collections of Kollontai's writings: the best is Alix Holt's *Alexandra Kollontai: Selected Writings*, (1977). The other, published in the USSR, *Alexandra Kollontai: Selected Articles and Speeches*, (1984).

Women in Workers' Liberty has a chapter on the subject in *Why Socialist Feminism?* (2016). Also relevant are Janine Booth, *Comrades and Sisters*, (2004) and Ann Campbell, 'The ICL and Women's Liberation', *International Communist* 4, (1977).

The Communist International: school of strategy

The resolutions and debates from the early Communist International are translated into English by John Riddell. These include: *Founding the Communist International, Proceedings and Documents of the First Congress, March 1919*, (1987); *Workers of the World and Oppressed Peoples, Unite! Proceedings and Documents of the Second Congress of the Communist International, 1920*, 2 volumes, (1991); *To See the Dawn: Baku, 1920 — First Congress of the Peoples of the East*, (1993); *To the Masses: Proceedings of the Third Congress of the Communist International, 1921*, (2015); *Toward the United Front: Proceedings of the Fourth Congress of the Communist International, 1922*, (2011).

The following from Workers' Liberty are relevant: Cathy Nugent, *Marxist Ideas to Turn the Tide*, (2013), Jill Mountford, 'The Case for a Workers' Government', *Workers' Liberty* 45, (1998), John Sterling, 'The Workers' Government (an historical excavation)', *Permanent Revolution* 2, (1974), Martin Thomas, 'The Workers' Government', *International Communist* 4, (1977), Chris Reynolds, 'The Revolutionary Programme', *International Communist* 7, (1978) and Stan Crooke, 'The Third International', *Workers' Action* 182, (1981).

Stalin's counter-revolution

The best introduction to what went wrong in Russia and the Trotskyist assessment is Sean Matgamna, *The Fate of the Russian Revolution Volume 1: Lost Texts of Critical Marxism*, (1998). The subsequent volume, Sean Matgamna, *The Fate of the Russian Revolution Volume 2. The two Trotskyisms confront Stalinism*, (2015) continues the story into the

1940s. Leon Trotsky, *The Revolution Betrayed*, (1937) and Max Shachtman, *The Struggle for the New Course*, (1943) explain what went wrong in Russia.

On the early degeneration see Sam Farber, *Before Stalinism* (1990). For the civil war, Jean-Jacques Marie, *Histoire de la guerre civile russe: 1917-1922*, (2015) and David Footman, *Civil War in Russia*, (1961). Also useful are Michel Reiman, *The Birth of Stalinism*, (1987), Tom Twiss, *Trotsky and the Problem of Soviet Bureaucracy*, (2014).

The following texts from Workers' Liberty explain how the experiences of the Russian Revolution are still relevant: Sean Matgamna, *Can Socialism Make Sense?* (2016), Cathy Nugent, *What is capitalism? Can it last?* (2012), Sean Matgamna, 'Looking backward', *Workers' Liberty* 3/26, (2009)., Sean Matgamna, 'The Bolshevik-Trotskyist tradition', *Workers' Liberty* 3/27, (2010), and Rachel Lever, Phil Semp, Sean Matgamna, 'What We Are and What We Must Become', (1966).

THE RUSSIAN REVOLUTION: WHEN WORKERS TOOK POWER

Index

Russian names are anglicised only in the most well-known cases (such as Trotsky, Kerensky).

Abortion 241, 258, 259,
Adamovich, Evgeniia 239
African-American 216
Agadzhanova, Nina 237
Agitation 165, 196, 210,
   Defined 84, 88, 96, 110, 277, 283
   Anti-war 181, 188, 192
   Among women 246, 248, 250, 252
Akimov, Vladimir 77, 94,
Alexinskii, Grigori 35, 99, 107, 109
Algebra of revolution 89, 281
All Power to the Soviets 33, 34, 41, 53, 127, 131-32
Alliance for Workers' Liberty (AWL, Workers' Liberty) 9, 11, 14, 144, 345-46, 353-58
Anseele, Edward 82
Anti-imperialist united front 268
Anti-semitism 12-13, 217-22, 223-24, 228-29
Antonov-Ovseenko, Vladimir 49, 55, 322, 325
Anweiler, Oskar 127, 130
Assimilation 219-20, 222-23
Armand, Inessa 81-82, 108, 179, 238, 240, 247-49
Austro-Marxists 214, 228
Avilova, Mariia 239
Avrich, Paul 311
Axelrod, Pavel 35, 74, 76-77, 82, 88, 144

Badaev, Aleksei 82, 108
Bakunin, Mikhail 23
Batkis, George 243
Bauer, Otto 214-15, 217
Baugy group 83, 188
Bauman, Nikolai 77
Bebel, August
   Anti-semitism 218
   Hirschfeld's petition 243
   SPD leader 83, 86-87
   Women 243-44, 252, 255
Berger, Victor 293
Bernstein, Eduard 90-91, 99, 101, 280
Birobidzhan 225, 227
Black Hundreds 109, 126, 209
Blagoev, Dimitar 74

Bleikhman, Iosif 34
Bloody Sunday (1905) 106, 144
Bochkareva, Mariia 239
Bogdanov, Aleksandr 80, 82, 99-100, 108
Boldyreva, Anna 75
Bolsheviks
   1905 revolution 127-28, 145-46
   1912 split 81-82
   1917 revolution 22, 29-30, 38-43, 48-50, 83, 130-32, 155-62, 235-40, 247-49
   Deputies 106-07
   Elections 108-10
   First World War 178-79, 187-90
   Internal discipline 101
   National question 208-11
   Origins 77-79, 97-99, 274
   Strikes 111-14
Bolshevichki (Bolshevik women) 235-40, 243-49
Bonapartism 37-38, 44-45, 328
Bonch-Bruevich, Vladimir 31
Bordiga, Amadeo 271, 290-91
Bosh, Evgeniia 239-40, 322
Braunstein, Mikhail 27
Bregman, Lazar 42
Brest-Litovsk treaty 193, 305-06, 317
Briggs, Cyril 294
British Socialist Party (BSP) 283-84
Broué, Pierre 269
Brusnev, Mikhail 74-75
Bubnov, Andrei 82, 322
Bukharin, Nikolai 271
   Anti-semitism 221
   Baugy 83
   Imperialism 183-84
   National question 212-13
   Right Opposition 325
   Transitional demands 288
Bulygin, Aleksandr 106
Bund
   Comintern 220, 225
   Economism 92
   Origins 75-79
   National question 222-23
   Russian Communist Party 224
   Second Congress 206-208
Bureaucracy
   Stalinist 221, 302, 322, 326-32
   Tsarist 156, 312-14
   Union 183, 277, 285

INDEX

Campbell, Grace 294
Capitalism 9, 19, 144-47, 177-86, 222, 253, 272-73
Cannon, James 271, 295
Carmichael, Joel 154
Central Committee of the RSDLP
    1912 split 81-82
    1917 revolution 34, 40, 44, 48, 50, 83, 162
    Origins 76-78
    Evolution 314-16
    Degeneration 322-25
Chamberlin, William 24, 26, 28, 44
Cheka 313, 316-17
Cherevanin, Fedor 24
Chernomasov, Miron 104
Chernov, Viktor 22, 30, 32, 34-36, 57, 128, 193
Chernyi Peredel 74
Chernyshevskii, Nikolai 87
Chkheidze, Nikolai 25-26, 30, 42, 131, 160
Class struggle
    Three fronts 11-14, 268, 342
    Economic front 111-114
    Ideological front 84, 89-104, 271
    Political front 104-111
Clausewitz, Carl 177, 197
Cliff, Tony 73, 96, 348
Collectivisation 301, 325, 331, 347
Comintern – see Communist International
Communist International Congresses
    First (1919) 193, 269-70,
    Second (1920) 104, 193, 225, 249, 270, 272, 274-76, 283-84, 294
    Third (1921) 193, 225, 250, 271-72, 276-78, 284-87, 294
    Fourth (1922) 193, 225, 251, 271, 273, 278-82, 288-92, 294
    Fifth (1924) 295
    Sixth (1928) 184, 295,
Communist League 269, 280
Communist Party (China) 324
Communist Party (Germany, KPD) 157, 269
Communist Party (Great Britain) 290
Communist Party (Palestinian, PCP) 225-226,
Communist Party (Russia) Congresses
    Seventh (1918) 269
    Eighth (1919) 193, 308, 317
    Tenth (1921) 308,
    Eleventh (1922) 314, 318
    Thirteenth (1924) 323
    Fourteenth (1925) 323
    Fifteenth (1927) 325
Communist Party (United States) 293-95
Conciliationism 22, 80, 99, 102-03, 161

Consistent democracy 13-14, 134, 203-05, 205-12, 215-16, 340
Cossacks 46, 52, 55-56, 129, 237
Cunow, Heinrich 182

Day, Richard 12, 143
Debs, Eugene 293
Defeatism 186-97, 345
Degenerated workers' state 195, 320-21, 328, 330-31, 347-48
Democracy 57,
    Bourgeois 104-08
    National question 13-14, 134, 203-05, 205-12, 215-16, 340
    Party 98, 317-18
    Soviet 126-130, 305-06
Democratic centralism 98, 275, 277, 343
Democratic centralist group 317, 323, 328, 330-31
Deutsch, Lev 74, 77
Deviatkina, Anastasia 237
Dictatorship of the proletariat 29, 41, 90, 147, 159-61, 249, 270, 283, 291-92, 328
Drabkina, Feodosiia 239
Draper, Hal 143, 186-87, 189-91, 193, 196-97
Dual power 24, 28, 138, 341
Duma 20-26, 78-82, 98-100, 103, 105-111, 113-14
Durnovo villa 32-34, 36, 57
Duxiu, Chen 271
Dybenko, Pavel 49, 55
Dzerzhinskii, Feliks 81

Eberlein, Hugo 271
Economism 76, 92, 247, 329
Efremov, Ivan 21
Eidelman, Boris 76
Ekaterinoslav 81, 219
Elizarova, Anna 240, 247
Elwood, Carter 12, 103, 249
Emancipation of Labour group 74, 87-89, 94
Engels, Friedrich
    On democracy 204-05, 218
    On war 177, 181, 187
    On women's oppression 252, 254
    SPD 83-84, 89, 105, 108, 112
    Three fronts of the class struggle 84, 95
    Working class socialism 9, 93, 143, 159, 165, 269
Erfurt programme 84, 93, 287
Evans Clement, Barbara 12, 235

Fascism 222-23, 226, 286, 296
Fedorov, G F 42
Field, Karen 254

INDEX

Finance capital 182-84
Finland 28, 43, 78-79, 103, 131, 146, 211, 306, 347
First International 125, 179, 205, 267, 280
Fischer, Lars 12, 218
Fischer, Ruth 271
Fort-Whiteman, Lovett 294
Fourth International 194-96, 296, 346, 348-49
Flakserman, Galina 48
Frankel, Jonathan 224
French revolution 10, 43, 143, 165, 257, 327
Friedrich, Anton 182
Frumkina, Maria 225

Gaido, Daniel 12, 143
Gallagher, Willie 283-84
Gapon, Father 126, 144
Germany
    Imperial 28, 74, 76, 85-86, 89, 112, 177-82, 183-85, 189, 244, 249, 305-06, 316
    Weimar 221, 252, 268-71, 274, 289, 291, 341
    Nazi 229,
Giliarova, Elena 239
Gompers, Samuel 112
Goncharskaia, Sofia 237
Gordienko, Ivan 237
Gramsci, Antonio 271
Grimm, Robert 180
Grynszpan, Herschel 222
Guchkov, Aleksandr 21, 25, 111, 131
Guomindang 323-24

Hanecki, Iakov 77
Healey, Dan 242-43, 259
Hearse, Phil 162
Hebron pogrom 226-27
Hegemony 88, 90, 100, 143, 149, 152, 166, 171, 268, 345, 347
Helsingfors (Helsinki) 24, 49, 79
Herzl, Theodore 227
Hilferding, Rudolf 182
Hillyar, Anna 235
Hirschfeld, Magnus 243
Huiswoud, Otto 294

Iakovleva, Varvara 36, 240, 322
Iarchuk, Efim 34
Ignatov, Mikhail 74
Imperialism 13, 83, 153, 180-87, 208, 212-14, 222, 225-26, 228, 272, 345-46, 349
Imperialism of free trade 345

Ioffe, Adolf 325
Iskra (*The Spark*) 76-78, 94-97, 99, 103, 207-08, 227
Iurenev, Konstantin 46, 50
Ivanovo-Voznesensk 35, 42, 46, 56, 75, 113, 126-27, 324
Ivanshin, Vladimir 94

Jenness, Doug 162
Jogiches, Leo 81, 102
July Days 33-37, 45, 57, 132, 136, 239

Kaclerović, Triša 178
Kamenev Lev 36, 42, 48, 50, 81, 101, 104, 157, 159-61, 163, 168, 308, 318, 322-23
Kamenska, Anna 179
Kamkov, Boris 193
Karelina, Anna 75
Karpinskii, V.A. 187
Kasparova, Varsenika 251
Kautsky, Karl
    Consistent democracy 204-06, 217-18, 222-24
    Permanent revolution 143, 150, 163, 167
    War and revolution 182
    Working class socialism 82, 84, 87. 92, 95, 99, 280
Kadets (Constitutional Democrats) 21, 30, 33, 36-37, 43-44, 53, 57, 79, 52, 107, 109, 111, 165-66, 204, 305
Kerensky, Aleksandr 21, 25-26, 30, 36-40, 43-45, 47, 50-52, 55, 132, 193, 195
Khaustov, Flavian 33
Khrustalev, Petr 128,
Kiev 20, 35, 42, 49, 75, 81, 129
Kishinev massacre 219
Knuniants, Bogdan 128
Koenen, Wilhelm 277
Koenker, Diane 12, 135-36, 309
Kohn, Michael 225
Kollontai, Aleksandra 13, 134, 235, 238, 240, 243-250, 252-55, 257-58, 260, 317
Konovalov, Aleksandr 21, 25
Konspiritsiia (conspiracy) 96
Koppelson, Zemah 91
Kornilov, Lavi 38-43, 55, 132
Krakow 82, 108
Krasikov, Petr 77, 128
Kremer, Arkadii 76-77
Krichevskii, Boris 94-95
Kronawetter, Ferdinand 218
Kronstadt
    Naval base 24, 34-36, 42, 49, 131, 239, 316
    Rebellion 310-12
Kropotkin, Petr 23, 316

INDEX

Kruglova, Arishina 237, 239
Krupskaia, Nadezhda 75, 77, 108, 240, 249, 271, 322
Krylenko, Nikolai 49
Krzhizhanovskii, Gleb 314,
Kshesinskaia, Mathilda 29
Kun, Bela 271, 285, 319
Kuskova, Ekaterina 90-92
Kuusinen, Otto 277

Labour aristocracy 183, 185
Labour Party (British) 283-85, 290, 292, 344
Lane, David 78
Lapčević, Dragiša 178
Lashevich, Mikhail 50
Lashkevich Captain 23
Lassalle, Ferdinand 83-84, 147, 271
Latvian Social-Democratic Labour Party 26, 79-81
Lazimir, Pavel 50
Le Blanc, Paul 12, 115
League for Women's Equality 238
League of Revolutionary Russian Social Democrats Abroad 76
Left Opposition 258, 293, 322-27, 331-32
Legien, Carl 291
Lena goldfields massacre 113
Lenin (Vladimir Ilich Ulianov)
   Consistent democracy 203-12
   Bureaucracy 326-32
   Defeatism 186-93
   Elections 104-111
   Ideological front 95
   Labour Party 283-84
   Strategy and tactics 281-82
   Strikes 112-14
   April Theses (1917) 29, 154, 157-59
   Friends of the People (1894) 89, 167
   Imperialism: The Highest Stage of Capitalism (1916) 182, 184
   Left-Wing Communism (1920) 274, 281, 283
   Socialism and War (1915) 190
   State and Revolution (1917) 312
   Two Tactics of Social Democracy in the Democratic Revolution (1905) 145-46
   What Is To Be Done? (1902) 76, 95-96, 103, 112
Lever 96, 275
Levi, Paul 285, 289
Liber, Mark 77, 81, 208
Liebknecht, Karl 178, 180, 193, 195, 269
Liebknecht, Wilhelm 83, 85
Liebman, Marcel 96, 154
Lih, Lars 12, 96, 163-69

Liquidators 22, 24, 80-83, 99-102, 104
Lorimer, Doug 162
Lozovskii, Solomon 290
Lunacharskii Anatolii 32, 99
Luxemburg, Rosa 143, 178, 180-81, 190, 192, 204, 212-14, 218, 228, 269, 280

Malaka, Tan 271
Malinovskii, Roman 81-82, 110
Mandel, David 12, 138
Mandel, Ernest 162, 346, 348
Manifesto of the RSDLP (1898) 76, 92
Marchlewski, Julien 271
Marinskii Palace 25, 30, 47, 52
Marot, John 12, 168
Marseillaise 10
Martov, Iulii 22, 35, 43, 53, 75, 77, 81-82, 97, 189, 207-08
Martynov, Aleksandr 77, 95, 97, 128, 145, 194, 208,
Marx, Karl
    Consistent democracy 204-05, 212
    Permanent revolution 125, 143, 148, 159, 165
    War 177, 187
    Working class politics 9, 83, 89, 93, 95, 105, 112, 252, 269, 303
    Capital (1867) 147, 303
    Communist Manifesto (1848) 89, 112, 165, 205, 218, 269
Marx and Engels 9, 83, 89, 93, 95, 105, 112, 159, 165, 177, 187, 204-05, 212, 252, 269
    Address of the Central Committee to the Communist League (1850) 143
    German Ideology (1845-46) 112
Matgamna, Sean 327
Mawdsley, Evan 306
McDermid, Jane 235-36, 238, 248
McKay, Claude 294
McLaine, William 284
Medem, Vladimir 77, 208, 217, 220, 222
Mehring, Franz 143
Mekhonoshin, Konstantin 50
Melancon, Michael 24
Mensheviks
    1917 revolution 22,24, 27-28, 32, 39, 42-43, 47, 53-54, 57, 77-79, 81, 132-33, 135, 157, 163, 306-07
    1905 revolution 144-45
    National question 214
    Under Bolshevik rule 316-17
    War 178
    Within RSDLP 97-98, 102, 104, 107-10, 127
Meyer, Ernest 271, 291
Miasnikov, Gavril 318
Mikhailichenko, Mitrofan 109

INDEX

Miliukov, Pavel 21, 25, 30, 38
Motteler, Julius 85
Mullin, Richard 12, 96-97
Muralov, Nikolai 322
Murphy, Jack 271

Narkomnats (Commissariat of National Affairs) 211, 220
Narodniks 21, 74
Natanson, Mark 22
Nemec, Antonin 82
Nevskii, Vladimir 31, 50
Nicholas II 21, 23
Nikolaeva, Klavdiia 240
Nimtz, August 12, 104, 107
Nin, Andreu 271
Nizhni Novgorod 35
Nogin, Victor 43, 102

Odessa 20, 46, 219
Okhrana 20
Ordzhonikidze, Sergo 81-82
Otzovism (recallism) 22, 80, 100
Ozolin, M.V. 81

Pankhurst, Sylvia 283-84
Pannekoek, Anton 275
Paris Commune, (1871) 148, 159-60
Parvus (Aleksandr Helphand) 143, 146, 158, 182
Pate, Alice 102
Peasants 11, 21, 45, 51, 53, 87, 109, 111, 129-30, 145-46, 149-152, 156, 158, 161, 166-67, 311, 326
Peasant Union 167
Pereverzev, Pavel 34-35
Permanent revolution 13-14, 88, 143-171, 191, 342, 347-49
Piatakov, Iuri 83, 213, 322, 325
Piatnitskii, Osip 37, 81
Pipes, Richard 203
Pirani, Simon 308-09, 318, 320-21
Plekhanov, Georgii 74, 76-78, 81-82, 87-92, 94-95, 97, 101, 103, 144, 206, 222
Poale Zion 224-25
Podvoiskii, Nikolai 50
Poland 75, 78-79, 179-180, 186, 207, 306
Politburo 315, 322-24
Popov, Dimitri 82
Poronin 82, 204, 209
Potresov, Aleksandr 75, 77, 83, 100-101
Prague 81, 87, 101, 108, 115
Pravda (The Truth) 29, 31-32, 35, 45, 57, 82, 103-04, 108, 110, 136, 157-59, 258, 317-18, 322, 325

Preobrazhenskii, Evgenii 271, 322, 325
Professional revolutionary 96, 98, 115
Prokopovich, Sergei 91-92
Propaganda 75, 87-88, 96, 106, 108, 110, 165, 189, 210, 248, 261, 277, 281-83, 293, 344
Pskov 76
Putilov works 21-22, 34, 50, 108, 125-26
Puzanov 126
Pylaeva, Liza 239

Rabinowitch, Alexander 12, 33, 40, 42, 307, 312
Rabotnitsa (Woman Worker) 29, 238, 247-48
Radek, Karl 180, 213, 225, 271, 273, 285-93
Raskolnikov, Fedor 35, 49, 57
Rakovskii, Khristian 325, 327-28
Rasputin 21
Read, Christopher 44
Red Guard 31, 40, 46, 52, 56, 238-39
Reed, John 52, 54, 294
Renjing, Liu 271
Renner, Karl 214-15, 217
Reval (Tallinn) 131
Revisionism 76, 90, 94, 99, 280
Riabushinskii, Pavel 21, 44
Riazanov, David 133, 135, 143
Riddell, John 12, 251, 268, 286
Riga 20
Rigby, Harry 312-13, 315
Rodichev, Fedor 39
Rodzianko, Mikhail 21, 24, 38
Romanov, A.S. 81
Rosenberg, William 12, 135-36
Rosmer, Alfred 186, 196, 271
Rowbotham, Sheila 259
Rowney, Dan 313
Roy, Manabendra Nath 271
Rozmirovich, Elena 239
Rubanovich, Ilia 82
Russian Social-Democratic Labour Party (RSDLP)
    First Congress (1898) 76, 92
    Second Congress (1903) 22, 77, 206-08, 220
    Third Congress (1905) 78
    Fourth Congress (1906) 78, 98, 110
    Fifth Congress (1907) 79, 150, 220
    Sixth Congress (1917) 41, 83, 193
    First conference (1905) 78
    Second conference (1906) 79
    Third conference (1907) 79
    Fourth conference (1907) 79

INDEX

Fifth conference (1908) 80
Sixth conference (1912) 81, 87, 101, 108, 115
Seventh conference (1917) 83, 160
Rykov, Alexei 42, 80-81, 102, 161

Samoilova, Konkordiia 240-41
Sapronov, Timofei 317, 322
Savinkov, Boris 38
Second International 82-83, 88, 92, 115, 143, 267, 275, 280, 283
    First World War 178-79, 181-83
    National question 205-06, 212
    Women 244, 249
Self-determination 19, 55, 83, 183, 203, 206-15, 217, 296, 346
Sen, Katayama 271
Serge, Victor 271, 311, 323
Shachtman, Max 186, 196, 329
Shatov, Bill 135
Shliapnikov, Aleksandr 168, 187, 317
Shurkanov, Vasilii 104
Shvartsman, D.M. 81
Skobelev, Matvei 25-26, 30, 133
Skrypnik, Nikolai 138
Slutskaia, Vera 240
Smidovich, Sofia 251
Smith, Steve 12, 126, 137
Smilga, Ivan 325
Smirnov, Ivan 82
Smirnov, Nikolai 129
Smirnov, Vladimir 317, 322, 325
Social-Democratic Party of the Kingdom of Poland 75, 78-79
Social-patriotism 180, 189-91
Socialist Revolutionaries (SRs) 13, 21-23, 25, 29, 32, 35-36, 39, 41-45, 47, 50, 53-54, 56-57, 82, 128-33, 162, 164, 193, 259, 304-06, 316-18
Sokolov, Abramovich 75
Sokolov, Nikolai 27, 43, 75
Souvarine, Boris 271
Soviets
    1905 revolution 78, 100, 113, 126-28, 144, 150
    1917 revolution 19-20, 24-29, 31-34, 37-41, 43-53, 56-58, 125-26, 129-32, 156-61, 168-69, 237
    Weakened 304-08
Sovnarkom (Council of Peoples' Commissars) 54, 304, 307-08, 315-16
Sozialdemokratische Partei Deutschlands (SPD)
    Party model 74-75, 83-87, 90, 92-95, 98, 114, 267, 274
    War 178, 182
    Weimar 269, 289-91
    Women 235, 243-44, 253, 261
Spartacus League 180, 269, 287
Spiridonova, Maria 22, 57

Stal, Liudmila 238
Stalin, Josef
    1917 revolution 32, 48, 163, 168
    Anti-semitism 218, 220-21, 226-27, 229
    National question 216-17
    Pre-revolution 102-04,
    Short Course (1938) 24, 73,
    Socialism in one country 165, 184
    War and defeatism 186, 194-95
Stalinist bureaucracy 11, 13, 257-58, 280, 293- 295, 301-359
Stalinist history 36, 48, 50, 73, 115-16, 155, 162, 184, 203-04, 236, 296
Steinberg, Isaac 316
Stites, Richard 236
Stolypin, Pyotr 79, 99, 107, 109, 134
Strategy
    Anti-bureaucratic 326, 330
    Electoral 104
    Permanent revolution 144, 147, 154, 156, 163, 168-69
    Political 12, 29, 49, 58, 73, 88-89, 95-96, 102, 197, 204, 280-86
Struve, Petr 76, 92
Sturm, Hertha 251
Sukhanov, Nikolai 22, 26, 28, 30-32, 36, 39-40, 42-43, 45, 47-48, 50, 53
Sverchkov, Dmitrii 128
Sverdlov, Iakov 41, 104
Swabeck, Arne 271

Tactics 12, 29, 49, 58, 73, 88-89, 95-96, 102, 280-86
Tailism 88
Takhtarev, Konstantin 77, 92
Tammerfors (Tampere) 78-79
Tauride Palace 24-25, 31, 34, 38, 57, 107, 238
Teplov, Pavel 94
Tereshchenko, Mikhail 30, 32
Terracini, Umberto 225
Thalheimer, August 271, 288, 295
Thermidor 221, 257, 311, 327-28
Third camp 13, 111, 186, 197, 205
Tikhomirnov, Viktor 103
Tomskii, Mikhail 80
Totalitarian economism 329
Totalitarianism 11, 73, 301, 329, 331, 339, 348
Transitional demands 14, 196, 261, 268, 286-88, 290, 295-96, 344
Traverso, Enzo 12, 220, 223
Tresso, Pietro 271
Trotsky, Leon
    1917 revolution 20, 22, 27-29, 31, 33-34, 35-37, 41-44, 47-54, 56, 151-53
    1905 revolution 128, 144-49
    Anti-semitism 218-22
    Bolshevik government 304, 306, 308, 310-11, 315, 318

INDEX

    Bureaucracy 321-330, 347
    Comintern 270-73, 276, 279-80, 286, 288-89, 293-96
    Consistent democracy 207-08, 215-16, 218, 228-29, 346
    Left Opposition 302, 322-25
    Permanent revolution 13, 88, 102, 111, 144-71, 347
    RSDLP 73, 77, 80-82, 343
    War 179-180, 184-87, 189-97, 346
    Women 242, 257-58
    Zionism 222-28
    History of the Russian Revolution (1931-33) 11, 27, 29
    History of the Russian Revolution to Brest-Litovsk (1918) 51
    On Lenin (1924) 48
    Results and Prospects (1906) 148-49
    Stalin (1940) 196
    The Lessons of October (1924) 323
    The New Course (1923) 322
    The Revolution Betrayed (1937) 329
    War and the International (1914) 179
    War and the Fourth International (1934) 194-95
    What Next? (1917) 152
Trotskyists 12, 73, 154-55, 158, 160, 162, 196, 218, 296, 311, 330, 331, 347-49
Trudoviks 21, 26, 109, 111, 167, 204
Tsereteli, Iraki 28, 30, 32, 36, 107, 109
Tugan-Baranovskii, Mikhail 92
Turton, Katy 12, 235
Tverdaia (steadfastness) 240

Ulianov, Dmitri 77
Ulianova, Mariia 240
Uneven and combined development 13, 20, 144, 147, 153-54, 170, 182-85, 345, 347
Union of Russian Social-Democrats Abroad 75-76, 94
Unions of Struggle for the Emancipation of the Working Class 126
United front 14, 268, 286, 288-90, 292-93, 296, 344
United States of America 151, 216, 222, 228, 273, 293-95, 306
United States of Europe 191
Urbahns, Hugo 271

Van Ravesteyn, Willem 225
Vandervelde, Emile 82
Varentsova, Olga 75
Varga, Eugen 271
Vigdorchik, Natan 76
Vilna (Vilnius) 75
Vladimirskii, Mikhail 82
Vydrina, Mariia 237

Weinstein, Simon 39
Winter Palace 38, 52-53, 144, 239, 305

Wistrich, Robert 328
Women's liberation 13, 235-36, 245-46, 251, 253-60, 268, 340
Wood, Elizabeth 258
Woods, Alan 331
Worker intelligentsia 88, 90
Workers' control 12, 14, 19, 31, 46, 55, 126, 133-34, 137-39, 289, 306, 312
Workers' government
    1917 government 19, 54-55, 133, 137-38, 203, 211, 223, 227, 242, 257-59, 303-04, 310, 320
    Permanent revolution 149-52, 156, 158-60, 164-67, 171
    Slogan 14, 255, 268-69, 286, 290-93, 296, 344
Workers' Group 318
Workers' Opposition 317, 323

Zasulich, Vera 74, 77
Zborovski, S. 127
Zetkin, Clara
    Comintern 249-52, 271, 289, 292-93
    SPD 178-79,
    Women 243-44, 249-52, 61
Zevin, V. 81
Zhelezniakov, Anatoli 34, 57
Zhenotdel (women's section) 248, 252, 257
Zhitlovsky, Chaim 224
Zimmerwald 28, 179-80, 191-92, 267
Zinoviev, Grigorii
    1917 revolution 36, 48, 50, 133
    Bureaucracy 308, 318, 322-23
    Comintern 270-76, 285, 288, 290-92
    Opposition 323-25
    RSDLP 81-82, 96
    War 194
Zionism 217, 222, 224-29
Zubatov 126
Zumoff, Jacob 293-94